No Remedy Left Behind

No Remedy Left Behind

Lessons from a Half-Decade of NCLB

Edited by Frederick M. Hess
and Chester E. Finn Jr.

The AEI Press

Publisher for the American Enterprise Institute

WASHINGTON, D.C.

Distributed to the Trade by National Book Network, 15200 NBN Way, Blue Ridge Summit, PA 17214. To order call toll free 1-800-462-6420 or 1-717-794-3800. For all other inquiries please contact the AEI Press, 1150 Seventeenth Street, N.W., Washington, D.C. 20036 or call 1-800-862-5801.

NRI NATIONAL
RESEARCH
INITIATIVE

This publication is a project of the National Research Initiative, a program of the American Enterprise Institute that is designed to support, publish, and disseminate research by university-based scholars and other independent researchers who are engaged in the exploration of important public policy issues.

Library of Congress Cataloging-in-Publication Data

No remedy left behind : lessons from a half-decade of NCLB / edited by Frederick M. Hess and Chester E. Finn Jr.
   p. cm.
  ISBN-13: 978-0-8447-4255-7
  ISBN-10: 0-8447-4255-4
  1. Educational accountability—United States. 2. United States. No Child Left Behind Act of 2001. 3. School improvement programs—United States. 4. Education and state—United States. I. Hess, Frederick M. II. Finn, Chester E., 1944-

  LB2806.22.N625 2007
  379.1'5--dc22

                         2007027471

12 11 10 09 08 07   1 2 3 4 5 6

Printed in the United States of America

Contents

PREFACE   xiii

INTRODUCTION, *Frederick M. Hess and Chester E. Finn Jr.*   1
     A Brief Recap   3
     NCLB Accountability   5
     Itemizing the Remedies   7
     Organization of This Volume   10

PART I: THE BIG PICTURE   15

1. NCLB IN THE STATES: FRAGMENTED GOVERNANCE, UNEVEN
     IMPLEMENTATION, *Paul Manna*   17
     Expectations for NCLB's Remedies   18
     Choice and Supplemental Educational Services   21
     Corrective Action and Restructuring   33
     NCLB in a Fragmented Intergovernmental System   41

2. AMERICA'S GREAT CITY SCHOOLS: MOVING IN THE RIGHT
     DIRECTION, *Michael Casserly*   43
     Status of NCLB in the Great Cities   44
     Discussion   61

3. THE POLITICAL ECONOMY OF SUPPLEMENTAL EDUCATIONAL
     SERVICES, *Jeffrey R. Henig*   66
     SES: The Basics   67
     SES as a Major Policy Intervention   68
     The Origins of SES: Complicated Politics and Undigested Ideas   71
     Controlling Metaphors: Markets and the Limits of Localism   75
     Early Readings from an "Immature" Policy Regime   82
     SES as a Local Contracting Regime   90
     Implications for the Politics and Policies of SES Reform   92

4. THE PROBLEM WITH "IMPLEMENTATION IS THE PROBLEM"
   Michael J. Petrilli   **96**
   Stump the Chumps: Three Policy Paradoxes *97*
   Conclusion: Of Hubris and Humility *114*

PART II: REMEDIES IN THE STATES   **119**

5. CALIFORNIA: DOES THE GOLDEN STATE DESERVE
   A GOLD STAR? *Julian Betts*   **121**
   Setting the Scene: Accountability in California *122*
   NCLB Choice in California *126*
   NCLB Supplemental Educational Services in California *132*
   NCLB Remedies for Local Educational Agencies in Need
     of Improvement *139*
   NCLB and the State Department of Education *143*
   Unintended Consequences *145*
   Conclusion *148*

6. NEW JERSEY: EQUITY MEETS ACCOUNTABILITY, *Patrick McGuinn* **153**
   State Education Profile *154*
   Implementation of NCLB in New Jersey *155*
   Conclusion *173*

7. COLORADO: THE MISAPPLICATION OF FEDERAL POWER,
   Alex Medler   **179**
   The Limits of Federal Power *179*
   The Colorado Context *181*
   Revisiting Initial Challenges of NCLB *183*
   Schools Identified in Need of Improvement *186*
   Costs of NCLB Interventions *192*
   District Case #1: Denver Public Schools *194*
   District Case #2: Cortez *197*
   Conclusion *199*

8. MICHIGAN: OVER THE FIRST HURDLE,
   David N. Plank and Christopher Dunbar Jr.   **202**
   NCLB in Michigan: The Political Context *205*
   How Many Michigan Schools Face Sanctions? *206*
   The Implementation of NCLB Sanctions in Michigan *207*

State-Level Strategies for Restructuring Low-Performing
  Schools *212*
District Implementation *215*
Institutionalizing NCLB *221*

PART III: REMEDIES IN THE DISTRICTS   223

9. **RURAL KENTUCKY DISTRICTS: "DO-IT-YOURSELF" SCHOOL
    IMPROVEMENT,** *Stephen Clements*   225
  Kentucky and Its School Reform Efforts *226*
  NCLB Comes to the Commonwealth *229*
  Rural Districts in Focus: Three Case Studies *230*
  Discussion: The Feasibility of School Improvement
    Mandates in Rural Areas *241*

10. **MIAMI-DADE COUNTY: TROUBLE IN CHOICE PARADISE,**
    Jane Hannaway and Sarah Cohodes   244
  Miami-Dade County Public Schools *245*
  School Choice in Florida *246*
  School Choice in Miami *250*
  NCLB School Choice *253*
  The Bases of Choice *259*
  Supplemental Educational Services *261*
  Conclusion *263*

PART IV: RESTRUCTURING DISTRICTS AND SCHOOLS   265

11. **REMEDIES IN ACTION: FOUR "RESTRUCTURED" SCHOOLS,**
    Julie Kowal and Bryan C. Hassel   267
  Methodology and Overview *270*
  Case Study #1: Buchanan Elementary School *271*
  Case Study #2: Balboa Elementary School *274*
  Case Study #3: Milwood Magnet School *278*
  Case Study #4: Gompers Middle School *282*
  Common Lessons and Conclusions *285*

12. **DISTRICT ACCOUNTABILITY: MORE BARK THAN BITE?**
    Joe Williams   290
  NCLB Accountability for Districts: How It Works *292*

"Corrective Action"   *294*
How It Plays Out   *296*
Supporting District Stability   *299*
Case Study: Baltimore City Schools   *300*
Conclusion   *307*

**CONCLUSION: CAN THIS LAW BE FIXED? A HARD LOOK AT THE
NCLB REMEDIES,** *Frederick M. Hess and Chester E. Finn Jr.*   **309**
Recommendations   *319*
Closing Observations   *327*

NOTES   **331**

ABOUT THE AUTHORS   **373**

INDEX   **379**

Tables and Figures

CHAPTER 1: MANNA

Figure 1-1   School Districts and Title I Schools in Improvement
              by Number of States, 2004–5   *20*

Figure 1-2   Final State AYP Determinations, 2006   *23*

Table 1-1   Excerpts from Model School Choice Parental
              Notification Letters   *24*

Table 1-2   Excerpts from Model Supplemental Educational
              Services Parental Notification Letters   *28*

Table 1-3   Information in State Lists of Approved Supplemental
              Educational Services Providers   *31*

Figure 1-3   Title I Schools in Improvement Stages by Number of
              States, 2004–5   *34*

CHAPTER 2: CASSERLY

Table 2-1   NCLB Transfers, 2002–3 to 2005–6   *47*

Table 2-2   Supplemental Educational Services, 2005–6   *51*

Table 2-3   Strategies Used by Responding Districts with Schools
              in Corrective Action or Restructuring   *59*

CHAPTER 3: HENIG

Figure 3-1   Students Receiving SES over Time   *70*

Figure 3-2   Major Newspaper Coverage over Time   *72*

Table 3-1   Program Elements Reviewed by States and Districts
              Monitoring Providers, 2005–6   *84*

Table 3-2   SES Providers by States in Which Approved   *87*

Table 3-3   Providers by Type   *88*

CHAPTER 5: BETTS

Figure 5-1   School and District AYP Expectations in California   *124*

Figure 5-2   Percentage of Title I Schools by Program Improvement
                (PI) Status, 2006–7 *127*

Table 5-1   Number of Students Participating in NCLB School
                Choice by Year, and as a Percentage of Eligible
                Students and All K–12 Students *128*

Table 5-2   Number of Students Participating in NCLB Supplemental
                Educational Services by Year, and as a Percentage of
                Eligible Students and All K–12 Students *133*

CHAPTER 6: MCGUINN

Figure 6-1   Adequate Yearly Progress of 2,400 New Jersey
                Schools *157*

Figure 6-2   NCLB School Choice in New Jersey, 2004–5: Eligible
                and Transferred Students *159*

Figure 6-3   Supplemental Educational Services in New Jersey:
                Eligible and Served Students, 2003–6 *166*

Figure 6-4   "In Need of Improvement Status" of New Jersey
                Schools *171*

CHAPTER 7: MEDLER

Figure 7-1   Colorado School Ratings: SAR and AYP, 2005 *184*

Table 7-1   Demographics of Colorado Schools *186*

Figure 7-2   NCLB-Identified Schools by Mean Percentage of
                Minority Students, 2005 *187*

Table 7-2   Denver and Non-Denver School Demographics, 2005 *188*

Table 7-3   Mean Cost and Revenue for NCLB-Identified
                Schools *193*

CHAPTER 8: PLANK AND DUNBAR

Table 8-1   Comparison of Schools by AYP Phase 2006
                and 2005 *208*

CHAPTER 9: CLEMENTS

Table 9-1   Kentucky's State Test (CATS) Configuration,
                Spring 2006 *228*

Figure 9-1   Kentucky School Districts *231*

CHAPTER 10: HANNAWAY AND COHODES

Table 10-1   AYP by School Grade, All Florida Schools *248*

Table 10-2 Enrollment in School Choice Programs 251
Table 10-3 NCLB School Transfers, Miami-Dade County 254
Table 10-4 AYP by School Grade, All Miami-Dade County
Schools 254
Table 10-5 School Choice Capacity 256
Figure 10-1 School Choice Application Windows 258
Table 10-6 AYP and School Grades: Percentage of Transfers
by Sending/Receiving Schools 260
Table 10-7 Supplemental Educational Services 262

CHAPTER 11: KOWAL AND HASSEL
Figure 11-1 Buchanan Elementary School: Percentage of Students
Meeting State Standards 272
Figure 11-2 Balboa Elementary School: Percentage of Students
Meeting State Standards 275
Figure 11-3 Milwood Magnet School: Percentage of Students
Meeting State Standards 279
Figure 11-4 Gompers Charter Middle School: Percentage of Students
Meeting State Standards 283

Preface

Like everyone else engaged with U.S. education policy, we have spent a great deal of time over the past five years talking, thinking, and writing about the intricacies of the No Child Left Behind Act (NCLB). In 2002 and 2003, when states and localities were first struggling with its implementation, discussion with policymakers, educators, reformers, and analysts helped clarify for us the challenges inherent in the "remedy" provisions of that law—the parts meant to revamp low-performing schools and create educational alternatives. Given the larger significance of those remedies for school reform, and our hope that careful scrutiny might help prevent a repeat of missteps that plagued the first decade of the old Elementary and Secondary Education Act (ESEA), we assembled a team of researchers who could illuminate the implementation and impact of the NCLB's remedy provisions as they were coming into effect. The result was the book, *Leaving No Child Behind? Options for Kids in Failing Schools*, published by Palgrave Macmillan in 2004, which offered an initial assessment of NCLB's remedies and some guidance for policy and implementation.[1]

The present volume builds on that earlier effort, taking a hard look at these provisions five years after enactment of NCLB and as the law enters the reauthorization process. We seek to provide guidance and insight for those now struggling to make the law work as intended. Again, by tracking the remedy provisions in real time, we hope this volume will help policymakers and educators improve NCLB's design and implementation.

The chapters that follow were first presented at a research conference at the American Enterprise Institute (AEI) in Washington, D.C., in November 2006. There the authors and editors benefited from much constructive feedback. We particularly acknowledge with thanks the contributions of the conference's designated discussants, including John Winn, then Florida's commissioner of education; Alan Bersin, then California's secretary of education; Morgan Brown, assistant deputy secretary of the U.S. Department of Education; Kati Haycock, director of the Education Trust; Diane Ravitch, senior fellow at the Brookings Institution and the Hoover Institution; and Marshall Smith, director of the education program at the William and Flora Hewlett Foundation.

We also express our appreciation to the Koret Foundation and to AEI's National Research Initiative for the generous support that made the conference and this volume possible. We offer special thanks to Rosemary Kendrick for the stellar job she did in coordinating the entire project, planning the conference, overseeing the preparation of this volume, and keeping the trains running on time. We also note with gratitude the worthy contributions of Jennifer Leischer, Juliet Squire, and Morgan Goatley.

Introduction

Frederick M. Hess and Chester E. Finn Jr.

American education has nothing like the Food and Drug Administration to ensure that its treatments are safe and effective. The FDA is charged with protecting us from unsafe, unreliable, and ineffectual products, be they medicines that don't work, pharmaceutical devices that cause more problems than they solve, tainted food, mysterious ingredients, or adulterated canned goods. In general, the FDA won't approve drugs or medical devices for routine use by physicians until they have been shown, through careful testing, to be both safe and effective. Many products never pass that dual test.

Education has no comparable watchdog. The goofiest nostrum, the most bizarre innovation, or the riskiest intervention may be undertaken in curricula, pedagogy, school operations, and classroom practice—even undertaken on a vast scale, potentially affecting the lives of thousands of teachers and millions of pupils—without ever having to demonstrate its effectiveness, its reliability, or its freedom from troubling side effects.

This situation is at best strange, at worst inexcusable. One can reasonably assert that the "interventions" introduced by the No Child Left Behind Act (NCLB)[1] are as important for the well-being of millions of U.S. children as the medicines they take and the food they eat. With that sobering reality in mind, in 2006 we commissioned a select group of scholars and close observers of the education scene to examine NCLB's remedy provisions as they are being carried out, to help us render a preliminary judgment on their implementation today and, looking ahead, to how safe and effective they will likely prove to be for America's children. The goal was not so much to issue a definitive evaluation but to glean insights into the remedies' design and impact that could inform their redesign and execution.

1

Passed by Congress in late 2001 and signed into law by President George W. Bush one year after his inauguration, NCLB is the most ambitious federal education statute ever enacted. Most observers—whether they like it or not—regard it as the Bush administration's signature domestic accomplishment, aside from tax cuts.

NCLB's sprawling 1,100-plus pages radically overhauled Washington's role in education, rewrote the rules, and reassigned power—including more to Uncle Sam than ever before—while striving to boost overall pupil achievement, narrow a host of learning gaps, and assure every student a highly qualified teacher. The legislation's main engine, however, is a historic attempt to impose a results-based accountability regime on schools across the land.

Radical as it is, NCLB was no start-from-scratch law. It was the (much delayed) reauthorization of the nation's most important K–12 statute, the Elementary and Secondary Education Act, first passed in 1965 when Lyndon B. Johnson was president.[2] ESEA, already extensively modified by many previous renewals, provided the superstructure to which NCLB was attached. (Whether that superstructure could reasonably be expected to support the weight added by NCLB is an important question that we revisit below.)

Given near-universal assent to NCLB's goal of educating all American children and general agreement that U.S. schools can and must do better, even the law's harshest critics typically voice support for its objectives before citing concerns about its mechanisms, timetables, regulations, or funding. And NCLB's ardent champions are wont to acknowledge missteps in execution—"weak implementation"—as a way to deflect criticism of the law's basic design.

Who is right? After five years of life with a statute that aims to produce "universal proficiency" (in math and reading, mainly in grades 3–8) by 2014, with reauthorization looming, and with advice about revamping it pouring into Congress from many directions, it is time to scrutinize the reality of NCLB as it has unfolded on the ground. In this volume, we focus explicitly upon its remedy provisions. We do not seek to evaluate their academic effects so much as their operations, their implementation, and the *likelihood* that they can bring about the ambitious changes in education practice and performance that their ambitious creators intended.

A Brief Recap

During the 2000 presidential campaign, both candidates promised aggressive action on the issue of education. George W. Bush, then governor of Texas, promoted as a national model his state's strong and relatively successful standards-based accountability program, leavened with charter schools and other elements of school choice. His opponent, then Vice President Al Gore, struck a remarkably similar note when he said, for example,

> I propose that we require every state and every school district to identify failing schools and work to turn them around, with strict accountability for results, strong incentives for success and more help to get the job done. If failing schools don't improve quickly, they will be shut down and reopened under a new principal.[3]

Gore also favored limited forms of school choice.

The outward kinship of the Democratic and GOP positions resulted from both teams having embraced essentially the same analysis of what ailed American K–12 education—and how to cure it. This diagnosis hearkened back to the celebrated 1983 report, *A Nation at Risk*, and the Washington-driven remedies urged in its wake by George H. W. Bush and Bill Clinton.[4] The former called his plan "America 2000," while the latter termed his "Goals 2000"; but few observers could spot big differences. Both proceeded from the belief that U.S. schoolchildren were not learning enough, especially when it came to the "three R's," and that this could be set right by inducing states to set explicit academic standards, deploy tests to determine whether and how well students and schools were meeting those standards, and create behaviorist "accountability" mechanisms, whereby rewards would come to schools that succeeded, and interventions, embarrassment, and sanctions would befall those that failed. Well before NCLB, governors of both parties had embraced this basic policy framework, and a number of states had acted upon it, albeit with varying degrees of enthusiasm. Though conservatives and liberals bickered about how far Washington should go in prodding laggard states, by 2000 the federal statute books already contained much prodding, notably a pair of laws that Clinton nudged through Congress weeks before the 1994 GOP takeover.

NCLB can fairly be termed the feisty progeny of those earlier measures, yet, in other respects, it has no precedent. It creates stern federal directives regarding test use and consequences; puts federal bureaucrats in charge of approving state testing systems and accountability plans; sets a uniform nationwide timetable for boosting achievement and closing gaps; and prescribes specific remedies for underperforming schools—and the children in them. In other words, NCLB is both an evolutionary development and a revolutionary departure.

The central challenge of making NCLB work arises from the mismatch between its vaulting ambitions and the extent of Washington's actual authority over K–12 education. Federal funds amount to barely eight cents of the public school dollar, giving Congress limited fiscal leverage. Constitutional responsibility for education is vested in state capitals, while Americans cherish "local control" of public schools, and the "education establishment's" formidable lobbying operation is known for its tenacious defense of the status quo.

In 2001, seeking to clear the obstacles that had blocked earlier federal efforts to boost pupil achievement, George W. Bush promoted a more forceful role for Uncle Sam—one that would use mandated tests and consequences to compel state and school cooperation, while increasing parental choice of schools and granting states more freedom in spending their federal aid. Within days of taking office, he dispatched to Capitol Hill a legislative blueprint that drew heavily on his experience in Texas. From the outset, however, Bush also insisted on bipartisan support, and his legislative strategists pressed for that. The complex law that resulted accordingly drew in ideas from left, right, and center—often without reconciling their inconsistencies.

After nearly a year of negotiations, administration and congressional leaders hammered out a bipartisan measure that commanded support not only from most Republicans but also from such prominent Democrats as Massachusetts Senator Edward M. Kennedy and California Representative George Miller, then the ranking members of Congress's two education committees and now their chairmen. In December 2001, the No Child Left Behind Act was adopted on a 381–41 vote in the House of Representatives and by 87–10 in the Senate. The price of that broad support, however, was a major reshaping of the original White House proposal. The compromise bill joined Bush's results-centered approach to a host of equity-oriented provisions that ranged from the performance of racial groups to the assignment of teachers, while sharply curbing the White House's school choice and state flexibility proposals.

Though NCLB is routinely labeled a Bush law—in no small part because the White House has proclaimed it a great domestic achievement while prominent Democrats have been far more equivocal—in fact its provisions are a Rube Goldberg–like assemblage of administration proposals, "New Democrat" schemes, favorite liberal ideas of Messrs. Kennedy and Miller, and proposals and cautions introduced by countless other constituencies, all superimposed upon programmatic habits, architecture, and rules that had accumulated like reefs since LBJ worked in the Oval Office. Indeed, from the outset, it was clear that implementing this mishmash would recall the phrase that the late Daniel P. Moynihan used to describe LBJ's multifaceted community action program: "maximum feasible misunderstanding."

Nowhere was this clearer than in the cascade of "remedies" for low-performing schools (described below), which borrow from multiple theories, display innumerable compromises, and are grafted onto four decades of prior processes and regulations.

NCLB Accountability

NCLB's accountability engine is driven by two pistons: the insistence that states adopt systematic standards and testing for schools and districts, and the intervention in ineffective schools and districts, executed while providing immediate relief for their pupils. The federal government has charged states with defining and adopting the standards and tests while it spells out the remedies that states and districts are responsible for providing. Yes, the statute contains hundreds of other provisions. But if its two main pistons aren't firing well, this complex engine won't budge the massive barge that is American schooling—much less render it a more agile craft.

On the assessment front, NCLB requires that all public schools annually test all their students in grades 3–8 in reading and math, and that every state measure whether its public schools are making "adequate yearly progress" (AYP) toward universal proficiency in those core subjects by 2014. Each school must meet steadily rising goals in every demographic subgroup: by race, disability, English-language status, and so on. Schools are then evaluated on the past year's achievement of each category in which their enrollment meets or exceeds a minimum number of students (that number being determined by the state, subject to federal approval). If a school fails to "make AYP" in any of those categories for two consecutive years, it is judged to be "in need of improvement"; if that school is the recipient of Title I dollars (federal money set aside for low-income students),[5] it is then subject to a cascade of sanctions and interventions that grow more draconian with each additional year of failure.

The testing issues that arise from NCLB have received extensive attention. State and federal officials and platoons of academics have spent five years debating cut scores, proficiency targets, sample and population sizes, confidence intervals, value-added metrics, and similar concerns. Receiving far less attention has been the remedies side of the equation. In this volume, we do not focus on the standards, the tests, or the definition of AYP, though we touch on them when necessary. Instead, we examine the seven-year sequence of remedies prescribed in the law, whereby a Title I school that fails to make AYP is subject to interventions designed to change it and give new options to its students and their families. Our aim is not to evaluate the overall impact of NCLB but to provide a more penetrating picture of the remedies than currently exists.

After all, NCLB's remedies are meant to do far more than pour money into needy schools (as the original ESEA did) or pour sunshine onto school performance (as measures adopted in the 1990s had attempted). In 2001, lawmakers sought to *change* ineffective schools, not merely illuminate their derelictions. NCLB promised not just to identify schools "in need of improvement" but also to intervene in multiple ways to correct their shortcomings, while providing escape hatches for youngsters trapped in them. Toward that end, Congress mandated the remedy cascade. This was a novel role for Washington, and one fraught with challenges.

The approach was borne of massive frustration among both Republicans and Democrats with the pace of school improvement across America. Republicans, in particular, had historically been leery of Uncle Sam's wading into state and local educational responsibilities. Yet in the face of what it saw as inertia, resistance, and excuses from the nation's educators, Congress's historic reticence crumbled. In creating NCLB's cascade of remedies, lawmakers sought to construct a uniform, predictable, and logical framework for school improvement, while sending educators a message that the status quo would no longer be tolerated.

Itemizing the Remedies

What does this "cascade" of remedies actually entail? If a federally aided (Title I) school fails to make AYP for two consecutive years, its students are supposed to be offered public school choice, enabling them to attend other public schools in their district. Under that provision, the district is to provide each such child with a choice of alternative public schools (including charter schools) that *are* making suitable progress. Meanwhile, schools identified for improvement must draft or update a multiyear improvement plan and receive technical assistance to address the problems that led them to fail to make AYP.

If a school falters for a third straight year, its district is supposed to provide pupils with the opportunity to obtain supplemental educational services (SES)—essentially, free after-school tutoring—from diverse providers, including private firms. This tutoring is to be paid for with a portion of the school's federal dollars—a sort of minivoucher. In addition, because the remedies are cumulative, qualifying students continue to be eligible for NCLB school choice.

If a school fails to make AYP for a fourth year running, its district is to take "corrective action." This can entail replacing school staff, implementing a new curriculum, reducing the school's management authority, extending the day or year, appointing an outside expert to advise the school, or reorganizing the school. Qualifying students in year 4 schools also remain eligible for NCLB school choice and supplemental educational services—and do so as long as their schools fail to make AYP.

If it fails to make AYP for a fifth consecutive year, a school's district must (during year 6) prepare a restructuring plan for it. This may include reopening it as a charter school, replacing its principal and staff, contracting with a private management company to run it, turning it over to the state, or any other major restructuring of school governance. If the school fails to make AYP for a sixth year, the restructuring plan is to be implemented by the beginning of the following (that is, the seventh) school year. Various regulations govern how districts are to manage these processes, how states are to oversee districts, and so forth.

On paper, this all proceeds in an orderly and familiar top-down sequence, with federal rules spelling out what states are to do, states telling districts what to do, and local school systems having the primary obligation to repair their faltering schools (and offer options to pupils). State education departments are charged with setting standards, creating tests, intervening in districts that themselves fail to make AYP, and generally overseeing matters. That hierarchy of responsibility—from Washington to state capital to local school system to schools and, finally, to classrooms—has been the basic architecture of federal education policy for decades. But it was never designed to support a results-based accountability system, to make effective repairs to faltering schools and lagging districts, or to function in an environment peppered with education novelties such as charter schools, home-schooling, and distance-learning.

Yet, to the best of our knowledge, none of NCLB's architects even paused to ask whether a hierarchy decently suited to distribute money according to certain formulae and rules could also handle the challenges of school reform and the implementation of a very different and much more aggressive federal role.

Upon examination, the NCLB remedies prove to contain elements of at least four different theories of education change. One is to boost achievement by helping children to leave ineffective schools for better ones—and to obtain remedial tutoring from education providers other than the (ineffectual) school itself. A second is creating market-style competitive pressures (via the exit of students and dollars) to motivate weak schools or districts to improve. A third is to effect desired improvements by furnishing low-performing schools with technical assistance, guidance, and support in developing and implementing their own reform plans. And a fourth, in the event that the previous steps do not yield the desired gains, is to intervene forcibly and "restructure" low-performing schools through district and/or state-level action.

Alternatives. Competition. Help. Intervention. Over the seven-year time-frame elaborately constructed by NCLB, and with various options at each step along the way, all four types of education reform—and the quartet of change theories that undergird them—were to be imposed on schools "in need of improvement."

Thus, NCLB's remedies are more an assemblage of reform ideas than a coherent scheme. They were adopted with scant attention to how they would fit together, what resources or authority they would require, or whether they could be deployed sensibly through the available machinery. For instance, furnishing assistance and technical support to low-performing schools requires providing them with new resources, which undercuts efforts to make the consequences of mediocrity painful for educators in those same schools. Enabling children to leave troubled schools may remove both money and some of the internal pressure (for instance, from unhappy parents) to set the schools right.

Moreover, many of the specific policies and practices ultimately inscribed in NCLB are wan versions of their own underlying theories and pale shadows of the original proposals considered by Congress; a vivid example of this is the intradistrict public school choice provision, which was adopted in lieu of vouchers or other far-reaching choice-based reforms. Furthermore, at key junctures the remedy cascade provides schools and districts with options that range from mild to severe and from vague to specific, thus blurring both theory and remedy. Finally, all the remedies assume that someone—schools, districts, states, tutoring providers, families—possesses both the capacity and the will to carry them out with skill and gusto.

The result is messy and confusing at best, the product of much compromising on Capitol Hill and mixing and matching of theories and remedies, and all part of a massive congressional smorgasbord of programs, incentives, interventions, and sops to ideologies, advocates, and interest groups.

After a decade of uneven efforts with "standards-based" reform, the most contentious question in 2001 was, what should states be expected—or required—to do when their tests indicate that some schools or districts are persistently failing? That question had long perplexed education reformers and federal policymakers. NCLB undeniably sought to answer it. The question before us in these pages is how satisfactory the answer has turned out to be in practice—that is, how well the NCLB remedies are working on the ground.

Relevant data are depressingly elusive. The lassitude with which local, state, and federal officials have approached the task of collecting information on the NCLB interventions is, frankly, stunning—and extremely disappointing, the more so in an era marked by ceaseless talk of research, evidence, and program effectiveness. As readers will see in the chapters ahead, simply locating descriptive data on the workings of NCLB's remedy provisions is no easy task—and trying to assess their impact has barely been contemplated. Consequently, our authors were forced to glean what they could from various methods, sources, and locales. In doing so, they exhibited admirable tenacity and pioneered a variety of thoughtful ways to answer the question posed. The result is the assembly and presentation of data available nowhere else, and some data-collection efforts that may become models for methods Washington and the states can pursue in more systematic and comprehensive ways.

Organization of This Volume

From here, the book proceeds in four parts. The first four chapters provide the broad national picture. The next four look at how public choice, supplemental educational services, and NCLB's restructuring provisions are playing out in California, New Jersey, Colorado, and Michigan. The third and fourth sections consist of four chapters that take a closer look at developments in districts and schools across the nation. Finally, the editors draw some conclusions and offer our own thoughts on the design and implementation of the NCLB remedies circa 2007.

Readers should bear in mind that we did not ask authors to "evaluate" those remedies, so much as to attempt to understand and describe them. In social scientese, their assessments are more "formative" than "summative." The authors do, however, take a careful, nuanced look at how the NCLB remedies are playing out in schools, districts, and states, and at the U.S. Department of Education. This research is instructive not only for future policy deliberations regarding NCLB, but also—because NCLB's remedies include such high-profile reform strategies as public school choice, charter schooling, and state takeovers—for school improvement more broadly.

In chapter 1, Paul Manna of the College of William and Mary provides an overview of how all fifty states have guided implementation of NCLB's remedies for troubled schools and districts that fail to make adequate yearly progress. He finds that states vary tremendously in how enthusiastically they have pursued the NCLB remedies, with implementation in many so spotty that it is unlikely the various remedies can be made to work properly at the local level. He offers several reasons for these difficulties, some attributable to NCLB itself and others to the structure of the U.S. federal system.

In chapter 2, Michael Casserly, executive director of the Council of the Great City Schools, provides the most comprehensive look to date at how the remedies are being implemented in the nation's major urban school systems. Casserly reports on low but slightly improved participation rates in NCLB school choice, major changes in who provides supplemental educational services, and the onset of school restructuring in the major cities. He concludes that NCLB is both living up to many of its promises, as its strongest proponents hoped it would, and encountering many of the pitfalls that its harshest critics warned against.

In chapter 3, Columbia University professor Jeffrey R. Henig examines the political economy of NCLB's supplemental educational services (SES) provision. Henig argues that the politics behind SES were influenced by two simplifying images: the "image of obsolescent localism" and the "market metaphor." These served different purposes for Republican and Democratic proponents, but they converged on one key point: The role of conventional local school districts should be less central and more circumscribed. As NCLB unfolds, however, Henig argues that SES is better understood as a local contracting regime. Rather than being marginalized, local politics and governance are playing a modified but no less consequential role.

In chapter 4, Thomas B. Fordham Foundation vice president and former U.S. Education Department official Michael J. Petrilli looks critically at the design and implementation of NCLB. He notes the argument made by many NCLB advocates that, with the right people calling the shots in the Department of Education and making good decisions, the NCLB remedies will work as intended. In other words, they say, "implementation is the problem." Petrilli challenges this contention when it comes to NCLB choice, SES, and school restructuring, concluding that the law's failings are due not primarily to faulty implementation but to constraints in the federal system.

In the second part of the volume, the contributors look more deeply at developments in four states. In chapter 5, Julian Betts, of the University of California at San Diego, examines NCLB school choice, supplemental educational services, and local educational agency remedies in California. He finds that student-participation rates in choice and SES are still low and explains barriers to increasing them. Betts observes that California's Department of Education bears a huge information-gathering burden and may need additional personnel or outside help to focus on NCLB. He suggests altering parental notification practices so as to employ shorter, more direct letters, and allowing higher-income but low-achieving students in failing schools to participate in NCLB choice and tutoring if the programs fail to attract enough low-income participants.

In chapter 6, Drew University's Patrick McGuinn considers implementation in New Jersey and finds decidedly mixed results. Initially, the state Department of Education failed to provide clear and timely AYP determinations or adequate guidance and supervision for underperforming schools. The small size of most New Jersey districts has combined with the lack of a law regarding interdistrict choice and a difficult chartering process to make school choice virtually nonexistent. Districts have used their discretion over SES processes to constrain the entrance and expansion of private providers. The state has created a new process for monitoring and intervening in struggling schools but has been reluctant to impose major restructuring changes. McGuinn illustrates just how challenging it can be for states with strong local control to respect that tradition while complying with the NCLB remedies.

In chapter 7, Alex Medler of the Colorado Children's Campaign concludes that, in Colorado, NCLB is nearly powerless to effect the desired behavior changes. He reports that the state has a great deal of public school choice, some tutoring, and a few districts that have embraced school restructuring. But he finds that very little of this activity can be attributed to NCLB, and, to the extent that it can be, most of it happens in settings like Denver, where it was occurring anyway. He concludes by suggesting alternative interventions to promote local action that would not happen otherwise, that would affect more children, and that would be more likely to increase performance.

In chapter 8, David N. Plank, of Policy Analysis for California Education (and formerly director of the Education Policy Center at Michigan State University), and Christopher Dunbar Jr., of Michigan State University, examine Michigan's implementation of NCLB sanctions and deem it half-hearted at best. State and local officials have preferred the gentler interventions, focusing on the closer alignment of curriculum and instruction and the provision of coaching and other forms of technical assistance. Even so, in 2005–6 more than half of the state's lowest-performing schools made AYP for the second consecutive year, resetting their sanctions clock to zero. The authors conclude that the credible threat of sanctions has focused Michigan officials' attention on the state's least successful schools, though the strategies they have adopted to turn these schools around are very different from those foreseen under NCLB.

Chapters 9 through 12 probe more deeply into developments in districts and schools across the nation. In chapter 9, Stephen Clements of the University of Kentucky profiles three remote districts in that state that have struggled with the NCLB remedies. He finds them implementing various remediation measures arising from Kentucky's school improvement planning process, but almost no evidence of NCLB school choice. Similarly, SES is rare, with only a few eligible students participating and few vendors seemingly willing to work in these locales. Clements raises the question of whether the cascade of remedies is suited to the needs of rural students and schools.

In chapter 10, Jane Hannaway and Sarah Cohodes of the Urban Institute provide eye-opening new data on the implementation of NCLB choice and supplemental educational services in Miami-Dade County, Florida. While 22 percent of Miami-Dade students are enrolled in school choice programs, fewer than 1 percent of eligible students use NCLB school choice, and fewer than 12 percent use SES. The authors explore possible reasons and conclude that, in the case of the school transfer option, the low rate of participation is due to a restrictive timeline for NCLB choice and the failure of the AYP designation to offer a meaningful signal regarding school quality.

In chapter 11, Julie Kowal and Bryan C. Hassel of Public Impact profile four schools that restructured during 2005–6. Their case studies make clear that, while NCLB provides an *opportunity* to reshape a school radically, its requirements offer districts wide flexibility on how to proceed. The authors conclude that the impact of NCLB restructuring is indeterminate and depends on many factors. Besides NCLB, these schools and their districts are responding to a complex set of political and market pressures and struggling with a web of constraints on the actions they can take.

In chapter 12, Joe Williams of Democrats for Education Reform addresses NCLB's call for the restructuring of low-performing school *districts*, focusing on the case of Baltimore. He reports that nearly five years after NCLB was adopted, not a single school district has been subjected to radical restructuring—or even been taken over by the state—under NCLB's corrective-action provision. Due to federal guidelines that offer tremendous wiggle-room and the reality that districts themselves frequently take the lead in determining what remedies are necessary, Williams finds little evidence that NCLB is bringing dramatic change to those that fail to make AYP.

Finally, in the conclusion, we try to make sense of this wealth of research and analysis, providing some closing thoughts and recommendations for policymakers and practitioners.

PART I

The Big Picture

1

NCLB in the States: Fragmented Governance, Uneven Implementation

Paul Manna

Many people claim that the No Child Left Behind Act of 2001 (NCLB) has revolutionized federal education policy. Whether or not the law is a true breakthrough for Washington, NCLB's prospects still rely heavily on state government actions. In fact, one could easily argue that state policy is the fuel that powers the federal NCLB engine. This overview chapter examines how all fifty states have guided implementation of NCLB's remedies for troubled schools and districts that fail to meet annual achievement goals known as adequate yearly progress (AYP).

The chapter relies on several sources, including documents and press releases from state education agency websites, federal reports, popular press coverage of NCLB, and correspondence with state education officials in eight states during October and November of 2006. The evidence shows much diversity in how states have carried out NCLB's remedies. Some appear to be doing yeoman's work with this complicated law, but many continue to struggle. That diversity suggests several challenges for federal policymakers, who, despite claims to the contrary, remain fundamentally limited in their ability to engineer major changes in American schools. The

The author offers many thanks to officials in eight states who offered valuable insights. He also received superb feedback on earlier drafts from Dane Linn, Jason Palmer, Frederick M. Hess, Chester E. Finn Jr., and participants at the American Enterprise Institute/Thomas B. Fordham Foundation's "Fixing Failing Schools Conference." Last, but certainly not least, Chad Aldeman provided outstanding research assistance.

overall result is perhaps not surprising, given NCLB's ambitious goals, its dynamic nature, and the fragmented intergovernmental system in which it is unfolding.

Expectations for NCLB's Remedies

NCLB's remedies for schools and districts not making scheduled progress are a cornerstone of the law's theory of action, and they represent a key difference between the current law and its immediate predecessor, the Improving America's Schools Act of 1994 (IASA).[1] The idea that real consequences must ensue if schools and districts consistently fail to make AYP contrasts with more "suggestive" versions of accountability, such as using student testing to provide teachers and parents with information about school performance, but then relying on informal pressure or added support to prompt improvement. With a suggestive approach to accountability, critics argue that consequences are more ambiguous and lack the needed bite of high-stakes measures.[2]

Under NCLB, schools repeatedly missing AYP are subject to a cascade of remedies. These include allowing students to transfer to another public school and receive supplemental educational services, as well as reforming schools through corrective action and more major restructuring. Many people forget that the law also requires entire school districts to make AYP. Those failing to do so for two consecutive years must craft an improvement plan. After two more years of missing AYP, districts enter their own version of corrective action, which can include adopting management, organizational, or curricular reforms at the district level, or experiencing greater state involvement in the management of district operations.

Even with more high-stakes accountability for troubled schools and districts, implementing NCLB has required federal officials to balance their ambitions for greater control with efforts to persuade other government leaders to follow along. In other words, high-stakes accountability has joined, rather than replaced, the suggestive accountability regime that had dominated previous iterations of the Elementary and Secondary Education Act (ESEA).[3] That combination and the institutions governing NCLB suggest several reasons to expect state implementation of the law's remedies to vary.

First, even with added accountability measures compared to previous ESEAs, fundamentally NCLB is organized around a series of grant programs, most notably in Title I, that can be challenging for federal overseers to manage. Money is supposed to entice states and localities to adopt goals that federal officials are unable to accomplish without substantial help. In many policy areas, not just education, grant recipients often use that fact to gain leverage by extracting concessions from grant providers as they push their own agendas.[4]

Second, NCLB creates a long delegation chain that places states in a difficult middle-management position. State leaders are agents of federal principals in Washington, charged with implementing a complicated law, but they are also principals over their own agents—local school districts and schools—who must simultaneously carry out federal and state education policy. States will differ in how they manage these arrangements, which can alter how NCLB's remedies unfold in practice.[5]

Third, in saying that NCLB relies heavily on the "states," one should remember that state governments are not unitary actors. While their education departments are the primary agents overseeing federal education policy, they operate within complicated policy networks. Governors, legislatures, courts, and state boards of education all can influence the state-level policy infrastructure that supports NCLB. With so many cooks in the kitchen, and different formal and informal arrangements connecting them, some states will likely be more successful than others at managing the coordination problems, political disagreements, and transaction costs associated with implementing NCLB's remedies.[6]

These three reasons suggest that the impact of NCLB's remedies will vary across states. Figure 1-1 provides an initial glimpse at that variability, which this chapter examines.[7] Part A of the figure shows the distribution of school districts that have consistently failed to make AYP by number of states. The spike at the left side of part A shows that over half the states have a very small percentage of their districts in improvement status. In fact, eleven of those states have no districts in improvement. A relatively small number of states have over half of their districts in improvement, which makes them subject to NCLB's district-level remedies.

Part B shows the distribution of Title I schools in improvement status, again by number of states. Singling out schools that receive Title I money is

FIGURE 1-1

SCHOOL DISTRICTS AND TITLE I SCHOOLS IN IMPROVEMENT
BY NUMBER OF STATES, 2004–5

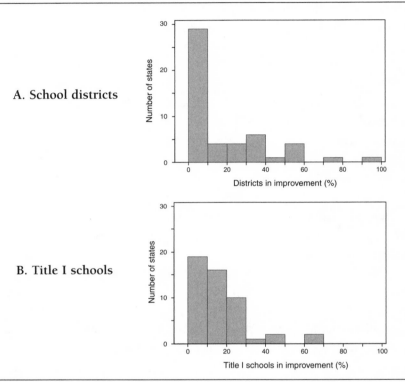

A. School districts

B. Title I schools

SOURCE: Adapted from U.S. Department of Education, National Center for Education Evaluation and Regional Assistance, Institute of Education Sciences, *National Assessment of Title I Interim Report: Volume I: Implementation of Title I*, by Stephanie Stullich, Elizabeth Eisner, Joseph McCrary, and Collette Roney (Washington, D.C.: Government Printing Office, 2006), exhibits 31 and 33.

NOTES: The tallest bar in part A reads that twenty-nine states have fewer than 10 percent of all school districts in improvement status. The second tallest bar in part B reads that sixteen states have at least 10 but less than 20 percent of Title I schools in improvement. The Title I schools are subject to NCLB's cascade of remedies. See figure 1-3 for a breakdown of the remedies currently being implemented in these schools.

important because even though all schools are rated for AYP, NCLB's remedies only apply to those that receive Title I funds. The variability in Part B shows that most states have relatively small percentages of their Title I schools in improvement status, as evidenced by the clustering between 0 and 20 percent. Only a few have larger percentages, as revealed by the two small bars in the 40 and 60 percent range.

Part of the variation across states is no doubt related to actual school quality. However, one could safely attribute much of it to how state policy defines what it means for a school or a district to make AYP. Variability in these state definitions—the fuel for the NCLB engine—in turn produces variability in how many districts and schools must implement NCLB's cascade of remedies.

Choice and Supplemental Educational Services

In theory, NCLB school choice and supplemental educational services can empower parents and students, providing students who are attending struggling schools with opportunities to improve their academic fortunes. Simultaneously, both mechanisms offer a form of "exit," through which parents' choices can put pressure on struggling schools to change.[8] Thus, these two remedies can serve not only the individual students who use them, but also those who remain in schools that respond to the parents' signals. States perform important functions that can help the choice and supplemental educational services remedies succeed.

Timely Notification of AYP Results. State testing and accountability systems determine whether schools have made AYP and, therefore, whether they must offer NCLB school choice or supplemental educational services. Because most students take state tests in the spring, states must process the results swiftly and accurately and then calculate AYP results. It is hard to overemphasize how crucial this timing is to the proper functioning of NCLB's remedies, especially those that depend upon parents making choices for their children. Without timely notification, it is virtually impossible to expect smooth local implementation.

Technically speaking, NCLB requires school districts, not states, to notify parents if their children can exercise choice or use supplemental educational services. Before that can happen, though, states must administer tests, score them, compute AYP results, offer schools and districts time to appeal the calculations—which NCLB requires—and make any needed revisions. All these steps take time. Ultimately, then, states are responsible for ensuring that these remedies work by offering timely notice to districts, schools, and parents.[9]

Recent research suggests that state and local officials disagree about whether the timeliness of AYP notifications is a problem. In a study of NCLB for the 2004–5 school year, the Center on Education Policy found that "identifying schools for improvement prior to the start of the school year" was a top challenge mentioned by local districts in implementing NCLB's public school choice remedy. In contrast, when querying state officials, the center's researchers uncovered an interesting disconnection, given that "only a handful of states mentioned the timing of state AYP determinations as a challenge to choice."[10]

More than four years since NCLB became law, the evidence shows that states still struggle to determine AYP results in a timely manner. Figure 1-2 illustrates these difficulties by plotting the date on which each state made publicly available its final AYP determinations, based on performance from the 2005–6 school year. Notably, three states do not appear because, as of November 30, 2006, they still had not calculated final AYP results for all their schools. Of the remaining forty-seven, twenty-five produced these results in August. Others released them in September (ten states), October (four), or November (three). Only five states—North Dakota, Wisconsin, Florida, Georgia, and Hawaii—announced their final results before the end of July.

States have offered different reasons for these delays.[11] Some delays involved errors from contractors hired to score and compile test results. Others occurred because states were in the midst of transitions to new testing systems. Recognizing the importance of producing timely results, some states have been reporting provisional AYP determinations to specific schools likely not to make progress. However, these provisional assessments can change, causing problems for local school personnel who must inform parents about their children's eligibility for NCLB school choice or supplemental educational services.

Implementing NCLB School Choice. Most federal guidance for implementing NCLB school choice targets local school districts, not states. That is because districts have perhaps the most demanding responsibilities for this remedy, and thus, in practice, states work at arm's length on this provision. The primary state role, as noted in the previous section, is to provide timely information on schools identified as needing improvement so districts can inform parents of their options.

FIGURE 1-2
FINAL STATE AYP DETERMINATIONS, 2006

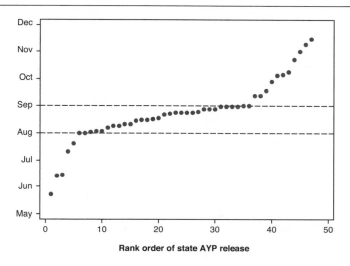

Rank order of state AYP release

SOURCE: Author's calculations based on information in various state educational agency press releases and newspaper stories.
NOTE: Each data point represents an individual state. The vertical axis specifies the date by which each state released its final AYP results. The horizontal axis orders the states from the earliest to the latest release of final AYP results for schools and districts. There are three states missing from the figure because, as of November 30, 2006, final AYP results were not available from their websites. Illinois and Montana had not released any AYP results, and New York had results available only for high schools.

Many states have developed "tool kits" of documents, answers to frequently asked questions, and other guidance to help local districts carry out the law. Often these kits include model letters that states have crafted and local districts can adapt to inform eligible parents about NCLB school choice. These letters are worth considering because they represent a concrete way in which states help implement this otherwise locally dominated NCLB remedy.

The actual letters that districts produce have created controversy in some places where, critics have claimed, they are confusing, or even discourage parents from exercising this option. Poor letters can at least partially explain the relatively low student participation in NCLB school choice, these critics say. Some states have been proactive in this regard. One official from Delaware told me that the state actually monitors the letters local districts send to parents. Still, it is worth considering whether potential problems may begin in language that states themselves suggest to local districts.[12]

TABLE 1-1

EXCERPTS FROM MODEL SCHOOL CHOICE PARENTAL NOTIFICATION LETTERS

Opening paragraph	Words preceding sentence with choice option
West Virginia. West Virginia's public schools have been working hard to improve the performance of our students in reading, writing, and mathematics. On state tests, most students are scoring well and are achieving mastery in these core subjects. Our schools have shown that they can and will rise to high standards.	92
Delaware. Your child's school has been designated under the *No Child Left Behind Act of 2001* (NCLB) as a Title I School Improvement School. This designation alone does not indicate a failing school, but provides for a focus on areas of school improvement by principals, teachers, and parents. Identified schools become eligible for additional support from the school division and state as they work together to improve teaching and learning especially in the areas of reading and mathematics. Under the federal NCLB legislation, when a Title I school is identified as in need of improvement, parents have the option to: 1. Remain at the school and participate in the school improvement process; or 2. Seek enrollment in one of the designated schools below.	112
Washington. As part of the "No Child Left Behind Act (NCLB) of 2002" school districts are required to notify parents/guardians when schools that their children attend have not made Adequate Yearly Progress (AYP) for two consecutive years. AYP is the level of proficiency that schools must achieve on an annual basis. It is determined by a matrix of "cells" that include the percentages of participation, as well as proficiency of students in reading and math along with unexcused absences and graduation rates for secondary students. Those percentages are calculated across categories that include student ethnicity and socioeconomic status. Districts are also required to inform you of options that you have as a result of your child's school not making AYP.	163
Iowa. Many of you are aware of the federal No Child Left Behind (NCLB) Act, which requires schools to assess students annually and to meet student achievement goals. If a school does not meet those assessment and achievement goals (termed "adequate yearly progress" or AYP) for two consecutive years, and if the school receives federal Title I funds, then it is placed on a federal "Schools in Need of Assistance (SINA)" list and subjected to federal sanctions. Schools or districts are cited if they a) don't meet 95 percent participation rate for	172

(continued on next page)

(Table 1-1 continued from previous page)

Opening paragraph	Words preceding sentence with choice option
assessments, b) don't meet student achievement goals, or c) don't meet attendance rate for elementary and middle schools or graduation rate for high school.	
Connecticut. Our school is committed to providing all students with an excellent education. (SCHOOL NAME) has strong, dedicated teachers, who want to help your child succeed.	270

SOURCES: West Virginia Department of Education, "Parent Letter for School Choice," http://wvde. state.wv.us/titlei/documents/ParentLetterforSchoolChoice06.doc; State of Delaware Department of Education, "Parent Notification: Public School Choice, Sample 1," http://www.doe.k12.de.us/SchoolImprovement/Choice/choicesampleletters.doc; Washington Office of Superintendent of Public Instruction, "Schools Identified for School Improvement—Step 1—Public School Choice 2005," http://www.k12.wa.us/ESEA/models/parentschoolchoiceletter05-06.doc; Iowa Department of Education, "Notice of AYP, Sample Letter B," under NCLB Reporting Requirements, AYP Notifications Under NCLB, Communication Guidelines for Local Districts to Use with Parents, http://www.iowa.gov/educate/content/blogcategory/497/921/; and Connecticut State Department of Education, "Sample Letter of Parent/Guardian Notification of Public School Choice for Elementary and Middle Schools Identified as 'In Need of Improvement'—Year 1," http://www.csde.state.ct.us/public/cedar/nclb/sip/resources/sip_guide/templates/parent_letter_Elem_Midd_year1.doc (all accessed June 13, 2007).

Excerpts from five state model letters appear in table 1-1. These letters were downloaded from state education agency websites in October 2006 and were chosen to provide examples (not a random sample) of states with different geographic and population characteristics. Table 1-1 presents the opening paragraph of each state's letter. It also indicates the number of words parents must read before seeing the sentence that explicitly states their child qualifies for NCLB school choice. Without examining the actual letters that parents receive, one cannot know for sure if local districts are actually using these templates when they develop their letters. Some local letters may be better, others worse, than the state models.

These examples suggest that many state templates do not lead with perhaps the most important piece of information—namely, that parents can exercise NCLB school choice. Connecticut's and West Virginia's letters may be most striking in this regard. Both open with several lines that emphasize strong performance in the public schools generally (West Virginia's letter) or in the particular school the child attends that is missing

AYP (Connecticut's letter). Other letters open by generally discussing NCLB, and explaining how AYP works. The sometimes complicated language demonstrates the difficulty some states have experienced in accurately describing the law in lay terms.

Some letters also take longer than others to mention NCLB school choice explicitly. Even though West Virginia's letter opens with a generally positive statement about the state's public schools, it is the swiftest at alerting parents to this option. A parent needs to read only 92 words, the rough equivalent of a four- or five-sentence paragraph, before learning about NCLB school choice. Connecticut's template takes the longest to mention NCLB's choice remedy; parents learn of it after reading 270 words.

Other state actions also can affect how NCLB's choice remedy plays out. In particular, implementation can chafe against other state laws or priorities. Sometimes, though not always, federal law affirms that state priorities can take precedence. That variability in NCLB itself has created confusion for states and local districts.

Florida's Polk County School District provides an example of how state and federal law can collide to complicate implementation of NCLB school choice. In 2002, Florida's voters enacted a constitutional amendment to limit class sizes across the state. Four years later, in August 2006, Polk County was required to offer NCLB school choice to approximately 34,000 students who attended twenty-nine schools not making AYP. Even though barely 2 percent of those students requested transfers, it was enough to throw the district out of compliance with the state's class-size amendment.[13] Federal guidance for NCLB's school choice remedy is explicit about which state laws can alter the implementation of choice. It says:

> The only type of State law that can limit or exempt an LEA [local education agency] from implementing the Title I public school choice requirements is a law that specifically prohibits public school choice through restrictions on public school assignments or the transfer of students from one public school to another. Other laws, such as those that mandate specific student–teacher ratios, may make providing choice options more difficult, but may not be used to prohibit parental choices.[14]

Whether Florida's *constitutional* provision should be considered different from a state *law* is unclear. The school district's lawyer, Wes Bridges, noted that, as a practical matter, the district would have to obey one policy and disobey the other. "We have to make a choice, which spanking hurts worse," he said.[15]

Beyond that difficulty lies a further challenge. Like many states, Florida maintains its own accountability system, separate from NCLB, to rate school progress. In Polk County, twelve of the twenty-nine schools required to offer NCLB school choice also scored an "A" or "B" using Florida's accountability metric. That can complicate matters for districts attempting to inform parents about district progress and parents' options under NCLB.[16] It would likely confuse parents to receive a notice that their child's school rated an "A" by the state's measure, but learn through a different mailing that their child can transfer because the school did not make AYP.

Implementing Supplemental Educational Services. Unlike NCLB's school choice remedy, which places most responsibility on local districts, states must complete many specific tasks to support supplemental educational services. In general, federal guidance says that the state education agency (SEA) "must identify providers, maintain a list of providers, and monitor services." In developing a state-approved provider list, the guidance explains, state departments of education should ensure that parents have as many choices as possible. States also must remove providers from their lists who for two consecutive years cannot show evidence of increasing student academic proficiency.[17]

For this remedy, states have also developed model letters districts can use to inform eligible families about supplemental educational services. Table 1-2 presents excerpts from a convenient sample of these letters. Interestingly, unlike the excerpts from table 1-1 regarding NCLB school choice, these letters tend to be much more direct. Massachusetts's model letter is the most direct of all. Its opening paragraph simply states: "Your child may be eligible for tutoring that takes place outside of regular school hours, at no cost to you." What makes that line particularly clear, and perhaps slightly more effective than New Jersey's also quite direct opening, is that the lead paragraph is a single sentence that stands alone. It also uses the common word "tutoring" rather than the law's technical term, "supplemental

TABLE 1-2

EXCERPTS FROM MODEL SUPPLEMENTAL EDUCATIONAL SERVICES
PARENTAL NOTIFICATION LETTERS

Opening paragraph of letter	Words preceding sentence mentioning services option
Massachusetts. Your child may be eligible for tutoring that takes place outside of regular school hours, at no cost to you.	0
New Jersey. This letter is to notify you that, if your child is eligible for free or reduced lunch, he/she is eligible for free supplemental educational services this academic year. These services will be provided before school, after school, and/or during the summer. The services will be in addition to the regular instruction that your student receives during the school year.	0
Colorado. Welcome back to [school name]! In January 2002, a new federal education law was passed called No Child Left Behind. The law requires that schools in their 2nd year of school improvement or on corrective action offer tutoring to students in need. [School name] is in its 2nd year of school improvement. This letter is to inform you that your child may be eligible for free tutoring services. Listed below are important facts about the tutoring services:	52
Delaware. The highest priority for the *[INSERT DISTRICT NAME]* is to improve students' achievement. We firmly believe that all children can learn and will achieve when parents are actively involved with their children's education. Our schools are currently engaged in special efforts to improve student performance in our Title I schools that have not made adequate yearly progress for a period of three years. *No Child Left Behind* legislation encourages educators, parents and approved supplemental educational service providers to work diligently together to incorporate additional services in these schools.	88
Iowa. Many of you are aware of the federal No Child Left Behind (NCLB) Act, which requires schools to assess students annually and to meet student achievement goals. If a school does not meet those assessment and achievement goals (termed "adequate yearly progress" or AYP) for two consecutive years, and if the school receives federal Title I funds, then it is placed on a federal "Schools in Need of Assistance (SINA)" list and subjected to federal sanctions. Schools or districts are cited if they a) don't meet 95 percent	214

(continued on next page)

(Table 1-2 continued from previous page)

Opening paragraph of letter	Words preceding sentence mentioning services option
participation rate for assessments, b) don't meet student achievement goals, or c) don't meet attendance rate for elementary and middle schools or graduation rate for high school.	

SOURCES: Massachusetts Department of Education, http://www.doe.mass.edu/ses/results.asp (accessed October 2006); New Jersey Department of Education, *A Toolkit for Schools, Districts, and Providers to Implement Supplemental Educational Services Under NCLB*, school year 2004–5, 18, http://www.state.nj.us/education/title1/program/toolkit.pdf; Colorado Department of Education, "Sample Parent Letter," http://www.cde.state.co.us/FedPrograms/improvement/download/SS_ParentLetter.pdf; Delaware Department of Education, "Sample Parent Letter," http://www.doe.k12.de.us/SchoolImprovement/SES/Sample%20Parent%20Letter%202006%202007.htm; and Iowa Department of Education, "Notice of AYP, Sample Letter C," under NCLB Reporting Requirements, AYP Notifications Under NCLB, Communication Guidelines for Local Districts to Use with Parents, http://www.iowa.gov/educate/content/blogcategory/497/921/ (all accessed June 13, 2007).

educational services." Parents would likely find the opening of Massachusetts's letter very easy to understand, which might motivate them to read on.

Because school districts can adapt the state examples for their own use, local letters may be better or worse than the state models. A U.S. Government Accountability Office (GAO) study has noted that some providers are dissatisfied with actual district letters, although the problems may not be entirely attributable to state and local decisions. The reason is that guidance from the U.S. Department of Education, which also provides a sample letter, "does not clearly specify all of the key elements required by SES [supplemental educational services] law and regulations. For example, the sample letter does not include information on provider services, qualifications, and effectiveness." The study also reported, "a few state and district officials commented that, when followed, the Title I regulations governing SES yield a letter that is unreasonably long and complex, which may be difficult for parents to understand."[18]

NCLB does not require states to provide model letters, but it does compel them to develop a list of state-approved supplemental educational services providers. Among other things, federal guidance instructs states to incorporate several items into these lists that describe the providers' programs, their records of effectiveness, and their modes of instruction. Analyzing the published lists illustrates how well the states are meeting these requirements.[19]

Table 1-3 presents results from a systematic analysis of these provider lists, which were obtained during October and December 2006 from state education agency websites. A state received credit for each item in table 1-3 if its provider list presented an explicit field with the specified information. The information might have appeared for some providers in another form even if a state did not get credit based on the coding rules that generated table 1-3. That is because some state lists included provider narratives that mentioned some of the specific elements in table 1-3. In other words, a state list might not have an explicit field indicating grade levels served, but a particular provider might have mentioned grade levels in its narrative. In that case, a state would not have received credit for the grade-level item, which appears in the eighth row of table 1-3, for two reasons. First, it is not clear that the state explicitly called for this information, so it is not clear whether all provider narratives included it. Second, and more important, the list is less user-friendly without a specific field for the grade-level item. Practically speaking, it would be much easier for parents to find a field labeled "grade levels served" and to read quickly down to eliminate providers not serving their child's grade. Wading through individual narratives—especially in states with dozens of providers—makes things quite complicated for parents who want to comparison-shop.

Table 1-3 illustrates that some states have crafted more detailed and systematically organized provider lists than others. Substantively, at least three main findings stand out. First, nearly all states do a good job of helping parents initially sort providers by key criteria. In 82 percent of states parents could quickly learn if a provider served their geographic area; in 80 percent parents could see if a provider served their child's grade level; and in 78 percent parents could easily discern for which school subjects the provider offered instruction.

Second, information on specific curricular or instructional matters was less frequently present. For example, 52 percent of state provider lists explicitly identified the student populations, such as disabled, limited English proficient, or low-income, that each provider specialized in serving. Further, several items that would probably interest many parents appeared inconsistently. The mode, time, and venue of instruction appeared around half the time (on 48, 52, and 58 percent of provider lists, respectively), while only around a third of these lists included fields addressing teacher

TABLE 1-3

INFORMATION IN STATE LISTS OF APPROVED SUPPLEMENTAL EDUCATIONAL
SERVICES PROVIDERS

Provider information item	States including item (%)
Basic information	
Name of contact person	82
Full mailing address	72
Phone number	88
Fax number	38
Email address	74
Website address	48
Clientele served	
Geographic area (e.g., school districts, counties, specific schools)	82
Grade levels	80
Student populations (e.g., disabled, low-income, limited English)	52
Curriculum and instruction	
Subject matter covered (e.g., math, reading, other)	78
Mode of instruction (e.g., small group, one-on-one, via Internet)	48
Time of instruction (e.g., days per week, before school, after school)	52
Venue of instruction (e.g., school, student home, provider office)	58
Teacher/staff qualifications	34
Teacher to student ratio	32
Other information	
Cost of services	42
Method of reporting to parents/schools	16
Frequency of reporting to parents/schools	16
Transportation (e.g., provides transportation, doesn't provide)	28
Evidence of effectiveness	24
Space for provider narrative description	48

SOURCES: Author's calculations based on provider lists available from state education agency websites in October and December 2006.
NOTE: Percentages are based on N=50.

and staff qualifications (34 percent) and teacher to student ratio (32 percent). Fortunately, nearly all states, 88 percent, did include a provider telephone number that would enable parents, or their advocates, to discuss these items. Still, it is surprising that provider phone numbers did not appear on all state lists.

Finally, most states offered little information regarding accountability. Only 24 percent of provider lists included explicit information on providers' effectiveness in improving student academic outcomes. Anecdotally, some providers did incorporate that, along with other information, in their open-ended narratives, which 48 percent of states allow a provider to include. Still, because the main point of supplemental educational services is to improve student achievement, it is unfortunate that more states do not explicitly single out information on effectiveness. As noted above, only a fraction indicated the method and frequency with which providers reported student academic progress; those items each appeared only 16 percent of the time.

The minimal information on accountability is perhaps not surprising, given that states themselves have had trouble developing methods for ensuring that providers improve academic performance. A recent study from the GAO considered this issue for the 2005–6 school year by examining several different methods states have used to hold providers accountable for increasing student achievement. Even though larger percentages of states said they planned to use these methods eventually, the actual number monitoring achievement during GAO's survey, conducted between January and March 2006, was quite small. Only 15 percent, for example, required the provider to document evidence of increased student achievement on statewide assessments. Other work has reported parallel findings, and some state officials have admitted that these monitoring issues have been rather challenging.[20]

One state official from North Carolina explained to me why monitoring provider performance is not easy. In this person's words, "It is really difficult to separate out the effect of one intervention when simultaneously the regular classroom teacher is providing instruction on a daily basis. Who gets the credit for the growth in academic performance that might be demonstrated?" Monitoring the quality of communication between providers, districts, and parents, this official continued, can also be challenging when providers reside outside the districts they serve.

Corrective Action and Restructuring

Unlike NCLB school choice or supplemental educational services, which rely heavily on parental decisions, the law's corrective-action and restructuring provisions take shape primarily when state and local officials act. Importantly, NCLB offers many options at these stages of improvement. How corrective action and restructuring actually unfold can vary tremendously across states and within them. Figure 1-1 has already illustrated that variability for districts, with part A documenting that most states have very low percentages of districts in improvement status.

Figure 1-3 provides additional information about Title I schools that have consistently missed AYP. Specifically, the figure shows the percentage of those schools, by number of states, that reached various stages of improvement status during 2004–5. For example, the bar furthest to the right in part A shows that seventeen states had at least 90 percent of their Title I schools in improvement at the year 1 or year 2 stage. In contrast, the leftmost bar in part B says that twenty-nine states had fewer than 10 percent of their Title I schools in improvement at the corrective-action stage. Finally, part C shows thirty-six states having fewer than 10 percent of Title I schools in improvement facing restructuring.

Two key conclusions emerge from figure 1-3 and provide an overall backdrop for this section. First, only a few states possess much experience working with Title I schools at the corrective-action and restructuring stages. Looking at the actual numbers that generated part B reveals that eight states had no Title I schools in improvement that had reached corrective action; for part C there were twenty-one states with no Title I schools in improvement at the restructuring stage. Those results were due in part to real differences in school performance, but also, and perhaps most significantly, to how states calculate AYP.

The second conclusion emerges when one compares part A of figure 1-3 with parts B and C. Even though many states have had limited experience with school corrective action and restructuring, many will likely face larger numbers of Title I schools reaching these stages in the future. The distribution in part A indicates that most Title I schools in improvement in 2004–5 were at the year 1 or year 2 stage. If those schools continue to struggle, states will start seeing more enter corrective action and restructuring. That

FIGURE 1-3

TITLE I SCHOOLS IN IMPROVEMENT STAGES BY NUMBER OF STATES,
2004–5

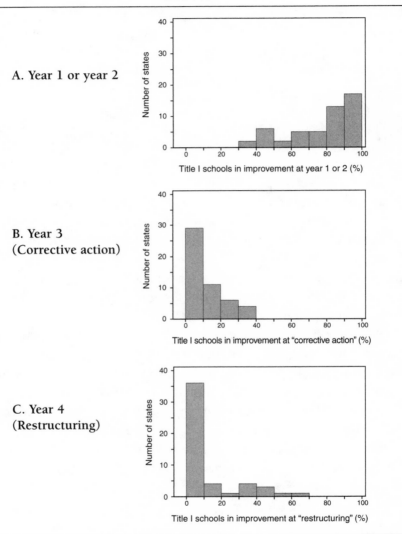

SOURCE: Adapted from U.S. Department of Education, Institute of Education Sciences, *National Assessment of Title I Interim Report to Congress: Volume 1*, by Stephanie Stullich, Elizabeth Eisner, Joseph McCrary, and Collette Roney, NCEE 2006-4000, February 2006, exhibit 31, http://ies.ed.gov/ncee/pdf/20064000.pdf (accessed May 4, 2007).

NOTE: Percentages apply to Title I schools subject to NCLB's cascade of remedies. For example, the tallest bar in part B reads that twenty-nine states have less than 10 percent of Title I schools that are in improvement and have reached corrective action.

will place new demands on state officials as they attempt to implement these remedies.

State Oversight of Corrective Action and Restructuring. To understand the states' role in corrective action and restructuring, one should remember that NCLB defines local school districts as the primary change agents for schools in these stages of improvement. The law outlines support roles for state education agencies at all levels of improvement status, but in general, as federal guidance indicates, a local school district has "primary responsibility for assisting its schools that do not make adequate progress toward meeting established student academic achievement targets."[21] Comments from Patti Hammel, a local school official in South Carolina's Georgetown County Schools, suggest as much. "Corrective action does not mean state intervention," she said. Rather, "It's a district-wide look at programs and how to allocate resources."[22] Even during restructuring, theoretically the most demanding NCLB remedy, federal guidance says that NCLB "does not require the LEA [local education agency] or a school to submit to the SEA [state education agency] a restructuring plan or a report describing the alternative governance arrangements the LEA is implementing in a school identified for restructuring."[23]

But given the states' overall responsibility for public education, NCLB does stipulate that states can become more deeply involved in the improvement process. According to federal guidance, at the restructuring stage of improvement the state "may choose to have more significant involvement in district decision-making, such as by collecting and reviewing plans or participating in plan development, modification, and monitoring." Some states monitor more aggressively than others.[24]

In contrast, NCLB does outline very specific responsibilities for state education agencies dealing with local school districts that reach corrective action. Beyond providing technical assistance, the required corrective actions can be quite dramatic. At this stage of district improvement, state education agencies must do at least one of the following: defer program or administrative funds; require the district to adopt a new curriculum; replace key district personnel who are preventing the district from making AYP; remove specific schools from the district's jurisdiction; strip the local school board and superintendent of their power and appoint a receiver or trustee to administer the district; or abolish or restructure the district. Importantly, state education agencies must act in ways "consistent with State law."[25]

Versions of Corrective Action and Restructuring. High-stakes accountability and NCLB's cascade of remedies imply that schools and districts repeatedly missing AYP should experience the most dramatic consequences. By that logic, schools entering corrective action or restructuring should feel greater pressure than those at earlier stages of improvement. But that might not always occur in practice. Schools in restructuring might close and reopen as charter schools—a very radical change—while others might opt for a lesser consequence that is nevertheless consistent with the law's restructuring options. Hoping to avoid disagreements with district officials, and believing that support rather than coercion will improve schools, many states have used NCLB's corrective-action and restructuring remedies in ways that avoid more radical reform measures.

In some instances, state personnel appear to oppose drastic action on philosophical grounds. In Illinois, for example, Becky Watts, chief of staff for the state Board of Education, has argued against state takeovers of schools because "Illinois is a local control state, and schools are best run by local school districts and local communities."[26] Dana Tofig, spokesman for the Georgia Department of Education, appeared to agree. Despite having eighty-five schools slated for restructuring, Tofig noted that the department would not take over any because "Our focus is on helping schools."[27] Oregon's state school superintendent, Susan Castillo, said that she would not take over a school even if state law allowed it because "As long as we have schools that are trying, that are making progress, then we need to support them. If all you use is the stick, you are not going to get anywhere."[28]

Those philosophical arguments are sometimes rooted in disagreements over the appropriate way to hold schools accountable for results. Comments from John Winn, education commissioner of Florida, illustrate that line of thinking. In comparing Florida's approach to accountability to that of NCLB, Winn said, "We have schools that are doing very well that are closing the achievement gap and achieving at high levels and still not making AYP. . . . I'm going to be hard-pressed to put the federal sanctions ahead of our state accountability system."[29]

When states do intervene during corrective action or restructuring, typically they offer added support to schools and districts. Although Iowa has not had many schools enter corrective action, a state official there told me that the "most appropriate action" for schools at that point "seems to be the curriculum review and redesign." Another state official in North Carolina told me that the state approaches corrective action by providing "direct assistance to the schools that miss the greatest percentage of their AYP targets." Consistent with the remarks of education commissioner Winn, Florida, which shows schools making strong progress on its own metrics but has increasing numbers of schools missing AYP, has been quite lax with those reaching the restructuring phase. Even though several Florida schools should have been well into that phase of improvement status as the fall 2006 school year began, the state was giving districts until January 2007 to devise school restructuring plans and until August 2007 to implement them.[30]

A popular approach has been for states to send "turnaround specialists" into schools and districts needing corrective action. These individuals might be state agency employees, private consultants, or former expert teachers or principals. Such supportive measures foster direct state involvement that is less coercive than other NCLB options. Some states dispatch these advisors with much deference to local prerogatives. In Pennsylvania, for example, the state division chief for district and school development, Sally Chamberlain, explained that even this sort of measure "is a cooperative thing" because a school district "has to agree to allow the team to come in."[31]

One thing facilitating more supportive or suggestive measures, rather than high-stakes ones, is a major loophole in the NCLB school restructuring requirement. Section 1116(b)(8)(B) of NCLB allows schools in restructuring to employ "any other major restructuring of the school's governance arrangement that makes fundamental reforms" to help the school make AYP. What these other major reforms are is open to interpretation. A study in California found that this was the most popular option by far. During 2005–6 it was chosen by 76 percent of schools reaching the restructuring stage and involved measures including "hiring coaches who will help teachers work together in new ways" and "appointing a leadership team to oversee school operations." Those moves fall short of what lay observers might consider "restructuring," but technically they could still be consistent with the letter of the law.[32]

Despite generally favoring more supportive approaches to corrective action and restructuring, some states have gotten tough by directly intervening or withholding funds. An Alaska official told me that for school districts entering corrective action, the state has required specific elements in a districtwide improvement plan, and that NCLB funds are "prorated and released upon completion of key milestones." At the start of the 2006–7 school year, at least four Pennsylvania school districts, including Philadelphia, were under some form of state control for failing to make AYP.[33] And in California, despite the somewhat lenient measures described above, the existence of that state's charter school law helped enable the California Charter Schools Association in October 2006 to win a multimillion-dollar federal grant to open fifty-two new charter schools, ten of which were traditional public schools slated for restructuring under NCLB.[34]

Perhaps the most aggressive attempted use of NCLB's remedies by a state official occurred in Maryland. During the spring of 2006, the state Department of Education, led by superintendent Nancy Grasmick, tried to take over eleven Baltimore schools that had failed to make scheduled progress. The state legislature blocked that move and gave these schools another year before the state agency could assert its power in this way. The result was a district corrective-action plan that, among other things, required curricular changes, training, and a study to determine if academic leaders in the school district should be replaced, changes that fell short of more radical measures that might have ensued under more direct state control.[35]

Explaining Choices for Corrective Action and Restructuring. States have tended to favor less dramatic reforms at the corrective-action and restructuring stages for several reasons. A lack of political will to make tough choices is likely one, but at least three others are relevant, too.

First, state policies often do not support the more demanding remedies that NCLB suggests. Recall that NCLB and its accompanying guidance say that the remedies states choose must be consistent with state law. That can prevent several measures from gaining traction. Not all states allow state education departments to take over struggling local districts or schools, for example.[36] Additionally, even though many states have charter school laws, some make it rather difficult for charters to form, or they even cap the number of charter schools that can operate.[37] State policy can also limit the introduction of private management companies into struggling public schools. Such companies cannot participate in major restructuring efforts in Kentucky, for example, because the state has not developed regulations to govern how they would be paid for their efforts.[38]

State policies governing teachers present a related obstacle that can limit corrective-action or restructuring measures. Laws that guarantee teachers a right to collectively bargain, and in turn produce binding teacher contracts, can make radical changes to school personnel difficult. Further, state policies governing teacher licensing can narrow local options. Certification requirements sometimes discourage individuals from becoming teachers, creating major problems in communities that already have a limited teacher pool from which to choose. As it may be extremely difficult for those communities to restructure schools by replacing entire school staffs, local leaders may consider the other, less radical remedies that NCLB allows.[39]

Second, state education agencies possess varying capacities to intervene aggressively in low-performing schools and districts. In part, these capacity challenges persist because the capabilities of state education agencies have not kept pace with their evolving roles.[40] Many state officials told me that the increasing numbers of schools and districts entering corrective action or restructuring have significantly stretched their limited capabilities. One Iowa official explained to me that "Looking at the overall curriculum, instruction, and assessment for a district," which state support teams do in troubled districts, "is a demanding task that doesn't fit well in the timeframe dictated in the federal legislation [NCLB]." These difficulties exist, the official noted, even though the state already has a relatively well-established network of support units, called area education agencies, to serve local districts.

A North Carolina official explained to me that the "capacity to provide assistance" is a major challenge because "There are not enough staff members at the state level to address the needs in all the districts/schools in improvement." The official expected those challenges to intensify, given "the exponential increase in the number of districts entering improvement. Last year, there were forty-four districts, this year there are sixty-two." Ironically, one related issue, further straining state capacity, has been the incremental flexibility that federal officials have offered to states as they implement NCLB. As the North Carolina official noted, "In our state alone, there have been twenty-nine changes in how the AYP rules have been applied in our accountability workbook." Those changes, while designed to ease burdens on states, can actually create more work, as state officials must communicate these adjustments to local districts and then help districts and schools incorporate them into their improvement plans.

Even when states provide support to help districts and schools analyze their weaknesses, local leaders sometimes get little guidance about what to do next. In Massachusetts, for example, one researcher has found that "The state has done a good job . . . at the identification phase. They're less clear what you actually do about it . . . The reality is that the state doesn't have enormous capacity right now to engineer significant interventions for turn-around schools."[41] State officials in Alaska and Delaware expressed similar sentiments about capacity in exchanges with me.

A third reason limiting the use of more radical options is that corrective action and restructuring depend not only on state capabilities but on local ones, too. Federal policymakers rely heavily on states for NCLB's success, and the law's delegation chain means that states in turn lean heavily on local ideas and leadership.[42] A state official in Connecticut explained to me why this is often difficult. Typically, school principals "were trained to be managers and not instructional leaders," this person noted. "It is difficult to assist with systemic change in school districts when the leaders in the district do not have the technical skills to lead large-scale organizational change." Connecticut has tried to ameliorate these problems by recruiting retired, successful urban principals to advise current officials managing the corrective-action and restructuring processes. In West Virginia, a state official relayed a similar story to me, saying how "developing [local] leadership for change and school improvement [and] training schools and districts to make data-based decisions" are two of the major challenges the state has faced in trying to implement NCLB's cascade of remedies.

These comments suggest that local districts and schools are experiencing some of the same administrative growing pains as states themselves. Moving from a compliance- to a performance-oriented mindset within schools and districts, especially where student achievement has suffered for several years, is a steep challenge. North Carolina's strategy, noted earlier, of targeting the most robust state assistance to the districts performing the most poorly seems to recognize this fact. The state's approach appears premised on the belief that low district capacity, which targeted state assistance can ameliorate, is a major barrier to improving student success.

NCLB in a Fragmented Intergovernmental System

Despite Washington's growing role in education, NCLB's cascade of remedies will succeed or fail in large part based on how well state officials strategically apply the high-stakes and supportive measures that the law allows. Reasonable people can disagree on how to strike that balance. But without a major revolution in educational governance in this country, federal and local officials will continue relying heavily upon state policy and leadership to improve the educational fortunes of thousands of American children who attend struggling public schools. Put another way, the persistence of state power in education means that NCLB's ambitions and federal officials' promises to enforce the law strictly will continue to collide head-on with the primary institutions that control American schools. NCLB has provided Washington with a stronger lever to press for change. But given the law's lengthy delegation chain and the reluctance of federal officials to assert real control through a national curriculum and national exams, federal officials' options remain limited.

If it is difficult for Washington to guarantee real high-stakes accountability and consequences for low educational performance, there are several ways that national policymakers can use the logic of suggestive accountability to improve state implementation of NCLB's remedies. Even though NCLB is now more than five years old, it is still quite difficult for even experienced researchers, let along casual observers, to determine at any given moment how many schools and districts in each state are at each level of improvement status. Simply knowing those totals and being able to compare them across state lines would provide lay observers and policymakers with important information about where and how NCLB's remedies are taking hold across the country. Without clear data on how states are shepherding implementation of NCLB, it will be impossible for policymakers at any level of government to judge the effectiveness of the law's remedies.

Overall, NCLB's ambitious approach to accountability has created new challenges and opportunities for education reformers across the United

States. Despite the high-stakes logic that motivates the law's remedies, the evidence reveals that state implementation has varied tremendously. The states' internal political climates, their own policy choices, and their capabilities have had a tremendous impact on how the law's remedies are taking shape. That is not surprising, given NCLB's many moving parts and the challenging position that states occupy in the nation's intergovernmental system.

2

America's Great City Schools: Moving in the Right Direction

Michael Casserly

No Child Left Behind (NCLB), the nation's boldest reform of federal education policy, is over five years old. And it is becoming increasingly evident that this landmark legislation is both living up to many of the promises its strongest proponents hoped for and encountering many of the pitfalls its harshest critics warned against.

The promise of NCLB, of course, rests in its pledge to attain academic proficiency for all students by 2013–14. The law sets bold goals, mandates extensive testing, requires greater transparency in public reporting, offers parental choice, and holds school officials accountable for results. At the same time, it has attracted widespread opposition, has spurred what some see as an overemphasis on test preparation, has narrowed curricula, and has encouraged new ways of gaming the system.

So far, test scores in reading and mathematics have increased—at least in some places. Reading scores in large central cities show significant increases on the National Assessment of Educational Progress (NAEP), but scores nationally remain flat. Math scores, for their part, are going up everywhere. More importantly, the country's largest central city school systems are narrowing gaps between themselves and the nation in both reading and math.[1] It is not clear that the new federal law drove those gains, but it may have helped to sustain them.

Five years after the law's enactment, it is clear that a school and school district may be in full compliance with NCLB and still not be raising student achievement. Conversely, it is quite possible to raise student achievement substantially without complying with any of the law's requirements. This anomaly is critical for both proponents and opponents of NCLB to reconcile if recommendations for the law's reauthorization are to make sense.

This chapter examines the status of No Child Left Behind in America's Great City Schools, considering in particular the law's cascading accountability system. It includes an inventory of schools in "improvement" status; examines school choice and supplemental educational services and how they have evolved over time; and focuses on the law's "corrective action" and "restructuring" provisions and how urban school systems are implementing them. A final section discusses the overall status of NCLB in city school systems and summarizes persistent problems.

Status of NCLB in the Great Cities

In June 2006, the Council of the Great City Schools, a coalition of the nation's largest urban public school systems, administered a twelve-page survey to its sixty-six-member urban school districts to gather data on various aspects of the implementation of the No Child Left Behind Act.[2] The council also asked districts to provide copies of letters to parents, provider contracts, and evaluations. Forty districts (60.6 percent) responded with data on school years 2002–3 through 2005–6.[3]

The districts responding to the survey enroll more than 5.8 million students (not counting preschool students). Of these, 65.9 percent are eligible for free or reduced-price lunch, 18.3 percent are English-language learners, and 13.0 percent are students with disabilities.[4] The districts operate 8,523 schools, enrolling an average of 683 students per school. Some 6,780 of these schools (79.6 percent), enrolling about 3.5 million students, are Title I schools subject to NCLB's accountability provisions.[5]

Adequate Yearly Progress (AYP). School year 2002–3 was the first in which districts were subject to NCLB's requirements to report test data on the academic progress of all major student subgroups. The results were used to determine which schools would undergo school improvement, corrective action, or restructuring, the three main stages of sanction under NCLB.

In school year 2005–6, 616 schools in the forty districts on which we have data were in their first year of school improvement because they had not made adequate yearly progress (AYP) for two consecutive years. Some 762 additional schools were in their second year of school improvement because they failed to make AYP for three consecutive years. Another 505 schools were identified for corrective action, and 646 were in restructuring status—the last stage of NCLB's accountability system.

In all, 2,529 schools in these districts were placed in various improvement categories in school year 2005–6. This number had increased from 1,378 schools in 2002–3, when NCLB first went into effect, and constitutes 29.7 percent of all schools in these districts and 37.3 percent of Title I schools in the big cities. About 29.9 percent of schools nationwide in "need of improvement" are in one of these forty cities.

Survey results also showed considerable variation from city to city in the numbers of schools designated for improvement in 2005–6. The largest cities tended to have the most schools in "need of improvement." But the cities show considerable variation in the percentage of their schools needing improvement—a variation that may have little to do with their relative performance. For example, the Boston and San Diego school districts had similar reading and math scores on the NAEP, but 47 percent of Boston's schools were in school improvement status, compared with 15 percent of San Diego's.

The data also indicate that only 332 schools in the forty districts failed to make adequate yearly progress in 2005–6 because their testing rate was below the 95 percent required under NCLB. On the other hand, 2,412 schools failed to make AYP because of reading, and 2,016 did not make their math targets. An additional 443 schools were "in need of improvement" because they missed their AYP targets in one subgroup only. Most common were schools not making AYP solely because of low performance among their limited English proficient students or their students with disabilities.

Conversely, 444 schools made enough progress to be placed "on hold" by making AYP for one year after initially being tagged for improvement. Sanctions were lifted from 161 schools after they made AYP for two consecutive years after first being identified for improvement, while 229 schools made their reading targets and 215 made their math targets using "safe harbor," the smallest increment of gain needed to avoid sanctions.

In addition, twenty-five urban school districts indicated that their states identified schools as low-performing under an accountability system that was separate from the one under NCLB.

Finally, most of the forty responding districts—twenty-five in all—were now designated by their states for "district improvement." Sixteen of the twenty-five were in districtwide sanction for not having attained state-set proficiency bars in reading; eighteen had not met goals in math. Twenty-one had not met performance targets for various subgroups, mostly poor, disabled, and limited English proficient students. Sixteen had not met their goals for African-American students, and eleven had not done so for their Hispanic students. Most districts under sanction had been in this status since 2003–4 or 2004–5, and five had been in "need-of-improvement" status since 2002–3. Most districts expected to remain under sanction through the 2006–7 school year.

Public School Choice. The law requires schools that have not made AYP for two years in a row to plan for improvement, receive technical assistance, set aside funds for professional development, and offer all students (regardless of achievement level or income) the opportunity to transfer to another school that has not been designated for improvement. In this section, we look at participation rates and trends for the period 2002–3 to 2005–6; methods school districts used to inform parents about their options; and restrictions districts placed on the process, the period during which parents had to make choices, and the number of receiving schools.

Transfer rates. Data from the responding districts indicate that the number of students transferring from one school to another under NCLB was relatively small in 2005–6, compared with the total number enrolled in the eligible schools.

All but two of the responding districts—Omaha and Salt Lake City— had at least one school in "need of improvement" and were required to offer transfers under NCLB. Of the approximately 1.3 million students enrolled in one of the 2,529 school-improvement schools, 27,445 requested a transfer, and 23,000 (1.8 percent of the total eligible) actually moved to other schools—up from 12,539 in 2002–3 (see table 2-1).

Table 2-1

NCLB Transfers, 2002–3 to 2005–6

2002–3	2003–4	2004–5	2005–6		
	Transfers		Eligible for transfer	Transfers requested	Transfers
12,539	22,970	19,524	1,315,090	27,445	23,000

Source: Council of the Great City Schools, "No Child Left Behind Reauthorization in the Great City Schools," unpublished internal survey, 2006, 5,6.

The upward trend in transfer rates between 2002–3 and 2005–6 suggests that districts may have gotten somewhat better at identifying available space and informing parents about their options than in previous years, and states have gotten better at providing at least preliminary data by the start of the school year. Still, the number of requests for NCLB transfers remains low and may have leveled off over the last two years.

City and school officials, community groups, and others have cited several factors contributing to this low participation rate, none of which fully explains it. They note that some parents do not want their children taking lengthy bus trips or riding public transportation, while others may not have gotten their first choices of schools. Some parents may not think the available options are any better than their current situations, and some may be frustrated by the application procedures.

Methods for notifying parents. Thirty-seven districts sent letters to parents informing them of their options, with thirty-two supplementing the mailings with at least one other method of communication: parent and community meetings in twenty-two cities, notices and websites in seventeen, flyers home in ten, vendor fairs in eight, public service announcements in seven, partnerships in one, email in one, and other methods in seven cities.

The survey also asked districts into how many languages they translated materials when notifying parents about their choices. The average district indicated it put its transfer notices into three languages. The New York City and Philadelphia school districts translated their notices into nine languages; those in Los Angeles and Boston into seven; the school district in

Detroit into six; and the districts in Anchorage, Columbus, Fresno, and Portland into five languages each. Only four districts did not translate their notices into languages other than English, and none of them had sizable numbers of English-language learners.

Still, some parents and groups indicated that they did not get the information, or that insufficient notification was provided. It is likely that parents were missed. Mailing addresses are often incomplete, and mobility rates in cities are often high, making some difficult to locate. We did not find any pattern between the number of transfer requests and the methods districts used to disseminate information.

We also looked at the wording of the correspondence sent to parents about their options. Several groups have charged that letters to parents are often convoluted, jargon-filled, lengthy, and self-serving.[6] Our scan of letters sent to parents in the various cities showed a range of features.[7] Some were written better than others. None was longer than two pages, although some school districts did not articulate the nature of the choice until the second page. Most explained, correctly, that the schools available through choice might or might not have services that parents would want. All pointed out that the district would provide transportation, if required. And most had some information about the schools to assist in making choices.

Numbers of choices and restrictions. All of the responding districts gave parents a choice of one or more schools to which they could transfer their children. The norm was to grant four or more options, at least at the elementary school level. The number of choices appears to have increased since 2002–3, when the norm was two or three options. Most districts limited choices by zone, geographic region, feeder patterns, or clusters, however. Several paired one school in "need of improvement" with several other receiving schools from which parents might choose. Some also built special considerations into their options, such as the desire of parents to keep siblings together or the capability of particular schools to handle certain types of disabilities.[8]

Most districts also offered non-NCLB choices that allowed more numerous and open-ended options than those available under NCLB. Depending on the district, students often were granted access to at least some of these choices, including charter schools in twenty-five cities, open-enrollment options in eighteen, cross-district transfers in twelve, magnet schools in twenty-five, open-enrollment zones or areas in nine, and other options in twelve. Only five of the surveyed school districts reported that they had no options beyond those required under NCLB.

Moreover, the survey indicated that 470,323 students—or about 8 percent of all students—in the responding districts (not counting New York, which did not respond to this item) took advantage of some form of non-NCLB transfer option in 2005–6—about twenty times the number of students participating in choice under the law. If one adds to this rate the numbers of students choosing nondistrict charters and private schools, then overall choice rates exceeded 35 percent.

Period to choose. We also looked at the timing of parental notifications. First, we examined the dates on which spring testing data were returned to the districts, when the data were finalized, and when parents were first notified about their options. Second, we looked at how long the window remained open for parents to make their selections.

Five districts received their initial 2004–5 test data before the end of the school year, twenty in June or July 2005, ten in August, and three after the 2005–6 school year began. Although these results represented an improvement over 2002–3, when a substantial number of districts reported having received their initial test results after the beginning of the school year, thirty-two districts were given fewer than the thirty days specified in the law to review their test results, make corrections, and submit changes. The average review period was eighteen days.

The data review process is important because states may not know whether a child has been in a particular school for an entire year and should be scored against that school's AYP targets or the district's—or both. None of the districts had final data determining the number of schools in "need of improvement" before the end of the 2004–5 school year. Nine districts had their data finalized by the state by the end of July and eighteen by the end of August. Eleven did not receive their final data until after the beginning of the 2005–6 school year. The results indicated that, generally, districts were getting their final data earlier than they did in 2002–3, but thirty reported that they did not have adequate time to make program changes.

Moreover, only six of the districts informed parents about their options before the end of the previous school year, 2004–5, and six in June or July

2005—a process apparently based on preliminary data from districts' Title I (phase 1) reports, which are filed in early summer. Sixteen districts informed parents about their options in August, and ten had to wait until after the beginning of the 2005–6 school year. Even so, these numbers also suggest somewhat earlier notifications of parents about their choice options than was the case in 2002–3.

We looked as well at how long parents were given to make their selections. Twenty-two districts gave parents a month or more to make a choice about transferring schools, and another eight provided three weeks to a month. Eight districts provided between a week and two weeks to choose, while no districts restricted parents to a week or less.

School capacity and choice. Another issue was the capacity of receiving schools to accommodate students. The responding districts reported that they had identified 2,219 higher-performing schools (1,567 elementary, 215 K–8, 252 middle schools, and 185 high schools) as potential receiving schools. Districts with the most difficulty identifying schools to which students could transfer were those that lacked the physical capacity, had large numbers of their schools identified for improvement, or had small numbers of schools eligible to receive students.

When asked about challenges in meeting the choice requirements under NCLB, the responding districts rated the timing of the NCLB choices as the greatest problem, followed by parental communications, the limited number of higher-performing schools in specified grade bands, and available space. Issues presenting the least problems were surrounding school districts, desegregation issues, and funds. Most districts reported having had sufficient funds to implement NCLB's choice provisions, but had had almost no success in getting the surrounding districts to take any of their students.

Supplemental Educational Services. In addition to offering choice, the law requires schools that have not made AYP for three straight years to receive technical assistance, devote funds to professional development, and offer tutorial services. Parents select from a state-approved list of public or private providers of tutorial services, with whom school districts are then required to contract. This section looks at participation rates, notification

TABLE 2-2

SUPPLEMENTAL EDUCATIONAL SERVICES, 2005–6

Students eligible for SES	Students receiving SES	Schools with SES	SES students per school
1,383,877	229,057	1,913	120

SOURCE: Council of the Great City Schools, "No Child Left Behind Reauthorization in the Great City Schools," unpublished internal survey, 2006.

methods, numbers and types of providers, periods for choosing providers, contracts, services, and expenditures.

Participation rates. All but three of the forty cities (Omaha, Norfolk, and Salt Lake City) for which we have data had at least one school that was required to offer supplemental educational services under NCLB. These districts, which had 1,913 schools in the second stage of school improvement, indicated that they served 229,057 students in 2005–6 in a supplemental educational services program—a rate of about 120 students per eligible school, or about 16.6 percent of all those eligible (see table 2-2). This participation rate was up from about 124,000 students, or about 93 students per school, in 2003–4, when SES programs began in earnest.

Approximately 208,375 students—or about 91 percent of all students participating in SES in the forty responding city school districts—received their services from private providers. Only 20,682—or 9 percent of those participating—received services from a school or district provider.

The significance of these data rests in the fact that most districts that were providing SES on their own in 2003–4 were not doing so in 2005–6. (Two districts—Chicago and Boston—were allowed to provide their own supplemental educational services in 2005–6 under a special arrangement between the Council of the Great City Schools and the U.S. Department of Education.)

Preliminary data from the survey indicated that cities where districts were allowed to offer their own services provided them to a higher proportion of eligible children (25.4 percent) than those where districts were banned by Department of Education regulation from providing these services (10.9 percent).

Methods for notifying parents. The majority of districts responding to the survey used the same methods to inform parents about supplemental educational services as they did to inform them about school choice, including letters in thirty-seven cities, flyers home in thirty-two, parent and community meetings in thirty-one, vendor fairs in twenty-six, notices in nineteen, public service announcements in twelve, partnerships in eleven, email in one, and other methods in fifteen. The data also showed that districts used more methods to inform parents about SES in 2005–6 than they did in 2003–4, and they used more methods to inform parents about SES than about transfer options. Most districts used at least four different methods of notifying the public about tutoring options in 2005–6, compared with one or two in 2003–4. Some notified parents of both opportunities in the same correspondence, while others did separate notifications.

A spot check of the correspondence sent to parents indicates that school districts did provide most of the required information.[9] Some appeared to steer parents to specific SES providers. Some provided little information besides the state's list of providers, while others prepared comprehensive directories containing information about the kinds of services offered by each provider; the experience, qualifications, and effectiveness of the providers; and contact information. Sometimes, the names of the providers were simply presented in checklist fashion with no other information. Parents wanting services were usually asked to complete forms or sign up at specific locations.

Finally, the survey results indicated that districts translated their SES notices to parents into languages other than English in approximately the same ways and in about the same numbers as they translated their notices about choice.

Numbers and types of providers. While the council's survey did not explicitly ask about the number of providers available in each district, it did ask districts whether there were more or fewer external providers in 2005–6 than in previous years. Thirty-four of the forty responding districts indicated that there were more providers now than before. Three districts indicated there were fewer.

The types of providers varied somewhat from city to city. The Indianapolis school district, for instance, had a list from which parents could select that included large national tutorial services, such as the Princeton Review, Newton Learning, Education Station, PLATO Learning, Club Z, Babbage Net School, Socratic Learning Inc., and Brainfuse. A number of local and regional providers were also on the list, including Boys and Girls Clubs of Indianapolis, Dyslexia Institute of Indiana, the Midwest Life Enhancement Services Inc., and the Indiana State Council of Opportunities Industrialization Centers of America. A look at most provider lists showed many of the same companies city to city.

Some companies and providers specialized in a single content area, such as reading, and others concentrated on particular grades or grade spans. Few colleges, universities, or faith-based groups appeared on any of the state lists. Moreover, only a few private school management firms, such as Edison, were evident. Five districts indicated that their teachers union was a state-approved SES provider.

Districts were also asked about areas in which there were particularly acute shortages of providers. Respondents indicated that external providers were in short supply for English-language learners (eighteen cities), students with disabilities (seventeen), and middle and high school students (nine).

All city school systems that were not in "district improvement" status were approved to be their own supplemental educational services providers. Eleven cities were on their respective states' provider lists; twenty-nine were not approved providers.

Period to choose providers. Because of the logistical and contractual arrangements involved with SES, the time taken by the districts to inform parents about the eligibility of their children for supplemental educational services and for parents to make their selections was generally longer than the time it took to implement the choice provisions. Six districts were able to give parents SES options before the end of the previous school year (2004–5), and fifteen were able to notify parents over the summer months. Seventeen districts informed parents after the beginning of the 2005–6 school year.

The city school districts seemed to be leaving the selection window open for longer periods than afforded under the choice provisions. In addition, the SES windows appeared to be open longer in 2005–6 than in 2002–3. In twenty-five cities, parents had a month or more to choose a provider. Seven districts gave parents three weeks to a month, and four gave one or two weeks. One district gave parents less than a week. And several districts instituted rolling enrollment opportunities over the course of the school year.

Start dates, duration, and nature of services. Most supplemental educational services are now provided by external or private providers, and they begin at various points in the first semester of the school year. In the survey, only three school districts said they began SES in September; eleven began in October; and thirteen began in November. The remaining districts started services in December or January. Those that were allowed to provide their own services started at about the same time as the private providers.

Still, the timing of school improvement services continued to be a problem for school districts. Under the law, districts are allowed thirty days to review state test data for errors. Schools are then given three months after first being tagged for not making AYP to develop a plan for improvement, and another forty-five days to review and modify the plan. For most districts, this would mean putting a program into effect in mid-January if state test data were returned by the end of August—not enough time to produce any impact on spring test scores before triggering the next round of sanctions. On the other hand, districts that implement programs in October or November are not devoting the time the law allows to adequate planning for improving test scores.

The council's survey also asked districts about the duration of their own services and those of the private or external providers. On average, the private providers' tutoring sessions lasted about eighty minutes, generally ranging from about forty-five minutes to two hours. The external providers typically offered two tutoring sessions a week for each participating child, for an average of seventeen and a half weeks.

The length and duration of services for district providers were similar to those offered by external providers. No provider—private or district—offered services for periods shorter than six weeks or longer than thirty-six weeks, including some Saturdays.

In addition, twenty-two cities reported that external providers offered their services to students in groups of five or more; only two cities indicated that their external providers did one-on-one tutoring. The seven districts providing their own SES did so for groups of five or more students. None provided one-on-one tutoring.

Districts reported problems with students showing up for tutoring sessions, but district providers reported a somewhat higher attendance rate than external providers. Attendance rates at sessions provided by the districts averaged about 70 percent, while rates at sessions provided by external providers averaged about 63 percent.

When asked whether they allowed external providers to offer their services on school grounds, thirty of the responding districts indicated that some or all providers were permitted to tutor students in school classrooms—a substantial increase since 2003–4.

The issue of instructional alignment remained a critical problem as well. NCLB states clearly that supplemental educational services providers are to ensure that their services are consistent with the instruction provided by the local educational agency (LEA) and are aligned with state academic standards. Nevertheless, it seems unlikely that all the approved providers in each city are aligned with state standards to the same degree. Indeed, most providers use the same packaged program, regardless of the city they are in or the students whom they tutor. The problem is compounded as the number of providers and the variety of student skills-deficits grows.

Twenty-seven districts reported that they were attempting to solve this problem by requiring external providers to align their programs with the districts' curriculum, but the extent and depth of alignment undoubtedly varied from city to city and from provider to provider within the same city.

Finally, districts were providing external SES providers with more assessment data on the performance of participating students. The practice is tricky because there are confidentiality issues requiring parental consent. Still, twenty-eight of the responding cities said they provided state assessment data, nineteen provided grades, sixteen provided standardized test scores, seven provided sample student work, and seven provided quarterly test scores to external providers for individual students or groups of students—a new development in the provision of supplemental educational services.

Evaluation of services. The law requires that supplemental educational services be evaluated, providers be assessed, and approval of providers be withdrawn if success is not evident for two consecutive years. Thirteen responding districts indicated that they knew of private providers that had been removed from the approved list for one reason or another.

The law is ambiguous, however, on how evaluations are conducted and what success means, and most states clearly have not pursued these assessments actively. To districts and schools, success means making adequate yearly progress on state tests, but it may mean something else to outside providers. Most providers prefer using their own evaluation tools to assess the effectiveness of their services. These tools may or may not be aligned with the state assessments, however, and may or may not have the requisite technical strength to measure academic gains reliably.

The council asked its districts about the evaluation of SES. Twenty-three indicated they were conducting their own evaluations of SES, and twenty-one said their states were conducting or planning to conduct evaluations. Most of the local evaluations entailed site visits, parent or student satisfaction surveys, or other program-compliance assessments.

The limited number of evaluations of results suggests that tutorial sessions have had modest effects on student achievement, at best. An analysis conducted by the Denver school system, for instance, showed that its external providers improved state test scores only marginally over those of students who received no services. Some providers produced significant gains, while others saw declines in state test scores. Denver cannot provide its own services. An evaluation in Minneapolis also showed limited impact.

A report by the Chicago school district showed that its SES program ranked in the middle of all external providers in terms of effectiveness—that is, the district improved achievement more effectively than about one-half of the providers, but less effectively than the other half. Otherwise, evaluations of these services remained scant.

In implementing SES, respondents indicated that their toughest challenges involved what they described as "unscrupulous" vendors, student attendance at tutoring sessions, and parental communications. Seen as less troubling were the numbers of providers available to provide reading and math services, and services for English-language learners and students with disabilities.

Contracts. The law is clear about the responsibility of school districts to inform parents about the nature of SES and enter into contracts with private providers, yet it is largely silent about the mechanics. As a result, school districts and potential providers have found themselves tussling over the length of the contracts, pupil fees, billing and payment procedures, staff qualifications, union rules, and similar issues.

For instance, supplemental educational services providers and urban school districts often disagree about the logistics and conditions of delivering services. Many providers would like to receive a portion of their fees before work begins, but districts often prefer to pay as the work proceeds. The providers would like to charge the districts a flat fee for the number of students enrolled in the tutorial sessions, but the districts think they should be charged only for the number who actually attend. The providers would like to build transportation fees into their overhead charges, but the districts generally disallow these expenses because the law does not authorize them. Some providers would like to provide their services on school grounds, while the districts want the option to charge a reasonable fee for the use of their facilities.

Conflicts have also arisen about educational aspects of the supplemental educational services. The providers would like to provide their services as they were packaged, while the districts want them to be aligned with district curricula. The providers sometimes want to reject English-language learners or students with disabilities because they require specialized services and facilities that the providers lack. The districts would like the providers to serve *all* eligible students.

A scan of sample contracts in districts found that they contained standard clauses, including a description of services to be provided, educational goals, and payment schedules and methods. Contracts also covered topics such as progress reports, indemnification protections, insurance, access to and confidentiality of student information, criminal background checks, and assurances against discrimination and drug use. Other standard clauses dealt with audits and inspections, subcontracting limits, deliverables, workers compensation, nonperformance, and termination. Some of the contracts were as short as three pages; others were fifty pages or more. Such terms, involving sometimes complicated contractual and financial arrangements, illustrate why supplemental educational services take longer to implement than the public school choice option.[10]

Expenditures. We know that both the supplemental educational services provision and the choice requirement affect Title I expenditures. However, the law does not appear to be having any impact on districts' general-fund expenditures, because the vast majority of cities use only Title I funds to pay for these programs.

While most such funding came out of regular Title I dollars at the time of the survey, ten districts did use non-Title I funds. Thirty were told by their states to reserve 20 percent of their Title I allocations for supplemental educational services and choice. In Denver, for instance, 54 of its 170 schools were in school improvement status in 2005–6. The district set aside $3 million for its choice program and $2.7 million for its SES program—20 percent of its Title I allocation in all. The district eventually spent $2 million on transfers and $2.1 million on SES—or 15 percent—in response to demand. Overall, districts budgeted the equivalent of 17.4 percent of their Title I allocations for choice and supplemental educational services.

Finally, districts were asked about the average per-pupil costs of supplemental educational services they provided and those provided by external providers. Providers may charge the Title I per-pupil allocation or the cost of the service, whichever is less. Results indicated that, on average, the cost of services offered by external providers ran two to three times more per child than did the costs for district or school providers.

Corrective Action and Restructuring. In addition to requiring that schools that have not made AYP for four consecutive years continue to receive technical assistance, offer transfers, and provide supplemental educational services, No Child Left Behind calls upon them to undertake at least one of the following corrective actions: replace relevant staff, implement a new curriculum, decrease management authority, appoint an outside advisor, extend the school day or year, or reorganize. Approximately 505 schools in the forty responding districts were in "corrective action" status.

The Council of the Great City Schools asked its member districts which actions they took with schools in this stage of sanction in 2005–6. The results indicated that the majority of responding districts provided technical assistance to schools in corrective action, afforded schools professional development, instituted new research-based curricula, developed joint school improvement plans, and notified parents about the status of the schools.

A modest number of districts appointed outside experts to advise the schools, replaced the principals, extended the school day, or decreased the management authority of the schools. Few districts contracted with a private

TABLE 2-3

STRATEGIES USED BY RESPONDING DISTRICTS WITH SCHOOLS
IN CORRECTIVE ACTION OR RESTRUCTURING

Strategy	Corrective action	Restructuring
Provided professional development	29	19
Provided technical assistance	27	18
Notified parents about status of schools	27	19
Developed joint improvement plan	21	19
Appointed outside advisor	18	14
Implemented new research-based curriculum	17	15
Decreased management authority	12	12
Extended school day	10	8
Restructured internal organization	10	11
Replaced principals	9	11
Replaced relevant staff	8	10
Extended school year	4	2
Replaced all or most staff	3	8
Reopened schools as public charters	2	3
Contracted with private entity to run schools	1	1
Turned schools over to state	1	0

SOURCE: Council of the Great City Schools, "No Child Left Behind Reauthorization in the Great City Schools," unpublished internal survey, 2006, 9.
NOTE: The two columns on the right indicate the number of responding districts that took each type of action while in the "Corrective action" and "Restructuring" phases.

entity to operate the schools, replaced all the staff at the schools, or turned the schools over to the states (see table 2-3).

Schools not making AYP for five straight years are placed into "restructuring" status. This designation requires them to carry out the sanctions from the previous stages and make necessary arrangements for alternative governance. Approximately 646 schools in the forty responding districts were in restructuring status.

Districts appeared to be most inclined to provide additional technical assistance and professional development, and to conduct additional planning. A modest number implemented somewhat tougher sanctions, decreasing management authority at the schools, replacing the principals and relevant staff, restructuring or reorganizing the schools, or appointing outside advisors of some sort.

It was clear that most districts stayed away from the more punitive sanctions, such as reopening the schools as charters, replacing all or most of their staffs, contracting with private entities to run the schools, or turning the schools over to the state. Some of this reluctance may be based on simple pain avoidance; some may be borne of political experience. Getting rid of ineffective staff is harder than it should be, given that most districts are required to find new positions for dismissed personnel in restructured schools. In addition, most states have been reluctant to seize schools, and most districts lack confidence that the states would know what to do with them if they did. Finally, many cities have considerable experience contracting out selected schools to private providers, and the results are often mixed. The record of many charters and private providers is not much better than that of regular schools in improving student achievement.

District Improvement. Some twenty-five major urban school districts were in "district improvement" status in 2005–6. Asked about how their respective states had intervened, eight indicated that their states required them to implement a new curriculum; four said their states had reduced or deferred some funding; five indicated that the states had required some restructuring; and two districts noted that the states had required replacing some district personnel. None of the districts reported that their NCLB improvement status had resulted in their state's takeover of individual schools or the appointment of a receiver or trustee to manage the district.

All but six districts also indicated that they were receiving technical assistance from their respective states on developing improvement plans, recruiting highly qualified teachers, implementing choice and supplemental educational services, and analyzing assessment data. Just over one-half of the districts indicated that they had received technical assistance from their states aimed at improving student achievement in reading and math, addressing the needs of English-language learners or students with disabilities, or providing professional development. Most cities said the assistance they received from their states involved regulatory compliance or school improvement grants of varying amounts, rather than direct instructional guidance.

Most districts receiving assistance from their states rated the quality of that assistance as "moderate." The Indianapolis school district reported that the assistance it received on data analysis was particularly helpful. The Philadelphia school district also rated its state's assistance as helpful. However, most districts did not have high expectations that their states had the capacity or expertise to provide adequate assistance in raising student achievement.

Finally, districts in "improvement" status were pursuing a number of steps to raise achievement and avoid sanctions. Most of these efforts were systemic in nature, rather than focused on individual schools. They included clearer goal-setting, better improvement planning, more stringent internal personnel accountability and evaluation systems, upgraded curricula, better instructional interventions, closer alignment with state standards and assessments, more targeted professional development, more directly aligned supplemental materials, more benchmark testing, greater focus on data analysis, more intensive coaching and instructional monitoring, and other, similar strategies.

Discussion

No Child Left Behind is now over five years old, and states and school districts across the country have struggled to implement the law to the best of their ability. Testing systems in the states are largely in place, and local programs have been reoriented to fit the framework of the act. In fact, considerable progress has been made in a number of areas over the past five years. But the steps forward appear to be accompanied by new complications.

First, states are returning spring testing data to their districts earlier than they were when the act was first being implemented. They also appear to be making AYP determinations earlier, and districts seem to be somewhat better positioned to use the data to make program decisions. At the same time, evidence shows that some states have moved their spring testing dates to late winter in order to get results back to the districts before the next school year, thereby reducing the amount of instructional time before assessments are given and sanctions are levied. Experience also suggests that the data states are returning to districts are often in very crude form, and it is clear that cities are being given less time in which to review the data for errors or adjustments than was the case when the law first went into effect.

Second, participation rates in NCLB transfer options, while still low, have increased substantially. The data suggest that districts are providing somewhat longer windows of time for parents to make choices and are attempting to communicate with them using a wider variety of methods than they did at first. In addition, districts appear to be notifying parents of their options somewhat earlier and are doing so in more than one language. Districts also appear to be giving parents more options than before.

Overall, however, NCLB transfer rates remain low, for a number of reasons related to capacity, information, and demand. As the number of schools tagged for improvement increases, the number of receiving schools from which to choose dwindles. Moreover, letters to parents could be clearer, although the large amount of information they are required by law to contain does not facilitate brevity or simplicity. And it is still not clear how eager parents are to send their children to schools outside their immediate neighborhoods.

Nonetheless, districts indicated that their biggest challenge in boosting NCLB options was rooted in the timing of the various choices. Parents normally receive information on options for magnet schools, open-enrollment, charters, and the like well before the close of the previous school year—and considerable numbers of students take advantage of them. In contrast, parents do not receive information on NCLB choices until the end of the summer at the earliest, and sometimes not until after the school year begins. By that time, those who were inclined to move their children to other schools may already have done so, or their options may be more limited.

Third, supplemental educational services have also made some headway. The variety of methods now used by districts to inform parents about tutoring options is considerably better than it was at the start of the policy. The number of providers remains high. Contracting has become somewhat more routine, windows in which to choose providers are open longer, assessment data are being shared more regularly across school and provider lines, and districts are far more likely to allow some providers onto school grounds to offer their services. These are not small steps.

The number of students participating in SES has apparently also increased, but participation rates have not grown much beyond what might be expected from the larger numbers of schools required to offer the services. This finding is unexpected, so we offer a number of hypotheses as to why the pattern may be occurring. One possibility is that school districts have increased their resistance to SES in order to hold onto as much of their Title I funding as possible. The evidence, however, does not support this explanation, in that districts seem to be doing more to put the program into place. It seems unlikely, moreover, that greater resistance would have prompted a smaller increase in participation rates. If anything, the pressure brought to bear over the past several years on school districts to accommodate private services providers has resulted in somewhat greater acceptance of the services themselves.

Another possible reason for the slow-growing participation rates is the decision by the U.S. Department of Education to bar school districts in "improvement" status from providing their own supplemental educational services—a ban not contained in the law itself. About 91 percent of students receiving SES in the responding districts now get their services from private providers. The assumption by SES proponents has been that students would move to private providers on a one-to-one basis as districts were barred from providing their own services. This assumption may be wrong, as the higher costs per child that most private providers charge may not accommodate the same number of students as the districts can. The numbers of students participating in SES would have grown by about 50 percent if all districts were able to provide services regardless of their improvement status.

One further reason for low participation is that some districts have begun to operate their own after-school programs with general funds. These programs, where they exist, now compete against the private providers without Title I funds being counted against NCLB.

Fourth, the past couple of years have seen the beginning of corrective-action and restructuring efforts. These sanctions are prompting some of the "softer" sanctions beyond choice and supplemental educational services, such as additional professional development, technical assistance, and school planning. Use of tougher punishments, like chartering or privatizing a school, is still limited. It is still too early to tell what the impact of these varied efforts will be. But experience outside of NCLB with many of the stiffer sanctions suggests that districts should either be given clearer authority to override local collective bargaining agreements in order to restructure schools, or they should engage in a more convincing partnership with the unions to get the job done.

Fifth, and finally, the effect of all these cascading sanctions on student achievement remains unclear. At the very least, the federal law deserves credit for extending the standards movement and underscoring the need to improve academic performance for all children and youth. The paradigm shift from universal access to universal proficiency has been an important one.

Student achievement in the nation's urban schools, in particular, has increased over the last several years, but it is impossible to attribute all the gains directly to NCLB. It is certainly conceivable that NCLB—or some portion of it, like Reading First—helped produce the academic improvements, but it is also possible that the law had little to do with them. A district could be in technical compliance with NCLB's provisions and not see gains in student achievement, despite the ever-stiffer punishments that would ensue. A district could also be raising student achievement without being in strict compliance with the law. Most city districts indicate that their gains are the result of more systemic instructional reforms beyond those called for in NCLB. Nonetheless, we are inclined to give NCLB the benefit of the doubt.

It is certainly not clear that NCLB-mandated sanctions, as currently defined and structured, are responsible for the gains. The research so far does not indicate that school choice under NCLB has produced increases in test scores on a broad basis in either sending or receiving schools, much less district-wide. In addition, research on the effects of some of the corrective-action and restructuring sections of the law on student achievement is still not very convincing.

Supplemental educational services have the potential to boost performance, but across-the-board gains seen in city schools cannot be attributed specifically to them. A cursory inspection of the data suggests that SES participation rates are not correlated with the academic gains of various cities. Moreover, the preliminary evaluations emerging from local sources indicate that gains are modest at best, and often vary by provider. This effect may be the result, in part, of loose eligibility criteria set by the states for who can actually provide services. The irony is that most district programs, where they exist, seem to do as well as the average private provider.

Congress faces critical questions about the accountability system under NCLB as the law comes up for reauthorization: Are the sanctions doing anything more than punishing schools for poor performance? Are the sanctions the most effective ways of leveraging faster academic gains from the schools? Should the sanctions be redefined to put more emphasis on instructional intervention? Is it counterproductive to have districts in charge of picking and administering their own sanctions? Are we spending too much or too little on the sanctions for them to benefit students? Has the law devolved into an exercise in compliance rather than being a lever for improving academic performance?

It is also worth considering whether the cascading nature of the sanctions—and not the sanctions themselves—are a drag on the districts. Many districts complain consistently about not having enough time to implement one set of strategies before they have to start putting another into place.

Answering these and similar questions is important if the law is to be more than a regulatory document producing uncertain outcomes and divided loyalties. A paradigm shift such as that represented by No Child Left Behind was bound to produce unintended consequences, particularly in its first iteration, and a constructive balance may not have been struck the first time around. Yet it is worth the effort of people who want to see it succeed to figure out how the law could help accelerate achievement gains and attain real accountability.

In the meantime, NCLB continues to be a useful tool for the nation's big-city schools in their attempts to improve. Although it has proved complicated to implement and cumbersome to administer, it has helped America's urban schools direct attention to students who, for too long, were out of sight and out of mind. That alone has made NCLB worth the effort.

3

The Political Economy of Supplemental Educational Services

Jeffrey R. Henig

Building legislative coalitions sufficiently powerful to enact important policies requires enlisting support from politicians and interest groups that differ in their goals and their fundamental understanding of how the world works. As a result, the underlying theoretical rationales are often implicit at best, and frequently mixed and muddled. Such is the case with the No Child Left Behind Act (NCLB), which was supported by ideologically strange bedfellows ranging from conservative Republicans like Judd Gregg to liberal Democrats like Ted Kennedy. And such is the case in the more particular case of Supplemental Educational Services (SES), the component designed to expand out-of-school-time tutoring to students in poorly performing schools.

SES, as I argue in this chapter, is a major policy initiative with unusually thin and tangled intellectual roots. Its somewhat last-minute inclusion in NCLB is better understood as the outgrowth of inter- and intrapartisan maneuvering than the culmination of deep and consistent thinking about how children learn, how schools interact with families and communities, and how reforms take root and succeed. Rather than being guided by an overarching theory, the politics of SES were influenced by two simplifying images: the *image of obsolescent localism* and the *market metaphor*. These served different purposes for Republican and Democratic proponents, but they converged on one key point: The role of conventional local school districts in the future would be less central and more circumscribed.

While useful for understanding the national politics surrounding SES, both the image of obsolescent localism and the market metaphor are poor tools for predicting how the program will unfold at the street level, where everyday decisions by parents, providers, and public officials take place. In the discussion that follows, I first set out the key elements and origins of the program and summarize the available evidence about how it is unfolding. I then contrast the market metaphor and the image of local obsolescence with an alternative perspective that I refer to as the *political economy of the contracting regime*. We will see that consumers and providers, competition and "shopping around," all play a role in this perspective, but they do so within parameters that continue to be shaped by government and politics. The national government and the states play more prominent parts in setting the SES ground rules than has been historically the case with education policy in our federalist system, but when it comes to making the program work, local government is still the fulcrum. Rather than being marginalized, politics and governance—including local politics and governance—play a somewhat reconfigured but no less consequential role, potentially for the better but also potentially for the worse.

SES: The Basics

Defined in its broadest terms, supplemental education refers to the "formal and informal learning and developmental enrichment opportunities provided for students outside of school and beyond the regular school day or year."[1] Some define these opportunities very broadly to include home and family supports, as well as community resources such as libraries, museums, and participation in "various folk and 'high' cultural events and faith-based activities" that influence the "development of proactive and engaged dispositions toward academic learning."[2] As a public policy, the idea is to use the levers of government to expand and make more equally available such outside-the-school supports for learning.

SES as a concrete program is a more focused and instrumental representation of that broad idea. The primary emphasis is to make after-school, weekend, and summer tutoring available to low-income students in low-income schools that are failing. Under NCLB, the SES provisions normally come into play when a Title I school fails to make adequate yearly progress (AYP) for three or more years.[3] At that point, the district must offer low-income students in that school the chance to enroll in supplemental educational services, with the district footing the bill. Districts can provide these services, unless they have themselves been found to be systemically failing, but so can a wide array of for-profit and nonprofit entities. States are responsible for approving a list of eligible providers and monitoring their performance to ensure they abide by various health, safety, and civil rights requirements, and that they actually maintain a track record of improving students' academic achievement. The fact that SES has the potential to shift funds away from low-performing schools and systems is a critical part of the program's appeal to some.

NCLB requires that districts set aside at least 20 percent of their Title I allocations to meet the combined costs of SES and any transportation costs associated with the law's choice provisions. Districts are required to inform parents when their children are eligible for SES, identify approved providers, and explain the process through which students may enroll. When families opt for private providers, districts are responsible for entering into contractual arrangements to reimburse the providers at rates set by them or by the state. These contracts may involve giving or renting to providers access to school buildings as tutoring sites, but tutors may also provide the services on their own premises, or in students' homes via onsite visits or distance-learning online. Private providers are free to hire public school teachers to do the tutoring; as we shall see, this option is often exercised.

As with other aspects of NCLB, the provisions are designed as part of a cascading series of steps schools and districts are required to take in order to ensure that all children are proficient in reading and mathematics by 2014. Districts and schools may see these steps as unwanted constraints on their ability to decide how best to help the children for whom they are responsible. The more schools that fail to meet AYP, the more families that opt for SES, and the more they choose private providers, the more the inroads on the budget that district officials otherwise would control.

SES as a Major Policy Intervention

SES is, by almost any standard, a major policy intervention. In an era when policymakers are seeking to limit entitlements, SES creates a new entitlement.[4] Against a backdrop of limited national government involvement in K–12 education, SES represents a new arena for clashes with states and localities over the proper dimensions of federalism. In a time when "privatization" of public services has become the scrimmage line for partisan battles between the right and left, SES is an apparent endorsement of the notion that for-profit providers may hold answers that direct public provision does not.

Measured in terms of people served, dollars spent, and the probability of future program expansion, SES is shaping up as a bigger commitment than other, more widely discussed aspects of education reform. The parental choice provisions of NCLB, for example, were much more visible in the NCLB debate and were structured to go into effect a year before SES. In the 2004–5 school year, over 430,000 children received SES.[5] But in 2003–4, the second year in which choice provisions were in effect, the U.S. Government Accountability Office (GAO) estimated that only about 250,000 students nationwide were exercising the option, representing about 1 percent of those eligible.[6]

SES has dramatically expanded both the supply and demand sides of what was already a growing private-sector market in educational services. Parents have the option under SES to select programs offered by charter schools, public universities, or a wide range of private-sector providers, including for-profit firms, social service or community-based organizations, and faith-based entities. Some of these providers had been in the tutoring business for years predating SES. Princeton Review, for example, began marketing its test preparation services in 1981. Like other for-profit companies, they had for the most part targeted higher-income families with the ability to pay. But some nonprofit social service and community-based organizations had worked with low-income, high-need students, sometimes relying on philanthropic support and sometimes working with contracts from local school districts. Sylvan, earlier than most of the other corporate providers, had been trying to partner with districts to make its services available to less advantaged families.

Because the number of students eligible depends on the number of schools failing to make AYP, it is difficult to assess with accuracy the full potential on the demand side. GAO estimates that slightly more than four out of five of those eligible in 2004–5 did *not* receive the services. Currently, there

FIGURE 3-1
STUDENTS RECEIVING SES OVER TIME

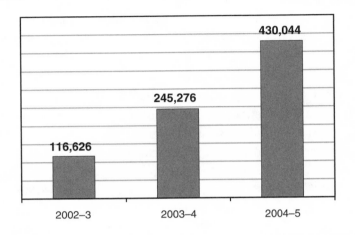

SOURCE: U.S. Government Accountability Office, *No Child Left Behind Act: Education Actions Needed to Improve Local Implementation and State Evaluation of Supplemental Educational Services*, GAO-06-758, August, figure 1, http://www.gao.gov/new.items/d06758.pdf (accessed June 13, 2007).

are over 2.1 million students eligible, and that number is likely to increase as more districts and schools are required to provide SES. As indicated by figure 3-1, the growth rate so far has been dramatic, with the number of participating students increasing over 110 percent between the 2002–3 and 2003–4 school years and over 75 percent between 2003–4 and 2004–5.

The amount of money in play is also substantial. In 2005–6, Title I funds distributed to school districts amounted to about $12.7 billion.[7] Of that, 20 percent—the cap for SES and choice—was about $2.5 billion.[8] By way of comparison, the federal government spent $6.8 billion for about 907,000 children in Head Start, a huge program in place for more than four decades.[9] For private corporations the amount potentially available can be quite exciting and an inducement to invest in what is seen as a growing market. In September 2006, for example, Knowledge Learning Corporation paid about $18 million to acquire Education Station, one of the largest SES providers in the country.

Because of its size, growth, and particular approach to tapping into the private sector, SES has the potential to alter dramatically the relationship between families and school districts. In some people's minds, SES might provide a catalyst for an even more radical rethinking of the institutional arrangements by which we try to bring public goods and private needs into alignment. Siobhan Gorman writes that, although vouchers and charter schools dominate public attention, tutoring services provided under SES "arguably represent the federal government's largest free-market experiment in education."[10]

The Origins of SES: Complicated Politics and Undigested Ideas

Despite the program's significance, relatively little is known about the policy theory underlying SES. During the period when NCLB was crafted, SES received far less attention than other components such as testing, teacher quality, and school choice. Figure 3-2 presents the results of a series of searches using ProQuest, a web-based searchable database, to determine the amount and prominence of coverage of NCLB versus SES in major newspapers over time.[11] Although a small peak of attention to SES occurred in 2001, even in that year only 15 articles treated it prominently enough to be picked up in a search of titles and abstracts, while 74 mentioned it somewhere in the full article text. To put these figures into context, consider that during the same year, 3,397 articles mentioned Iraq in their titles or abstracts, and 713 mentioned the HBO television show *The Sopranos*.

This is not simply a case of communication failure between, on the one hand, a well-informed set of legislators who have pored over the details and, on the other, media and a public who are distracted or disengaged. Education reform was high on the public's agenda in the 2000 election; in August 2000, 91 percent of Americans indicated that K–12 education was either very important or extremely important to them, and in the Gore–Bush presidential election it was ranked first out of eleven issues as the nation's most important problem.[12] The public, therefore, presumably was primed to be attentive to major elements in the law that was to represent President Bush's delivery on a campaign promise. Even so, it appears that SES was low not just on the public's radar screen, but on that of Congress as well.

FIGURE 3-2

MAJOR NEWSPAPER COVERAGE OVER TIME

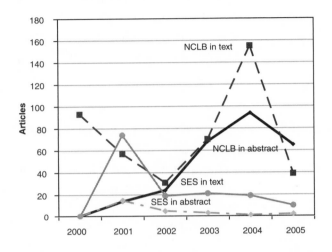

SOURCE: Author's tabulation based on searches of ProQuest Direct online database, http://proquest. umi.com.

Some who expect the policy process at least roughly to approximate a rational-comprehensive model of decision-making might find it hard to fathom that Congress could approve SES without thorough debate about its rationale and the evidence to support it. Those who follow national politics more closely, however, know that this would hardly be unique. Daniel Patrick Moynihan wrote a classic analysis of a similar occurrence: the inclusion of a highly ambiguous commitment to "maximum feasible participation" in 1960s War on Poverty legislation that established the Community Action Program. As Moynihan related, "The provision calling for 'maximum feasible participation' of the poor was utterly ignored" in the congressional hearings and debates.[13]

In the case of the Community Action Program, the core ideas that gave birth to maximum feasible participation had been harbored and honed in academia and then picked up by "guerrillas in the bureaucracy,"[14] renegade public employees whose interpretation of the program was more radical than that of the Congress that had enacted it. SES also had some history. But rather than a well-developed idea lurking close by until legislators found it useful, the notion of providing funds for tutoring was a vague one that appealed to legislators less on its own terms than as the tail on the dog of the bigger issue of whether funding should be targeted at districts and schools, as was conventionally the case, or at individual students, as would be the case with vouchers. Republican senators Judd Gregg and Charles Hagel had included something very much like it in their 1999 bill proposing the transformation of Title I into a "child-centered" program. Under their proposal, states and districts could convert their Title I funds into per-pupil allotments for each school-aged child living in poverty. This per-pupil allotment—essentially a voucher—would then, as Gregg explained "follow the child to the school they attend," and,

> since some schools continue to fail to provide high quality educational services to their neediest students, students could use their per-pupil amount to receive supplemental educational ("add-on") services from either their school or a tutorial assistance provider, be that a Sylvan learning center, a charter school or a private school. The idea behind this provision is to allow parents to use their per-pupil amount to purchase extra tutorial assistance for before or after school.[15]

In May of 2000, Democratic Senator Joe Lieberman included similar provisions for after-school tutoring in a bill offered by a group of moderate, so-called "New Democrats," in the hopes of combining Republican ideas for accountability and choice with mainstream Democrats' demands for substantial new spending. But in the run-up year to the 2000 election, neither Republicans nor Democrats were willing to forge a compromise for which their rivals might claim credit. The Gregg-Hagel bill died in committee. The Lieberman proposal won only thirteen votes, all from Democrats.[16]

SES did not emerge as a prominent piece of the NCLB package until the spring of 2001, and when it did so it was not because of its intrinsic appeal, well-defined elements, or compelling empirical support. As the political ground shifted in the aftermath of the 2000 election, SES became a useful piece in the construction of a political coalition. Rather than being a hindrance, its fuzziness at the margins probably helped at this juncture.

The bargaining leading up to NCLB hinged on a couple of key points. In the interparty bargaining, Democrats accepted accountability procedures and elements of privatization in return for gains in funding and the elimination of proposed voucher provisions. The Republicans accepted some incursions on states rights and a temporary hiatus in their campaign for vouchers in return for accountability measures that would "get tough" on unresponsive schools and districts, and a strong legislative victory on a campaign commitment to give the Bush administration momentum that might carry forward into other areas.[17]

But neither party entered the bargaining with a unified front. Many conservatives within the GOP remembered and were loyal to the goal of eliminating the U.S. Department of Education entirely—raised long ago by Ronald Reagan and then reaffirmed in 1994 with the Contract with America manifesto. They saw Bush as setting off on the wrong foot by expanding the powers of the national government and giving up too easily on the quest for vouchers. Many more liberal Democrats were reluctant to let Bush have a major win; some saw the accountability provisions as punitive and antiteacher, and they insisted it was critical to increase funding and capacity dramatically before insisting on overnight results.

In the intraparty bargaining among Republicans, SES ended up playing an important role in assuaging anger about the sacrifice of vouchers. Previously, for conservatives, tutoring was basically an add-on to vouchers, possibly included initially as part of a strategy to make vouchers less susceptible to constitutional challenge.[18] But SES, on its own, provided at least three benefits as seen from the political right. First, in its structures and principles it resembled key aspects of vouchers—portable aid; given to individuals, not schools; private-sector providers—and therefore could be regarded as moving in the direction of prescribing market-based solutions to social problems. Second, by expanding the market, it provided a nose under the tent for an emerging corporate sector which, as it became more muscular, might be a valuable ally in future battles to expand market-based solutions. Third, SES gave conservative Republicans a chance to claim they had had an impact on the law and retained enough political clout not to be dealt out in future battles.

New Democrats had already signaled a willingness to move in this direction. In late 2000, a group of them had been invited by Bush to a meeting in Texas, where they agreed to help pass NCLB as long as the incoming administration did not try to force them to swallow voucher provisions that would put them sharply at odds with their Democratic colleagues. Senator

Edward Kennedy was not invited to this meeting; but if there were to be a strong bipartisan vote for NCLB, he would be key. And Kennedy did not want to be dealt out of this important legislative initiative.

For Kennedy and mainstream Democrats, extracting the most funding possible was a primary focus. That meant finding a way Kennedy could support the bill and sell it to others, despite aspects of it that were disturbing to the teachers unions, who were key elements in the Democratic coalition. Several things about SES made it attractive as a piece to help close the deal. One central fact was that it was *not vouchers*. For at least two reasons, SES was considered less radical and threatening to Democrats and their allies. Because it focused on time outside conventional schooling hours, it did not present a head-on challenge to the existing mode of K–12 education or those who worked within it. And, unlike vouchers, which would simply *replace* public provision with private provision, SES would represent an *expansion* of public responsibility, generating new entitlements primarily for constituencies with whom liberals and Democrats traditionally identified—minorities and the poor. In this sense, SES was attractive not just because of what it was not—vouchers—but because of what it was: a tangible program aimed at Democratic voters.

In the end, SES provided cover to say "yes," both to Republicans who needed to show they were still fighting for market strategies and to Democrats who needed to show they were intent on providing real resources to high-need families. Andy Rotherham, who witnessed the early developments from his perch on the Clinton White House staff, concludes, "I think both sides frankly thought they'd snookered the other afterwards." Republicans thought they had "got something under the tent for vouchers." And Kennedy thought he'd got "a really good deal for kids. . . . And I think it is still too early to tell who is right and wrong on that."[19]

Controlling Metaphors: Markets and the Limits of Localism

Two simplifying images have dominated impressions about SES: the image of obsolescent localism and the market metaphor. The first helped provide a simple problem definition: Past efforts at school reform failed because local school governance is encrusted with parochial values, interest-group politics, over-bureaucratization, and reflexive loyalty to the status quo. The second provided a simple way of understanding SES as a part of a consistent policy package intended to bring about positive change. The image of obsolescent localism was shared by many key actors across the conventional ideological and partisan divides, and it helped overcome obstacles that normally might have doomed a plan so emphatically challenging to deep traditions of local control. The market metaphor helped to crystallize ideological differences separating the left from the right and was used tactically to rally and unify both conservative support and fragmented elements of the left in opposition. Combined, the two images created expectations that converged on one key point: The role of conventional local school districts in the future would be less central and more circumscribed.

Localism as obsolescent. The presumption that schooling should be a local concern has been a powerful force since public education took root in this country. It reflects a sense that schools are meant to transmit values that legitimately differ from place to place. This commitment to localism is different from the more formal, legal aspects of federalism that are based on the U.S. Constitution and guide relations between the national government and the state, but say nothing about localities. Localism remains strong, but it has been eroding.

The image of obsolescent localism is not a well-honed thesis but a collection of impressions based on demographic, social, and political changes that are associated with modernity and that weaken loyalties to small communities. We live in an increasingly mobile society, in which children leave home after high school and often never return, and the elderly often retire to communities distant from their children and grandchildren. Mobility of the young reduces the economic incentive of localities to invest in their schools because they can no longer count on the human capital the schools create becoming part of their infrastructure for economic development. Mobility of the old reduces local support for funding schools because older voters who no longer live near their grandchildren and other young relations are less supportive of bond referenda that will support local schools but raise their taxes. With the expansion of national media and the Internet, localized values are less distinct and protected. At the same time, localities have lost some of the claim they held on schooling because of major shifts in funding responsibilities to the states.

The images of obsolescent localism held by Democrats and Republicans differ somewhat in content. For critical decades during the twentieth century, the nonsouthern core of the Democratic Party supported a forceful national government willing to challenge "states rights" as a defense against racial desegregation. The wrenching battles over busing energized one part of the Democratic coalition but also weakened the party's hold in the South and spurred a shift in the party identification of many working-class whites, who felt the Democrats were not tending to their concerns. This view of localism as being associated with discrimination and control by parochial elites moderated somewhat as Democrats saw large central cities shifting to minority control, but the sense that the national government was a more reliable partner for redistribution and social justice remained strong. As battles over race became more muted, the role of suburban localism in generating and sustaining fiscal inequities became more prominent. For political reasons, Democrats could not afford to challenge suburban exclusionism and self-interest directly, but at least some in the party saw local control of education as a vestige that could and should dissipate as the nation marched into a future marked by greater geographic mobility and mass media.

If the *principle* of local control was weaker among Democrats than Republicans, the political link to large urban bureaucracies was not. When Republicans backed measures that encroached upon the local prerogative of central cities—as, for example, when conservative state legislatures moved to take over the running of central-city school systems—the conventional Democratic response was to cry foul. But softening the ground for support of state and national preemption of local control in the allocation of Title I funds was a sense among even some Democrats that even large urban school districts really *did* need to be held more strictly accountable, especially for improving services to minorities and the poor.

If Democrats attached the image of obsolescent localism primarily to southern bastions of anti-integration and suburban enclaves of privilege and metropolitan irresponsibility, for Republicans the central focus was the large central city. Large urban centers carry negative connotations for many Americans, who have seen them historically as nurturing grounds for amorality; but in recent years, this cultural aversion has been grafted onto a more political message. Cities, many Republicans came to believe, had become overly bureaucratized, and distracted by distributional battles over patronage, with possibilities for local coalescence around common interests stalemated. Local school boards in big cities were portrayed as a sad combination of meddling micromanagers and bickering politicians hoping to build political credibility to move into higher office.

Republicans, for the most part, still harbored fond feeling about localism as applied to the suburbs and townships where more of their constituents lived. But the image of obsolescent localism as manifested in large cities made it easier for them to accommodate policies that stripped school districts of some of their authority—especially when such stripping would be conditioned upon poor performance, as they believed would be the case with SES, and as they expected would not be a problem for suburban districts that they presumed were performing well.

The market metaphor. For the more moderate Democrats and Republicans who were trying to build bipartisan support for NCLB, the image of obsolescent localism helped defuse resistance based on appeals to localism, whether embedded in calls for states rights (Republicans) or for protecting big-city self-government (Democrats). The market metaphor proved useful in a different way, as partisans on each side used it to maintain enthusiasm in their activist base.

The market metaphor justifies SES as a way to give low-income families the ability to compete as consumers in a market that previously had been closed to them. This metaphor likens students and their families to consumers who, armed with a public subsidy, are freed to shop around for the best and most fitting educational enrichment, creating a competitive environment in which public and private providers are pressed to do more, do better, and be more responsive. It likens the school district to just one among a diverse array of tutoring providers.

Although the law explicitly identifies nonprofit organizations as potential SES providers, from the standpoint of the market metaphor it is the for-profits that are central. Some conservative supporters of SES were excited by the prospect of faith-based providers becoming involved, but most legislators who thought much about this at all were expecting established companies like Sylvan, Kaplan, and Princeton Review to have the capital and expertise to dominate the supply side. Indeed, in its early stages of discussion, SES was occasionally referred to informally as the "Sylvan Amendment." Some genuine market enthusiasts probably hoped and expected these more professional outfits to clear out much of the "Mom and Pop" trade, but, if so, this was a politically volatile point that was better left unstated.

For conservatives, the market metaphor provided a unifying theme that made it easier to incorporate disparate proposals into a simple and coherent privatization narrative. Republican spokespersons did not need to master the details of SES or any specific program. It was enough to recite a core speech about the benefits of flexible and responsive markets over sclerotic and special-interest-dominated government and then list SES among the initiatives that would move things in the right direction. In the maneuvering over NCLB, the incorporation of SES into this privatization narrative played an important role in easing the conservative wing's dissatisfaction with Bush's decision not to fight tooth and nail for vouchers. SES might be only "vouchers lite," but wrapping it in the market metaphor made it possible for conservative advocates to portray it as a small victory, instead of a large defeat, for the privatization movement.

Liberals tend to question the appropriateness of the market metaphor as a normative guide. They acknowledge that markets are appropriate means for allocating many goods and services, but see unregulated markets as a primary source of inequity and argue that government provision tends to be fairer and more reliable over the long run. Suffering from a number of painful political losses, the liberal wing found the market aspects of SES to be tactically useful as a symbolic target and rallying device. By characterizing it as part of a Republican giveaway to corporate supporters and a strategy to dismantle unions, they could incorporate attacks on SES into a set of themes that would unify discrete groups—unions, environmentalists, minorities, the working class, the elderly concerned about the privatization of Social Security—in resistance to a Republican administration they painted as being in the pockets of businesses and the wealthy.

What obsolescent localism and the market metaphor lead us to expect. The beliefs that local government was dysfunctional and inflexible and that markets were a rival to be welcomed (conservatives) or resisted (liberals) did more than help structure the dynamics of politics around SES. They also established some basic predictions about what would happen once the policy was put into place, including expectations in terms of the power and behavior of government and the contours of demand and supply within the supplemental education market. Though less tightly wrought than would be the case for the more developed causal theories that Pressman and Wildavsky suggested lay behind all policies, these predictions do provide us with some touchstones against which to begin evaluating the program. First, we can make the following three predictions about local districts:

- *They will be slow to respond.* Because they are crusty and overly bureaucratized, local districts will be slow on the uptake. Those that had already been offering some form of outside-of-school-hours tutoring will continue to do so, with little effort to reconceptualize their offerings in the face of new competitors. They will also be slow to put into place the operations the law requires of them, notably informing parents of their options and establishing contracts with state-approved providers.

- *They will be resistant.* The two images lead us to expect local districts to go beyond simple sluggishness to attempting actively to undermine the law. To maintain control over their Title I allocations, they will attempt to block private-sector competitors by misinforming parents, denying private providers access to students and schools, and erecting bureaucratic barriers. Gorman both predicted this and found evidence that some districts were behaving like "bullies" in the SES arena.[20]

- *They will be significantly and increasingly marginalized, along with local policymakers.* Local districts will become less important because power and authority will be simultaneously moving vertically up the ladder of federalism and horizontally from the public sector to the private one. Because public bureaucracies are enmeshed in regulations and staffed by persons cultivated to be careful instead of innovative, the market metaphor anticipates that in any fair and prolonged period of competition, districts will be unable to compete and, therefore, will hold only a small market share. This marginalization will accelerate as districts themselves are blocked from providing SES because they are deemed in need of corrective action, and accelerated further still as states turn to charter school and private-education management organizations (EMOs) as a form of corrective action as required under the law. "I think that the lawmakers thought that the districts would kind of just step aside," an SES provider explains. "There was this notion that the districts should not be really a factor here. That, in fact, if these schools have failed, then there is this sanction . . . and the districts are just going to have to make way for all of these providers."[21]

Three more predictions apply to market response:

- *There will be an active demand-side response.* Parents will exercise choice and be intrigued by the new private options. Conservative adherents to the market metaphor expect this because they believe only lack of money explains why low-income consumers normally content themselves with subpar services by public monopolies. At least some of those on the left anticipate strong uptake also, not because poor families are choosing wisely, but because market providers will offer glitzy services and aggressive marketing campaigns. After the local districts are marginalized, the SES provider cited above suggests, congressional supporters assume that "a market mentality is supposed to set in and parents [will] go shopping among the various state-approved providers and over time, the cream will rise to the top."[22]

- *There will be a vibrant and steadily increasing supply-side response.* Once the program becomes known and procedures are put into place, many organizations of various types will offer SES. Conservative adherents to the market metaphor expect this because they believe that the program creates an opportunity for entrepreneurs—whether in business or in the nonprofit social service, community organization, or faith-based sectors—and that the nature of entrepreneurialism is to respond to need and demand.

- *For-profit providers will have a competitive edge over district and nonprofit providers.* The market metaphor presumes that efficiency, quality control, product-branding, and organizational dexterity determine which providers will gain market share. Companies with established business sense, access to private capital markets, and complementary products like testing and curriculum design will win the battles for the bulk of the clientele. Liberal skeptics anticipate for-profit dominance for different reasons and through different behaviors. They expect corporate providers to use both economic *and* political resources to muscle aside smaller, community-based providers. Rather than expand by improving services and responsiveness to citizens, they suggest, for-profit corporations will become active lobbyists for further deregulation and marginalization.

Early Readings from an "Immature" Policy Regime

Trying to take the measure of new programs before they have had time to mature is hazardous. Administrative procedures and capacity may take awhile to come up to speed. Even well-conceived programs have wrinkles that need to be ironed out. Personnel have to be trained in new procedures. For these reasons, early returns on new programs may be disappointing.

But policies do not always get better with time. Often, new programs appear to work well out of the starting gate, benefiting from the burst of attention and information that accompanies their launching, from support from foundations and donors who want to be part of something exciting and new, and from the leadership of especially skilled and committed individuals. But they may decline in vitality as time goes on, with program effectiveness beginning to dim as interests and attention fade, donors finding new reforms to champion, and first-generation leaders, who got involved early because of their intense interest, burning out or moving on. Accordingly, the assessments made here are tentative.

Local Districts Still the Fulcrum. "Rumors of my death have been greatly exaggerated," Mark Twain is reputed to have said. Similarly, local school districts and their leaders might at this point claim that projections of their obsolescence are greatly overblown. While the conventional understanding of SES proposes states and the national government as the new venues for active school policy, in its day-to-day workings, SES may be empowering some local policymakers rather than dealing them out of the game.

Initially, local districts were scolded for being slow in notifying parents that their children were eligible for choice and SES. "Massive resistance might be too strong a term to describe the way in which local school officials are implementing these new options for parents. But not by much," wrote one observer.[23] To critics of past local district performance, this was a predictable outcome of the perverse incentives created by the law: If parents were not given due notice of their rights under the program, if the district were slow to identify failing schools or resisted providers' requests to use school facilities or hire local teachers, it would not be punished for bad behavior; rather, it would get to keep control of the greater portion of its Title I funds.

While some districts almost certainly dragged their feet, however, it appears that the delays in notification were frequently due to states being slow in providing them with information they needed. Early critiques of district response focused on the seemingly low participation rates, which observers attributed to district failures to promote the program. But participation rates have climbed substantially. Nationally the participation rate in 2004–5 was 19 percent, up from 12 percent the year prior.[24]

Despite the prediction that bureaucratized urban school systems would be the most intransigent, a number of districts—including some of those initially criticized—appear to have embraced SES and worked hard to shape it to complement their missions. Hannaway and Cohodes describe Miami-Dade's aggressive marketing of SES, including organizing fairs at which various providers could advertise and a phone operation in which taped recordings by Miami Heat players explained the program's benefits.[25] Rochester, N.Y., Toledo, Ohio, Los Angeles, and San Diego have also been noted for their proactive efforts.[26] One reason districts may have been willing to promote private providers is that they are less likely to see them as competitors than most observers expected; indeed, Casserly shows many large urban districts are staying out of the SES provision business entirely.[27]

Similarly, despite the notion that they were the more reliable partner in an era in which local districts were increasingly dysfunctional, many states have had at least as difficult a time stepping up to the demands of the

TABLE 3-1

**PROGRAM ELEMENTS REVIEWED BY STATES AND
DISTRICTS MONITORING PROVIDERS, 2005–6**

	States (%)	Districts (%)
Parent/student satisfaction with provider	27	34
Provider communication with teachers and parents	37	46
Extent to which a provider's program, as enacted, reflects its program design, as outlined in its application	19	30
Evidence of meeting academic achievement goals as stated on student learning plan	23	28
Evidence of improved student achievement based on any statewide assessment	15	26
Alignment of provider curriculum with district/school curriculum or instruction	25	35
Student attendance records	27	67
Evidence of improved student achievement based on provider assessments	27	39
Protection of student privacy	33	55
Adherence to applicable health, safety, and civil rights laws	29	48
Evidence of provider financial stability (e.g., audits, financial statements)	31	N/A
Evidence of improved student achievement based on grades, promotion, and/or graduation	12	23
Billing and payment for services	N/A	72

SOURCE: Adapted from U.S. Government Accountability Office, *No Child Left Behind Act: Education Actions Needed to Improve Local Implementation and State Evaluation of Supplemental Educational Services*, GAO-06-758, August, table 5, 34, http://www.gao.gov/new.items/d06758.pdf (accessed June 13, 2007).

NOTE: GAO collected these data before the end of the 2005–6 year and includes in the report results based on what states and districts said they "planned" to do before the end of the year. Those figures suggest a much higher level of activity is possible but, without evidence that the jurisdictions delivered on their promises, must be regarded with due skepticism.

program. Delays in processing test scores have already been mentioned. But possibly the biggest shortcoming has been in implementing rigorous procedures to make sure districts and providers are performing as they are supposed to—monitoring and evaluation tasks that NCLB assigns to the states. GAO found that most states were not conducting any onsite reviews of district implementation, and even those that were did so only in a few districts rather than comprehensively. Instead, states have largely relied on implementation data provided by the districts themselves.

Table 3-1 presents the GAO assessment of actual monitoring of provider activity carried out by states and districts in 2005–6. Two points stand out. First, at the time GAO performed its assessment, most states and districts had not yet collected this kind of information. Second, the districts were more active than the states. Here, again, it probably makes sense to regard this as a function of capacity more than will. Most large districts have bigger and more experienced bureaucracies to which to assign these tasks than states do, despite states' being charged with overseeing the much larger geographic area.

Local obsolescence was thought by some to be ensured by the Department of Education's prohibition against districts providing SES once they had been found in need of improvement. Paradoxically, the experience of large urban districts that have faced this sanction underscores that local districts have a more critical role than many expected. Chicago and Boston were among the first to "trip" the ineligibility to provide SES provision. But faced with the prospect of enforcing the law, with the likely attendant disruptions to children and the unlikely capacity of private providers to fully fill the gap, the DOE found it advisable to create an escape clause they could exercise selectively. They devised a "pilot program" that would permit districts to continue to provide SES, despite being in need of improvement or corrective action, as long as DOE was convinced that the districts in question were aggressively attempting to implement the SES provisions.[28] Some observers saw this as a pragmatic realization that federal and state policymakers need local districts as viable and cooperating partners if their reform visions are to be realized. Others saw it as capitulation by the DOE; an example of politically induced timidity that sacrifices local schoolchildren in order to make life easier for adults.

Market Reponses: Slow Uptake in Demand; Wild and Woolly on the Supply Side; and Partnership Favored over Competition. The market metaphor presents SES as driven by for-profit firms interacting with families-as-consumers. But early indications suggest there may be less pent-up demand than envisioned, that the development of SES may have as much to do with nonprofit organizations as for-profit ones, and that partnership relationships between providers and the local schools and districts may explain more about the way the program is evolving than a model focused on direct provider-to-consumer interactions.

The slow rate of early uptake has most often been attributed to local districts' failure to inform parents expeditiously of the program and their eligibility. But this explanation is losing traction as the program gets more familiar and as it becomes evident that participation lags behind expectations even in the districts that have been most responsible in getting out the word. Eligible families seem to need aggressive courting to get them to enroll, and both families and students need coaxing to assure the attendance of those who sign up. Because it has been difficult to entice families, providers have worked hard to be able to offer SES in children's home schools. Even with this advantage, maximizing enrollment has been difficult, as has been ensuring attendance once students are enrolled. Some providers have responded by offering families and students various selective incentives, much as local savings and loans companies used to offer families free toaster ovens or other appliances if they opened bank accounts. In some instances, these efforts have raised serious questions about the basic integrity of the operations. Investigators in New York City in March 2006 reported to schools chancellor Joel Klein evidence of "questionable business practices" by providers "in efforts to attain the maximum amount of Federal dollars available" under the SES program. These included "monetary donations to schools in order to gain access to on-site delivery, the procurement and use of confidential student information, improper parent and student solicitation, and the offer of money to parent coordinators for the enrollment of students."[29]

If the demand side has been more tentative than anticipated by the market metaphor, the supply side has, if anything, proved more elastic than expected. Many states were inundated by requests from potential providers asking to be approved for participation in the program. Since providers are

TABLE 3-2
SES PROVIDERS BY STATES IN WHICH APPROVED

States	Providers (%)
1	1,644 (92.9)
2	55 (3.1)
3–5	32 (1.8)
6–10	10 (0.6)
More than 10	29 (1.6)
Totals	1,770 (100)

SOURCE: Author's calculations based on data collected by American Institutes for Research, Supplemental Educational Services Quality Center, "SES by State," http://www.tutorsforkids.org/state.asp (accessed June 16, 2006).

approved on a state-by-state basis, compiling a national list can be difficult, and estimates of the number and types of providers vary. To get a clearer sense of the provider universe, I downloaded state lists of approved providers from the Supplemental Educational Services Quality (SESQ) Center, which was established by American Institutes for Research under a grant provided by the U.S. Department of Education. I integrated the lists and, based on available information that included the organizations' titles and facts gathered through website checks, I coded individual providers to identify the number of states within which each organization was approved for SES, and whether the provider was a unit of government, a corporate for-profit, or one of a range of different types of nonprofit organizations such as social services providers, universities, charter school, and faith-based organizations.

As measured simply by the number and variety of approved providers, SES stimulated a tremendous supply-side response. As of November 2005, there were 1,770 unique, state-approved SES providers. Much attention has been paid to the role of large national providers, who might bring high levels of capitalization and expertise to an area historically dominated by small-scale, community-based providers and "mom and pop" operations. Although there are some large providers focusing on national or regional markets, however, by far the bulk of operators are small and locally focused.

TABLE 3-3

PROVIDERS BY TYPE

Provider type	Number of providers	% of all providers	% operating in more than one state
True generic/uncodeable	615	34.7	8.3
Social services provider	232	13.1	1.7
Traditional public district	229	12.9	0.0
Academic	206	11.6	15.0
Faith-based	109	6.2	0.0
Traditional public school	98	5.5	0.0
Ethnic, race, gender, international	65	3.7	1.5
Neighborhood	55	3.1	1.8
University	51	2.9	0.0
Special needs	48	2.7	10.4
Online	47	2.7	27.7
Corporate	45	2.5	73.3
Vocational, job skills	32	1.8	3.1
Private school	23	1.3	0.0
Other public entity	23	1.3	0.0
Home schooling	10	0.6	20.0
Charter school	10	0.6	0.0
Union	9	0.5	22.2
Specialty	6	0.3	0.0
Total	**1,913***		

SOURCE: Author's calculations based on data collected by American Institutes for Research, Supplemental Educational Services Quality Center, "SES by State," http://www.tutorsforkids.org/state.asp (accessed June 16, 2006).
* Totals more than 1,770 because some providers fall into more than a single category.

As indicated in table 3-2, about 93 percent of the approved providers had been approved by only one state. Only about 2.1 percent were operating in six or more states. Of those operating in more than ten states, about one in four provided services online or in the form of packaged programs.

A diverse array of organizations has been approved, and not all fit the model of the entrepreneurial and consumer-responsive firm connoted by the market metaphor. Where possible, I coded organizational types based on their names. For example, a provider was coded as "faith-based" when the title included the name of a religious organization or figure; an organization was coded as "ethnic" if it included a reference to a specific race, ethnicity, gender, or foreign nationality. Other categories, similarly, were coded based on keywords. When terms were confusing or ambiguous, I attempted to find the organizations via Google web searches to obtain additional information.[30] Table 3-3 presents the results, in descending order of number of different provider types.

Of those with codeable names, the most common providers were social service agencies, traditional school districts, and organizations emphasizing academic achievement. Faith-based organizations were the fourth most common, but they were only about half as common as the three that were higher on the list. It is important to remember that some of these providers may be very small. One indication of the difference between number of providers and scale of the operation is shown in the column in table 3-3 indicating the percentage of the organizations of each type that were operating in multiple states. While only 2.5 percent of providers were recognizable for-profit companies, almost three-quarters of these were multistate operations. In contrast, all of the faith-based providers and more than 98 percent of the social services providers were approved only in a single state.

At this point, we do not really know how these providers are dividing the market, although it seems likely a small proportion accounts for a sizable majority of students actually receiving services. And it is simply too early to tell how this array of providers will mutate over time. One possibility is that larger corporate providers will use their depth of capital, name-brand recognition, staying power, and research capacity to provide scientific evidence of effect to muscle out the competition and expand their market shares. This is what appears to be occurring in the charter school and education management organization arenas more generally, and, arguably, this is akin to what has happened in the arena of health maintenance organizations, a public-private market with somewhat analogous characteristics. If these are also the best providers in terms of student outcomes and well-being, that will be fine and, indeed, what the market metaphor leads one to expect. But there are other possibilities.

SES as a Local Contracting Regime

> The naiveté of the lawmakers was in failing to realize that every-
> thing has to run through the district. And the thought that the
> district was going to kind of just step aside and let the money
> run right through them straight to the providers was kind of
> foolish in retrospect. . . . If you go inside of any, especially the
> big urban, school districts you will see that they are very much
> in control of the SES program. And increasingly so.[31]

The image of local obsolescence predicts that local government will be
pushed to the margins by a combination of market competition and preemption by state and federal actors. What seems to be developing, instead,
is the incorporation of SES into a model of service delivery that is common
in nonschool arenas of municipal government. Under this model, local government fully or partially cedes responsibility for direct delivery to private
firms that operate under contract to provide specified services to specified
populations for specified lengths of time. This raises questions about both
the prediction that local governments will be marginalized and the prediction that market dynamics will displace political dynamics.

NCLB, as we have seen, gives local districts a formal role in contracting
with providers. Within the contracting model, local school districts retain considerable say in the process of determining who will provide SES, under what
conditions, and with what degree of oversight. That local districts are still critical gatekeepers is partly due to their advantages over state and federal agencies
in terms of capacity and local knowledge. Compared to state and national
governments and bureaucracies, local municipalities have the on-the-ground
capacity to monitor performance and to meet and come to terms with the hundreds of SES providers approved to deliver services in their state. Moreover,
in practice, some of the functions formally allocated to the states are being
delegated to local officials to handle as "agents" for the state; in Paul Manna's
terms, the states may be "borrowing strength" from the districts.[32] Some
local districts may turn their backs on SES in the hope that it will go away;
in these cases they risk ceding authority and influence to others. But "CEO-
style" superintendents in some of the largest urban districts are aggressively

managing a portfolio of educational providers, including nonprofit and for-profit enterprises, that are constrained within a contracting regime.[33]

Besides on-the-ground capacity that states and the federal government lack, local districts have bargaining leverage because they control resources and points of access that private providers need or want. For various pragmatic reasons, providers often find it critical to enlist public-sector allies at the school and district levels. This is partially to ease the contracting process itself but goes beyond this to relate to the potential for profitability once a provider has a program in place. Providers need partnerships with local officials to market their products, to obtain cheap and convenient sites for delivering their products, to staff their operations, and to make it less likely that they will subsequently be disapproved for failing to meet NCLB standards.

Getting access to a school building as a delivery site and public school teachers as instructors can be critically important for a provider, in part due to the greater convenience to parents who would otherwise have to find a way to transport their child from school to a tutoring office. In inner-city districts, too, the greater safety in having one's child simply stay in his or her school building for longer is a huge bonus. But access to a school building can also substantially reduce cost and make it easier to recruit the school's teachers to work for the provider after hours. GAO found that over three-quarters of the providers they interviewed were delivering services at schools, and a majority were hiring teachers to do so.

Hiring local teachers makes SES programs seem more inviting to many families. It can also help providers by reducing their need to provide special training and professional development. Significantly, it also offers providers an easy way to demonstrate to local or state regulators that their programs are "aligned" with the official curriculum. At the same time, the providers' need for access to the districts' teachers and facilities gives the districts considerable leverage. Even districts that have been declared ineligible to provide SES themselves have chips they can play to influence private providers to operate on terms defined by local officials. Far from being marginalized, then, local regimes that are aggressive and astute have the potential to use their gatekeeper role to extend their influence over private providers and—depending on local proclivities—either build new capacity to improve the range and quality of services under their aegis or treat them as a new source of "goodies" to distribute to favored groups, communities, and firms.

The market metaphor suggests that activating parents as empowered shoppers is the key force driving a competition to improve supplemental education for students in low-performing schools. Within contracting regimes, however, providers have more incentive to attend to the needs and interests of public officials than those of the ultimate consumers of their services. Marketing SES directly to consumers is problematic. Since eligibility depends on what school a child attends as well as families' income, it is hard to target the message to the right audience. Newspapers, television, and radio would send the message too broadly; the providers would be paying rates based on much larger audience bases than would be potentially responsive to their offerings.

Moreover, some providers who have tutoring services they also offer to unsubsidized families might want to avoid a broader identification with the SES market. "I don't look at this as a retail business, like putting up billboards on the highways," a Princeton Review executive is reported to have said.[34] School-specific channels can be much more targeted—PTAs, principals' newsletters, teacher recommendations, and general word of mouth.[35] A set of case studies done for DOE's Office of Planning, Evaluation, and Policy Development found "principals in several districts [who] said they often helped with outreach efforts by calling the parents of students they believed could benefit from the services."[36] Teachers, moreover, are among parents' most trusted sources of information and guidance.

Thus, it should be no surprise if SES providers, by choice as well as necessity, spend as much or more time cultivating support among local politicians as they do in conventional market research or in cementing relations with their current clients.

Implications for the Politics and Policies of SES Reform

In place of a well-developed policy theory, the original support for SES rested on images of obsolescent localism and the market metaphor. Experience to date suggests that local governments have not been dealt out of the game; to the contrary, they retain a key gatekeeper role and have considerable leverage. And rather than being a part of a market regime in which the essential decisions are made in bargaining relationships between providers and consumers, private providers, due to a complicated mix of choice and necessity, find themselves bargaining more with central district and school-level leaders to get contracts, gain access to schools, recruit teachers, and construct a situation in which they can carve out a profitable market. For-profit companies are prominent players, but so are more parochial, community-based organizations and social service–oriented nonprofits. The latter have long traditions of working with local politicians and their own political constituencies, and in some instances are long-term members of the local governance regimes. Politics, not markets, are their métier.

What does this mean for the future of SES, and what should it mean for future policy? Contracting out is not a new function for local governments. Municipalities for decades regularly have contracted out for certain urban services, including trash collection, parking meter collections, data management, mosquito abatement, and the like. While privatization of core educational functions has been highly controversial and often blocked by local political resistance, school districts nonetheless have historically contracted with private firms for some important services, including food services, maintenance, security, and professional development. Recognizing this has some advantages. SES has expanded the contracting model into an arena traditionally reserved to educators employed by, paid by, certified by, and directly responsible to local government. Despite this being a departure from past practice, we are not without markers and roadmaps about what is likely to develop.

What can we learn from experience with contracting in other realms? I highlight four points here. First, contracting can be done well or can be done badly. When there are multiple providers to compete for bids, and when local officials have expertise and the capacity to monitor performance, contracting out can be a valuable tool for local leaders to consider. But the history of contracting out also indicates potentialities for corruption and ineffectiveness.

Second, contracting works best when there is agreement on the product that is to be produced and on a metric by which it can be measured. Measuring the performance of private firms contracted to pick up the garbage is relatively straightforward. Early experiments with the privatization of education ran into difficulties at least in part because the uncertainties about how to measure vendors' performance were so much more contentious and complex. Arguably, the sharp focus on test-score gains mandated by NCLB resolves some of the previous ambiguity, but that assumes a local consensus on the adequacy of test scores as the pivotal outcome of interest, and it is premature to accept that assumption as fact.

Third, providers in contracting regimes can become an attentive political constituency that uses its inside information and resources to shape the programs under which they operate, and do so in ways that meet their own interests and not necessarily those of their clients. Providers can be expected to act as lobbying groups with a stake in the legislative, regulatory, and financing details, as well as organizations with a product to sell.

Finally, the quality of a contracting regime depends ultimately on the character of the political and bureaucratic institutions within which it is embedded. Contracting out can provide local officials with tools that enable them to act more flexibly and efficiently. But it can also be a breeding ground for corruption and patronage. To the extent that supporters of SES have seen it as a way to get around the tough, often frustrating challenge of making local government work better, they may be missing a key point. Good contracting depends on good government; it is not a substitute for it.

That some localities are lax, irresponsible, or clueless cannot be denied. But the challenge is to bring them up to speed—not because that is easy, but because it is the only way to go. Helping local districts build and maintain healthy and productive SES contracting regimes would require, I think, a three-pronged approach. First, "Do no harm." Unrealistic and unachievable standards for obtaining 100 percent proficiency make local failures inevitable and ensure that even well-designed and well-supported initiatives will be put on the defensive.

Second, couple responsibility with room for local judgment and discretion. A "laser-like focus" on outcomes and the achievement gap can be valuable; but in order to build civic capacity, public officials need to be able to build local coalitions among groups that have varying interests, values, and priorities. That requires having something to bargain with and having a zone of discretion within which to shape locally varying responses.

Finally, when the problems are severe and endemic, wielding the "stick" of state intervention and local governance reconstitution may be pragmatic and appropriate. But this should not be the remedy of first resort. And when it is used, it needs to be done as part of a process of rebuilding local politics and governance so that a healthier regime can be handed back key reins of control. That means involving local stakeholders throughout the process and systematically seeking to strengthen local institutions for democratic decision-making and responsibility.

4

The Problem with "Implementation Is the Problem"

Michael J. Petrilli

It's popular in Washington to declare No Child Left Behind (NCLB) an excellent statute (even "99.9 percent pure," as Education Secretary Margaret Spellings claimed), but complain about its "implementation."[1] For example, Senator Edward M. Kennedy, one of the law's architects, recently said,

> The No Child Left Behind Act contains essential reforms for the nation's schools. It's time to keep the promise of those reforms for all students across the country. The Administration's implementation of the reforms has been inadequate and ideological . . . its ineffective implementation has undermined the reforms it said were so important.[2]

Representative George Miller, another of the law's creators, recently said at a Business Roundtable forum that "I think I would give it an A in terms of the goals that it has. . . . And on implementation, I would give it a C."[3] At a similar forum in 2003, civil rights advocate Kati Haycock gave the law "an A for grabbing people's attention" but "a C on implementation so far."[4]

Note that these are *proponents* of the law. Its opponents in the education establishment—such as the National Education Association—flog its implementation but don't even pretend to agree with its core provisions.

The author thanks Fordham research interns Jennifer DeBoer and Coby Loup for their research assistance with this chapter.

So, berating its "implementation" isn't just a cute way to voice opposition to NCLB. Many individuals on Capitol Hill and in advocacy groups appear sincerely to believe that with the right people calling the shots in the U.S. Department of Education, making good decisions, and acting wisely, the law could work as intended.

Examining whether this contention is right—at least when it comes to the law's public school choice, free tutoring, and restructuring provisions—is the aim of this chapter.

Stump the Chumps: Three Policy Paradoxes

The central task of NCLB implementation is translating its aspirational statements and bold principles into action in the real world. Sometimes this is easy, such as when the statute itself is very clear. But in many areas of the law, Congress left key issues unresolved. (One good example: NCLB says that teachers coming through alternate routes to certification can be considered "highly qualified," but it also decrees that teachers with "provisional licenses" cannot be deemed highly qualified. Yet most alternate-route teachers have provisional licenses. What exactly did Congress intend?)

This isn't terribly surprising. Indeed, NCLB was a hallmark bipartisan bill, and as such it aggregated myriad policy ideas from across the political spectrum, some complementary, some directly at odds with each other. Fundamental disagreements among lawmakers were often papered over. This is a predictable part of the democratic process. It's how laws get passed.

But for a statute like NCLB to work well at the local level, in real schools, affecting real children, its contradictions must be resolved; its fuzzy notions must be made crystal clear. This is the work of implementation—first and foremost the work of the U.S. Department of Education (DOE).[5]

How well is the DOE doing its job? From my perspective as a former Bush administration official with some responsibility for implementing NCLB's public school choice and supplemental educational services (that is, free tutoring) provisions, I examine how the department has tackled three key policy paradoxes embedded within the law:

- In order for NCLB's public school choice and free tutoring provisions to work, local school districts must take aggressive actions to inform parents of their options. Yet districts have little incentive to do so.

- Students in schools "in need of improvement" are to be provided with the option of better school choices within the same public school system. But in many big-city districts, there aren't enough good schools to go around.

- School districts are supposed to "restructure"—that is, overhaul—persistently failing schools. Yet these districts rarely have the inclination or political will to do so. Loopholes in the law make bold action even less likely.

What has the DOE done to untie these knots? How has policy evolved or changed since the arrival of a new education secretary in 2005? Are department actions working? And, most importantly, do these dilemmas have any chance of ever being resolved? If these riddles cannot be solved, the fault must be placed on the law itself—not just those charged with carrying it out.

Let's take a look.

Policy Paradox #1: How to Get Recalcitrant Districts to Inform Parents of Their NCLB Choice Options. It almost goes without saying: For parents to take advantage of school choice programs, they must know that they exist. Yet experience has shown that in the early days of any choice program, good parental information is scarce. That helps to explain why each of the nation's school voucher programs got off to such a slow start. In the first year of the federally funded Opportunity Scholarship program in Washington, D.C., for example, almost half of the available vouchers went unused because organizers didn't have time to inform parents adequately. Similar dynamics can be seen in other voucher and charter school programs nationwide.[6]

So under the best conditions, informing parents of their options under NCLB would be a difficult challenge. But the construction of the law presents a unique problem: It requires local school districts to inform parents of their options when doing so is at odds with districts' own interests. As will be explained below, many big-city districts don't have many school choice options to offer parents anyway, and few are eager for parents to use the districts' tutoring dollars on private providers outside the school system's domain. Plus, if districts don't spend the required amount on choice or tutoring (a sum equal to 20 percent of their Title I allocation), they can use these dollars for their own initiatives. In other words, it's not "use it or lose it," it's "use it for choice and tutoring or use it as you see fit."

Many analysts predicted these problems even before the law's ink was dry, and they help explain why so few students are participating in NCLB school choice. Let's examine what the DOE tried to do to address them—and consider why its efforts failed.

Strategy #1: Appeal to districts to do the right thing. The statute is relatively clear—though not elaborate—about districts' responsibilities when it comes to informing parents. They must provide information "in an understandable and uniform format and, to the extent practicable, in a language that parents can understand." They must explain why the child's school is "in need of improvement" in the first place, including "how the school compares in terms of academic achievement to other elementary schools or secondary schools served by the local educational agency and the State educational agency." They must make clear "the parents' option to transfer their child to another public school" or "to obtain supplemental educational services for the child."[7] These notices must come "not later than the first day of the school year" following the identification of a school "in need of improvement."[8] Districts obligated to provide supplemental educational services must annually give parents a "brief description of the services, qualifications, and demonstrated effectiveness" of each approved tutoring provider in the district.[9]

In the first version of its *Public School Choice Non-Regulatory Guidance*, published in December 2002, the DOE built on these basic statutory requirements to encourage districts to provide helpful information to parents: "The [local educational agency] should work together with parents to ensure that parents have ample information, time, and opportunity to take advantage of the opportunity to choose a different public school for their children."[10] That same month, in its *Supplemental Educational Services*

Non-Regulatory Guidance, the department encouraged districts to "consider multiple avenues for providing general information about supplemental educational services, including newspapers, Internet, or notices mailed or sent to the home."[11] These suggestions were hardly aggressive, though. At this critical early stage, the department failed to publish a model letter that districts could send to parents explaining their options; without such guidance, many districts wrote opaque missives full of jargon.

The DOE took another bite at the apple in August 2003, when it published an updated version of its supplemental educational services guidance. Clearly frustrated about the letters some districts were sending home that actually discouraged parents from taking advantage of free tutoring, the department added new language: "Any additional information in a notice should be balanced and should not attempt to dissuade parents from exercising their option to obtain supplemental educational services for their child."[12] But this mild rebuke—in the form of nonbinding "guidance"—was hardly going to spur districts to change course.

But the department didn't give up. Still trying to appeal to districts' better angels, in May 2004 it published *Innovations in Education: Creating Strong District School Choice Programs*.[13] This colorful booklet culled "best practices" from five school districts with vast experience implementing their own public school choice programs. Under headings like "Communicate Clearly About NCLB Choice Options" and "Provide Personalized Follow Up," it gave concrete, actionable advice to districts that wanted to implement the choice provisions effectively. Importantly, it also provided sample letters (from Milwaukee) that demonstrated how districts could communicate to parents in a straightforward, jargon-free way. The department printed fifty thousand copies of these booklets and distributed them widely, and posted a version online. It used the booklet in a variety of forums and conferences.

But from the DOE's perspective in Washington, boosting districts' know-how didn't seem to make much of a difference; those pesky perverse incentives hadn't gone away. So the department adopted another strategy: If you can't work through the districts, work around them.

Strategy #2: Empower the outsiders. Though many local school districts didn't seem to see much benefit in touting NCLB's choice opportunities, several advocacy groups did. Organizations such as the Black Alliance for

Educational Options (BAEO), the Hispanic Council for Reform and Educational Options (HCREO), and the Greater Educational Opportunities Foundation (GEO) viewed parental outreach as the key part of their mission. One of BAEO's objectives, for example, is to "educate Black families about the numerous educational options available."[14]

It made perfect sense, then, to support these organizations when they applied for grants under the DOE's Fund for the Improvement of Education (FIE), also known as "the secretary's discretionary fund." BAEO received grants totaling almost $1.5 million; HCREO received $900,000 and GEO almost $750,000.[15] Each of these groups set out to inform parents of their NCLB options in target cities. Nina Shokraii Rees, the head of the DOE's Office of Innovation and Improvement at the time, explains the department's thinking:

> Anyone who has spent any time in an inner city school district knows that the process of educating families about their rights under a complicated law like NCLB can be a time consuming task—and not one that a Title I director in a district office has the time or funding to focus on. Groups like BAEO and HCREO had experience in this area and because they were small and nimble they brought a greater entrepreneurial spirit to the task at hand.[16]

BAEO's "Project Clarion," for example, launched aggressive outreach campaigns in cities including Detroit, Atlanta, and Philadelphia. Using a mix of radio ads, grassroots communication, and media relations, it sought to inform parents of their NCLB school choice and free tutoring options. The project had some success: Knowledge of NCLB and its choices increased in BAEO's target cities from 37 percent to 72 percent over the three years of the initiative.[17]

But discretionary FIE funds were quite limited, and these targeted campaigns couldn't come close to having a national impact. There was a substantial amount of money (almost $40 million in 2006) for the DOE's Parent Information and Resource Centers (PIRC) program—except its name was a misnomer; it wasn't actually designed to inform parents about their school choice options. A holdover from President Clinton's Goals 2000 law, the PIRCs' primary role was to fund parent-education programs, with a focus on early childhood. Regardless, department officials used the grant application process to establish priorities (that is, bonus points) for PIRCs willing to do the work of informing parents of their options under NCLB. Soon the nation's seventy-odd PIRCs were engaging in parental information campaigns of one sort or another.

It's hard to know for sure whether any of these nontraditional methods worked. To this day there are no good, comparable city-by-city data on participation rates in NCLB school choice or supplemental educational services, so it's impossible to know if participation spiked in communities with stronger parental outreach. And in such a big country, with millions of children eligible for choice and free tutoring, even these activities have to be seen as mostly symbolic.

Strategy #3: Offer carrots. While the efforts of outside groups might have had their benefits, the DOE came to believe that what mattered most was whether districts "bought into" the choice and tutoring provisions and decided to launch aggressive outreach campaigns. After all, districts had some particular advantages. They had access to student information nobody else had, knowing exactly who was eligible for choice and tutoring. They had the power to send information home in students' backpacks, or, even more importantly, to instruct school principals, counselors, and teachers to give parents information about these options at back-to-school nights, during parent/teacher conferences, and so on. As the *Innovations in Education* booklets made clear, parents were most likely to trust and act on information coming from their child's teacher and principal.

So with the arrival of Secretary Margaret Spellings in the second term of the Bush administration, the DOE tried a new tack: Replace the law's perverse incentives (which pushed districts to avoid aggressive parental outreach) with different incentives—those that would encourage them to play ball. In other words, the department said, "Let's make a deal." It launched two different pilot programs. First, in August 2005, it allowed four districts in Virginia (and later another twelve districts in four additional states) to flip-flop the order of NCLB school choice and free tutoring. Now districts with schools identified as "in need of improvement" would have to offer supplemental educational services immediately, and could delay NCLB school choice for another year. In return, those districts had to engage in aggressive parental outreach, as tracked by significantly improved participation rates in the NCLB school choice and tutoring programs.[18]

The department launched a second pilot with the free tutoring provision. Four urban school districts (Anchorage, Boston, Chicago, and Hillsborough County, Florida) were given permission to serve as tutoring providers even though they were districts "in need of improvement" under the law. (In 2002, Education Secretary Rod Paige had issued a regulation that disallowed such districts from providing tutoring directly; to say this rankled the big-city districts is a vast understatement.) Once again, the deal was that these districts had to show significant progress with parental outreach and student participation. Specifically, they were required to

> notify parents of the availability of SES in correspondence that is simply written and in a language that parents can understand . . . notify parents of the availability of SES by letter to the student's home and by at least two other means . . . [and] broadly circulate information in the community about SES.[19]

These pilots certainly made political sense. Secretary Spellings was under heavy pressure from the education establishment to show greater "flexibility" with the implementation of the law. Even members of Congress had to come to agree that NCLB school choice should come after supplemental educational services. And Spellings felt she had to allow at least some big-city districts to serve as tutoring providers, in part to placate the Council of Great City Schools, which had been a vocal and courageous advocate for the law. So if she was going to make these policy changes anyway, why not get something in return?

But whether she got a good deal remains to be seen. As this book went to press, results from a third-party evaluation of these pilots had not yet been published. (And allowing districts to serve as tutoring providers has all kinds of deleterious effects on the supplemental educational services program. For example, a *Wall Street Journal* editorial reported that Chicago, Boston, and Hillsborough County were all using "administrative hurdles to make it very difficult for private and faith-based tutoring programs to reach students.")[20] Of course, no matter what the impact might be in a handful of cities, these pilots will not have had an effect on the larger national picture.

The dog that didn't bark: Wielding the stick. One strategy the Department of Education has still not adopted is getting tough with wayward states and districts. This isn't the case for the law as a whole; the administration has shown remarkable courage in withholding administrative funds from states for various infractions, such as not testing new elementary school teachers before they enter the classroom (as required under the law's "highly qualified teachers" provision) or failing to include English-language learners or special education students in the state's assessment system.[21]

So why did the DOE not take the same actions when it came to choice and tutoring? Simple—it's a matter of grey. The examples cited above are black and white: Either states tested their new teachers, or they didn't. The law was clear about what was required; enforcing the statute was fairly straightforward. This was not the case for parental outreach and information, because most districts were, in fact, living up to the *letter* of the law. They sent parents letters about their choices and posted information online. Sure, many letters were full of jargon, written to dissuade parents from taking advantage of their options, and a wholly inadequate mechanism for breaking through information overload anyway. But "going through the motions" is not illegal. Simply said, the department did not have grounds to take action.

As Rees explains,

> The Department (as an enforcement body) didn't have a track record for withholding funds from school districts which meant we needed to review all problems very carefully and ensure that we had the legal grounds to withhold money. . . . At the end of the day, we relied mainly on the bully pulpit. When we noticed instances of malfeasance, we sent letters to or called states asking them to look into the matter—these actions usually served their desired goals.[22]

In other words, the feds couldn't touch states or districts for failing to embrace the "spirit" of the law.

Which brings us back to the law itself. Perhaps it should have listed several explicit steps districts had to take beyond just sending letters home to parents. Perhaps it should have disallowed districts from keeping leftover choice and tutoring dollars, thus giving them less incentive to "hide the ball" from parents. Or maybe there's nothing the federal government can do to force districts to inform parents of options the districts would rather pretend didn't exist.

Policy Paradox #2: How to Make "Public School Choice" a Reality When There Aren't Enough Good Public Schools. We have already discussed the "demand" side of parental choice—the importance of informing parents of their options. But what about the supply side? Of course, in order for school choice to work, parents need choices—and not just any choices, but good choices. Thus, there needs to be "capacity" in good schools—in the form of empty seats—or the ability and incentives for good schools to expand their capacities (by growing, replicating, and so on) so they can serve more students.

Yet NCLB's public school choice provisions speak entirely to the demand side of school choice—by mandating that parents of children in struggling schools be given other options—while doing nothing to address the supply side. They simply assume that these other options are plentiful. But what if they are not?

Of course, that's not the worst part. As other commentators have noted, NCLB's choice provisions actually provide disincentives for schools to identify excess capacity, or to create such capacity.[23] Because many students eligible for NCLB school choice are likely to be low-performing themselves, potential "receiving" schools may be wary of accepting them for fear that their own tests scores will drop—putting them at risk for being labeled "in need of improvement." And these students don't bring any additional funds. So good schools have few incentives to 'fess up to empty seats if they have any, much less create new seats if they don't.

So if you're the federal agency charged with implementing this challenging provision, what do you do? Close your eyes and hope for the best.

"No excuses." The law's directive is clear enough:

> In the case of a school identified for school improvement under this paragraph, the local educational agency shall, not later than the first day of the school year following such identification,

provide all students enrolled in the school with the option to transfer to another public school served by the local educational agency, which may include a public charter school, that has not been identified for school improvement under this paragraph, unless such an option is prohibited by State law.[24]

Almost as soon as the law was passed, the heads of big-city school systems raised red flags, complaining that they didn't have enough schools "not identified for school improvement" to serve all their eligible children. As Arne Duncan, the head of the vast Chicago Public Schools, said later, "It's not like we have a lot of high-performing schools at 50 percent capacity."[25]

Senior officials in the Department of Education felt little pity for these leaders, since they were the same ones who had worked to defeat the president's original choice proposal, which would have expanded capacity by providing parents the option of choosing private schools. Drawing a line in the sand, the department worked quickly to make it clear that "lack of capacity is no excuse" for not implementing NCLB school choice. In June 2002, Secretary Paige sent a letter to all of the state chief school officers explaining that

a school district is obligated to provide choice to all eligible students, subject to health and safety code requirements (regarding facility capacity). Transferring students should be treated as students who have moved into the receiving school's attendance zone and allowed to enroll in class and other activities on the same basis as other children in the school."[26]

Despite this admonition, in the fall of 2002—as the first school year under the NCLB regime began—districts across the country used "lack of capacity" as an excuse not to provide public school choice to thousands of students. The *Boston Globe* told the story well in its August 2002 article, "Few So Far Use Law Allowing School Transfers." It explained, "In Chicago, 29,000 students were eligible for transfers, 2,400 sought them, and 1,165 got them. . . . Los Angeles United School District said it had room to move just 100 of the 230,000 eligible children."[27]

Clearly, district leaders hadn't bought into the provision, as is clear from a *Los Angeles Times* article, also from August 2002. "Just to move children from one building to another building does not guarantee that they are going to learn that much better," said L.A. superintendent Roy Romer. "We can take the existing school and make it work." Baltimore superintendent Carmen Russo concurred: "You want to live up to the letter and spirit of 'No Child Left Behind' as a school district. But in the long run, the answer to this is that all of our schools have to be better so no one has to flee them."[28]

These sentiments found voice in the many written comments submitted to the DOE in response to its draft Title I regulations. They are summarized in the discussion section of the final regulations, published in December 2002:

> Several commenters maintained that existing overcrowding of schools, teacher shortages, transportation difficulties, class-size limits, health and safety concerns, and other capacity issues may prevent many LEAs [local educational agencies] from implementing the public school choice option. . . . One commenter, for example, recommended that the final regulations permit LEAs to preclude transfers to schools that have reached their "maximum instructional capacity under State or local laws or ordinances."

These comments only stiffened the department's spine. It responded,

> The [Elementary and Secondary Education Act] does not permit an LEA to preclude choice options on the basis of capacity constraints. Rather, the statute requires an LEA to take measures to overcome issues such as overcrowding, class size limits, and health and safety concerns, that otherwise might prevent the LEA from complying with Title I public school choice requirements. . . . The expectation is that LEAs will need to find ways to provide choice, consistent with their obligations to provide a healthy and safe learning environment.[29]

It wrote a new regulation that was crystal clear: "An LEA may not use lack of capacity to deny students the option to transfer."[30]

It was a shot across the bow. But where, exactly, was this capacity to come from? The DOE didn't have any bright ideas. In its *Public School Choice*

Non-Regulatory Guidance, also published in December 2002, the department merely repeated itself: "If an LEA does not have sufficient capacity in
the schools it has offered under its choice plan to accommodate the demand
for transfers, the LEA must create additional capacity or provide choices of
other schools."[31]

A long, cold war between the department and the big-city districts
ensued. Administration officials repeated their mantra, "Capacity is no
excuse," at every possible chance. And districts just went on denying transfers to students, because there was nowhere for them to go. Yet, for all of its
big talk, the Department of Education never seriously threatened to take
away money. Why not? Rees explains:

> I think the capacity issue caused a political problem. It's one
> thing to ask districts to open the doors to tutoring when thou-
> sands of tutors are waiting to tutor kids but it's another to ask a
> cash strapped district to offer choice when it doesn't have many
> good schools to offer as an option—or the means to start a new
> school from scratch.[32]

To be sure, the DOE monitored the states' implementation of NCLB
school choice and, at times, sent letters requesting particular actions. For
example, when the Jefferson County school system (in Louisville) made
a unilateral decision to delay NCLB school choice for a semester, the
department contacted the Kentucky Department of Education requesting
an investigation. (Jefferson County reversed its decision.) Such black-
and-white situations were rare, though. As other districts went through
the motions, the department sat by and did little. After all, it couldn't
answer a basic question: How were districts supposed to create new seats
in good schools?

The Golden Rule. Meanwhile, as the "capacity is no excuse" position hard-
ened, the Office of Innovation and Improvement quietly set out to help
answer this question. In line with the Golden Rule—he who has the
gold makes the rules—it created priorities for scarce charter school and
magnet school assistance program grants that pushed states and districts
to target these dollars to communities with inadequate capacity for

NCLB school choice. (More fundamental changes would require a change in the statute.)

These efforts might have helped at the margins. Still, in order to solve the capacity challenge nationwide, someone needed to come up with better solutions. To that end, in its February 2004 update of the *Public School Choice Non-Regulatory Guidance*, the DOE offered ten ideas for districts befuddled by capacity constraints, including

> reconfiguring, as new classrooms, space in receiving schools that is currently not being used for instruction . . . expanding space in receiving schools, such as by reallocating portable classrooms . . . encouraging the creation of new charter schools within the district . . . modifying either the school calendar or the school day, such as through "shift" or "track" scheduling . . . easing capacity by initiating inter-district choice programs with neighboring LEAs or even by establishing programs through which local private schools can absorb some of the LEA's students.[33]

This last suggestion raised eyebrows among observers. Kristen Tosh Cowan, a partner with education law firm Brustein and Manasevit, told a May 2004 conference that "the guidance from the feds is quite interesting here," though, at the same time, "we've been hearing a lot of strong language, but we haven't seen any enforcement," even though "there's certainly a lot of fodder out there for enforcement."[34]

Indeed, it appears that these ideas disappeared into the ether. Districts ignored them and, with the 2004 election fast approaching, the DOE gave up any hopes of tough enforcement. After all, the administration had little appetite to explain to voters why their high-performing schools were being forced to go to a "shift" schedule, or why their school playgrounds had made room for portables. The truth was that all of these capacity-building strategies were either politically difficult, expensive, or took years to implement. (Creating new charter schools, for one, depended on getting state policy right: lifting caps, ensuring fair funding, helping with facilities, and so forth. Even then, creating new schools would take years.) So the department began to speak softly and threw away its big stick. Perhaps the lack of capacity was a decent excuse for not offering choice, after all.

Policy Paradox #3: How to Force Districts to "Restructure" Their Own Schools. While NCLB's public school choice and supplemental educational services provisions can be dressed up in the language of "options" and "opportunities," its restructuring provision is a cold, hard "sanction." It is meant to be a gun aimed at the heads of failing schools: Get better, or else. It is designed to put out of their misery those schools that have failed to make "adequate yearly progress" for six long years. But, importantly, it expects school districts actually to pull the trigger.

Here's how Congress said it:

> The local educational agency shall implement one of the following alternative governance arrangements for the school consistent with State law: (i) Reopening the school as a public charter school. (ii) Replacing all or most of the school staff (which may include the principal) who are relevant to the failure to make adequate yearly progress. (iii) Entering into a contract with an entity, such as a private management company, with a demonstrated record of effectiveness, to operate the public school. (iv) Turning the operation of the school over to the State educational agency, if permitted under State law and agreed to by the State.[35]

This is strong medicine, to be sure. But Congress went on to include two loopholes which would make much of this "tough love" approach crumble. First, the infamous fifth option for schools in restructuring:

> (v) Any other major restructuring of the school's governance arrangement that makes fundamental reforms, such as significant changes in the school's staffing and governance, to improve student academic achievement in the school and that has substantial promise of enabling the school to make adequate yearly progress.[36]

And second, the collective bargaining loophole (which had also been in previous versions of the Elementary and Secondary Education Act):

> Nothing in this section shall be construed to alter or otherwise affect the rights, remedies, and procedures afforded school or

school district employees under Federal, State, or local laws (including applicable regulations or court orders) or under the terms of collective bargaining agreements, memoranda of understanding, or other agreements between such employees and their employers.[37]

The implications of this statutory language are clear with a close read. First, the whole law's "get tough" approach rests on the willingness of school districts to implement aggressively one of four total makeovers: turn the school into a charter school; dismiss all or most of the staff; turn the school over to private management; or turn it over to the state. But districts aren't expected to do any of those things if they conflict with state law. In many states—those without charter school laws and those that have reached their cap on the number of charters—that means that the charter school option is out. Few states authorize state takeovers of schools, so forget that one. Private management might be possible, if unpopular, though the entire education management industry can only handle a few hundred new takeovers a year. And as for firing the staff? Collective bargaining makes that impossible in most places around the country.

Is it much of a surprise, then, that the administration has not made "restructuring" a top implementation priority? Let's take a look at what it has done to try to make lemonade out of these lemons.

Flip-flop-flip on collective bargaining. The administration quickly recognized that collective bargaining could be a big obstacle to the implementation of the law's restructuring (and corrective-action) provisions. Though the language cited above appears fairly restrictive, the DOE still wanted to push as hard as it could on the issue. So in its August 2002 "Notice of Proposed Rulemaking" (that is, draft regulations published for comment), it floated the following two aggressive regulations:

Any State or local law, regulation, or policy adopted after January 8, 2002 may not exempt an LEA from taking actions it may be required to take with respect to school or school district employees to implement [the law's improvement, corrective action, and restructuring provisions].

And:

> When the collective bargaining agreements, memoranda of understanding, [etc.] are renegotiated, an LEA must ensure that those agreements do not prohibit actions that the LEA may be required to take with respect to school or school district employees to implement [the law's improvement, corrective action, and restructuring provisions].[38]

The national teachers unions went ballistic. The American Federation of Teachers, for example, stated in its written comments that the proposed regulations "would attempt to work a retroactive application of a new rule, it would impinge on the sovereign power of states guaranteed by a federal form of government to construct their relationship with their employees, and it would impinge on the associational rights of school employees."[39]

The department caved, removing those regulations from the final package. To save face, it provided a legal explanation when its final regulations were published sans the collective bargaining policies:

> The Secretary believes that [the collective bargaining section of NCLB] was not intended to deny LEA and school leaders the management tools needed to implement effective LEA and school improvement measures, which may often involve changes in the assignment and duties of LEA and school personnel. However, the Secretary agrees that the proposed regulations arguably were inconsistent with a strict reading of the NCLB Act, and may have conflicted with applicable State and local laws.[40]

The teachers unions had won this battle, but some within the DOE continued to fight a guerrilla war. Soon after the regulations were final, Secretary Paige sent a letter on this topic to Michael Casserly, the executive director of the Council of Great City Schools, the substance of which was finally incorporated into department "guidance" in July 2006. It publicly reasserted that collective bargaining agreements were not supreme:

An LEA that accepts funds under Title I of the ESEA must comply with all statutory requirements, notwithstanding any terms and conditions of its collective bargaining agreements. Although section 1116(d) does not invalidate employee protections that exist under labor law or under collective bargaining and similar labor agreements, it does not exempt SEAs, LEAs, and schools from compliance with Title I, Part A. It is the Department's view that such agreements should not exempt school officials from any obligations related to the purpose of Title I, or the school improvement, corrective action, or restructuring requirements in section 1116.[41]

The unions were not impressed. "A letter to Casserly and a Q&A in guidance clearly do not have the same legal weight as the regs," Michele McLaughlin, assistant director for educational issues at the American Federation of Teachers, told the *Title I Monitor*. "If I were a state or district, I would be mindful of what ED said in the December 2002 regs."[42]

Indeed. While life may be full of second acts, if the department wanted a second chance at its policy on collective bargaining, it needed to revise the actual regulations. While the language in the guidance might be helpful to reform-minded superintendents who want to push the issue with their unions, in legal terms it represents little more than the DOE seizing the bully pulpit.

The infamous loophole. As this drama on collective bargaining unfolded, the DOE did very little to address the biggest loophole in the law—that allowing districts great leeway in identifying "any other major restructuring of the school's governance arrangement that makes fundamental reforms, such as significant changes in the school's staffing and governance." Its December 2002 Title I regulations did not attempt to narrow districts' range of options. Nor did its January 2004 *LEA and School Improvement Non-Regulatory Guidance*. It was not until its July 2006 update of this guidance that the department finally addressed the issue head-on—perhaps because by then it had become apparent that many districts were abusing this loophole to implement reforms much less aggressive than the ones lawmakers envisioned.

The guidance provides examples of what an "other major restructuring of the school's governance" might entail:

> Change the governance structure of the school in a significant manner that either diminishes school-based management and decision making or increases control, monitoring, and over-sight of the school's operations and educational program by the LEA; Close the school and reopen it as a focus or theme school with new staff or staff skilled in the focus area (e.g., math and science, dual language, communication arts); Reconstitute the school into smaller autonomous learning communities (e.g., school-within-a-school model, learning academies, etc.); Dissolve the school and assign students to other schools in the district; Pair the school in restructuring with a higher perform-ing school so that K–3 grades from both schools are together and the 4–5 grades from both schools are together; Expand or narrow the grades served, for example, narrowing a K–8 school to a K-5 elementary school.[43]

These are all reasonable ideas, and basically represent various forms of reconstitution and reopening. But as they are only found in "guidance," they are merely suggestions. Districts are free to ignore them, and there's lit-tle reason to believe that most districts will do anything else.

It's clear that on both the collective bargaining and the "alternative gov-ernance" fronts, the DOE failed to take aggressive action that might have mitigated the problems with the statutory language. But it's far from certain whether different policies would have helped. At the end of the day, is it possible to force fundamental reforms on districts that don't support them?

Conclusion: Of Hubris and Humility

Let's return to the original question posed by this chapter: Could NCLB work as intended with the right people calling the shots in the Department of Education, making good decisions and acting wisely? When it comes to the law's failings, is "implementation" really to blame?

To be sure, there have been missteps. Different actions might have helped at the margins. But they wouldn't have changed the basic storyline of the law's implementation. That doesn't mean, however, that changing the law is necessarily the solution (though I provide a few ideas below). There might be *no* solution to some of these problems because they are inherent in our federalist system. Federal policymakers should consider two lessons:

- *While it's hard to force recalcitrant states and districts to do things they don't want to do, it's impossible to force them to do those things well.* Put another way, the federal government can coerce states and districts to follow the letter but not the spirit of the law. So notes get sent home informing parents of their choice options, but they are filled with jargon and written in 8-point type. When it comes to identifying extra seats for the NCLB school choice program (much less expanding capacity), districts go through the motions. And when it's time to "restructure" persistently failing schools, districts choose the path of least resistance. There's very little the federal government can to do address this behavior—either through law or regulation.

- *The federal government is better at following than leading.* While NCLB deserves credit for being bold when it comes to expanding parental options and forcing radical change on persistently failing schools, it turns out that such boldness is less a blessing than a curse. Where the implementation of the law has gone most smoothly is where at least a handful of states and districts have already paved the way. It made sense for NCLB to adopt "standards-based reform" as its dominant strategy, as federal lawmakers could learn lessons from Texas, North Carolina, and other early adopters. But there were few models for how to force recalcitrant districts to implement choice programs they didn't buy into, or how to create a new marketplace of tutoring providers, or even what to do with persistently failing schools. As a matter of pragmatism, the federal government is better off following the lead of reform-minded states and districts, rather than breaking new ground.

Both lessons imply the need for greater humility when Congress reauthorizes NCLB. This is difficult for lawmakers and reformers to swallow. After all, the temptation to use federal policy to push for fundamental, transformative change is ever present. But wishing doesn't make something so, and the federal government can't snap its fingers and create schools of choice where they don't exist, or tough-minded superintendents where there are none.

What does this mean for NCLB's "cascade of sanctions"? Here are some suggestions, all of which require congressional action. First and foremost, the federal government should get out of the business of mandating school choice on a universal basis. Experience has shown that Uncle Sam does not have the tools to force districts to implement school choice when the districts don't believe in it. Instead, Congress could offer grants to willing districts (or even municipalities) that willingly embrace choice as part of their school reform strategies. (The DOE's $30 million Voluntary Public School Choice program already does this on a small scale; expanding it dramatically would be a good start.) Federal funds can provide a catalyzing effect, but they will only work with a willing partner on the ground.

The federal government should also acknowledge that school districts are not well-suited to be objective arbiters of information for parents, and should give the job of informing families to other organizations. The Parent Information and Resource Centers program, for instance, could be retooled and expanded to play this role.

Existing federal funds should be better targeted to the creation of new "capacity" for school choice. Charter School Program grants, especially, should be redesigned to focus predominantly on boosting the supply of high-quality schools of choice in communities desperately lacking them.

Congress should fix some of the law's disincentives by allocating funding specifically for choice and tutoring, and not allowing districts to use leftover money for anything else. If "use it or lose it" is the order, districts will be more likely to use it—and to provide real choices to parents.

Finally, Congress should offer incentives to districts willing to intervene aggressively in failing schools, including extra money or regulatory relief, or allowing them to drop the "needs-improvement" label from schools as soon as they are restructured.

None of these incremental reforms is as bold and exciting as NCLB's promise that every child trapped in a failing school would have an exit, or its admonition that bad schools must get better or be shuttered. But they are more in line with the capabilities and political realities of the federal government. Meanwhile, most reforms are going to have to develop the old-fashioned way—from the bottom up. Perhaps that's not such a bad thing, after all.

PART II

Remedies in the States

5

California: Does the Golden State Deserve a Gold Star?

Julian Betts

The goal of this chapter is to assess the implementation of provisions of the No Child Left Behind Act (NCLB) relating to school choice, supplemental educational services, and local educational agency (LEA) remedies, in the context of the state of California. California provides a challenging testing ground for NCLB's provisions for a number of reasons. First, it has a large population of English learners (EL), which makes particularly daunting the challenge of having every student in the state reach proficiency in reading and math by the target date of 2013–14.

Second, state departments of education are expected to play a major role in implementation of NCLB. They define the proficiency standards, set the timelines for adequate yearly progress (AYP) by which schools are judged, and administer tests and then use the results to judge schools. In addition, the state Department of Education is responsible for vetting providers of supplemental educational services (SES) and for ensuring that individual districts are administering the various components of NCLB in the spirit and letter of the law.

In Rhode Island, one can almost imagine a room big enough for the state to bring all the relevant players together. But in California, which in

The author thanks Chester Finn for helpful comments. He is very grateful to the many people he interviewed for sharing their valuable time to participate. In alphabetical order he thanks, without implicating, Karen Bachofer, Wendy Harris, Ann Just, Camille Maben, Christine Quinn, Steve Schneider, Mariam True, Dale Vigil, and Charles Weis. Several others around the state preferred to speak to him anonymously, but this in no way diminishes his gratitude to them.

2005–6 had roughly 6.3 million students, 9,600 schools, and 1,000 public school districts,[1] the challenge is obviously of an entirely higher order. The question is clear: Can a state bureaucracy centrally implement the federal accountability guidelines in an efficient and fair way?

Third, California has a reputation for having set relatively high standards for students to be labeled proficient or better in math and reading. Many states have received criticism for watering down their academic standards as, year by year, the number of schools deemed "in need of improvement" has grown. California has largely escaped this pattern of retrenchment.[2]

The following will provide a description of California's accountability system and how it relates to the system required by NCLB, and how the NCLB school choice, supplemental educational services, and LEA improvement programs are being implemented. The objective is to present a discussion, based on data as well as a series of interviews, of the extent to which California is realizing the promise of NCLB, and the degree to which experience in California points to reforms to NCLB that might make the federal law more effective.

Setting the Scene: Accountability in California

What is the educational setting in California, and how does it affect NCLB? In addition to the large English-learner population and the sheer size of the state, perhaps the most relevant issue is that California was one of the states that embarked upon its own accountability system well in advance of the passage of NCLB. The Public School Accountability Act of 1999 (PSAA) and subsequent legislation created a system of measuring educational outcomes at each school, along with a cascading series of interventions for schools and districts that failed to keep pace. Also included was a series of financial rewards for schools that met achievement targets and for staff at those schools. (The financial rewards were short-lived, being canceled after roughly two years because of budgetary issues.)

The setup of the state's accountability system differs in important regards from the federal system. At the heart of the state system is a single number, the Academic Performance Index (API), which varies between 200 and 1,000. All schools are expected to reach a score of at least 800 by the year 2020. Most important, the state system gives a "passing" grade to any sub-800 school that narrows by at least 5 percent the gap between the prior year's base API and the long-term goal of 800.[3] In sharp contrast, the federal requirement that schools make adequate yearly progress (AYP) is really a stipulation that in a given year a predetermined percentage of students must have test scores at or above cutoff points set by the state. These cutoffs do not change over time, but the proportion of students required to score at or above the cutoffs rises gradually to 100 percent in 2013. The California accountability system emphasizes *growth* in achievement, while the federal system as implemented in California emphasizes the percentages of students who meet proficiency targets, with these percentages changing only every few years.

The difference between these two systems has led to considerable public confusion. High-scoring schools with slow growth might make AYP but fail to improve enough to meet the state's expectations; conversely, low-scoring schools that are improving rapidly would fail to make AYP but would be given high grades in the state system. This confusion is relevant if one believes that accountability systems must be transparent in order to receive widespread support and have the maximum effect.

One aspect of NCLB that is not widely understood is that this federal law grants to states the right to dictate what students should know in each grade, what test(s) the state will use to determine student proficiency, the percentage of students required to be proficient in a school for the school to make "adequate yearly progress," and the rate at which the proportion of students must rise to reach the federally mandated requirement of 100 percent proficiency by 2013–14. Figure 5-1 shows the percentage of students in California who must demonstrate proficiency in math and English language arts in an elementary or middle school or district in order for the school or district to make adequate yearly progress, by year. As the figure shows, the state has set the initial percentage quite low and gradually, in step-like fashion, raises this percentage until it reaches the required 100 percent by 2013–14. (Requirements for high schools are similar, but the percentage of students required to be proficient is initially slightly lower than in elementary and middle schools.) The figure shows that California's schools are given considerable leeway in the first six years to adjust to the

FIGURE 5-1
SCHOOL AND DISTRICT AYP EXPECTATIONS IN CALIFORNIA

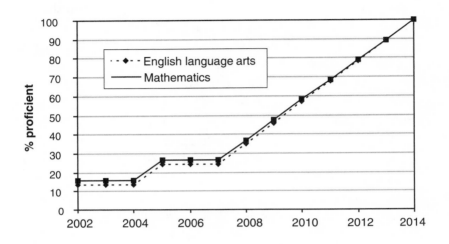

SOURCE: California Department of Education, *2006 Adequate Yearly Progress Report Information Guide*, 2006, http://www.cde.ca.gov/ta/ac/ay/documents/infoguide06.pdf (accessed August 2006).

AYP regime, in that the rather low initial AYP target is increased only once between 2002 and 2007. But then, starting in 2008, California steeply accelerates these requirements, so that the percentage of students expected to be proficient increases linearly to 100 percent in 2014, as required by NCLB.

This pattern does not mean that California has low standards. On the contrary, several studies suggest that California has relatively high standards. For instance, in 2006, *Education Week* gave California's standards a rating of B+. Only eleven states out of fifty had higher grades, and thirty-two had lower grades.[4] Similarly, in comparisons between scores on the National Assessment of Educational Progress (NAEP) test with those required for students to be deemed proficient on each state's grade 8 math test, McLaughlin and Bandeiro de Mello ranked California's standards the thirteenth most rigorous in the country.[5] Since California has relatively high absolute standards for what it deems student proficiency, all figure 5-1 shows is that the state has set the percentage of students required to meet these demanding proficiency standards quite low through 2007.

Under NCLB, a school must do more than meet the proficiency targets in math and English language arts each year. It must also reach a 95 percent participation rate among students for each test, and it must meet both proficiency and participation targets for up to ten student subgroups, which may include any of seven racial/ethnic groups plus economically disadvantaged students, English learners, and special education students. Enough students need to participate in each group for test results to be "numerically significant," in which case the given group will be included in the school's required targets.

In addition to these forty-four potential goals, California has designated two targets of its own. The first, in a tip of the hat to the state's preexisting accountability system, requires the school's Academic Performance Index to be at or above a certain minimum, or show growth of at least one point. The second is a fairly lax high school requirement for at least 0.1 percent growth in the graduation rate each year. Thus, the number of hoops through which a school must jump varies with its size and diversity. A large high school with a diverse student population would, in theory, have to satisfy forty-six requirements to make adequate yearly progress in any given year. Conversely, a small elementary school that is demographically homogeneous could face as few as five requirements (related to proficiency and participation rates in the math and English language arts tests and the API requirement).

The steep impending increase in the percentage of students who must be deemed proficient, along with the sheer number of targets, implies that the much-anticipated drama of a majority of schools and districts eventually being labeled as "failing" under NCLB will likely not take place in California until around 2009 or 2010. Once the California definitions of AYP begin to ramp up sharply in a few years, as shown in figure 5-1, districts may quickly use up their Title I apportionments for busing and supplemental educational services, and shortages of buses and outside providers of tutoring could emerge.

Seen in this light, any problems with a lack of funding, buses, or outsider providers of educational services to meet the demand for services from students in "failing" schools today would be a grave harbinger of shortages in the future.

NCLB Choice in California

After having failed to make AYP two years in a row in a given subject, a Title I school is placed into year 1 of program improvement (PI). Such a school must immediately begin offering district-funded busing to allow students to attend other, non-PI, schools. It must continue to offer choice until it gets out of program improvement, which is accomplished by making AYP for two years in a row.

Thus, the total effect of NCLB school choice on students in California is a function of several factors: how many schools enter PI status, how many schools stay in PI status, how many students at each PI school opt for the choice program, and, finally, the effect of school choice on the achievement of those who switch. While we know a lot about the number of schools in PI status and overall student participation in NCLB school choice, almost nothing is known statewide about whether those who switch schools boost their achievement.

Figure 5-2 shows that of 6,059 schools that receive Title I funding, 37 percent were in PI status in fall 2006. This amounted to about one-quarter of *all* California schools, including 3,600 schools that were not Title I schools.

About one in three PI schools were in the first year of PI status, and so had to offer NCLB school choice, but were not yet required to offer supplemental educational services. As shown by the column on the right in figure 5-2, 1.3 percent of schools were not yet in PI status but were at risk of entering it in 2007 because they had failed to meet AYP in 2006. This is a fairly small proportion of all Title I schools when compared with the 5–12 percent shown in the left-hand column that entered PI status in each of the past five years. This dropoff largely reflects the fact that most schools that were challenged by the proficiency standards shown in figure 5-1 got into trouble with meeting AYP long before 2006. Nonetheless, the sharp and steady increases in the proficiency standards that will begin in 2008 will no doubt greatly increase the share of Title I schools in PI status.

Moreover, the fact that roughly 25 percent of Title I schools were already in year 2 or higher of PI status suggests that many of these PI schools will *never* make adequate yearly progress again.

FIGURE 5-2
PERCENTAGE OF TITLE I SCHOOLS BY PROGRAM IMPROVEMENT (PI)
STATUS, 2006–7

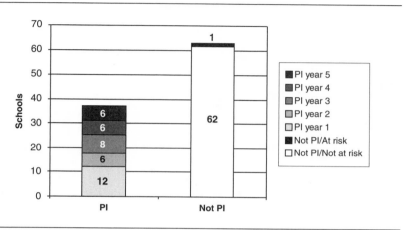

SOURCE: Calculations are based on data from California Department of Education, "2005–06 School Program Improvement Status," Title I Program Improvement Status Data Files, http://www.cde.ca.gov/ta/ac/ay/tidatafiles.asp (accessed October 2006).
NOTES: Non-PI schools are divided into those that were or were not at risk of entering PI status in 2007 or failure to make AYP in 2006. Four Title I schools for which PI status was pending as of October 2006 were omitted from the analysis.

To judge whether this prediction is overblown, we can ask how many schools exit from PI status after making AYP for two years. In 2006, 104 schools exited PI status, or about 6 percent of the schools that had been in PI status the year before. Most were in year 1 or 2 of PI status, which indeed suggests that many schools get into PI status and have a very difficult time getting out. In addition, about one-sixth of schools in PI status in 2005 made AYP in 2006, meaning that if they make AYP in 2007 they, too, will exit PI status.

Overall, these figures suggest that although most Title I schools in California are not yet in PI status, the net percentage is growing and will probably continue to grow markedly in 2008 and 2009. Already, 37 percent of Title I schools must offer choice to their students.

The next question is how many students at eligible schools are opting into the NCLB school choice program. Table 5-1 shows that the numbers of students participating in NCLB school choice in California to 2004–5 have been very small. For the one year in which the California Department

TABLE 5-1

NUMBER OF STUDENTS PARTICIPATING IN NCLB SCHOOL CHOICE
BY YEAR, AND AS A PERCENTAGE OF ELIGIBLE STUDENTS
AND ALL K–12 STUDENTS

Year	Number of students participating in NCLB school choice	Number of students eligible	Percent of eligible students participating	Percent of all K–12 students participating
2002–3	3,139	N/A	N/A	0.05
2003–4	3,609	1,124,591	0.3	0.06
2004–5	8,509	N/A	N/A	0.13

SOURCES: Data for 2002–3 and 2003–4 from the California State Department of Education, Consolidated State Performance Reports, http://www.cde.ca.gov/nclb/sr/rt/index.asp (accessed August 16, 2006); data for 2004–5 courtesy of Ann Just, director of Title I, California Department of Education.

of Education has provided an estimate of the total number of California students who were eligible to participate in NCLB choice, 2003–4, we find that a mere 0.3 percent elected to leave their schools. As shown in the rightmost column, when we instead calculate participation among *all* K–12 students, rates are even smaller—around 0.1 percent or less.

Why are these numbers so low? Part of the problem is clearly that the timetable for enrolling students in NCLB school choice in the first year that a school is in PI status is completely unworkable. Betts and Danenberg report that in San Diego the district had approximately a week after new PI schools were announced before fall classes started.[6] In this period they were expected by the law to develop bus routes, advertise them, and enlist participants. Reportedly, it took some time for parents at these schools to learn about the choice option, and many were unwilling to send their children to other schools after the school year was already well under way. Such problems have persisted. In 2006, the state Department of Education issued its press release describing annual accountability results on August 31, only then making clear which schools had entered and exited PI status.

But by 2006, problems with introducing choice at newly designated PI schools could not have been the main explanation for such low participation rates. Figure 5-2 shows that of the 37 percent of Title I schools that were in

PI in 2006–7, 25 percent, or about two-thirds, were in years 2 through 5. This means that the majority of schools that were required to offer school choice in 2006–7 had been doing so for anywhere from one to four years. Even in 2004–5, the last year for which we have data on participation in NCLB school choice, it is likely that between half and two-thirds of PI schools had already been required to offer busing for one to two full years. We infer that timing problems in schools in their first year of PI status cannot be the primary cause of low participation, and suggest some other possible explanations:

- Districts fail to send letters to parents informing them of the school choice program.

- The letters do not state clearly that parents can elect to have their students bused to other, "nonfailing" schools.

- Many parents whose first language is not English cannot interpret the information in the letters clearly.

- Districts have had trouble offering sufficient busing services.

- There have not been enough non-PI schools, or spaces at non-PI schools, to meet parents' demand.

- Parents, although well informed of their choices, have simply not been very interested in having their children bused out of their neighborhoods.

I know of no statewide studies of any of these issues.

Federal and state policymakers have certainly focused on the possibility that parents at PI schools are not receiving invitations from districts to enroll their children in other schools, or, if parents do receive the invitations, that they are not clearly worded. Districts are required by federal law to send such letters, and the California Department of Education provides templates on its website in both English and Spanish. This letter explains PI status, how a school can enter PI status, and the parents' options quite clearly.[7] A weakness is that the California Department of Education, in trying to follow guidelines from the U.S. Department of Education, has produced templates that quite simply lack marketing pizzazz. For instance, it is not until the top of page 3 of the letter that parents are told of the school choice option. One can imagine a parent receiving this longish letter and never making it to the end. A simple fix would be to change the template to state in bold print at the top of page 1 that the student in question has the right to transfer to another school, before getting into the detailed explanation of PI status and its implications.

It is hard to know whether family notification has been a significant problem in many or most districts in California, but the U.S. Department of Education has set out to determine this by asking the largest districts in the state to provide it with all versions of notification letters. Furthermore, a group of pro–school choice lawyers, led by Clint Bolick, sued the Los Angeles Unified School District and the Compton Unified School District in March 2006 for failing to provide adequate choice provisions to families. According to press coverage by David J. Hoff, the Bolick complaints alleged in the case of Los Angeles that parents received notifications late and had only a few weeks to make decisions, while Compton Unified was said to have failed to notify parents at all.[8]

The possibility that parents whose first language is other than English are reluctant to send their children to schools out of their neighborhoods gains some credence from a 2006 study of non-NCLB school choice programs in San Diego.[9] The authors model the probability that students apply to each of the choice programs as a function of the characteristics of the student, of his or her local school, and of the schools that the student could apply to in the given program. The analysis shows that English-learner students are significantly less likely to apply to leave their schools than otherwise similar students. This result cannot be explained by poor publicity, because the district distributes a detailed choice pamphlet to every district family annually and includes materials in Spanish. One possible explanation is a lack of adequate information networks among such families.

Ventura County schools superintendent Charles Weis told me that choice had not yet proved very popular in Ventura County. When I asked him why, he replied,

> It's because most people want their local school to be successful, and because they don't find it convenient to get their children across town. Also, choice has its biggest impact when the choice

schools have a different program [than the local school]. NCLB choice is within the same district and is not distinct. Also, the choice schools may have fewer supports for EL [English learners] and other struggling students than does the local school.[10]

Weis reported that a lack of spaces at non-PI schools and difficulty in finding busing had not been problems so far.

In Hayward Unified School District, an urban district in the San Francisco Bay area, a mere ten students opted for NCLB choice in the 2006–7 school year. With about half of the district's schools in PI status, this number is very low. Hayward's associate superintendent of educational services, Christine Quinn, believes that the main explanation for low participation is a district open-enrollment policy that already meets parents' needs adequately. By the time the district identifies parents in PI schools, verifies home addresses, and sends out notification letters by late September, "people who want to move have already moved," she reports.[11]

Will public school choice boost achievement for those who switch? Given the small numbers of enrollees and the need to study the longer-term effects, convincing evidence is probably years away.[12] However, the 2006 San Diego study cited above does examine preexisting choice programs in that district. The research uses "gold-standard" experimental approaches that take advantage of lotteries conducted by the district administration to decide which applicants to choice programs will be admitted. The analysis statistically compares the outcomes of lottery winners and losers one, two, and three years after the lottery. Betts and coauthors find little evidence that those who win lotteries for the district's traditional busing program, its magnet program, or its state-mandated open-enrollment program perform any differently than lottery losers on a variety of math and reading tests.[13] The main exceptions are numerous cases in which winners fare worse one year after the lottery but later recover, perhaps due to adjustment costs when students switch schools, and magnet high schools, where some evidence emerges that winners fare better in math two and three years after the lottery.

This study is particularly relevant to NCLB school choice in San Diego because the district implemented the new NCLB program by piggybacking it on the existing voluntary busing program; that is, under NCLB choice, students at a given school had exactly the same set of schools from which to choose as under the preexisting busing program. Put differently, in the first few years NCLB choice more or less funded the expansion of a preexisting program. Because for those years the two programs were identical, it is highly likely that the results from this experimentally based study will closely mirror the results for NCLB school choice in San Diego, at least through 2003–4, the final year of the study.

NCLB Supplemental Educational Services in California

NCLB requires that Title I schools in year 1 and higher of program improvement status offer choice. In year 2 and higher of PI status, these schools must also offer supplemental educational services—that is, tutoring—to students who remain at them instead of opting for NCLB choice. It is clear in California and nationally that NCLB has thus far provided school choice to only a very few of the students who are eligible. This, plus the relatively low cost of supplemental educational services (SES) relative to busing, suggests that SES could ultimately provide services to far more students than school choice.

As we saw in figure 5-2, in 2006–7, 25 percent of Title I schools in California were in year 2 or higher of PI status, and therefore required to offer SES to their students. To compare SES participation with participation in school choice, we return to table 5-1, which shows the numbers of choice participants together with the total number of those eligible for choice in 2003–4. SES participation rates in that year, shown in table 5-2, were not huge, at 7.0 percent, but they were markedly higher than the 0.3 percent participation rate reported for choice. The same point can be made in a slightly different way by comparing the numbers of students enrolled in NCLB school choice and SES in 2004–5: Only 8,509 California students had enrolled in school choice (table 5-1) compared to 98,403 students enrolled in SES (table 5-2).

Except for public schools in PI status, any entity can apply to provide supplemental educational services. The California Department of Education is required to evaluate and approve applications from potential providers. The 2006–7 application booklet, including instructions and forms, is somewhat daunting at twenty-eight pages. But most of the information applicants are asked to provide seems reasonable, ranging from letters of reference to

TABLE 5-2

NUMBER OF STUDENTS PARTICIPATING IN NCLB SUPPLEMENTAL
EDUCATIONAL SERVICES BY YEAR, AND AS A PERCENTAGE
OF ELIGIBLE STUDENTS AND ALL K–12 STUDENTS

Year	Number of students participating in supplemental services	Number of students eligible	Percent of eligible students participating	Percent of all K–12 students participating
2002–3	30,049	N/A	N/A	0.5
2003–4	41,198	588,388	7.0	0.7
2004–5	98,403	N/A	N/A	1.6

SOURCES: Data for 2002–3 and 2003–4 from the California State Department of Education, Consolidated State Performance Reports, http://www.cde.ca.gov/nclb/sr/rt/index.asp (accessed August 16, 2006); data for 2004–5 courtesy of Ann Just, director of Title I, California Department of Education.

details on academic focus and financial viability. A representative for the applicant must also sign off on a long list of assurances such as, "Provider assures that the instruction provided is secular, neutral, and non-ideological," and "Provider agrees to ensure it does not disclose to the public the identity of any student eligible for or receiving supplemental educational services without the written permission of the student's parents."[14]

As of 2006–7, California's Department of Education reports 286 providers as having been approved by the state. The breakdown of providers is quite interesting. Although most are entities other than public schools or districts, districts and related entities are important providers. Ten county offices of education, thirty-six districts, and nine schools are among the state-approved providers. Granted, these public school providers comprise only about one-seventh of all providers, but it is likely that they supply a disproportionate share of supplemental educational services. Among the remaining six-sevenths, both nonprofit and for-profit entities are well represented. California Department of Education figures suggest that, overall, 42 percent of providers are for-profit entities.

Betts and Danenberg report that in 2003, San Diego Unified School District administrators went to considerable lengths to find out which of the state-approved supplemental educational services providers were willing to work in San Diego. At the same time, administrators expressed concern that the state provided districts (and by extension parents) with virtually no information on the capabilities and background of each provider.[15]

A reasonable hypothesis is that if such information bottlenecks persist, they could reduce the demand for SES not operated by districts. As of 2006, the state Department of Education had improved considerably the online information it supplied about each provider. Anybody with a web connection can see the list of providers, along with contact information, a list of subject areas, grades, times and modes of delivery of services, date approved by the state, and districts currently served for each. It would be easy to criticize this list as superficial, but the information provided should still be of considerable help to both districts and parents.

Because the new application requirements were put in place after most providers were approved, however, online information is missing on many of these items for many of the providers. There is clearly room for further improvement in disseminating information on SES providers, and as providers come up for their renewal every two years, the more detailed application forms now required will help accomplish this. Camille Maben, director of the School and District Accountability Division of the state Department of Education, and Ann Just, director of Title I for the state, told me that the information will improve in future years, and that they listened carefully to districts' requests for information while heeding concerns of some of the for-profit providers about posting detailed proprietary information on teaching methods on the web.

I asked Maben and Just what they had heard from the field about how well districts and SES providers were working together. They said some SES providers had expressed concern at a lack of district responsiveness, but often had not complained to the state Department of Education, going instead directly to its federal counterpart. Some of the most typical complaints were:

- that the level of liability insurance required by districts was exorbitant;

- that some of the largest districts got notification letters out to parents too late in the school year, and sometimes after providers had already held fairs for parents; and

- that some districts did not allow providers to use district property.[16]

The response of the California Department of Education to this last problem has been that whatever policy a district has on allowing outside groups to use school facilities must, in fairness, be applied to the SES providers as well.

The varying complexity from one district to another of coordinating SES providers may explain why some allow providers to use school facilities. One provider told me that his organization built a direct relationship with a single school and worked so closely with its staff that administrators freely offered access to facilities after school. Similarly, in the Hayward Unified School District, only seven SES providers signed contracts for 2006–7, and so it was reasonably simple to allow each access at least to certain schools. But in the San Diego Unified School District, which by fall 2006 had thirty-seven external SES providers, providers were not allowed onto school sites. Mariam True, executive director of teacher preparation and student support for San Diego, told me that the district had allowed providers onto school campuses several years ago when there were only a few of them, but problems quickly cropped up. Use of classrooms sometimes clashed with extracurricular activities or teachers' own preparations for the next day's classes. Sometimes the provider's tutor would not show up, and no school staff would be available to supervise the classroom. In a few instances, providers asked school staff to run off copies of the provider's own teaching materials, at the school's expense. But the biggest concern, True told me, was that as the number of providers mushroomed to thirty-seven, there was no way to assign scarce classroom space in a way that would be seen as equitable. As a result, SES providers now mostly work by coming to students' homes or by meeting in other public locations, such as churches.

Partly in response to such frictions reported by both districts and providers, the state Department of Education has posted on the web a list of twenty-one quality-assurance factors that SES providers must meet, along with districts' implicit responsibilities to check on these factors in a timely fashion.[17] For example, the state requires districts to provide specific steps for SES providers to take under a formal complaint process. The state Department of Education will intervene only if provider complaints are not resolved at the local level.

At the department, Maben and Just have also heard many complaints from districts about failings of SES providers, including the following:

- Some districts complain of "bait and switch" tactics, where what is promised is not delivered.

- Similarly, some providers have failed to send out tutors after signing up students, or have started too late in the school year.

- Some providers have done end-runs around district procedures, such as going to shopping malls to obtain parent signatures on signup sheets that are supposed to go to the district. This has produced headaches for districts that have to go through these signup sheets name by name, only to find that some students are not even in the district, or that they are district students but are not eligible because they are not enrolled in PI schools, or are enrolled in PI schools but are not eligible because they are not low-income students.

- Some districts have complained to the state about what they viewed as excessive incentives being given to families to sign up, such as computers and, in an extreme case, free trips for four to Disneyland. The state has since issued new regulations that place a cap on the monetary incentives that can be given to families. The issuance of computers caused some districts particular difficulty because some families who found the computers unreliable or could not afford to pay for Internet service providers came to the district expecting them to fix these problems.

- Some districts have complained that SES providers bypass rural areas.

- Some SES providers have ignored standard procedures to protect children from potentially abusive situations, for instance, by ignoring requirements that an adult be present if a tutor provides in-home instruction. In another case, a provider was unable to comply with standard background checks because all of the tutors working for the online company lived outside the United

States. Mariam True of San Diego Unified related to me the story of one out-of-state provider that claimed to have done its own background checks of its employers. When district staff saw samples of these background checks, their reaction was that the provider "basically just Googled the people." Since then this provider has agreed to use the FBI to do criminal checks.

- Inadequate provider quality is another concern. True described asking one potential provider for evidence of student progress based on pre- and posttests. The best the provider could muster was a copy of a high school economics exam, which was puzzling, as this provider was proposing to work with elementary school children. She told me that she had concerns about whether the state Department of Education was adequately vetting providers. Hayward Unified's associate superintendent of educational services, Christine Quinn, told me similar stories, and concluded, like True, that she is

> not convinced that these providers are really doing an advanced curriculum. The biggest problem is a lack of program evaluation by the state. The CDE [California Department of Education] should do more to evaluate providers at the start. For instance, we want to know things like whether the service provider will provide students with work aligned to CST. [CST is the California Standards Test that has become the backbone of the state's accountability system.]

Although participation in SES is much higher than in NCLB school choice, it is still surprisingly small, which begs the question of why.

Mariam True does not believe that a lack of providers or poor or late parental notification were factors in San Diego, with its thirty-seven outside providers. Parents there receive in September a detailed booklet explaining the offerings of each provider, both in text and with a quite handy two-page checklist that allows them to make comparisons. In addition, parents are given three weeks to sign up.

Instead, she cited as the main impediment to greater participation the formal letters of notification:

The U.S. Department of Education has a long list of things that need to go into the letters to parents. This is one of the biggest barriers to getting students interested. What I know about getting people to read information is that if it is in simple language and concise, they will read it. But if the letter does not get to the point quickly they are going to toss it.

San Diego has attempted to get the word out to parents more effectively, by mailing its annual booklet describing SES providers in plain English. Indeed, the front cover states in large bold type: "FREE TUTORING!" and the booklet is noticeably lacking in "legalese." (The booklet is available in other languages, as well.)

True additionally recommends that SES be extended beyond students who are eligible for free or reduced-price meals because, at least as of fall 2006, San Diego was still spending only about three-quarters of its SES budget. (In spite of intentionally overbudgeting by about $250,000 last year, actual costs came in under budget because many students dropped out of the services.) Her reasoning is that relatively affluent parents become confused as to why other parents at the same school are receiving invitations to enroll their children in SES while they are not. True argues it would be better to offer these services to all low-achieving students, and only resort to income preferences once the program becomes oversubscribed.

In other cases, delays may reduce student interest. Hayward Unified's associate superintendent Quinn claimed that slowness in receiving funding from Sacramento was a big contributor to her district's problems with getting SES going early in the school year. In 2006, the state Department of Education did not notify the district of its SES allocation until November.

Another distinct possibility is that students and parents are not particularly interested in more schoolwork after school. One SES provider in northern California had developed a good relationship with a single school, but withdrew because of inadequate demand from parents. This provider felt that the school had gone out of its way to notify parents and to obtain parental buy-in. The school even provided free space. Student interest in staying late to do more academic work, however, was very low.[18]

This provider's impression—that low demand for SES largely reflects families' unwillingness to participate—was echoed in conversations I had with officials at the California Department of Education. Reasons they had often heard for low participation rates included conflicts of after-school programs either with bus schedules or with after-school sports programs, a lack of enthusiasm among parents for the providers' academic offerings, and a tendency of some students, once enrolled, to dislike the program and drop out.

Apart from the question of participation rates, can supplemental tutoring work? An ongoing RAND Corporation national study should eventually shed some light on this question. In San Diego, we can say something about SES as provided by the San Diego Unified School District itself. The study by Betts and Danenberg cited earlier found that the district's own Extended Day Reading Program (EDRP) accounted for 99.9 percent and 74.0 percent of supplemental educational services provided in 2002–3 and 2003–4, respectively. Betts, Zau, and King assessed this and other parts of the district's former Blueprint for Student Success and found, using student fixed-effect models, that EDRP had been quite effective in boosting reading achievement in the district.[19] (Ironically, the district decided to stop participating as an SES provider. One reason was complaints from some external providers that there would not be enough students left over for them, even though the district had yet to spend a full 5 percent of its Title I allocation on SES.)

NCLB Remedies for Local Educational Agencies in Need of Improvement

Just like individual schools, districts and county offices of education that accept Title I money must meet all of the test-score and student-participation criteria to fulfill the NCLB's adequate yearly progress requirements. Any of these local educational agencies (LEAs) that fail to meet criteria in the same subject for two years in a row will be placed into program improvement (PI) status. As of fall 2006, 162 LEAs were in PI status. Of these, 61 were in their first year, and 101 were in their second year.[20]

The state Department of Education expects to have some LEAs entering their third year of PI status in 2007–8, at which time the state will announce the corrective actions to be taken. According to Wendy Harris of the Department of Education, no decisions have yet been made on what these actions will be.

What happens when a local educational agency is designated in need of improvement? NCLB requires a number of steps, to which California law has added others. First and foremost, under federal law, a newly identified LEA has ninety days to produce a new plan of action that incorporates results of a self-evaluation of educational needs. Next, the LEA must contract with the county office of education or other outside provider to verify that the LEA has correctly identified its needs and then to support it as it attempts to improve its educational offerings.[21] The state legislature allows LEAs under PI status to apply for grants of $50,000, plus $10,000 per Title I school, to help it implement reforms, with this funding available for up to two years per LEA.

California provides several tools to help LEAs in the process of self-evaluation. It sends Title I schools and schools with low API scores an "Academic Program Survey" that gauges each school's alignment with nine program components defined by the state.[22]

The district then completes a separate survey called the District Assistance Survey (DAS), again designed by the state Department of Education.[23] This survey focuses on the provision of math and English language arts classes and asks the district how it supports these efforts in terms of curriculum and assessment, professional development and human resources, data-driven monitoring, parental involvement, and several other categories of assistance. The survey is fourteen pages long and quite detailed, and administrators are expected to consult widely before answering it. As the instructions state, "Older students, parents, teachers, administrators, board members, and key community leaders should be consulted to inform DAS results. Use of a representative district group will help build ownership and facilitate needed district changes." The survey results are intended to point to areas for improvement as the district (or county office) writes up its own LEA plan.[24]

The answers to the DAS given by a district in PI status must be "verified" by an outside agency, which is typically the county office of education. This external contractor verifies that the diagnosis of LEA weaknesses and the prescription for reform are both accurate. It then helps the LEA to implement the plan.

Is the DAS, which in turn builds upon data from school-level Academic Program Survey, likely to help districts? My impression is that if key district players are united and focused on improving academic outcomes, the detailed self-analysis required to answer the DAS could do much to identify areas of weakness and to generate support for reforms. A district that viewed this exercise as undesirable meddling by outsiders, however, would probably find it quite easy to avoid identifying its weaknesses. Indeed, there may be strong incentives to do exactly that: If an LEA fails to move out of PI status, one of the potential corrective actions is for the state to remove "local educational agency personnel who are relevant to the failure to make adequate yearly progress," or to appoint a receiver for the LEA.[25] Clearly, if one feels one's job is threatened, there is little incentive to be frank on the survey about the district's greatest weaknesses, especially if one lacks confidence about being able to move the district out of program improvement status.

Insights provided by Charles Weis, superintendent of education for Ventura County, strongly confirm my hypothesis that the effectiveness of the District Assistance Survey and related planning exercises could range from very high to very low, depending on the reactions of district leadership. His county office has worked as an external evaluator for several districts in Ventura County and elsewhere, and Weis has gleaned lessons from this experience, as well as from county offices elsewhere in the state:

> I was initially skeptical of the DAS, but I have now seen examples of how it really can be helpful. One district we are working with saw PI status as an opportunity to really dig into [and find ways to improve] subgroup support that it had previously ignored. But other districts have said, "Oh God, another report to the state," and so did not get very far with self-diagnosis. I know of one district where the self-diagnosis was found by the external contractor to be wrong. They [district administrators] had lied to themselves: They had claimed that formative assessments were in place, but they turned out really to have been implemented in only one place. They did not see this until the external evaluator came along and pointed out the problem. . . . Overall, Oxnard High worked its way out of PI status because they viewed [the reform effort and DAS] seriously. Others in the county are trying to take reform seriously, too, but sometimes there are some blind spots. Sometimes districts don't want to dig into pet projects.[26]

Superintendent Weis's main suggestion for the DAS was that the state Department of Education supplement it with a menu of reforms for which there was solid evidence of success, and let the local district choose a reform path from this menu in collaboration with the outside evaluator.

A separate question concerns whether the external evaluator can simultaneously be knowledgeable about the LEA and serve as an independent, arm's-length evaluator. First, suppose the district hires an evaluator that is truly arm's length in the sense that it has had little experience with the district. This evaluator's lack of inside knowledge could impair its ability to vet the district's responses to the survey and to spot overly rosy responses. This is partly so because most of the questions in the DAS are quite qualitative. A typical question in the survey asks respondents to assess whether

> the district clearly communicates with all stakeholders, especially teachers, students, and parents, (e.g., by means of publications, parent information nights, internet, mail, etc.) regarding: standards-based grade-level expectations.[27]

Two rational and well-informed people could review whatever evidence is available on such a topic, apply their own standards, and come to entirely different conclusions about whether the district was accomplishing this goal.

Suppose, on the other hand, that a district instead hires a contractor with which it has worked in the past. Though perhaps better able to spot errors in the survey responses, such a contractor might lack the independence necessary to challenge the district on them. One district in PI status reported to me, for instance, that it had hired as its outside evaluator a private-sector contractor that had already worked with the district for several years. The advantage, administrators said, was that the evaluator had been sitting in on key committees for some time and so really knew how the district's reform efforts were set up. But might not this contractor have undergone "agency capture"—that is, come to identify so closely with the district that it could no longer objectively identify blind spots in its self-evaluation? I have no evidence on this, but the possibility seems apparent.

The Association of California School Administrators (ACSA) recently issued forty-three recommendations for reform to NCLB, some of which shed light on widespread concerns among California school administrators about the treatment of districts in PI status. Among the concerns is that the time NCLB gives LEAs and schools to get out of PI status "is far too short, and [that] the timeframes are not founded on scientifically based research." In addition, the ACSA document argues, "The corrective actions for school districts in particular, are extremely rigid and limiting. NCLB should be amended to add 'and any other corrective action deemed appropriate by the appointed state agency in consultation with the school district.'"[28]

NCLB and the State Department of Education

A key question in California concerns whether the informational demands created by NCLB's accountability requirements can be met by the various players. Given the coverage in this chapter of the response of California as a whole, I focused on the state Department of Education's ability to meet the demands from parents, schools, districts, and the federal Department of Education for information.

As an intermediary, the state Department of Education is clearly in a bind. The problem is perhaps worse in California than in most other states for two reasons. First, California is much bigger than most states, so that a proportionately larger amount of information must be centralized and processed. Second, the U.S. Department of Education has asked California to provide additional information regarding provision of information by districts to parents about NCLB school choice and SES.

Ann Just, the state's director of Title I, painted for me a detailed picture of the demands placed upon her office, which has eleven employees focusing on all aspects of Title I apart from the financial issues. Her office deals with forty-nine separate tasks related to Title I, only two of which involve SES and NCLB school choice. Yet, she says, even if her staff worked full time on SES and choice, they would still not meet the demand. In 2006, they participated in seventy-one compliance reviews around the state and spoke at many conferences for administrators, in addition to handling questions that came directly to the department.

The heaviest burden has come from the federal government, which, in 2006, directed the state to document in detail the efforts being made to notify parents of their rights under NCLB school choice and SES provisions.

The U.S. Department of Education asked the twenty largest districts in the state to provide, via the California Department of Education, templates of their letters of parental notification and timelines for implementation. Ann Just told me that for six weeks in summer 2006, all of her staff focused exclusively on working with districts on their notification letters. The California department was further required to write three reports providing updates on district implementation plans and then to check whether the districts were maintaining their proposed timelines. After providing the district templates in August, the state was asked to gather the specific letters from every school, signed by the principal or designee. In addition, it was to verify that parents had read the letters.

How do administrators at the county and district levels in California view their interactions with the state Department of Education? I have already discussed concerns raised by several interviewees that the state issues news of which schools have entered and exited PI status, as well as details on allotments of NCLB intervention funds, too late in the school year.

Ventura County superintendent Weis told me, "Our CDE [California Department of Education] is one of the smaller per capita in the nation. It is evident to me that in the case of complex reforms like NCLB, they are not equipped to help schools." He saw two alternatives. One was to increase staffing at CDE; but his preferred route was to improve coordination between the state Department of Education and the county offices of education, and to do more to have each county office in the state standardize its assistance to districts related to NCLB.

Numerous district administrators echoed concerns that the state Department of Education has not been able to keep up with their need for accurate and timely information on implementation of NCLB. Superintendent Dale Vigil of the Hayward Unified School District expressed dismay that he had taken several staff out of the district for an NCLB briefing by state Department of Education officials, only to find that his people were more knowledgeable about certain aspects of the reforms than were the briefers from the state.

Administrators in several districts reported to me that they would like to get more information on SES providers from the state, that they would like to see stronger vetting of SES providers by the state, and that they would like more timely updates on both process and current regulations from Sacramento. One district administrator told me, for example, that the district learned when the state increased reimbursement rates for SES providers not from the Department of Education, but indirectly from the providers themselves. The lack of notification embarrassed district staff who had questioned the providers' most recent billing rates.

Unintended Consequences

NCLB has been associated with a number of unintended side effects, of which three already seem apparent. A fourth has probably not occurred yet, but it is likely to as the AYP requirements become stiffer.

The first unintended effect is that the public is greatly confused by the differing visions and terminologies in the state and federal accountability systems. I recently wrote about an attempt by the San Diego Unified School District to come up with a unified framework for ranking schools on their performance based on both the state's growth-oriented accountability guidelines and the federal government's approach of absolute standards that increase over time, and to provide one overall ranking of school progress. The district proposed to use this system to reward top-performing schools with more flexibility, while providing additional district oversight and assistance to those performing poorly according to both sets of guidelines.[29] Tellingly, when I presented this idea at a conference in 2004, the superintendent of a California district outside San Diego told me that San Diego's effort, although laudable in intent, was "doomed to fail" because it added yet another layer of complexity onto a situation that the public finds "hopelessly confusing."

This general refrain—that the state and federal systems are incompatible—is heard over and over again. For instance, annual press releases from California's state superintendent of public instruction, Jack O'Connell, on state accountability results are notable for the attention they devote to explaining the differences between the two systems. The 2005 release made clear O'Connell's unhappiness with the way NCLB is implemented. "It is important to remember the dramatic escalation in the AYP targets when viewing this year's results," he noted. "The dichotomy in the progress reports released today underscores why we support our state API growth model as a more accurate reflection of trends in our schools."[30] Ventura County superintendent Weis echoed these concerns. He told me: "The press and radio stations have a hell of a time understanding the difference between the state and federal systems. How do we explain to the public that a school has made big gains in API, but the federal government [system] says that this school is in program improvement?"

Ironically, although California was one of the states calling most loudly for the U.S. Department of Education to move from an absolute standards model to a growth model, when the latter recently allowed states the option of creating an alternative "growth" model of accountability, California did not even apply. The federal authorities decided that growth models should be student-based, and California is not in a position to do this because it has dragged its heels on creating a longitudinal system that follows individual students' progress over time as the students switch among schools and districts.

A second unintended consequence of NCLB that has emerged is its apparent conflicts with the federal Individuals with Disabilities Education Act (IDEA). The latter law requires that students with disabilities be given access to modifications during any testing period. Examples include giving these students additional time to do the test or reading the questions aloud. NCLB states that students who receive such accommodations cannot be counted as having participated in NCLB testing. Recently, San Diego's newly appointed superintendent, Carl Cohn, spoke out forcefully against this policy. In an op-ed, he told the story of a local school with high test scores and participation rates that was labeled as "failing" because these students' tests were discounted, causing the percentage of students with disabilities who had officially participated in testing to fall below the 95 percent requirement. Cohn writes:

> For most people, this outcome must be hard to believe. Who could imagine that bureaucrats in the U.S. Department of Education would have the power to erase from existence the hard work of disabled children in Mira Mesa? Who would then suspect that this decision would have the power to ruin the hard work of an entire school community?[31]

This problem does not appear to be confined to San Diego. The Association of California School Administrators recommends that a reauthorized

NCLB should "allow students' scores who test with 'modifications or accommodations' as allowed by IDEA, to count toward the participation rate." Similarly, they argue that students with disabilities should have until age twenty-one to be counted as high school graduates.[32]

A third unintended consequence of NCLB stems from the malleable composition of some student groups over time. For instance, it is clear that many schools will not make the 100 percent proficiency target for English learners in 2013–14 because many of these students will have just arrived in the country, with little knowledge of English. Similarly, the eventual exit of the best-performing students from English-learner status will mechanically lower the proficiency levels of the remaining group, erroneously implying that the school is doing worse over time with students in this group. This problem has partially resolved itself because the U.S. Department of Education allows districts to exempt English learners for up to three years. But this accommodation does not completely eliminate the problem; in California, the vast majority of English learners do not improve their abilities in English to the point of being redesignated as fluent English proficient within their first three years of schooling.

A related but more disturbing aspect of NCLB's definition of subgroups is that it sometimes creates a perverse incentive for administrators not to redesignate students, for fear of the percentage who are "proficient" falling below the state's requirements to make AYP. Conversely, schools that act faithfully to redesignate students whose achievement has grown sufficiently could, in theory, be cast into PI status, solely as a result of these redesignations lowering the percentage proficient for the subgroup. Both of these issues deserve further study.

The Association of California School Administrators notes its concern about this general problem, and states that

> dropping students out of a subgroup when they attain academic proficiency mitigates against schools and school districts reaching the 100 percent proficiency goal. Students who have been identified as English learners or in need of special education services should remain in the subgroup for NCLB accountability purposes "only," even after they have reached proficiency achievement levels.[33]

The sentiment of this recommendation seems reasonable, although one could easily quibble over whether redesignated students should forever be counted in the English-learner or special education subgroups, or only for a limited time, say, two years after being redesignated.

A fourth unintended consequence was mentioned to me by Ventura County supervisor Weis. He suspects that as more and more schools fall into PI status, and assuming that more students begin to leave for the non-PI schools, enrollment will shrink at the former and grow at the latter. Districts will be forced to transfer teachers from the PI schools to the very non-PI schools receiving students under NCLB school choice. In other words, teachers at failing schools will begin to follow in the footsteps of their students as they switch to schools with high test scores. If the drafters of NCLB anticipated that choice would allow students at PI schools to escape their teachers, in some sense this may not be entirely correct.

Conclusion

It is still too early to tell how NCLB-mandated school choice, supplemental educational services, and district remediation will affect student achievement. In California the state seems to be implementing all three with good intentions. Of course, good intentions do not earn a state a grade of A+, or a "gold star," as suggested in the title of this chapter. However good the intentions, capacity problems in Sacramento, timing problems, and a lack of parental interest have limited the growth and effectiveness of these interventions. To answer convincingly the question, "Have these interventions provided a big boost to student achievement?" one needs to know participation rates and the effects on participants. In both the supplemental educational services and, especially, the NCLB school choice programs, student participation is still quite low. The rate for the latter program, at 0.1 percent of all K–12 students in 2004–5, is particularly worrisome.

Evidence of the effect on actual participants in NCLB school choice programs is fragmentary at present. Aforementioned experimental analysis in San Diego raises doubts about the ability of school choice to boost achievement by itself.

But even if the effects on individual students were sizeable, NCLB school choice is clearly at risk of becoming almost irrelevant to student achievement statewide. The reason is simple: Almost nobody is participating. Administrators I interviewed did not mention a lack of buses, a lack of slots at non-PI schools, or a lack of funding as barriers. Instead, what I repeatedly heard was that it is quite difficult to get parents and their children interested in choice programs.

Parents' confusion about the divergent methods and vocabulary of the state and federal accountability systems could perhaps explain why so few parents are signing their children up for school choice. Several quotations above obliquely support that argument. However, the U.S. Department of Education has allowed a handful of states to use student-level gains in achievement as an alternative way to measure adequate yearly progress and thereby reconcile the two systems. In California's case, the state system, established in 1999, is also a gains model, but it defines gains at the school level rather than the student level. Thus, California is unable to participate in this trial. For this, the state has only itself to blame, as it has resisted moving to a system of statewide student identifiers, and truly longitudinal information, for some time. This problem may resolve itself by around 2008, as the state tentatively promises to create such a system.

The picture seems less bleak for supplemental educational services, thanks to much higher participation rates. In 2003–4, 7 percent of eligible students statewide were participating, which amounted to 0.7 percent of all K–12 students. In 2004–5, participation more than doubled, to 1.6 percent of all K–12 students. But questions remain about whether there is an adequate supply of providers, especially in rural areas, and some administrators have raised questions about the quality of at least a few of the providers, at the same time calling for fuller vetting of potential providers by Sacramento.

As with NCLB choice, little research evidence on the effect of SES on test scores currently exists. In San Diego, evidence from earlier work by myself and coauthors uses quasi-experimental analysis of the district's own after-school reading program, which dominated SES provision in the first few years of NCLB. The results imply that, at least initially, SES in San Diego was probably quite effective.

Is Sacramento devoting enough resources to oversee NCLB? I find it hard to believe that a state with 6.3 million students can adequately handle all questions when its Department of Education devotes only eleven staff members to handling nonfiscal aspects of Title I. Several district interviewees told me that it has sometimes proved quite difficult to get answers to implementation questions from Sacramento. It would clearly be a huge misrepresentation, however, to describe the parts of the California Department of Education that deal with NCLB as a huge and unresponsive bureaucracy. Those in Sacramento who are responsible for administration and oversight are a committed but surprisingly small group. Clearly, more people are needed. Even so, none of the interviews conducted for this chapter yielded any hints as to whether more personnel in Sacramento could alone solve the bottlenecks, or whether there are more fundamental issues. Perhaps bringing county offices of education in to help districts interpret regulations and troubleshoot, in a way that is coordinated statewide, would help.

Compounding matters, California has received special scrutiny from the U.S. Department of Education, which has sought to determine whether the state's districts are complying with NCLB requirements to notify parents about students' rights to school choice and supplemental educational services. These compliance checks have created a large workload for the California Department of Education, crowding out much of the other Title I work that the state department is required to do. Will all of this pay off? If we see marked increases in participation in NCLB choice and SES in the next few years, the case could be made. However, the sharp focus on parental notification neglects other barriers to participation that could be equally or more important. As numerous district employees and an SES provider told me, the truth seems to be that even with adequate parental notification, it is quite hard to convince parents to enter these programs.

California, as an extremely large state, does not seem to have created clear channels of communication on issues of NCLB implementation and compliance among districts, county offices of education, Sacramento, and Washington. Players in each of these locations might find it tempting to "blame the other guy." Indeed, most of the district and county administrators with whom I spoke raised concerns about the California Department of Education's ability to convey rules on implementation to districts. But to claim that this is "just a Sacramento problem" would be highly simplistic. As noted, more should be done to bring county offices of education in as intermediaries between the state and the local districts.

Neither is Washington blameless. Several of the people I interviewed around the state felt that the enforcement of NCLB provisions by D.C. has been needlessly heavy-handed. One administrator told me that while it makes sense to set standards and let the local agencies define the processes, it does not make sense both to set standards and then define the program interventions that every district must implement, regardless of the local context. Another administrator in a different part of the state made a similar point: "Washington should focus less on process and more on outcomes." Or, as still another administrator in a different location put it more bluntly, "There is micromanagement [from D.C.] that goes almost beyond comprehension."

Congress is moving toward reauthorization of NCLB, perhaps as early as 2007, and one of the goals of this volume is to provide suggestions for fine-tuning NCLB. In conclusion, here are some of the ideas that have emerged from my conversations around the state:

- The NCLB choice program risks becoming irrelevant because of the extremely small student participation both in California and nationwide. The U.S. Department of Education has launched an audit of the notification letters being sent home by the largest California districts. But many other obstacles could prove to be more important. All the institutional fixes in the world will achieve little if parents truly do not care for school choice of the NCLB flavor. One option would be for the U.S. Department of Education to conduct a survey of parents who have refused offers to enroll their children in NCLB choice to find out what the barriers might be.

- Short lead times for parents offered NCLB school choice have clearly been a problem. A revised law could formally allow states or individual districts to implement SES in the first year that a school falls into PI status, leaving NCLB choice, which takes much longer to plan and implement, for year 2. Such a change would generalize the exceptions that the U.S. Department of Education has started to make in this regard for some locales.

- The U.S. Department of Education could move away from its insistence on detailed and formal letters notifying parents that students are eligible for SES or NCLB school choice. Instead, it could encourage and even *require* districts to adopt simpler notification forms that get to the point quickly and in plain language.

- Camille Maben of the state Department of Education reported to me that, everywhere in California, administrators ask her what is known about the effects of choice and SES on student achievement. The U.S. Department of Education, to its credit, has contracted with the RAND Corporation to conduct a rigorous evaluation of this question in a limited number of districts around the nation. It should be simple and inexpensive, relative to the cost of the SES and NCLB school choice programs themselves, to commission additional analyses from researchers who have worked both with states and individual districts, and to ensure that the results of this research, once peer-reviewed, are circulated widely in the policy community.

- The U.S. Department of Education could consider providing more guidance on district-level reforms that have been scientifically proven to boost achievement, and to provide information on these proven interventions both to the state departments that authorize SES providers and to the parents who must choose among them.

- We could address concerns in Washington that not enough students are availing themselves of SES and, especially, NCLB choice by dropping the stipulation that these services are to be targeted to low-income students in failing schools and instead making them available to *all* low-achieving students in these schools. Mariam True of San Diego Unified pointed out that such a change would enhance SES programs for the additional reason that parents would be less confused about who was or was not eligible to participate. To retain some of the original flavor in the current law of directing services toward low-income students, a mechanism could be put into place so that if and when a program became oversubscribed, first priority would go to low-income applicants, with lotteries assigning spots as needed. After all, not all low-achieving students live in poverty, and our end goal is to leave, quite literally, no child behind.

6

New Jersey: Equity Meets Accountability

Patrick McGuinn

Three features of the New Jersey educational policy context are distinctive: the historical attachment to municipal home rule, the enormous disparities in wealth across school districts, and the increasingly active role of the courts and the state Department of Education in school finance and governance. Although these elements may be found in other states, they are considerably more pronounced in New Jersey. The state has a powerful tradition of home rule, which over time has resulted in the development of a large number of small, mostly self-governing municipalities. Large differences in education spending across school districts prompted the state judiciary to mandate aggressive school finance reform in the 1973 *Robinson v. Cahill* decision.[1] The ruling pushed the legislature to enact the Public School Act of 1975, which increased the state's share of education expenditures, initiated statewide academic standards and a minimum basic skills test, and outlined a school accountability system.[2]

In the 1990 *Abbott v. Burke* decision, the state supreme court mandated that spending on general education programs in the state's poorest districts had to at least equal spending in the state's wealthiest districts. In 1998, the court moved beyond questions of funding to mandate substantive educational reforms in the state's poorest school districts (which became known as "Abbott districts").[3] New Jersey Abbott Commissioner Gordon MacInnes called the mandates—which included high-quality preschool, full-day kindergarten, small classes, and whole-school reform—"the most specific and prescriptive set of instructional measures ever handed down by a high

The author extends many thanks to Bobbie Downs for assembling the charts and tables contained in this chapter.

court." In 2006, the thirty-one Abbott districts enrolled a total of 275,000 K–12 students and 40,000 preschool students; this represented 20 percent of New Jersey's 1,381,000 students and 50 percent of the state's free or reduced-price lunch, African-American, and Latino populations. Abbott spending in 2004 was $5.4 billion, with the bulk (82 percent) paid for by the state, 7 percent coming from federal assistance, and the balance from local property taxes.[4]

The long and contentious struggle between the state judiciary and the legislature over school equity also pushed New Jersey to enact the nation's first state takeover law for public schools in 1987. The takeover of the state's three largest districts—Jersey City (1989), Paterson (1993), and Newark (1995)—was widely seen as a failure, however, and the state later opted for a more advisory role in Camden, Asbury Park, and Irvington. In 1996, the state Board of Education established compulsory curricular standards, and achievement tests were mandated in 1999. When the No Child Left Behind Act (NCLB) was passed in 2002, the state was testing its students in grades 4, 8, and 11. The state passed a charter school law in 1996; but, as of 2005, there were only fifty-one charter schools in the state, serving a total of 14,900 students.[5]

New Jersey's home-rule tradition continues to exert a major influence over education policy in the state. The existence of over six hundred small, independent school districts and the active involvement of the New Jersey Department of Education (NJDOE) and the courts in the Abbott districts have created a unique and fragmented governance structure, which has complicated compliance with NCLB.

State Education Profile

In 2005–6, New Jersey had over 1,380,000 pre-K–12 students, enrolled in 2,428 schools staffed by 109,000 teachers. The state has an extremely diverse student population—approximately 42 percent minority, 16 percent with disabilities, 12 percent in poverty, and 4 percent with limited English proficiency.[6] The average school district in the state received 55 percent of its funding from local government, 41 percent from the state, and 4 percent from the federal government. New Jersey got approximately

$825 million in federal education aid annually,[7] a considerable amount to lose if the state failed to comply with NCLB. In the 2004–5 school year, Title I distributed $253 million to New Jersey schools, and 498 of state's 668 local educational agencies (and 1,200 of its 2,400 schools) received such funds.[8]

While the Abbott rulings have been very contentious, they have succeeded in making school finance in New Jersey among the most equitable in the country. In 2004, for example, the poorest districts in the state had per-pupil expenditures of $13,227, while the wealthiest spent $11,646, and the overall state average was $11,156.[9] In 2006, *Education Week* ranked New Jersey's educational system the fourth best overall in the nation with the second-highest proportion of students scoring proficient on national standardized tests. The analysis gave the state's standards and accountability policies an above-average grade of B+ but criticized the state's large gaps in test scores between poor students and others.[10]

Implementation of NCLB in New Jersey

Like many states, New Jersey struggled to implement NCLB at first, and had to devote considerable time and energy to aligning its existing state standards, assessment, and accountability policies with the law's new mandates. This was particularly difficult in the state's Abbott districts, which, as noted above, were operating under detailed court-ordered school improvement plans; several observers noted that the Abbotts' whole-school reforms were often at odds with the dictates of NCLB.

This educational alignment was further complicated by the need to realign the state's school governance structures. Many of New Jersey's worst-performing schools are supervised by the state's Division of Abbott Implementation, but NCLB implementation is run out of the state's Title I office. According to Wayne Dibofsky, a lobbyist for the New Jersey Education Association (NJEA),

> We have too many chefs in the kitchen and not enough cooks;
> in many instances different agencies in the State of New Jersey
> have oversight of various aspects of NCLB but they don't talk to

each other; even within the Department of Education they don't talk to each other.[11]

Dr. Gayle Griffin, the assistant superintendent in Newark, concurs, noting that

in the State of New Jersey we have multiple plans—we have an Abbott plan, we have a Title I plan and they are not the same and the two offices, the Abbott office and the Title I office, at the state level don't quite see things the same way.[12]

A further complicating factor, initially, was that the New Jersey Department of Education (NJDOE), under commissioner William Librera, tried to implement a number of new state reform initiatives simultaneously with the rollout of NCLB, and this made for a confusing and fragmented approach to school reform.[13] New Jersey also faced a number of major problems with the collection and reporting of data at the school, district, and state levels in the first few years of NCLB implementation that muddled the state's efforts to identify schools and districts in need of improvement, or to initiate NCLB-mandated remedies and sanctions. Delays and errors in grading the state's new standardized test (the New Jersey Assessment of Skills and Knowledge, or NJASK) in 2004 and 2005 created confusion about which schools did and did not meet NCLB requirements for adequate yearly progress (AYP) and forced the state to revise its preliminary lists two separate times.[14] A federal audit in 2005 concluded that state assessment results were still "not in a format for the LEAs [local educational agencies] to easily determine the AYP status of its schools."[15] These issues caused considerable frustration and logistical challenges for school and district staff and reinforced the sense among many teachers and administrators that NCLB was an arbitrary and ineffective diagnostic tool. It also had a major impact on the implementation of the remedy and sanction provisions of NCLB. The federal audit noted that "since NJDOE did not have an adequate process in place to provide clear assessment results to LEAs prior to the 2004–5 school year, school choice and SES options were not timely implemented."[16]

As shown in figure 6-1, the percentage of schools making AYP in New Jersey has fluctuated over the past three years, from 75 percent in 2003–4, to 65 percent in 2004–5, to 73 percent in 2005–6, though there is no clear

FIGURE 6-1

ADEQUATE YEARLY PROGRESS OF 2,400 NEW JERSEY SCHOOLS

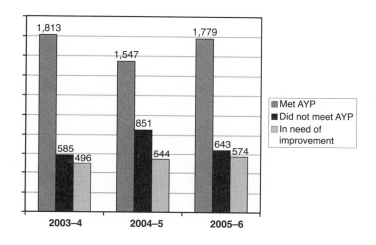

SOURCES: New Jersey Department of Education, "New Jersey 2004–05 No Child Left Behind Act AYP Report," press release, August 10, 2005, http://www.state.nj.us/njded/news/2005/0810aypreport.htm (accessed April 6, 2007), and New Jersey Department of Education, "New Jersey 2005–06 No Child Left Behind Act AYP Report," press release, August 22, 2006, http://www.state.nj.us/njded/news/2006/0822ayp.htm (accessed April 6, 2007).

trend. The number of schools identified as in need of improvement has grown marginally, from 496 schools in 2003–4, to 574 (25 percent) in 2005–6.[17] On both measures, then, New Jersey is faring worse than the national average, which is 75 percent of schools making AYP and 13 percent of schools in need of improvement.[18]

School Choice. Despite the mandate contained in NCLB, school choice essentially does not exist in the state of New Jersey. NCLB requires states to offer only intradistrict choice to students in failing schools, not interdistrict; and because most districts in the state are unusually small, intradistrict choice is essentially a nonstarter. Most suburban and rural districts are so small they have only one school for each level (elementary, middle, and high school). In most, if a school is labeled "in need of improvement," there is no other school to which a transfer can be made. The state's larger urban districts have multiple schools at each level, so choice is theoretically possible there; in practice, however, most if not all of them have failed to make AYP, and there are therefore few if any seats open in better schools to which to transfer. Choice is further constrained by the small number of existing charter schools (fifty-one) in New Jersey, and the arduous process for converting traditional schools to charter status.[19]

In spring 2002, 268 schools in seventy-one districts were placed on the "needing improvement" list because of their poor test scores. A survey by the state, however, found that only twenty-one of these—or fewer than one-third—offered families the option to transfer to better-performing schools as required under NCLB.[20] School system officials offered a variety of reasons choice was not implemented, ranging from transportation and space concerns to confusion about the requirements and timing of the law.[21] Almost half of the districts in the state reported they had "zero" capacity in their schools for offering school choice. Statewide, only 844 transfer requests were received by September 2002, and of these 504 (or 60 percent) were granted.[22] In 2003–4, 557 students were eligible to transfer, and 363 actually did so.[23]

The following year, the state saw an explosion in the number of students who were eligible for NCLB choice. During the 2004–5 school year, 105,986 New Jersey students were eligible to transfer to other public schools, but only 978 (0.9 percent) applied. Of those, 735 actually transferred (see figure 6-2), which represented 75 percent of the total applications, but only 0.7 percent of the eligible student population.[24] Choice data for 2005–6 are not yet available.[25] With fewer than 1,000 students—and less than 1 percent of those who were eligible—utilizing choice under NCLB in 2004–5, however, it is safe to say that this part of the law has failed to increase educational opportunity in New Jersey substantially.

The state has required districts that cannot offer choice in year 2 of improvement status to offer supplemental educational services (SES) instead. In general, however, the New Jersey Department of Education does not appear to have exerted sufficient oversight of district compliance with either the choice or SES provisions of NCLB. The 2005 federal audit criticized the NJDOE for delegating this responsibility to the county superintendents' offices without any "written policies or procedures on monitoring for compliance." The report found that, as a result of poor guidance and oversight, school districts in New Jersey had done an inadequate job of

Figure 6-2
NCLB School Choice in New Jersey, 2004–5:
Eligible and Transferred Students

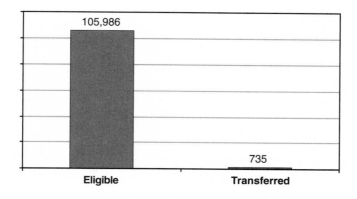

SOURCE: Data provided by Judy Alu, New Jersey Department of Education, Office of Title I Program Planning and Accountability, in correspondence with the author, November 13, 2006.

notifying parents of children in schools in need of improvement of their SES and choice options, declaring that

> for the 2004–2005 school year, NJDOE did not have an adequate process in place to review LEAs' compliance with AYP, Public School Choice, and SES. NJDOE also did not provide sufficient data for LEAs to timely determine AYP for schools, and had an inadequate process to timely monitor approved SES providers. As a result of NJDOE's inadequate process, all five LEAs reviewed did not comply with the Public School Choice and SES provisions of ESEA.[26]

In response to the highly critical audit report, in the summer of 2005 the NJDOE made a number of changes to its supervision of choice and SES across the state. It notified districts of their schools' AYP and accountability status on July 29, which was earlier than in the past and sufficiently in advance of the school year to permit schools to inform families of their eligibility for choice or SES. NJDOE also conducted training sessions about choice and SES for LEA and NJDOE field staff and required that districts henceforth use a standard parental notification letter created by the state to ensure that families received accurate and complete information about these services. A survey of a number of Abbott district websites, however, reveals that, as of this writing, information on choice (as well as SES) still had not been made as accessible for parents as it could be—none of the websites examined contained SES or choice forms or lists of SES providers or choice schools.

A closer analysis of Newark's experience with choice and SES helps to illustrate the challenges facing urban districts in the state. The federal audit found that the district sent a timely letter to parents, but that the letter only indicated that their child's school "may be" eligible for school choice or SES; and it was never followed up with any final determination of school status or student eligibility. The early letter also did not identify schools to which students could transfer or indicate that transportation would be provided to those exercising school choice. The district's revised 2006 letter indicated clearly that the recipient's child attended a school in need of improvement and had the option to be sent to tutoring or transferred to a high-performing school in the district. The letter contained a list of state-approved SES providers and their contact information, but did not indicate which of the providers were operating in Newark. An enrollment form for SES was not included with the letter, and parents were told they had to attend the district's SES fair in order to obtain one. These omissions appear to have unnecessarily burdened parents interested in utilizing SES.

Forty-six schools in Newark were identified as in need of improvement in 2006, and forty-one of those were in year 2 status or beyond, making parents of children in them eligible for choice. The options for choice, however, were quite limited, as only eleven of the eighty schools in Newark were designated as high-performing.[27] As with SES, no form was provided for parents interested in utilizing choice; rather, they were instructed to write a letter to their child's principal and to the assistant superintendent of their school leadership team for additional information.

The combination of communication issues and the lack of better schools to which to transfer within the district have made choice a nonstarter in Newark. Out of a total student population of forty-two thousand, a grand total of ten children have utilized school choice in the city over the past three years *combined*: one in 2003–4, none in 2004–5, and nine in 2005–6.

New Jersey's inability to offer meaningful school choice will become increasingly problematic as more schools move into NCLB's restructuring phase. Despite the virtual absence of choice, however, there has apparently been little discussion at the state level about changing state law in this area. In my discussions with educators from around the state, the lack of demand from parents for choice was frequently mentioned, but the impact that such a limited supply of high-quality choice options may have on parental demand was rarely noted. It is clear that unless major changes are made to state and/or federal law, NCLB's choice provision and the option of transferring to higher-performing schools will remain unrealized for most New Jersey students.

Supplemental Educational Services. Like many states, New Jersey was slow to comply with the supplemental educational services (SES) provision of NCLB. In the law's first year, 2002, the state Department of Education argued that it was not able to identify failing schools in time, largely because of the state's overhaul of its assessment system. While New Jersey was one of only fifteen states in the country to release a list of approved SES providers in 2002, errors in grading the state's new standardized test in 2003 and 2004 led to a delay in identifying schools in need of improvement and in informing parents and providers of student eligibility for choice and SES.

The state ultimately established several guidelines for SES that have had an important impact on how these services are provided and by whom. In addition to meeting all federal, state, and local health, safety, and civil rights laws, SES providers are required to ensure that their instruction is aligned with district and state standards and to provide parents, the school, and the district with monthly (and year-end) reports of student progress in the program. In response to the federal audit in 2005, the state also created a standard notification letter that schools are required to send to parents informing them of their children's eligibility for SES. The letter must be accompanied by a list of approved providers, and the state has established a timeline that schools must follow in processing parental SES applications. Despite this guidance from the state, schools appear to retain significant discretion over the administration of SES. As Mayra Rosner, Perth Amboy's director of federal programs, notes, "The state provides us with certain guidance and they have a lot of sample letters and things like that on the website, but they tend to be a bit ambivalent . . . In the end, it's up to the district what to do."[28]

The state's management of SES has been criticized by both educators and providers. Educators express concerns about the rigor of the state's approval and supervisory process for private providers. Sean Hadley a lobbyist for the New Jersey Principals and Supervisors Association (NJPSA), for example, remarks that

> the requirements for these providers are very lenient and in some cases nonexistent, and there's no real measurement of the outcome. And the providers on the list are not necessarily consistent from year to year, so there's also lack of consistency in who you can choose to be a provider and it's hard for districts to establish a relationship with them.[29]

District officials also complain that outside providers are not complying with state reporting requirements, that oversight from the state has been insufficient, and that the districts themselves have no power to regulate the providers. Perth Amboy's Rosner comments,

> I don't have a lot of faith in a lot of the private SES providers. I don't think some of them seem to have the capacity to manage the program. We don't get progress reports as we should, and the progress reports are very poor, but we don't have any leverage . . . all I can do is send a letter that says please remember to send progress reports every month, communicate with the child's teacher, but some of them don't. But we as a district cannot do much. We cannot require them to do certain things besides what the state has required them to do.[30]

Not surprisingly, providers have a very different set of concerns about the management of the SES process under NCLB. In their view, the biggest obstacle to the effective provision of SES and the emergence of a more robust SES marketplace in New Jersey has been the considerable discretion left to school districts and the state's unwillingness to hold districts accountable for the small percentage of eligible students they have enrolled to date. The state did little to regulate or standardize the SES process, particularly in the early years, and this resulted in tremendous variation in policies from district to district in New Jersey. The lack of consistency within and across districts has presented a major obstacle for private SES providers, particularly those that aspire to expand their programs statewide. Gene Wade, the director of Platform Learning—one of the largest SES providers in the state—remarked, "For the last few years, you had different policies in every school district and within a school district from year to year, and there have been yearly changes that have impacted whether or not parents can get through the registration process."[31]

Lack of transparency in the registration and approval process was cited as another major challenge for private SES providers. According to Wade,

> The approval process is a black box. The most challenging part of the registration process is where districts tell providers you can't see the form. The parent has to turn the form in directly to the school, so you have no way of knowing who signed up for your program.[32]

Districts were also criticized for their efforts at informing eligible families about the SES option; while all are required by the state to send out a standard SES eligibility notification letter, providers question its effectiveness, and whether it actually reaches parents. And, as noted above, most New Jersey school districts have not taken the relatively easy but important step of posting SES forms and information on their websites.

Tutoring companies are eager to market their services directly to parents but have found their efforts to do so limited by formal and informal rules laid down by the districts. As Wade observes,

> It is hard to get in front of the parents. Districts have an obligation to notify parents, but there's a big difference in SES between notification and marketing. . . . The devil of SES is in the details, and you're asking a district to play referee on that process and that is very problematic. We found that districts vary, and lots of times didn't vary at the policy level, [they] varied at the implementation level.[33]

While formal policies often permit SES providers to engage in direct marketing to parents, Wade says they often feel constrained because, "as a practical matter, if you tick off the district it's not going to help you very much. So when a district says we don't want you guys doing that kind of marketing, whether it's legal or not, we don't do it."[34] Lack of transparency creates an additional challenge for private SES providers: uncertainty. These companies must often attempt to prepare for the coming year—including hiring and training teachers and renting and outfitting classroom space—without advance information on student enrollment numbers. In addition, policies on payment schedules and documentation, and the release of student information such as test scores, all appear to vary considerably from district to district.[35]

The concerns of both the districts and the providers about the SES process in New Jersey were supported by the findings of the 2005 federal audit, which concluded that the NJDOE did not have an adequate process in place for monitoring the SES application process or provider activities. The state had established a four-part process for evaluating the performance of SES providers: a survey of school districts with input from parents, students, and teachers; a self-evaluation survey by providers; analysis of assessment results; and onsite visits by the NJDOE to a "selected sample" of providers. Federal investigators found, however, that as the 2005–6 school year got under way, the NJDOE was still in the process of evaluating the performance of the 2003–4 SES providers.[36] District communication with parents about the SES process was also found to be poor. All five of the local educational agencies (LEAs) investigated by the inspector general's office were found to have serious deficiencies in their SES notification letters. The report noted that the LEAs "were not aware of their responsibility for providing this information to parents, because NJDOE did not provide adequate guidance to LEAs regarding parental notification of SES."[37]

While much of the confusion and ineffectiveness of the SES registration process was attributed to the initial absence of state guidance or the learning curve of district administrators, some of the private SES providers had the perception that the districts viewed the entrance of private companies as ineffective and/or a threat to their interests, and actively worked to restrict their operations. Platform Learning's Wade observes that "we certainly saw times when we sat down and were basically signaled that you can only tutor X number of kids. Now that we're seeing the fact that a bunch of kids signed up for you, you can only have a certain number of kids and we're going to allocate the rest to somebody else."[38]

It is clear that many district educators and administrators do not see value in the provision of SES by private companies. One administrator, for example, says,

> We think it's just another distraction. They're not effective if you bring in a commercial package, drop them in, and bring teachers from different schools to supervise the homework and the game plan. The only chance you have for this to work is to have the districts themselves, including the failing districts, provide the tutoring themselves.[39]

Because NCLB places districts in the unusual position of being both SES providers and gatekeepers for the private providers, they have the ability and the incentive to restrict the participation of others. Districts are required under NCLB to set aside a portion of their Title I budget to pay for SES, but in New Jersey, as in most states, that money gets returned to the district budget if it goes unused. Whether they believe they are best equipped to provide SES, or they want to prevent a hit to their budgets, districts thus have reason to minimize the utilization of private SES providers.

The issues discussed above have created a number of operational challenges for private SES providers. Equally important, however, is that they have also discouraged potential providers from entering particular school districts or from entering the market at all. Despite the expectation that a competitive SES market would emerge in response to NCLB, this has not been the case in New Jersey.[40] The number of approved providers grew from 70 in 2002, to 116 in 2003, to 159 in November 2006; but in any given district the number of providers was typically quite small.[41] The mix of providers also changed from year to year, but in 2006, 40 percent were LEAs or high-performing schools, 33 percent were private for-profit companies, 23 percent were community, faith-based, or nonprofit providers, and a handful of colleges, private schools, and individuals rounded out the list.[42]

As shown in figure 6-3, during the 2003–4 school year, 63,467 children were eligible for SES, and 19,243 (30 percent) enrolled.[43] In 2004–5,

FIGURE 6-3

SUPPLEMENTAL EDUCATIONAL SERVICES IN NEW JERSEY:
ELIGIBLE AND SERVED STUDENTS, 2003–6

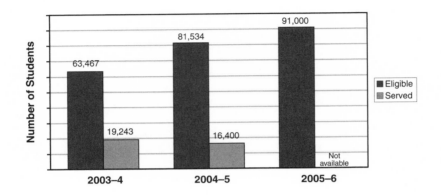

Source: Data for 2003–4 from John Mooney, "Rash of Tutor Programs Spurring New Concerns," *Star-Ledger*, December 22, 2003, 17; data for 2004–6 provided by Judy Alu, New Jersey Department of Education, Office of Title I Program Planning and Accountability, in correspondence with the author, November 13, 2006.

81,534 students were eligible, and 16,400 (20 percent) enrolled. Thus, the number of children receiving SES in New Jersey actually declined over the two years, despite a significant increase in the number of eligible students, and only a fraction of those eligible have received the services. The number of students utilizing SES during 2005–6 has not yet been compiled by the state, but approximately 91,000 were eligible.[44] Federal auditors found a similarly low rate of SES utilization; they sampled four school districts in 2005 and found that only 1,126 of 6,084 eligible students (18.5 percent) enrolled in SES.[45]

In Newark, the state's largest district, the number of students receiving SES grew considerably, from 1,639 in 2003–4, to 2,715 in 2004–5, to 4,325 in 2005–6.[46] Information on the number of Newark students who were eligible for SES was unavailable, so it is unclear what percentage of eligible students were served. The number of providers operating in Newark grew slowly, from thirteen in 2003–4, to fourteen the following year, to twenty in

2005–6. Many of these, however, enrolled only a handful of students; only eight enrolled more than thirty students, and only three enrolled more than a hundred. The biggest SES provider in the city was the district itself; its After School Youth Development Program (ASYDP) enrolled 2,438 students in 2005–6, which represented over 50 percent of the total. Platform Learning (1,103 students) and Education Station (330 students) were the next largest providers.[47]

The lack of a standardized process for SES has clearly had a dramatic impact on the number and kind of tutoring services made available to students in New Jersey. Like any business, a tutoring company must assess the demand, risk, and uncertainty of a new market when deciding whether or not to enter it. The difficulties encountered by prospective SES providers as the result of many district policies in New Jersey, however, have to this point made it difficult to ascertain demand, and they increase the risk and uncertainty of new investments. Platform Learning, for example, has focused its efforts on the state's largest Abbott districts and those that are supportive of SES. As a result, it is not offering services to smaller districts or those that have thrown up considerable obstacles to SES providers, which Wade estimates to be about 50 percent of the total districts in the state.

The combination of a hostile business climate that inhibits the entrance of private providers with the ban on failing districts offering SES has meant that eligible students may find few—if any—options for tutoring in their particular districts. As Sarah Kohl, a lobbyist for the New Jersey School Boards Association (NJSBA), notes, "Paterson had a problem with SES because not only did they not have enough schools that were not on the in-need-of-improvement list to provide supplemental educational services, but they didn't have enough private providers, and they were trying to figure out how they were going to arrange for these services because they had a lot of students who were eligible."[48] While there is a much greater utilization of SES than choice in New Jersey, it is clear that only a small portion of the eligible students are being served, and that the process by which these services are offered and supervised needs considerable refinement.

Corrective Action/Restructuring. While the New Jersey Department of Education has been only somewhat active in promoting the utilization of choice and supplemental educational services under NCLB, it has been much more active in assisting struggling schools. In 2003 the New Jersey NCLB advisory council identified several problems in the state's initial implementation of the law:

- A lack of collaborative planning and program delivery in schools across NCLB titles, which often resulted in duplication, unmet needs, higher costs, and poor student outcomes

- A lack of planning skills and strategies for conducting comprehensive needs assessments, identifying appropriate strategies for adequately addressing needs, and administering practical program evaluation as a planning tool

- A lack of understanding of the change process and strategies for facilitating change

- A lack of a basic understanding of NCLB requirements, purposes, and nonregulatory guidance

Perhaps most significant was the council's conclusion that the NJDOE "does not hold schools accountable for the requirements of NCLB. There is too much flexibility. DOE gives in or bends when it should remain firm for schools that are deficient, non-compliant or that cannot document progress."[49]

In response, the council outlined a more robust role for the state Department of Education in implementing NCLB and providing technical assistance to schools and districts. This vision became the basis for Collaborative Assessment and Planning for Achievement (CAPA) teams, which conduct week-long school reviews in low-performing Abbott and Title I schools. Based on the "scholastic audit" model developed in Kentucky, the CAPA process was initiated during the 2004–5 school year in New Jersey and is a collaborative effort between the state's Title I office and the Division of Abbott Implementation.[50] The CAPA teams do early intervention with struggling schools that are in year 3 or year 4 of "in need of improvement" status and then go back into schools that are in restructuring.

The teams then spend three days conducting interviews, making classroom visitations, and gathering and analyzing data.[51] Each team presents its draft report to school and district leadership in a "prioritizing meeting," and a final agreement lays out the steps the school will take to improve and describes the nature of ongoing technical assistance from the state. The state also recently initiated periodic "benchmark visits" by Department of Education staff about three times a year which analyze what is being done, what is working, and what may not be working in order to inform the kind of additional technical assistance the department should be offering. While the CAPA teams are state-run, a major goal of the review process has been to get the districts to play a bigger role in supervising and supporting their schools and helping them to meet their objectives. A particular focus is on equipping and encouraging district and school administrators and teachers to gather and analyze student performance data and to use those data to inform the instructional program.

As indicated in figure 6-4, the number of schools in New Jersey in year 4 corrective action under NCLB went from 271 in 2004 to 164 in 2005; the number in year 5 restructuring went from 8 to 17; and the number in year 6 restructuring went from 71 to 52. The number of districts designated as in need of improvement in the state fell from sixty-three in 2005 to sixty in 2006. Thirteen of these had not made AYP for four consecutive years and now face corrective action.[52] According to Patricia Mitchell, who supervises the CAPA process for the NJDOE, the department made 102 CAPA school visits in the program's first year (2004–5) and 77 visits in 2005–6.[53]

Because of the large number of school visits and insufficient staff in the NJDOE to conduct them all, the CAPA teams are comprised of volunteers from districts, many of whom are apparently retired teachers who have not been in the classroom for many years. Several observers have questioned the way in which the CAPA team members are selected and trained. Abbott commissioner MacInnes comments,

> Some of our teams are very good. But the first few years of these CAPA teams we were recruiting actively to try and fill the vacuum that had been created by this requirement and we had some great inconsistency and unevenness in the quality of our CAPA visits . . . but we started weeding out the really weak teams and I think their value is increasing with more practice.[54]

Initially districts were reluctant to embrace the CAPA process and resented what they saw as state intrusion in their schools, although Mitchell believes that

> we have overcome the resistance of the districts. They still get a knot in their stomachs when they see we're coming, but we don't get people writing to the commissioner anymore saying, "I want to appeal this visit."[55]

Many observers express doubt about whether the NJDOE—operating in recent years under budget cuts and a hiring freeze—has sufficient capacity to provide assistance to the growing number of schools that need it. The CAPA teams are expensive, at about $23,000 per visit, and Hadley noted that the state has been forced to redistribute federal School Improvement Grant money to pay for them. As Wayne Dibofsky of the New Jersey Education Association notes, "To meet all the mandates and provide all the additional assistance that is needed, especially in the Abbott districts, has been a real serious problem. There's not enough manpower in their CAPA teams to go out and perform all the tasks on hand."[56] His view is seconded by Andrew Babiak, counsel for the New Jersey Association of School Administrators (NJASA), who says,

> The department definitely faces a capacity issue. There are a lot of things that they have to do under NCLB, and they don't physically have the staff to go out and do everything so they are relying on volunteers from school districts to help staff these teams. We have over one hundred schools that need assistance, but they have limited resources and take a triage approach.[57]

While many observers praise the efforts of the CAPA teams in diagnosing school problems and making recommendations, their effect in securing meaningful change in schools or improvement in student performance remains ambiguous. It is unclear how binding CAPA recommendations are on schools, as schools and districts appear to have a great deal of discretion in determining whether and how to implement the reforms. Sarah Kohl of the New Jersey School Boards Association (NJSBA) remarks, for example,

FIGURE 6-4

"IN NEED OF IMPROVEMENT" STATUS OF NEW JERSEY SCHOOLS

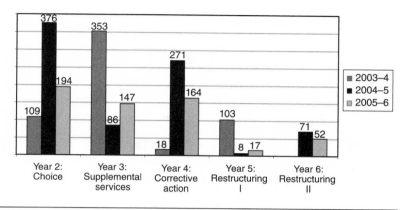

SOURCE: State of New Jersey Department of Education, "DOE Identifies 60 NCLB 'Districts in Need of Improvement,'" press release, December 5, 2006, http://www.state.nj.us/education/news/2006/1205dini. htm (accessed May 23, 2007).

that "the CAPA team recommendations are just that, they're recommendations. And the school or the district has the option of taking or leaving them."[58]

Others, however, see compliance with the CAPA recommendations as essentially required. NJPSA's Hadley, for example, calls the CAPA plans a "backdoor mandate" from the state to schools.[59] Nonetheless, when pressed, state education administrators and observers are unsure whether any consequences have ensued for schools that have not enacted CAPA recommendations. When asked whether the agreement was binding, for example, one state education official who works with CAPA schools indicated that he did not know, and that the follow-up supervision by the state of compliance of the plans was "spotty." Since no additional funding is provided by the state to implement the CAPA recommendations, there is no financial incentive for schools to comply.

In addition, the statutory language of NCLB gives schools that reach the restructuring phase (after five years of failing to make AYP) considerable latitude in terms of the steps they must take to improve. According to Andrew Babiak,

There are basically three options available to New Jersey schools. The first is the broad option, implementing any major restructuring of the school's governance that is consistent with the principles of restructuring. That is the number one choice for schools. Option two is to reopen the school as a public charter school. That's not going to happen, and nobody has selected that option. In order for a charter school to be established under New Jersey law the staff basically has to vote for it. The third option is to replace all or most of the school staff, which may include the principal. That option has been chosen, but basically it's been chosen in combination with option number one.[60]

While detailed information on school restructuring changes in New Jersey is not available, Mitchell says that "there were a lot of principal changes . . . Sometimes the CAPA report is what the district needed in order to make changes or convince the board that changes needed to be made."[61] In general, however, the state DOE seems to have focused its efforts on data analysis, curriculum, and professional development rather than on structural or organizational changes.[62]

The state's NCLB advisory council has recommended that districts be formally required to adopt all of the CAPA recommendations, but there is resistance to this idea both from districts, which do not want to lose their discretion, and from state officials, who are wary of taking on responsibility for more failing districts. As Sarah Kohl observes,

The only way it would become mandatory is if the CAPA teams were there as a state takeover instrument, and they won't do that. The NJDOE has takeover districts right now that they are trying to get out of and they don't want to be in the business of taking over districts anymore.[63]

CAPA director Mitchell reiterates this point, noting that "the likelihood of the state intervening the way it has in the past is very unlikely. The state needs to be involved in these districts but it can't be top down. It is intended to focus on capacity building."[64]

For both political and philosophical reasons, then, the NJDOE has thus far been largely unwilling to overrule districts' authority and mandate particular interventions in failing schools. The effect of the CAPA process on school improvement continues to be unclear—when pressed, the NJDOE could not point to any data demonstrating its impact (though the department indicated it is in the process of collecting some).

Conclusion

The success of NCLB implementation in New Jersey thus far has been decidedly mixed. As was made abundantly clear in the 2005 federal audit and in my interviews with educators across the state, the NJDOE initially failed to provide schools and districts with clear and timely data from state assessments with which to make AYP determinations. Adequate guidance for and supervision of compliance with NCLB's sanctions and remedies for underperforming schools were also clearly lacking. While the state appears to have rectified many of these initial problems and has taken a number of significant steps to improve its oversight and align its assessment and accountability systems with NCLB, the analysis of the application of NCLB remedies and sanctions provided above demonstrates that they have had a very uneven impact on school improvement efforts in the state.

The unusually small size of districts in New Jersey has combined with the lack of an interdistrict choice law and a difficult charter-conversion process to make school choice virtually nonexistent in the state. And, despite steps by the state to increase the supervision and standardization of the SES process, it appears that districts and schools have used their considerable remaining discretion over the process to constrain the entrance and expansion of private SES providers and the utilization of these services by students. The area of NCLB implementation where New Jersey has expended the most effort has been in intervening with failing schools during the corrective-action and restructuring phases. The CAPA process—and in particular the focus on early intervention—has provided unprecedented guidance from the NJDOE to schools and districts and pushed them to embrace a data-driven approach to school improvement.

Whether or not the CAPA process will generate substantial and lasting achievement gains for traditionally underserved student populations, however, remains to be seen.

A number of developments are underway in New Jersey that will have a major impact on the state's education reform efforts and its compliance with NCLB:

- Preschool and all-day kindergarten were recently initiated in Abbott districts, and hopes are high that this will boost academic achievement for traditionally underperforming groups and assist in meeting AYP proficiency targets under NCLB.

- In 2005, the Department of Education's monitoring and evaluation system was completely revamped with the creation of the New Jersey Quality Single Accountability Continuum (NJQSAC). The purpose of the NJQSAC is to eliminate the different standards for Abbott and non-Abbott districts and to better align the state assessment and accountability system with NCLB. The NJQSAC also calls for the development of a statewide student-level database that can provide more timely and comprehensive data about student performance to teachers and administrators. It is hoped that these data will enhance districts' ability to monitor the performance of schools and the state's ability to monitor the performance of districts, and permit New Jersey to move to a growth model under NCLB if such a model becomes permissible after the forthcoming reauthorization. The new system was field-tested during 2005–6 and is expected to be implemented statewide during the 2007–8 school year.

- During the summer and fall of 2006, New Jersey was engaged in a contentious debate over tax and spending policies and municipal governance that will have enormous implications for schools and the implementation of NCLB in the state. One proposal receiving serious attention is to consolidate many of the small school districts in the state, which could potentially make school choice a much more viable reform strategy.

- Another recent development was the filing in July 2006 of a law-suit by the Alliance for School Choice to gain private school vouchers for students in ninety-seven schools throughout the state which, the suit contends, have failed to provide the "thorough and efficient" education guaranteed by the state constitution.

A number of possible refinements to NCLB that could be made during the forthcoming reauthorization emerge from the analysis in this chapter and from my discussions with educators and administrators and members of the state's NCLB advisory council. While NCLB was widely praised for shining a spotlight on poorly served disadvantaged students and for engaging the state and districts more actively in helping them, there is concern that the law has not provided sufficient resources to build state and district capacity. Although many observers have been quick to discount educators' plea for more resources as a return to the old inputs versus outputs dispute and an attempt to escape accountability for student performance, the debate about school resources appears to have shifted in some important ways. The educators I spoke with did not, for the most part, talk about the need for smaller class sizes, better school facilities, or increased teacher salaries, but rather assistance with data collection and analysis, professional development, and interventions for underperforming students. With Democrats now in control of Congress, additional funding for education appears likely to be forthcoming, but the purposes to which these monies are targeted will be important to the future of NCLB.

There is clearly a major disconnection between the educational worldview of NCLB supporters—which is centered on school governance and accountability—and that of many educators in New Jersey who believe that the law has not focused enough on the pedagogical challenges presented by disadvantaged students. According to Abbott commissioner MacInnes, for example,

We have been trying to push that you need to change instruction not governance. . . . NCLB now focuses the attention on student achievement but in a way to punish schools and reorganize them as if organization is the problem. Actually pedagogy is the problem—it's instruction, it's knowing how to teach kids what they have to learn. . . . So I think you have a pretty good mismatch between what needs to get done on the ground and NCLB.[65]

The treatment of special education kids and ESL learners (who together comprise approximately 20 percent of the New Jersey student population), in particular, was highlighted by many observers as an area of NCLB in need of considerable revision. Administrators felt that the expectations for these populations were impossible to meet because of the students' educational challenges and the inability of many urban districts to attract and retain the specialized teachers who can serve them effectively.

More generally, there is the perception among many educators that NCLB is designed to fail, or rather that it is designed to show that schools have failed. Given the importance of NCLB "buy-in" by teachers, administrators, and state education departments to the long-term success of the law, such concerns should not be discounted. The credibility of the testing and accountability regime in NCLB is particularly important in this regard—it is imperative that it be viewed as a fair and accurate estimation of student and school performance, which is clearly not the case at the moment. There is strong support to expand on the pilot programs already in place by permitting all states to utilize growth models to track individual student progress within and across years and to reward states for improvement, as well as for meeting proficiency targets. Such a change would provide educators and administrators with an effective pedagogical tool as well as improve perceptions about the validity of the testing regime.

New Jersey observers are also frustrated by the ability of other states to game the system by tinkering with their standards, tests, "n size," and proficiency levels. While this flexibility was given to the states in the interest of minimizing federal control over schools, it has undermined the veracity of state-by-state educational comparisons and frustrated those states that are making a good-faith effort to raise rather than lower their expectations for students. Standardizing the n size for subgroups and providing a common yardstick (beyond the current limited use of the National Assessment of Educational Progress) for evaluating the education performance of all states—perhaps through a national test—are two steps that could be considered in this regard.

There was also widespread support for reversing the order of choice and SES and for creating a standardized assessment for measuring student progress and provider effectiveness in SES programs. One suggestion for addressing the financial disincentive for school districts to expand SES utilization was to adopt Florida's policy of rolling over unused SES money from year to year rather than returning it to the district. Continuing the district's double role as both provider and gatekeeper of SES also seems problematic and may best be resolved by increasing transparency or requiring states to take over the management of the application process rather than just approve providers.

Perhaps the part of NCLB in greatest need of revision is that which deals with the restructuring of schools that have failed to meet AYP for five or more years. While restructuring was intended to force persistently underperforming schools and districts to undertake major changes in their approach to school improvement, it is clear that this has generally not occurred. Though information here is sketchy, most "restructuring" schools in New Jersey appear to have avoided doing much serious restructuring, instead opting to replace their principals or adopt modest pedagogical or curricular changes. The existence of the option in NCLB to implement "any major restructuring of the school's governance that is consistent with the principles of restructuring" constitutes a major loophole that should be closed by requiring persistently failing schools to take more concrete steps to improve.

Some of the recommendations above involve greater centralization of educational authority from the states to the federal government, which is always a controversial proposition. Just as the federal government has walked a fine line with NCLB in balancing federal goals with state discretion, so, too, has New Jersey struggled to balance its efforts to comply with the law while preserving its historical tradition of local control of schools. Initially, the New Jersey Department of Education did not provide sufficient guidance or supervision for district compliance with NCLB's choice and SES provisions, which may help to explain why the usage of these services by eligible students remains quite low. In the past two years, however, the department has become much more active in implementing NCLB, and with the CAPA process has developed a promising—if as yet unproven—system for intervening in struggling schools. Due to judicial mandate, the state is one of the most equitable in the country in terms of education finance. Thanks to NCLB, equity has now been joined with accountability in New Jersey, but it appears that the state must increase its oversight further to ensure that schools are effectively deploying their resources to enhance student achievement and educational opportunity.

7

Colorado: The Misapplication of Federal Power

Alex Medler

In Colorado, the No Child Left Behind Act (NCLB) is raising important questions about students who deserve a better education than they are getting. When it comes to intervening in low-performing schools, however, the law appears nearly powerless to bring about the changes in behavior it was intended to produce. Power can be defined as the ability to get people to do something they would not otherwise have done. For example, there is no power behind a command to sit if the recipient either insists on standing or was already seated. Likewise, the interventions of NCLB are largely irrelevant in districts that are hostile to the federal law, and they are implemented seriously only by districts that were already using those strategies. As a result, NCLB's impact comes on the margins of more significant initiatives driven by state law and local initiative.

The Limits of Federal Power

In Colorado, the limits of the federal law's power to change state, district, and family behavior is demonstrated by the modest penetration of public school choice, supplemental educational services (SES), and school restructuring.

Public School Choice. NCLB has articulated and asserted a new right: Any child attending a school that is failing to educate its students deserves a chance to enroll elsewhere. The assumption is that the child will learn more in a new setting. In addition, advocates of school choice hope the exit of students will produce competitive pressure that stimulates improvement in the schools they left. But even if we accept the controversial proposition that choice benefits both the students who leave and the students who stay, too few Colorado children are choosing new schools because of NCLB to reap these benefits.

Outside of Denver in 2005, only 72 of the more than 22,000 students eligible for public school choice under NCLB transferred to other schools.[1] That is fewer than two students per identified school. In these communities, too few students are enrolling in higher performing schools for any individual student's potential increase in performance to solve the achievement problems. Collectively, not enough students are leaving to put real pressure on their former schools to improve. In Denver—which contains more than half of Colorado's schools identified as needing improvement under federal law—about 2 percent of the eligible children exercised choice through NCLB. However, more than 30 percent of Denver's students were already choosing their schools. It is possible that those choosing new schools under NCLB would have done so without the statute. Federal money may be subsidizing transportation for the district's preexisting, and much larger, public school choice program.

Supplemental Educational Services. Statewide, about 10 percent of eligible children receive tutoring under NCLB.[2] Some of Colorado's districts have almost no students using supplemental educational services (SES). Six of the districts with eligible students have participation rates of less than 1 percent. In another six, 10 percent or more of the eligible students participate. The state has similar programs, including other federally funded ones, that serve higher proportions of eligible children. In the districts with viable SES programs, the participation rates are high enough that effective services providers could have an impact on overall academic performance. Questions have emerged, however, about the efficacy of some of the more than fifty tutoring companies Colorado has approved. Any academic improvement among participants could be limited to a subset of the already modest number of students using the services.

Restructuring. Only three schools have begun restructuring under NCLB in Colorado.[3] A state law that preceded NCLB also forced action in these schools. Until 2006, Colorado law mandated a state-run chartering process for its worst-performing schools. Ironically, rather than encouraging profound restructuring, NCLB served as a model for policymakers interested in providing schools with more flexibility to select the changes they could implement to qualify as having restructured.

In addition to helping the state relax its definition of restructuring, NCLB has "commanded" restructuring in a district, Denver Public Schools, that had already embraced the process. In Denver many schools are planning and implementing restructuring efforts using several local options.[4] The NCLB-driven mandate to restructure will catch these schools midway through their locally initiated version.

In sum, Colorado has little new behavior that can be attributed to NCLB interventions. In the long run, new interventions may have more influence on local behavior and student performance than those currently applied under the law. Hopefully, the examination of the limits of federal power in Colorado presented in this chapter will inform efforts to design interventions under the next version of the Elementary and Secondary Education Act (ESEA) that will produce more progress toward the commendable goals of NCLB.

The Colorado Context

Colorado's public school system serves more than 780,000 students in 1,689 schools spread among 178 districts.[5] The state's public school enrollment is 63 percent white, 27 percent Hispanic, 6 percent black, 3 percent Asian, and slightly more than 1 percent American Indian.[6] Statewide, 34 percent of the state's students qualify for free or reduced-price lunch (FRPL).[7] Colorado has more than 43,000 students identified as English-language learners, and that number has increased rapidly in recent years.

These numbers mask regional differences. The Denver metropolitan area has more than half the state's students and most of its larger school districts, including more than 430,000 students in fifteen school districts.[8] Denver Public Schools (DPS) serves more than 73,000 students, 80 percent of whom are children of color.[9]

Colorado's geography also affects its education system. The state has about ninety rural districts and seventy districts that serve fewer than four hundred students each.[10] Many of these small districts have only one class-room per grade, decreasing the viability of school choice. Great distances separate districts in the eastern plains. Daunting passes divide mountain communities. The resulting isolation creates obstacles to providing both choice and tutoring. Some rural communities serve large proportions of low-income, Hispanic, and Native American students.

The Policy Environment. Colorado mixes local control and decentralized governance with a growing array of accountability and school choice poli-cies. Historically, local control by district officials outweighed both state authority and parental choice. Over time, state authority was expanded through the creation of accountability measures, while parental authority increased as more families exercised public school choice.

Local control. In Colorado, district power is established in the state's consti-tution and given rhetorical deference by elected leaders from all levels of government.[11] This deference to local control sometimes constrains educa-tion reform. For example, the state legislature established a voucher pro-gram that would have allowed students in low-performing public schools to attend private schools at public expense. The program was overturned by the state's supreme court based on language in the state constitution mandating district control of educational programs. Meanwhile, new accountability policies have expanded the state's role while choice programs have increased parental control. Collectively, these steps have diminished district power to a small extent.

Choice. Colorado has a great deal of school choice. Even excluding intradis-trict choice, which is difficult to quantify, about 18 percent of the state's school-age children are choosing charter schools, private schools, attending schools outside the districts where they live, or being home-schooled. In 2005–6, 120 charter schools spread among forty-seven districts served 44,250 students.[12] More than 42,000 students currently attend public schools outside the districts where they live.[13] In 2005, 56,665 students were enrolled in private schools,[14] and about 7,000 were registered as home-schooled.[15] The number of families exercising choice is even higher because of locally designed, intradistrict open-enrollment programs.

Accountability. Like most states, Colorado had a far-reaching accountability system in place prior to NCLB. The Colorado Department of Education (CDE) uses test results from the Colorado Student Assessment Program (CSAP) to publish School Accountability Reports (SAR). CDE also uses the CSAP scores to calculate adequate yearly progress (AYP) and incorporates them into state accreditation. Under the SAR system the state designates schools as unsatisfactory, low, average, high, or excellent. The SAR system differs from NCLB because it does not disaggregate performance for various groups of students. But, like the AYP calculation, the SAR rating triggers interventions if performance stays too low for too long.

Revisiting Initial Challenges of NCLB

Colorado educators have five years of experience with NCLB. The challenges they are encountering now are different from those that emerged earlier. In a 2004 case study of Colorado's implementation of NCLB,[16] three issues emerged:

- Conflicts between state and federal designations of struggling schools

- Long timelines for determining each school's status

- Relevance of NCLB interventions in Colorado's rural districts

Conflicts between SAR Ratings and AYP Designations. Analysis in 2004 identified inconsistencies between state and federal designations of struggling schools. Schools that scored low on the state SAR system passed the federal AYP, while some that scored high on the state system failed to make AYP, according to NCLB. These inconsistencies remain. In 2005, 2 of the 17 schools rated "unsatisfactory" and 132 of the 348 schools rated "low" in the SAR made AYP. Of the schools that scored "high" on the SAR, 56, or 10 percent, failed to make AYP. Of schools rated as "excellent" on the SAR, 7 failed to make AYP (see figure 7-1).[17] These contradictions roughly mirrored the proportions in 2004.

The contradictions stem from differences in how the SAR and AYP address diversity. The state's reporting system does not disaggregate performance by

FIGURE 7-1

COLORADO SCHOOL RATINGS: SAR AND AYP, 2005

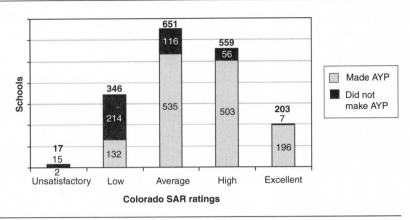

SOURCE: CCC dataset. See endnote 17 for details.

different types of students, while the designation of AYP gives no credit to schools that do an excellent job with most students if others are still "left behind." Of the seven schools that were rated as excellent in 2005 by the state system but did not make AYP, six were high schools with a large number of "target groups" under NCLB. These seven schools averaged 23.7 NCLB targets. Meanwhile, the 196 "excellent" schools that made AYP faced an average of only 13.9 targets.[18] NCLB identifies larger schools with diverse enrollments in which strong performance by most of the students masks unacceptable performance by students with particular backgrounds. These two systems provide insight into school quality and could complement one another. However, differences between them continue to undermine the credibility of both.

Timeline for Designating Schools. Earlier analysis identified a problem in the state's timeline for designating each school's AYP status which can slow down the implementation of public school choice and SES.[19] AYP designations are based on results from the Colorado Student Assessment Program (CSAP). These results are not available until August, meaning that each school's official AYP designation does not come until the late fall of the next school year. District officials must decide whether to provide transportation for NCLB-funded choice in the fall following a state test without knowing if their schools made AYP. In most districts this means NCLB-funded choice does not begin until the school year that starts seventeen months after the test. The delay also means that districts are likely to offer transportation for one year more than is necessary under the law if a school improves enough to make AYP, because they are unlikely to cancel choice programs after designations are released in the middle of the school year.

Since 2004, Colorado has accelerated its designation timeline by about two weeks.[20] According to CDE staff, the state is unlikely, despite federal pressure, to accelerate the process further because of challenges presented by the timing of the test and the technical aspects of cleaning and analyzing data. As Paul Manna points out, at least forty-three states have found ways to overcome these challenges and speed up their timetables considerably.[21] Colorado should borrow strategies from these faster-moving states. In addition to helping districts comply with the letter of the federal law, quickly returning all available CSAP data would help educators meet the more important objective of improving instruction.

NCLB and Colorado's Rural Districts. Colorado's geography frustrates NCLB implementation. In many small districts, intradistrict choice is impossible. In some sparsely populated districts, choice options technically exist but remain impractical. Small rural districts with no more than a handful of students interested in tutoring have difficulty recruiting SES providers. These challenges have convinced many rural Coloradans that NCLB is poorly designed for their communities.

Although small rural schools generally have fewer targets to achieve under NCLB for specific subgroups of students, some fail to make AYP. These schools comply with their obligations to notify parents of their rights. CDE has prepared model letters for districts to use when they must notify parents of the choice options to which their children are entitled, and according to CDE staff, most of these schools comply with their obligation to send them—even when those choices do not exist. The state has also worked to ensure that at least one SES provider can work face-to-face in each district with NCLB-identified schools. Despite these efforts to meet the letter of the law, very little action occurs in Colorado's rural districts.

Some rural districts do resist NCLB. The Kit Carson District turned down its share of Title I funding under NCLB ($25,000) and then asked

TABLE 7-1

DEMOGRAPHICS OF COLORADO SCHOOLS

Subgroup	All schools (%)	NCLB-identified schools (%)
American Indian	9,178 (1)	703 (1)
Asian	25,460 (3)	1,093 (2)
Black	46,465 (6)	6,322 (11)
Hispanic	211,314 (27)	38,577 (68)
White	487,916 (63)	9,106 (18)
Total	780,333	55,914
Free/Reduced Lunch	262,036 (34)	41,267 (75)

SOURCE: CCC dataset. See endnote 17 for details.

local voters to pass a levy that raised enough money to replace the lost funding. Kit Carson is located on Colorado's southeastern plains. It has a single school building, serving ninety-four students across all grades, and has never had a grade level not make AYP. The district's superintendent also lobbied the Colorado legislature to enact legislation making it easier for school districts to opt out of NCLB. His legislative proposal was defeated.[22]

Schools Identified in Need of Improvement

In the 2005–6 school year, Colorado had 105 schools identified as needing to improve under NCLB. Thirty-six schools were in the first year of school improvement, thirty-one were in year 2, twenty-two were in corrective action, thirteen were in the stage of restructuring-planning, and three were implementing restructuring plans.[23]

For most of the analysis that follows, a subset of one hundred schools was included. The smaller subset was necessary because of issues with comparability of datasets.[24] The hundred schools were spread unevenly among twenty districts. Most were concentrated in Denver and a handful of surrounding districts. These hundred schools served approximately 55,900 students in 2005–6, representing 7 percent of the state's enrollment and

FIGURE 7-2

NCLB-IDENTIFIED SCHOOLS BY MEAN PERCENTAGE OF MINORITY STUDENTS, 2005

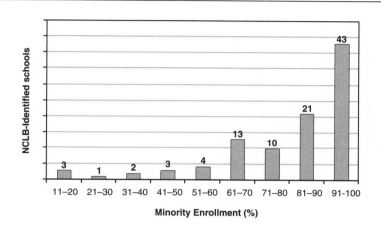

SOURCE: CCC dataset. See endnote 17 for details.

about 6 percent of the state's schools (see table 7-1).[25] Denver Public Schools had fifty-four identified schools, or 36 percent of all DPS schools. The DPS schools identified served a total of about 33,300 students, or 46 percent of the total DPS enrollment. Four of the identified schools were charter schools.

Demographics. Students in the NCLB-identified schools were more likely than those in nonidentified schools to live in poverty. About 75 percent of the students in identified schools qualified for free or reduced-price lunch (FRPL), compared to 34 percent of all students statewide (see table 7-1).[26] In NCLB-identified schools, 68 percent of students were Hispanic, compared to 27 percent in all Colorado schools, and 11 percent were black, compared to 6 percent statewide. Only 18 percent of the students in identified schools were white, compared to 63 percent in all Colorado schools.

The minority students were concentrated within the NCLB-identified schools. The enrollment of forty-three of the identified schools was greater than 90 percent minority (see figure 7-2). Only nine NCLB-identified schools served majority-white populations.[27]

TABLE 7-2
DENVER AND NON-DENVER SCHOOL DEMOGRAPHICS, 2005

	Denver Public Schools (DPS)		Non-Denver public school districts	
Subgroup	% of students in NCLB-identified schools	% of students in district	% of students in NCLB-identified schools	% of students in state excluding DPS
American Indian	1	1	2	1
Asian	2	3	2	3
Black	15	18	7	5
Hispanic	76	58	58	24
White	6	20	31	67
Free/Reduced Lunch	80	67	67	30

SOURCE: CCC dataset. See endnote 17 for details.

Denver serves the largest minority population in the state and has more than half of the schools included in this analysis. The identified schools in DPS are presented separately from those in the rest of the state (see table 7-2). Compared to the rest of the schools in Denver, the fifty-four NCLB-identified schools in the district in 2005–6 served much larger percentages of low-income and Hispanic children.[28] While enrollment in the average school in DPS was 20 percent white students, the district's NCLB-identified schools served an average of 6 percent white students. In DPS, the percentage of FRPL-qualifying students was 13 percent higher in identified schools than in other DPS schools.

The applicability of choice and SES under NCLB was not equal for Denver's different racial and ethnic groups. Only 14 percent of Denver's white students attended schools identified as failing under NCLB.[29] Of the district's Hispanic students, 61 percent attended schools where the choice or SES options of NCLB were offered, as did 35 percent of its black students.[30] Thus, for six out of seven white families in Denver, NCLB was an abstraction. Meanwhile, for the majority of the district's Hispanic families, and for a third of the black families, NCLB had been a tool, however modest, for serving their children.

The overrepresentation of low-income and minority students was not confined to Denver. The other forty-six NCLB-identified schools in Colorado were in nineteen districts spread across the state.[31] Three larger districts in the Denver area each had six identified schools, Colorado Springs had four, and the fifteen remaining districts had three or fewer. Outside DPS, the NCLB-identified schools served more than twice as high a percentage of Hispanic and low-income students as the nonidentified schools. When DPS schools were excluded from the analysis, the identified schools served, on average, fewer than half as many white students as the nonidentified schools (see table 7-2).

Choice. The Colorado schools where choice was viable enrolled a total of 53,290 students in 2005–6.[32] In 2005, 875 children exercised choice through NCLB, an average participation rate of 1.4 percent.[33] Denver accounted for about 800 of those choosing under NCLB. If we exclude DPS, only 72 out of more than 22,000 eligible students in the rest of the state exercised choice through NCLB.[34]

Statewide, NCLB produced only about 1 percent of the choice generated by Colorado's charter schools and interdistrict transfers. Fifty-eight schools had participation rates of less than 1 percent. Fewer than 2 percent of students chose in another nineteen. In only twenty-three of the hundred schools did the participation rate in choice programs rise above 2 percent. Twelve schools had more than 3 percent of their students exercise choice through NCLB. And of the five schools with more than 5 percent exercising choice, three were small high schools that were generated from the breakup of Manual High School.[35] The exodus of students from the small (and shrinking) schools at Manual was likely due more to the schools' failed reform (which has been documented extensively)[36] than to their NCLB designations.

Supplemental Educational Services. Of the one hundred schools in this study, sixty-seven were required to provide SES because they were in the second year of school improvement or later in the process.[37] These schools served 36,400 students, of which 27,880 qualified for FRPL and SES. Compared to school choice under NCLB, the SES appeared relatively popular.

In 2005, 2,960 students used SES, or 10.6 percent of the eligible enrollment of all the identified schools.[38]

As was the case with choice, many of these schools had few or no students using SES. Eight had no students using SES, and eighteen had between 2 and 5 percent of their students using services. Twenty-seven schools had more than 10 percent participation rates.[39]

Other programs in the state provide services that are similar to NCLB's SES programs. The 21st Century Community Learning Centers, for example, operate in forty schools in nineteen districts and serve about 6,800 students.[40] The state also runs a youth development program, the Tony Grampsas Youth Services Program, which operated at more than a hundred sites with $3.4 million in 2005.[41] Many districts with schools providing SES under NCLB also have sites with Tony Grampsas and 21st Century Community Learning Center grants.

Colorado has an annual request for proposals (RFP) in which potential SES providers apply for approval from the state. Since the passage of NCLB, Colorado has approved a total of fifty-six providers.[42] In 2006, forty-three remained on its official list. In 2004, CDE staff had found it difficult to judge the effectiveness of providers without track records.[43] They also reported that would-be providers regularly enlisted political leaders to lobby on their behalf. While CDE staff was quick to note that the lobbying efforts were not effective, the state approved nearly all applicants in the initial years.

In the 2006 RFP, CDE turned down a larger proportion of SES applicants. Staff suggested that adding face-to-face interviews to the selection process had increased the likelihood of weak applications being rejected. Some approved providers also removed themselves from the list for a variety of reasons. For example, some national providers faced unexpected difficulty in finding acceptable facilities without district support.

Staff at CDE still say it is hard to ensure quality among tutoring companies. The state has contracted with a third-party evaluator to use state assessment data to evaluate various aspects of the supplemental services delivered through NCLB by comparing statewide the performance of children who participate in the program with that of similar students who do not. This should provide insight into the various programs' accomplishments. While this evaluation does not completely remove doubts about the efficacy of some providers, it helps increase the state's confidence that in the long run their SES offerings will improve.

Restructuring. Both NCLB and Colorado law require failing schools to restructure. And both laws have, thus far, been irrelevant to all but a handful of schools. Under a 2000 Colorado law, schools that the state labeled "unsatisfactory" were supposed to be converted to charter schools if they did not improve within three years. In the first few years, most unsatisfactory schools managed to improve enough to reach the "low" level and avoided reconstitution. The law did force the chartering of one school in 2005, Cole Middle School. Three schools statewide, including Cole, also faced restructuring under NCLB in 2006. Twelve more face restructuring under NCLB in 2007.[44]

Cole is now affiliated with the Knowledge Is Power Program (KIPP).[45] The school operated in 2005 as a "KIPP Transition School." It did not implement the traditional KIPP approach entirely in its first year but is scheduled to begin operating as a KIPP school in fall 2007. An evaluation of the initial year of the Cole transition process found significant implementation problems at the school, district, and state levels.[46] However, the report also showed significant improvement in the academic performance of the students attending the school in its first year of transition. As a vignette on DPS later in the chapter will explain in more detail, Denver has a variety of restructuring options available to its schools outside of NCLB and fewer schools restructuring through NCLB than through the local options.

In 2006, the Colorado legislature revisited the law mandating the forced chartering of schools and weakened it considerably. The revised law still allows for the potential chartering of failing schools, but it no longer mandates chartering by the state as the only option. Colorado law now allows schools and districts to pursue a full range of restructuring activities similar to those under NCLB.

Despite the differences between the state and federally mandated restructuring efforts, there is still too little experience to judge the efficacy of either approach. The main lesson to be gleaned so far is that policymakers have little stomach for requiring dramatic restructuring. For public school choice and tutoring, NCLB presented a marginal addition to a more substantive state- and district-initiated system. For school restructuring,

NCLB provided a model state leaders could use to dilute a more intense state approach that predated the federal law.

Costs of NCLB Interventions

For each of the one hundred schools included in this analysis, the annual direct cost of implementing the interventions of NCLB was calculated by multiplying the number of students participating in choice and SES by the estimated cost of providing that option to one student.[47] Based on this analysis, the total estimated cost of transporting students in 2005–6 was $6,295 per school, or a total of $629,500 statewide. In no case did NCLB-mandated transportation cost a school's district as much as 1 percent of that school's operating budget.[48] In only thirty cases did the cost reach more than one-tenth of 1 percent of the school's operating budget.

If we examine the sixty-seven schools that were required to provide SES, the estimated costs of the SES provided in 2005–6 and the requisite mailings totaled $63,644 per school, or $4,264,201 statewide. This represented 2 percent of the total budgets generated for these schools by their per-pupil operating revenue. Seven schools spent more than 5 percent of their operating budgets on SES. In thirty-one schools, the portion of the operating budget spent on SES did not reach 1 percent. In thirty-six schools, it accounted for more than 1 percent. If we add the total costs for SES and choice among all one hundred schools, the cost for the state was $4,893,370, and the average cost per school was $48,937.[49]

School Improvement Grants and Calculating the Annual Gain or Loss for Schools Identified under NCLB. Colorado awards School Improvement Grants (SI Grants) to many of its NCLB-identified schools. The awards are generally two-year grants of $150,000. While these grants arguably reward failure, the state also awards smaller grants to schools that look likely to fall into school improvement status in future years. In the first years these grants were offered, the DPS leadership discouraged schools from seeking them.[50] As a result, only eight of the initial thirty-eight SI grants awarded to schools in this study went to DPS schools.[51] Outside Denver, thirty of forty-six identified schools received them. After a change

TABLE 7-3

MEAN COST AND REVENUE FOR NCLB-IDENTIFIED SCHOOLS

	DPS schools ($)	Non-DPS schools ($)	All schools ($)
Choice	9,031	3,084	6,295
SES	53,768	29,580	63,644
Total cost	62,799	32,664	48,937
School improvement grant revenue	11,111	48,913	28,500
Total gain (loss)	(51,688)	16,249	(20,437)

SOURCE: CCC dataset. See endnote 17 for details.

of leadership, Denver's schools are now encouraged to apply for these grants and are increasingly winning them.

The total costs to a school of being identified under NCLB can be calculated by treating each SI Grant as an addition to revenue and by counting the costs of providing choice and SES as expenses. The provision of the SI Grants allows for a calculation of the financial impact on schools of NCLB sanctions. By subtracting the net costs of the SES and choice services as calculated above from $75,000 (one-half the amount of the $150,000 two-year grant), we can derive a rough estimate of the overall annual costs to schools of being identified under NCLB. These estimates are admittedly crude, as the overall costs of SES and choice are not necessarily limited to two years.[52]

If we examine the schools outside Denver, where districts welcomed SI Grants in 2005–6, the average NCLB-identified school gained $16,249, an increase in its respective budget of seven-tenths of 1 percent. Within Denver, where the chances of receiving an SI Grant in the initial years were slim and the average costs were higher, the net results are negative. The average school lost $51,688, or 1.6 percent of its operating budget, as a result of its NCLB identification. If we assume each Denver school were to receive the amount of money the average non-DPS schools received through the SI Grants in 2005, the average Denver school would still lose $13,886, or about one-half of 1 percent of its operating budget. The financial returns for schools inside and outside Denver and for all schools statewide are reported in table 7-3.[53]

District Case #1: Denver Public Schools

DPS is a single district serving the city and county of Denver. The district is Colorado's second-largest, serving 73,000 students in 151 schools.[54] Its students are about 80 percent minority and FRPL, and 57 percent Hispanic, 19 percent black, 20 percent white, 3 percent Asian, and 1 percent American Indian. It has experienced a significant increase in its Hispanic population recently, and 20 percent of the students are English-language learners. DPS received nearly $28 million in Title I funding in 2006,[55] which is up from $15.5 in 2001. No other district in the state received even a third as much.

Denver has the largest number of schools that are identified as struggling under both state and federal provisions, with fifty-six in some form of identification under NCLB.[56] In 2005, DPS had sixteen schools in the first year of school improvement and twelve in year 2, eleven schools in corrective action, twelve planning for restructuring, and three implementing restructuring plans. Under the SAR system, Denver had five unsatisfactory schools, and 58 percent of the schools were rated as low, compared to 16 percent statewide.

Denver has a great deal of school choice. The district emerged from court-ordered desegregation in 1997 and sought to diversify its schools through a mixture of magnet schools, neighborhood schools, and extensive public school choice. This approach has not succeeded in solving its problems with racial, ethnic, and economic stratification; outside evaluators documented significant resegregation.[57] It has, however, generated school choice. DPS officials report that about 32 percent of the current enrollees exercise intradistrict choice and attend a DPS school other than the one they would attend according to residence.[58] In addition, 5,464 Denver residents attended public schools in neighboring districts in 2005—almost 7 percent of potential DPS enrollees. The district has nineteen charters, nine magnets, and several alternative and contract schools serving specific special populations.[59]

Implementing NCLB in Denver. DPS leaders have tried to implement the public school choice, SES, and restructuring aspects of NCLB. However, in each case, similar efforts are already underway through state law and local initiatives that operate at greater scales.

Choice. According to state officials, DPS had 800 students exercising choice under NCLB in 2005–6, representing 2 percent of the enrollment of the identified schools.[60] This compares to roughly 26,500 students exercising other forms of choice in DPS (including both intra- and inter-district choice).[61] The choice driven by NCLB in DPS has increased each year in the district, and district officials expect it to continue to rise. District officials attribute the rise to several district-level policy decisions. For example, the district provides transportation to students throughout their entire enroll-ment in the receiving school, regardless of any subsequent improvement in the sending school's designation. It also offers transportation to students who are too young to have yet attended the NCLB-designated school, but who would have potentially entered the low-performing school the next year. The district makes this offer even if such children live in attendance areas where their residence entitles them to choose from among several neighborhood schools, regardless of whether one of the other neighborhood schools was performing well enough to not be identified under NCLB.

To manage the logistics of choice, the district offers transportation to participating students based on existing transportation routes serving its magnet schools. DPS gives high school students city bus passes.[62] Thus, the incremental costs of busing the NCLB students is less than it would be if routes were created from scratch.

The district mails packets written in English and Spanish to all eligible families. They include information on all 151 of the district's schools, as well as application materials. The completed forms are due at the same time as all other applications for the district's open-enrollment process, but the district gives priority to students in NCLB-designated schools.

SES. DPS had 1,953 students receiving SES in 2005, or 10.7 percent of the 18,234 eligible students in the district.[63] Denver enjoys the largest number of approved SES providers in the state—twenty-six. As is the case with school choice, DPS has a great many other tutoring and after-school programs in place besides the tutoring under NCLB, with at least ten other district-run after-school programs operating in 178 schools.[64] Numbers on total participa-tion are unavailable, but general reports indicate a pattern similar to that for school choice. DPS facilitates NCLB tutoring, but the scale of NCLB-mandated services is smaller than that of similar district-administered programs.

Restructuring. Denver is also home to a variety of restructuring initiatives in addition to those mandated by NCLB. As noted, Denver was the site of Colorado's one and only forced chartering of a school under the state's accountability law. The district's voters also raised their property taxes to provide money for "revitalizing" low-performing schools, which use the funding to support external consultants who assist with a strategic planning process. And DPS is creating a set of "Beacon" Schools, modeled on Boston's Pilot Schools, that will enjoy freedom from some rules and regulations in exchange for heightened accountability and their commitment to implementing reform. The district has a vibrant charter sector, and it contracts with outside providers to run schools, generally serving special populations, such as pregnant students and students who are parents.

These options create many ways to create new schools and reform existing ones. More than forty DPS schools are engaged in one or more of these strategies. Previously, the district resisted funding and technical assistance from outside providers—not only from NCLB, but also from change advocates like the Bill and Melinda Gates Foundation—preferring to support locally initiated reform mechanisms. Under new leadership, DPS is now encouraging schools to add Title I resources to these efforts.[65] Thus, NCLB is adding resources and a new rationale to local restructuring initiatives.

Discussion. DPS has worked to implement the interventions for struggling schools mandated by NCLB. People in Denver no longer debate the problems with student performance identified by NCLB, and the menu of strategies they consider as they work to address these challenges includes all of those from NCLB. Compared to the locally initiated versions of reform, the work linked to NCLB is modest, but it is real.

The NCLB interventions are helping the district's school improvement efforts. Federal mandates are producing slight increases in public school choice and SES participation, and they may add money to restructuring efforts pursued through state law and local initiative. However, it is difficult to determine what would be different in DPS without NCLB. The same local conditions that help DPS implement NCLB more vigorously than other Colorado districts could easily have produced these outcomes themselves. In this case, the apparent power of NCLB may reflect a false positive. The behavior sought by NCLB is taking place, but there is little reason to believe federal law produced it.

District Case #2: Cortez

Cortez is a small town located in the southwest corner of Colorado. It is the gateway to the Mesa Verde National Park, home to ancient Indian cliff dwellings. The town has about 8,000 residents. The school district of Montezuma-Cortez serves 3,264 students in the city and surrounding rural areas.[66] About 10 percent of these students are American Indians and 12 percent Hispanic,[67] and 49 percent qualify for FRPL.[68] Two district-run elementary schools in the town are identified for school improvement under NCLB.[69] While the Cortez district contains twelve schools, including two charters, this total overstates the potential for choice, as three of the schools are one-room schoolhouses located in remote areas.

Implementing NCLB in Cortez. Colorado's districts that have only one elementary school can easily ignore NCLB. Cortez is just big enough to have to deal with it. The district is also big enough to have its own programs competing with NCLB provisions. As it turns out, these local programs are more significant than the NCLB interventions.

Choice. The Cortez district has had few families exercising intradistrict choice by transferring to district-run schools within the town. However, 233 students, or about 8 percent of school-age residents, attend schools in nearby districts,[70] and 190 students in the district attend two independently managed charter schools also located in the district. According to district officials, a new online charter school operating statewide is also attracting local students. The district's enrollment declined by about two hundred students between 2005 and 2006, which district leaders attribute to declining population and the availability of the online charter school. The district plans to expand its own online program to try to win back these students.

Two elementary schools in town were identified under NCLB. Kemper and Manaugh, both in the corrective-action phase of school improvement in 2005, serve more than three hundred students. Manaugh's student population is 23 percent American Indian, 12 percent Hispanic, and 53 percent FRPL. Kemper is about 3 percent American Indian, 12 percent Hispanic, and 77 percent FRPL.[71]

Under NCLB, students at Kemper and Manaugh could choose either of the other elementary schools in the town that were not identified. In 2005, only one student exercised this option.[72] The student's family received $527 dollars, at forty cents a mile, to subsidize transportation. As of October 2006, no students had decided to transfer under NCLB for the 2006–7 school year.

Supplemental Educational Services. SES generates a little more interest in Cortez than choice. The district has an online provider approved for the area as well as a local provider of SES with a history of working with the district. District officials speak favorably of the organization. "We've done grants together and have a relationship," explains the district's Title I coordinator and assistant superintendent, David Cruz. Under NCLB, the district provided services to a total of twenty-five students in 2005, spending $14,500 on all SES.[73] As of October 2006, two students had signed up for NCLB tutoring for the 2006–7 school year. District leaders do not use deadlines for funding SES tutoring. Instead, they allow all interested eligible families to work with the provider all year until their budgetary allotment is used up for each student. They expect total usage in 2006 to be similar to that of the previous year. According to Cruz, SES under NCLB did not stir up much excitement. As he summarized, "We had room for a lot more, and kids didn't jump on that option."

The community is interested in after-school programs and tutoring, just not NCLB. The district's 21st Century Community Learning Centers (CCLCs) serve 363 students in Kemper and Manaugh.[74] This is more than fifteen times as many as served by the NCLB provider in the two NCLB-identified schools. These programs are funded by grants that provide about $50,000 per year to each school.

The most significant impact of NCLB on the district has been additional funding. Both Cortez schools received $150,000 School Improvement Grants under NCLB.[75]

Discussion. For Cortez, implementing the interventions required by NCLB has not been punitive. Taking into account the expenses of choice and SES and the income from new grants, the district appears to gain about $135,000 a year by having two schools identified as failing under NCLB. The community does not appear either enraged or inspired by this designation. The funding, meanwhile, is perhaps more important to the long-term benefit of Cortez's children than the choice and SES provided by federal law.

Tutoring and choice exist in Cortez, but both are driven more by factors outside NCLB than by federal law. Colorado's charter school program, interdistrict choice, and geography generate more choice than NCLB. Furthermore, district-run tutoring programs, like Cortez's 21st Century Community Learning Centers, provide a great deal more service. The difference between SES under NCLB and other supplemental programs is stark, given that the approved SES provider in Cortez is a historical partner welcomed by the district. In small communities like Cortez, NCLB appears to be too weak a lever to boost reforms that already had momentum on their own.

Conclusion

If public school choice, SES, and school restructuring are the tools for improving school performance, NCLB appears to be a clumsy way of extending their reach. Most of the analysis above has focused on process rather than performance. It is still too early to judge the connections between these interventions and academic achievement. However, there are clues in their implementation that arouse concern.

NCLB generates too little choice in Colorado to expect any appreciable increase in student performance overall, even if these choices produce tremendous gains for the few students who exercise them. More students participate in SES programs, but the total is still only about one-tenth of those eligible. This participation rate seems significant only in comparison to the failure of NCLB to increase choice in Colorado. The large number of SES providers and the questionable efficacy of some make it likely that any increases in performance among students receiving tutoring will be unevenly distributed. This could mean that the total number of students who benefit academically from effective tutoring will be a small subset of an already modest total. School restructuring is also affecting too few schools in Colorado at this point to hold out much hope for increasing achievement. In sum, NCLB interventions produce little action—and what does occur is not likely to improve academic performance significantly.

The current interventions under NCLB all provide students in struggling schools with alternatives and hope of a better education. That is enough to recommend that the nation continue to provide them for now. Further evaluations focusing on the links between the interventions and improved performance are also necessary. And several adjustments to the current interventions could be made now that might increase their impact. For example, to increase participation in SES programs, districts should be required to select at least one provider to locate services in the school; alternatively, districts could remain eligible as providers or be allowed to partner with outside providers regardless of their AYP status, as is the case in 21st Century Community Learning Centers. And, as many have suggested, NCLB's fifth school restructuring option of "other major restructuring" should be removed or refined, or incentives created to encourage schools to pursue more profound versions of reform.

But more should be done. If the federal government intends to promote action in schools and districts to improve performance, evidence from Colorado suggests that additional interventions are required. Rather than forcing schools to do a little bit more of things they are already doing, NCLB would have more impact on its stated goals if federal authority were used to compel states and local communities to implement effective reforms that they are not doing now, or that are difficult for them to do through state law or local initiative alone.

Future interventions should be judged on their ability to

- serve significantly more of the students who are most at risk of falling behind;

- help those students achieve at higher levels; and

- promote new action rather than rely on or duplicate state and local initiatives that are already underway.

By these criteria, the current mix of interventions is not faring well. Several possible interventions would meet the criteria above. These same proposals have the added advantage of supporting another education reform that is gaining momentum nationwide. The changes would strengthen student transitions between grades and help states build school systems that serve children from preschool through college, or "P–16" systems. These new interventions could include, first, providing high-quality, full-day preschool for three- and four-year-old children, as well as full-day kindergarten for all low-income children in the neighborhoods surrounding elementary schools that are identified as needing improvement. Preschool providers could include centers not operated by the district, as well as district-run facilities. Second, the public school choice provisions of NCLB could be expanded to include mandatory interdistrict choice and postsecondary open enrollment.

These recommendations differ from the current interventions in that they are difficult for districts and local schools to achieve through their own initiative. Federal power could be used to good advantage by forcing states to step in and orchestrate these options. In the absence of outside authority, individual districts are unlikely or unable to pursue them because they require action by other parties, including local K–12 schools, neighboring districts, preschool providers, and higher-education entities. Ironically, the difficulty of implementing these actions is precisely what makes them better candidates for federal coercion. The combination of federal pressure and state authority could make local implementation of these reforms more likely and effective than would be the case without the federal pressure.

While there is controversy on whether public school choice will improve performance for either the students who leave or those who are left behind, high-quality preschool programs have a strong correlation with improved academic outcomes. Of course, states would still have challenges similar to those with SES in fostering quality among preschool providers and in aligning preschool instruction with kindergarten standards in developmentally appropriate ways. Expanding choice to include postsecondary and interdistrict options may improve performance. In addition, it would at least provide more students an option to supplement their educations or flee schools that are failing to educate them. Other options should also be considered. Sticking with the current slate would be a disservice to the children who we know deserve more.

8

Michigan: Over the First Hurdle

David N. Plank and Christopher Dunbar Jr.

How can we make persistently ineffective schools effective? How can we create consistently successful schools for severely disadvantaged students? At present no one knows the answer to these questions. Policy initiatives aimed at raising achievement levels in low-performing schools have instead relied upon two competing sets of hypotheses. On the one hand, some scholars have argued that "turning around" schools where performance persistently fails to meet expectations depends on the provision of technical assistance: new knowledge, and support for translating new knowledge into practice.[1] Improving performance therefore requires additional resources and training, backed up by research aimed at learning how to move schools from failure to success. On the other hand, a variety of critics have argued that the persistent failures of schools serving poor and minority youngsters originate in the perverse incentives and bureaucratic strictures that characterize urban school systems, which fail to put children's interests first.[2] Improvement therefore requires the disruption of prevailing relationships and routines, and the introduction of more powerful sanctions and incentives.

Traditional approaches to the problem of persistently low-performing schools have been guided by the first set of hypotheses. Under versions of the Elementary and Secondary Education Act previous to No Child Left Behind (NCLB), for example, funds were allocated to individual schools to enable them to hire aides, purchase professional development services, and

The authors would like to thank Monica Evans, Derrick Lopez, and Laura McNeal for their assistance with the research on which this chapter is based.

otherwise enhance the knowledge and skills of local educators. In contrast to the traditional ESEA approach (often construed by critics as "rewarding failure"), NCLB exhibits a preference for sanctions that originate in the second set of hypotheses, shifting resources away from failing schools and seeking to punish failure by dismissing ineffective staff and enhancing incentives for success in meeting performance expectations.

One way of evaluating the NCLB hypotheses is to ask whether the cascading sanctions foreseen by the law have been implemented in good faith. After all, we will only know if the school reform strategy proposed in NCLB works if the sanctions are systematically put into practice. From this perspective, as we shall argue below, the implementation of NCLB in Michigan has fallen far short of expectations, and in some instances even of legal requirements.

In the absence of strong prior evidence about whether the NCLB sanctions will work, however, it might be argued that the critical question is not whether the sanctions prescribed under NCLB have been faithfully implemented in Michigan or elsewhere, but whether performance has improved in schools that are "in need of improvement" under NCLB criteria, regardless of the strategies adopted by state and local policymakers. Policy judgments from this point of view place Michigan in a more flattering light, as school districts across the state have successfully met the act's adequate yearly progress (AYP) standard and moved significant numbers of low-performing schools off the "critical list" of persistently low-performing schools maintained by the Michigan Department of Education (MDE).

In this chapter we review the ways in which the MDE and selected Michigan school districts have responded to NCLB sanctions, with a particular focus on their implementation of the mandate to restructure schools that have failed to meet AYP targets for four years or more. We conducted interviews with MDE officials, and with district and school administrators in the Flint and Grand Rapids school districts.[3] We also examined the response to NCLB sanctions in a Michigan charter school (legally equivalent to a school district) that had failed to make AYP for four consecutive years, conducting interviews both with school officials and with senior administrators in the Charter School Office at Central Michigan University.

The Michigan story reflects an irony: Weak implementation of NCLB has led to the accomplishment of NCLB's central goals. The school improvement strategies adopted by MDE officials and their district counterparts are, at best, a pale reflection of the robust sanctions prescribed under federal law. Officials have almost uniformly demonstrated a preference for gentle interventions, eschewing approaches that threaten staff, deprive schools of resources, or disrupt established routines. Preliminary evidence on the effectiveness of these approaches nevertheless suggests that they are working reasonably well, as many of the most troubled schools in Michigan have made AYP for two consecutive years and reset the sanctions clock to zero.

The question then becomes whether the implementation of the prescribed "sanctions cascade" matters in itself, or whether the implementation of alternative strategies that lead to positive outcomes reflects a sufficient level of compliance. The spotlight that NCLB shines on the performance of schools, coupled with the *threat* of sanctions for those that persistently fall short, appears to have persuaded schools to systematically improve their own performance, despite the subjection of only a handful of schools to significant sanctions.

We argue, in conclusion, that the goals and expectations introduced by NCLB have begun to be institutionalized in Michigan's education system, with positive consequences for the state's schools and students. The breadth and depth of this institutionalization will be tested in the next few years, however, in three ways. First, the height of the AYP hurdles that schools must clear will increase with time, and it remains to be seen whether the strategies preferred by MDE (or the strategies mandated by NCLB) will serve to sustain and accelerate recent performance gains. Second, getting middle and high schools over the AYP and other hurdles that still lie before them presents challenges that are significantly more complex and difficult than the state has faced in improving the performance of elementary schools, and it is uncertain what strategies will improve the performance of schools serving older students. Finally, current efforts by schools and school districts to improve their own performance are apparently motivated at least in part by the threat of sanctions, but the efficacy of this threat depends on the state's credible commitment to imposing significant changes on schools that continue to fall short of NCLB goals. With some schools now in their eighth consecutive year of failure to make AYP, MDE must soon demonstrate that the threat of sanctions has real force behind it, or else run the risk that the energy driving current reform efforts will dissipate.

NCLB in Michigan: The Political Context

In contrast to the period immediately following the law's adoption in 2001, NCLB has, for the most part, moved off the political and policy radars in Michigan. Despite the continued hostility of the state's teachers' unions, NCLB is now largely taken for granted as the central element in the state's accountability system. Such controversies as do arise emerge over technical issues, including the definition and adoption of confidence intervals on students' and schools' test scores and the development of appropriate assessment instruments for English-language learners and children with special needs. These engage the attention of officials in Lansing and in Washington, but they rarely rise to public attention and attract no comment from the governor or the legislature.

In the recent electoral campaign, for example, U.S. Senator Debbie Stabenow endorsed the "good intentions" that motivated NCLB, while asserting that the law has been "poorly implemented," both in terms of insufficient funding and "overemphasis on standardized tests." In her endorsement interview with the Michigan Education Association (MEA) she pledged to seek full funding for the law.[4] Governor Jennifer Granholm has been supportive of NCLB from the beginning.[5] She also was endorsed by the MEA, but was not even asked about NCLB in her endorsement interview.[6] Unlike Tom Watkins, who preceded him as Michigan's superintendent of public instruction, current superintendent Mike Flanagan has focused on effective implementation of NCLB, rather than public resistance to the law's provisions. The early conflict over NCLB in Michigan originated in part in the state's simultaneous efforts to implement NCLB and its own accountability system (known as *Education YES!*).[7] The discrepancies between the two systems are no longer a matter of great concern, except within the Michigan Department of Education, which is responsible for administering both.

Education YES! determines whether Michigan schools are accredited or not, and awards letter grades to schools based on a number of different criteria, including student progress and schools' self-reports on local conditions for learning. In fact, however, most Michigan schools continue to seek accreditation from the North Central Association (which will, according to one MDE official, "accredit *anyone*"), with the result that most schools can claim to be accredited without regard to their grades under *Education YES!*

Beyond this, *Education YES!* has been plagued by conceptual and implementation problems from its inception. The problems include statistical and measurement issues related to the evaluation of change in the performance of schools and students, along with opportunities that the system provides to schools and districts to game the system and avoid the lowest grades through their self-reports.[8] According to a senior official in the MDE, "only a handful" of districts pay attention to the letter grades produced under *Education YES!* and most of these are high-performing suburban districts anxious to ensure that all of their schools are graded "A." As a result, judgments based on schools' success or failure in making AYP under NCLB clearly take precedence over the grades produced by *Education YES!* in the perceptions of educators and parents. According to one parent, "I don't think parents understand what [the grades] are. I don't think *Education Yes!* is parent friendly, and I don't think a lot of parents pay attention to it."[9]

Despite their initial resistance to NCLB, many Michigan educators now acknowledge that the federal law has had a salutary effect on the state's schools. As one administrator in an urban school district stated, "Four years ago I couldn't see anything good in NCLB. But it has forced us to focus on what's taught and learned in our schools, and it has supported our efforts to align teaching with our curriculum standards."

How Many Michigan Schools Face Sanctions?

Michigan has had a statewide testing regime since the mid-1990s, well prior to the adoption of NCLB, and the state is consequently ahead of many others in the timeline of NCLB sanctions. When NCLB was initially implemented in 2002, Michigan had more than two hundred schools that had failed to make AYP for as many as four years, and nearly one hundred of these schools were immediately subjected to the full array of NCLB sanctions.[10] For the same reason, Michigan now has more than thirty schools facing restructuring, including a significant number that have reached their seventh or eighth year of failure to meet AYP targets. These schools have been placed on MDE's "critical list," where they are subject to close scrutiny and supervision by state officials.

In 2005–6, there were 343 Michigan schools "identified for improvement" under NCLB, having failed to make AYP for at least two years (see table 8-1). This represented approximately 10 percent of all Michigan schools. Of these, 207 were in the first two phases of sanctions, obliged to provide transportation to students who wished to transfer to higher-performing schools (105 schools) or to fund transportation and supplementary educational services for their students (102). Of the remaining schools, more than half (79) were in phase 3, which required them to take "corrective action" to improve the performance of their students.

As table 8-1 shows, in 2005–6 there were fifty-seven Michigan middle and elementary schools that had failed to make AYP for six or more years. Thirteen of these schools were "in delay," having successfully made AYP at least once since they were identified for improvement. The remaining forty-four schools had failed to make AYP for at least six years; more than half (twenty-five schools) found themselves on the critical list, having failed to make AYP for seven or eight consecutive years. All but one of these schools were in seven high-poverty urban school districts, with more than two-thirds located in Detroit. NCLB requires these schools to implement significant changes in their governance arrangements.

An additional fifty-five schools that had reached the restructuring phase of NCLB sanctions had been removed from the list of schools facing NCLB sanctions. Having made AYP for two consecutive years, their sanctions clocks had been reset to zero.

The Implementation of NCLB Sanctions in Michigan

In Michigan the implementation of the sanctions cascade prescribed by NCLB has been half-hearted at best. There is no evidence that any child in Michigan has requested or received funding from a local school district to pay for transportation from a school subject to NCLB sanctions to a more successful school. The provision of supplementary educational services has been subject to a variety of administrative and other problems that have prevented many children from receiving services and made it virtually impossible to assess program impact. At the same time, however, the significance attached to schools' success or failure to make AYP, combined with the threat of restruc-

TABLE 8-1

COMPARISON OF SCHOOLS BY AYP PHASE 2006 AND 2005

School Phase 2005	School Phase 2006								Total schools by 2005 phase
	0 Not identified for improvement	1 School improvement: Choice	2 School improvement: Choice and SES	3 Corrective action	4 Restructuring	5 Implement restructuring plan	6 Unspecified under the law	7 Unspecified under the law	
0 Not identified for improvement	3,244	56							3,300
1 School improvement: Choice	78	49	75						202
2 School improvement: Choice and SES	11		25	76					112
3 Corrective action	19		1	3	8				31
4 Restructuring	26		1		7	11			45
5 Implement restructuring plan	29				1	4	21		55
6 Unspecified under the law							1	4	5
Total schools by 2006 phase	3,407	105	102	79	16	15	22	4	3,750

■ Schools no longer identified for improvement (off the list)—163 schools

▨ Schools in delay (met AYP one or more years since initial identification)—92 schools

▢ Schools progressing along NCLB sanction path (no AYP since initial identification) —251 schools

SOURCE: Unpublished data provided by the Office of Educational Assessment and Accountabilily, Michigan Department of Education.

NOTE: When a school or district becomes subject to a new phase of remedies at the end of a school year, that phase's requirements take effect beginning the following school year. NCLB explicitly prescribes remedies only for the first five years of school failure. Schools that have continued to fail beyond those first five years enter phases with no additional specified remedies under the law.

turing, appears to have concentrated the minds of officials at both state and district levels, and focused their attention on the state's lowest-performing schools. The strategies they have adopted have departed fairly dramatically from the expectations articulated in NCLB, but they nevertheless appear to have been effective in motivating many schools to make AYP and remove themselves from the critical list.

NCLB School Choice. As in other states, the choice provisions of NCLB have proved inconsequential in Michigan. There are two main reasons this is so. First, school choice is so pervasive in Michigan that the opportunities to switch schools provided under NCLB disappear into irrelevance. Michigan has one of the nation's most permissive charter school laws. There are nearly two hundred charter schools in operation, with most located in the state's main metropolitan areas where most low-performing schools are also located. In addition, Michigan has adopted policies that allow virtually unrestricted interdistrict choice. State law permits students to transfer to any school that offers places in their own or any contiguous intermediate school district (ISD).[11] In addition, most of Michigan's urban school districts have adopted open-enrollment policies that permit students to enroll in any school in the district with space available. In consequence of these policies, students who wish to transfer to different schools already enjoy a wide variety of choices, and the transfer options offered under NCLB add little or nothing to the array.

Second, in Detroit, where publicly funded opportunities to move might conceivably make a difference for some students, the number of places in schools that are *not* under NCLB sanctions is too small to accommodate eligible pupils. The problem is compounded by a weak public transportation system, by an intractable budget crisis (which has virtually eliminated the district's ability to provide transportation to students under any circumstances), and by rules imposed by the Detroit Public Schools (DPS) that limit the number of schools to which eligible students might transfer.

Apart from these obstacles, school districts and charter schools have displayed little enthusiasm for the school choice provisions of NCLB. School officials are careful to comply with the law's requirements, sending letters that inform parents of their options under the law, but the burden of subsequent action is clearly left to the households of children enrolled in low-performing schools.

Supplemental Educational Services (SES). The supplemental educational services program was previously isolated from other offices within

MDE concerned with NCLB, and treated as a compliance problem rather than as an opportunity to provide additional services to students in low-performing schools. As a result, according to a senior official, the SES program was characterized by "a complete lack of clarity or responsibility." The department is just beginning to "get our [act] together," and officials are currently searching for a short-term consultant to "get the SES provider chaos organized and evaluated." As a result of both inattention and incapacity at the state level, neither MDE nor local school districts have made much effort to ensure that eligible children have access to SES.

There are 117 approved providers of SES in Michigan, ranging from small "kitchen table" operations with only a single tutor to national corporations, including Edison Schools and Sylvan Learning Systems. The list includes a dozen Michigan school districts, along with four intermediate school districts. According to current MDE data, 87 of these providers were actively engaged in offering SES to students in the 2005–6 school year.[12]

As we have discussed in a previous study, problems on both sides of the market continue to limit the number of Michigan students who take advantage of SES.[13] Students lack information about SES opportunities. In contrast to California and other states, the state's NCLB website supplies almost no information that would be useful to parents beyond phone numbers (and sometimes web addresses) for the providers that the department has approved.[14] School districts are required to provide some additional information in the letters they send to parents informing them of SES opportunities, but the primary burden of choosing providers and enrolling students continues to fall on parents. The number of children who enroll consequently remains small, relative to the number who are eligible for services.

Some providers are reportedly disenchanted with SES. Though the numbers of children eligible to receive subsidies to participate in SES are large, the amounts of money available to provide the subsidies are considerably smaller. In Detroit, for example, NCLB regulations require districts to set aside 20 percent of their Title I appropriation to pay for transportation and SES, which comes to approximately $13 million. Even if a district spends nothing at all on transportation (as appears to be the case), the funds that are set aside cannot nearly support SES for all eligible students, supposing even minimal costs per student. The economics of SES are made even less attractive by requirements included in the contracts negotiated between SES providers and some districts that providers rent space in district schools or hire district employees to serve as SES tutors.

As a result of these problems, relatively few Michigan students are taking advantage of SES opportunities. In 2005–6 approximately 12,500 Michigan students received tutoring services funded with Title I resources. Nearly three-quarters of these students were in Detroit, with an additional 12 percent in Flint. Statewide, students participating in SES received an average of thirty-two hours of tutoring, with those in Detroit and Flint receiving approximately the average number of hours. Elsewhere the number of hours varied widely. Students in the Highland Park school district received less than ten hours of SES on average, while students in Albion received more than sixty. In some Michigan districts with schools in which students were eligible to receive SES in 2005–6, including Benton Harbor and Lansing, no students received tutoring services. This means that these districts spent none of their Title I funds on transportation or SES, despite the NCLB requirement that they set aside 20 percent of the funds for these purposes.[15] At the local level, one principal whose school offers SES to its students was dismissive of the program: "The Supplemental After School [SES] Programs directed by Bush and NCLB are really not doing anything to help us with our kids." In her view, the idea that children who do poorly in school during the day will perform better in an after-school program that resembles the day-school program and often features the same teachers is "simply misguided."

NCLB requires states to evaluate SES in 2006, and MDE has contracted for an evaluation by a private-sector policy research firm in Lansing. Because there is no field for SES participation in Michigan's student data system, however, the evaluation is unlikely to provide any useful information on the question of whether SES produces learning gains among students who take advantage of these opportunities.

Restructuring. The sanctions imposed by MDE on schools that have failed to make AYP for four years or more have, for the most part, been considerably more district-friendly than the "tough love" foreseen by the framers of NCLB, relying on self-diagnosis and self-medication rather than external intervention. They have, for now, converged around a set of approaches that emphasize the acquisition of knowledge about effective practice by current

school personnel and the development of local capacity to translate knowledge into action.

The sanctions foreseen under NCLB have the potential seriously to disrupt the lives of educators in low-performing schools, challenging the comfortable assumptions on which they base their claims to professional
authority or even costing them their livelihoods. Putting this kind of shock
therapy into practice is likely to generate widespread anxiety among them,
and active opposition by their unions. As a result, both state and local officials in Michigan have proved deeply reluctant to pull the trigger on the
harsh changes in governance and leadership proposed under NCLB, opting
instead for a far gentler set of remedies.

Despite their general failure to comply with the "restructuring" requirements laid out under NCLB, however, the gentle approaches adopted by
MDE and district officials have worked well enough that fully half of the
schools engaged in the restructuring process have made AYP for two consecutive years and removed themselves from the department's "critical list."
Even in Detroit a number of elementary schools have significantly improved
their academic performance. In middle and high schools throughout the
state, in contrast, the process has yet to show similar results.

In the sections that follow we describe the key elements of the MDE strategy for restructuring low-performing schools and describe the ways in which
restructuring has been implemented in two urban school districts and one
urban charter school. We conclude with a discussion of the ways in which
NCLB is becoming institutionalized in Michigan's education system.

State-Level Strategies for Restructuring Low-Performing Schools

The implementation strategies adopted by the Michigan Department of
Education are attributable to two principal constraints. The first is institutional. MDE has virtually no capacity to oversee what is happening in
school districts and schools, or to ensure district compliance with federal or
state policy directives.[16] The department has devoted substantial resources
to enhancing capabilities in the state assessment program, and the reliability and timeliness of reports to schools have improved dramatically. The
devotion of scarce resources to strengthening assessment has limited the

resources available for other critical tasks, however, with the result that the department has come to rely almost entirely on short-term consultants funded by soft money from federal grants in its efforts to fulfill critical obligations, including the oversight of NCLB. Consequently, oversight is generally weak and sporadic, even in schools on the "critical list" to which MDE devotes the most attention, and MDE is obliged to rely on the good faith of local officials to ensure policy implementation.[17] The second constraint is political, and it originates in a widespread disinclination at both state and local levels to confront Michigan's teachers' unions, or to disrupt significantly the professional lives of their members.

The department's strategy for implementing NCLB is therefore district-friendly, relying on exhortation and conceptual guidance for local school improvement efforts rather than direct interventions or the imposition of sanctions. In addition, the department has found itself obliged to work with and through a variety of partners, including intermediate school districts and charter school authorizers. Key elements of the strategy focus on enhancing knowledge and capacity at the local level, to enable school districts to diagnose their own weaknesses and adopt locally devised measures to address them. At the same time, however, the department has at least begun to explore the possibility that more rigorous sanctions will be required to turn around Michigan's least successful schools.

Building Knowledge and Capacity. The foundation of the MDE's school improvement strategy is the "Michigan School Improvement Framework." The framework is contained in a relatively brief (twenty-page) document that summarizes "current research and best practice" pertaining to the school improvement process.[18] To encourage local educators to consider alternative strategies to enhance the effectiveness of their schools, MDE has also developed a user-friendly "toolkit for school reform" known as MI-Map, which offers instruments for self-diagnosis at the school level, along with "ruthlessly practical strategies" for school improvement.[19] A friendly cartoon character shaped like a map of Michigan encourages schools to begin their work with MI-Map by bringing all personnel in a school together to play the "fun and easy" MI-Map game, which structures opportunities to discuss a school's strengths and weaknesses and identify areas in which improvement is needed. In 2004–5 MDE provided training in the use of MI-Map for all schools in the first two phases of NCLB sanctions, in the hope of encouraging them to improve student performance, make AYP, and avoid the obligation to restructure.

In keeping with the department's focus on enhancing local knowledge and building local capacity, one strategy for turning around low-performing schools that has received particularly warm support is the provision of "coaches." A consortium of educational organizations, including the Michigan Education Association and Michigan State University, has worked to recruit and train coaches and to place them in schools. Schools throughout the state have, in turn, used their Elementary and Secondary Education Act (ESEA) funds to hire coaches to work with principals and school staffs to help focus their efforts and improve their schools' performance. Some ISDs and school districts have also adopted the coaching model, putting their own resources into coaching and technical assistance for low-performing schools.

To date there has not been much systematic evaluation of the effectiveness of the coaches' network, or of the strategy of relying on coaches, but officials at all levels of the education system remain enthusiastic about the program. The emerging consensus asserts that ex-principals make the best coaches; that coaches are most effective when they work directly with school principals rather than entire staffs; and that they must spend at least a hundred days in a building to make an appreciable difference in school performance. According to an MDE official who generally subscribes to these conclusions, however, the consensus has its origins in a number of "great stories" about coaches who are making a difference, and not in data on the performance of coaches or the schools in which they work.

Contemplating Sanctions. Because Michigan inaugurated its state testing program well in advance of the adoption of NCLB, four schools (three middle schools and one elementary school, all in Detroit) now find themselves in phase 7 of NCLB sanctions. This means that they are in their eighth consecutive year of failure to make AYP, on the far side of the restructuring process. NCLB is silent on what is to be done with these schools.

According to officials in the MDE, the department is considering two main approaches to schools in phase 7 which depart fairly dramatically from the relatively gentle remedies that have been implemented to date. On the one hand, the department's current advice to districts is to "shut down" schools where the restructuring required by NCLB does not produce adequate progress toward the NCLB goal of proficiency for all students, reopening these schools with an entirely new staff. MDE has not yet put this advice into practice, however.

On the other hand, MDE is considering the appointment of takeover trustees for schools that enter the "twilight zone" of phase 7. These schools would reopen as "hybrid charters," under the administrative authority of one of Michigan's many charter school authorizers.[20] Establishing such schools would require the state legislature to raise Michigan's current cap on the number of charters that can be issued, or to create a separate cap for these new schools. It would also render existing labor agreements null and void for employees in these schools, as already happens in schools that receive an *Education YES!* grade of "not accredited" for three consecutive years.[21] According to a senior figure in the charter school sector, however, the plan has met with considerable skepticism among charter school authorizers. They are not convinced that the department will be able to overcome the opposition of unions and their political allies in the legislature and on the state Board of Education to transferring the degree of discretionary authority that would be required to "break the bonds of dysfunction" in persistently low-performing schools.

District Implementation

Like the restructuring strategies employed by the state, those adopted at the district level have relied on relatively gentle sanctions rather than the more disruptive governance changes foreseen under NCLB. As one senior administrator from Flint put it, "We never entertained the possibility of closing schools or replacing staff." Instead, districts have emphasized direct efforts to improve teaching and learning, working for the most part with current personnel to focus their attention on key learning goals. The strategies adopted in different districts vary in the details of implementation, but they converge on four critical features:

- Alignment of instruction with key learning objectives

- Frequent assessments of student performance

- Use of assessment data to target instruction

- Employment of turnaround specialists or coaches to provide guidance and advice to principals, and to help them focus their attention on the improvement of student achievement

These measures correspond weakly at best to the governance changes foreseen under NCLB, but they have proved surprisingly successful in improving performance in elementary schools across the state. Many of these schools, faced with the threat of restructuring, have made AYP targets for two consecutive years, thus resetting the NCLB clock to zero. The absolute level of student achievement in these schools often remains low, and it is too early to say whether their relatively modest accomplishments can be sustained as AYP requirements continue to rise.

Flint. Because of the precipitous decline of the local auto industry, Flint has experienced a dramatic and continuing loss of population. This has produced a steady fall in enrollment and a permanent budget crisis in the Flint City School District. The district now enrolls approximately twenty thousand students, of whom 80 percent are African-American, and nearly two-thirds are eligible for free or reduced-price lunch.

District officials in Flint based their restructuring strategy on two priorities: the "taught curriculum" that is delivered in classrooms, and school leadership. They defended their strategy against the governance changes proposed under NCLB, which they characterized as "just moving people around." In both areas they gave primary attention to school principals, providing them with guidance and training aimed at shifting their focus from "administrivia" to instructional improvement. According to one district official, the message to principals was, "We're not here to beat you up, or take your job. We're here to support you."[22] The district has also provided targeted professional development for both principals and teachers, and is considering opening schools that will be segregated by gender, having experienced some success with gender-segregated classrooms.

On its own initiative, the Flint City School District reallocated ESEA funds to finance a contract with a private-sector firm that provided coaches to work with principals, explicitly arguing that coaching would be more effective in changing principals' behavior than closer supervision. Most of the coaches were retired educators, but some came from business and other backgrounds. The district has also organized several leadership forums each year, offering guidance to school-level administrators on topics including parental involvement, data use, effective teaching strategies, and the conduct of administrator "walk-throughs" to assess teaching and learning in individual classrooms. Principals are required to participate in regular "peer review" meetings with their supervisors, a fellow principal, and a representative from the ISD, in which their plans for school improvement are presented and evaluated. Information from these meetings must be shared with teachers and parents in their schools.

School improvement strategies have had to be negotiated with the teachers' union in Flint. Administrators praise local educators for voluntarily adding minutes to the school day, along with additional workdays dedicated to the discussion of student achievement. At the same time, however, the union has complicated the district's strategy by demanding strict adherence to the prerogatives of seniority. Efforts by the district to place excellent teachers where they are most needed, or to transfer ineffective teachers, have encountered resistance from the union.

At one time, twenty-one Flint schools were subject to various levels of NCLB sanctions. The district's middle and high schools continue to struggle, and two middle schools remain on MDE's critical list. Among the district's elementary schools, however, all but one have made AYP for two consecutive years and reset the sanctions clock to zero. In their interviews with us, district administrators acknowledged that "scores are not where we want them to be," but affirmed that their schools are now moving in the right direction.

Grand Rapids. Grand Rapids is the main city in southwest Michigan, where the local economy has remained relatively healthy. Despite generally favorable economic circumstances in the region, however, the Grand Rapids Public Schools (GRPS) have experienced a steady decline in enrollments, losing students to charter schools and suburban school districts. A substantial majority of the children who remain enrolled in GRPS are poor, with more than three-quarters eligible for free or reduced-price lunch.

District officials acknowledge that their current strategies for improving student performance originated in the "urgency" imposed by NCLB. Senior administrators characterize their approach to low-performing schools in these terms: "We're here to help, but there will be consequences." They have changed the leadership teams in some schools, including the middle school that remains on MDE's current critical list.

Frequent assessment of student performance and regular analysis of test-score data are the core components of the GRPS response to NCLB sanctions. According to the district's chief academic officer, some formal assessment takes place "almost every day" in the city's lowest-performing schools. Every six weeks, administrators in these buildings are required to conduct "data-review meetings" attended by the chief academic officer himself, along with other senior officials, including representatives from the intermediate school district. The purpose of these meetings is to review student test scores, plan intervention strategies, adjust instruction, and assess the effectiveness of previous adjustments.

Principals have found these meetings helpful. As one stated, "It helps us to reach our goals because we have people to examine data more closely. We have a person to help us with the data. If you know exactly what kids need to focus on, you can move them in a direction that will address their specific needs. . . . This is one thing that really works for us." According to another, the data review meetings have immediate consequences: "Fridays we look at progress . . . and move kids around to where they need to be. This has helped out a lot!"

In addition to their focus on assessment and data analysis, members of the central office staff also serve as coaches in troubled schools, with both advisory and supervisory responsibilities for turning these schools around.[23] All schools are also required to convene annual meetings with parents, at which they present student performance data and explain the school's AYP status.

Changes spurred by NCLB increasingly have been woven into the regular administrative and instructional practices of the school district. Though senior administrators continue to focus their attention on the most troubled schools in the GRPS, all are now required to administer a variety of standardized assessments and to conduct regular data-review meetings with central office staff. The district is moving toward the implementation of a "defined instructional model" that includes explicit learning expectations, pacing guides, and assessment tools in core areas of the curriculum. Teachers have received professional development aimed at familiarizing them with the new instructional model, and the district is currently developing procedures to ensure they deliver the prescribed curriculum to their students. In association with the district's new emphasis on assessment and accountability, these changes have produced an unprecedented shift, focusing teachers' attention on the performance of their students and their schools.

Grand Rapids has closed several persistently low-performing schools, or merged schools on MDE's critical list with more successful schools nearby. As a result, only one middle school in the district is currently engaged in restructuring. The district's middle and high schools continue to face difficulties in making AYP, but all but two elementary schools in Grand Rapids have made AYP for at least two consecutive years and are no longer subject to NCLB sanctions.[24] District officials acknowledge that NCLB has served to motivate positive changes in their schools, but they remain troubled by the "inconsistency" in the way their diverse, high-poverty district is treated when compared with wealthier and more homogeneous suburban districts.

Bayard Rustin Academy. The Bayard Rustin Academy is a charter school located in a midsized Michigan city, with a charter authorized by the Charter Schools Office at Central Michigan University.[25] The school enrolls approximately 225 students in grades K–6. Virtually all of the students at Bayard Rustin are African-American, and all are eligible for free or reduced-price lunch. The school has made AYP in each of the last two years, and is now off MDE's critical list with the sanctions clock reset to zero.

According to the Charter Schools Office at CMU, their main concern is not with whether the schools they authorize are making AYP, but rather with whether they are fulfilling the terms of their charters. Schools that fail to do so may have their charters revoked by CMU, which gives the Charter Schools Office considerable leverage when performance falls below expectations. Federal and state accountability policies including NCLB and *Education YES!* provide additional leverage to their planning process, but the threat that a charter might be revoked is the more powerful inducement to change. After several years of failure to make AYP at Bayard Rustin, CMU's "turnaround team" recommended a curriculum audit to the Bayard Rustin board, which was a key element in the school's subsequent improvement.

According to the principal of Bayard Rustin, the school's turnaround was attributable to three related changes. First, following the advice of CMU, the school conducted a curriculum audit which established the foundation for more "systematic" instruction, with a particular focus on reading and language arts. Individual teachers became more familiar with grade-level expectations for their students, and learned how to identify gaps and weaknesses in their students' learning. The introduction of clearly defined curricular expectations also made it possible for teachers to learn what their colleagues in earlier and subsequent grades were teaching, in order to coordinate their instructional goals better.

Second, the school used Title I money to hire coaches, who helped teachers focus on school improvement and take responsibility for successes and failures in their school. The coaches hired from outside were not as helpful as the principal had hoped, but two stellar teachers served as role models for the rest of the staff. "They [the teachers] showed everybody how it could be done," by modeling appropriate teaching and focusing on the needs of children.

Finally, Bayard Rustin Academy greatly increased the amount of time spent preparing students for the state's standardized assessments, commonly referred to as the MEAP (Michigan Educational Assessment Program) test. To this end they made use of a program called Edvisions (provided by CMU) that allowed students to take practice tests online. They brought in consultants to train teachers in the knowledge and skills required for success on the MEAP. They required teachers to fulfill a provision in their contract obliging them to contribute time toward tutoring students in preparation for the MEAP. They also held several assemblies prior to test administration in an effort to raise expectations and assure students that they would be successful on the exam.

The principal at Bayard Rustin also offered praise to her charter school board. The board "did not panic," instead adopting a "hands-off" approach that allowed her to implement changes with due deliberation and care. She affirms that the lessons learned over the past two years "serve as a template for future years" as the school seeks to move all students toward the goal of proficiency.

Institutionalizing NCLB

The Michigan case study provides an ambiguous account of NCLB implementation, featuring two contrasting stories. On the one hand is a story of half-hearted implementation and outright noncompliance, rooted at the state level in a lack of capacity to oversee effectively what's going on at the district or school level and, at the district level, in an unwillingness to upset educators and their unions by making harsh judgments about local schools. The main consequences from this point of view include overt but superficial compliance with NCLB mandates, accompanied by the adoption of restructuring strategies that only weakly reflect or even run counter to those prescribed under the law. The strategies adopted by MDE and by district officials have generally aimed to avoid tough choices or conflict with unions, and much of the guidance provided to schools seems "vapid and obvious" (as a senior MDE official remarked), even to those sponsoring the programs.

A second, very different, story also emerges from the Michigan case study, however. In this account, the state's weak implementation of the cascading sanctions mandated by NCLB matters less than the fact that officials at both state and district levels have accepted the legitimacy of the AYP criterion for judging the success or failure of local schools. In response to the bright light cast on school performance by NCLB, state and local educators have begun to focus attention and resources on the schools most in need of improvement. In this view, the sanctions prescribed by NCLB should be viewed as one among several possible strategies for accomplishing the goal of academic proficiency for all children by 2014. The failure of Michigan educators to make a good-faith effort to implement NCLB sanctions is less important than their apparent success in encouraging persistently low-performing schools to reach their AYP targets.

We are inclined to the latter view, but we acknowledge the danger inherent in allowing states and districts to pick their own strategies when it comes to implementing NCLB. The success even of Michigan's district-friendly, essentially hands-off strategy is ultimately dependent on the prospect of meaningful sanctions, and the credibility of the threat depends in turn on the state's thus-far unproven willingness to wield the sanctions hammer in schools that fail to improve.[26] Nevertheless, the Michigan case study suggests that the public "naming and shaming" that resides at the heart of NCLB, accompanied by the threat (however distant) of meaningful consequences for persistent failure to improve, has brought about a significant change in education officials' approach to persistently low-performing schools.

Regardless of which story is chosen, Michigan's education system is increasingly oriented toward the task of meeting NCLB benchmarks, and MDE has incorporated tools and approaches closely tied to NCLB into its long-term strategies for managing the system. For example, department officials have begun working with schools in their first year of failure to make AYP in an effort to keep them out of the sanctions process, and they are working with districts to design contracts that allow the necessary flexibility to implement effective restructuring plans several years in the future.

Despite these positive developments, many of the educators we interviewed continue to regard NCLB as a guarantee of failure for virtually all of the state's schools. As several noted, there are nearly fifty ways to fail under NCLB, and only one way to succeed. Their initial efforts have gotten them over the first hurdle and put many previously low-performing schools on a trajectory of improvement. Achievement in these schools remains very low, however, and confidence that recent improvements can be sustained is not widespread. There are also doubts that strategies that have proved effective in elementary schools will work in middle and high schools. Administrators across the state continue to decry the law's "unfairness" to urban school districts, and to call for a less punitive and more "humane" approach to accountability.

Still, outright rejection of NCLB has, for now, given way to skepticism about its long-term prospects for success, and significant numbers of previously low-performing schools have gotten themselves over the first AYP hurdle. This must be counted as progress.

PART III

Remedies in the Districts

9

Rural Kentucky Districts: "Do-It-Yourself" School Improvement

Stephen Clements

Although the No Child Left Behind Act (NCLB) was arguably designed with urban and suburban school districts in mind, thousands of America's schools are still located in rural outposts. Using a fairly stringent definition of rurality, just over 3,200 of the nation's 16,000 school districts are included in this category.[1] A heavily rural state like Kentucky has an even higher proportion of such districts. The commonwealth sprawls across almost four hundred miles of the Ohio Valley, touching Appalachian West Virginia in the east, Missouri in the west, and five other states in between. According to 2003 data, 77 of Kentucky's 175 school districts are heavily rural, and another 27 have populations of less than 19,999, but are adjacent to metropolitan areas.[2] Kentucky is as rural as North Dakota, and only six states have populations that are more rural.[3]

This chapter focuses on the particular challenges rural communities face in responding to NCLB pressures, using case studies of three remote school districts in Kentucky. The Bluegrass State is an ideal location for such an inquiry because it is so heavily rural, and because it has one of the more-developed, long-lived state accountability systems in the country. In fact, prior to passage of the No Child Left Behind Act, a distinct accountability environment already existed in Kentucky, onto which NCLB's accountability features have been layered in the past few years. The story of how these rural school districts are grappling with competing state and federal accountability demands will unfold here with, first, some brief background on Kentucky's school improvement efforts of the recent reform era, followed by an examination of three rural districts, their progress under both the state accountability system and NCLB, and how remedies are being implemented. The chapter will conclude by discussing what these cases suggest about the local and state capacity for school improvement in the current accountability environment.

Kentucky and Its School Reform Efforts

In spite of its geographic spread, slightly fewer than 4.2 million people live in the Commonwealth of Kentucky, with about one-third living in or near the "Golden Triangle" area of Louisville, Lexington, and northern Kentucky, just south of Cincinnati. Kentucky is home to an array of businesses, including United Parcel Service, Humana, and Toyota, as well as traditional industries, such as coal mining, horse racing, aluminum, and energy production. But agriculture remains the backbone of the rural economy. While its economic base has grown considerably over the past few decades, Kentucky's gross economic output is far surpassed by its neighbors to the north, particularly Illinois and Ohio. In 2002, for example, total manufacturer shipments and retail sales in Kentucky amounted to about $129 billion, whereas comparable figures for Illinois and Ohio that year were $320 billion and $364 billion, respectively.[4]

Kentucky has also struggled mightily, and with some success, for nearly two decades to improve its public schools, just over 1,100 of which are scattered across the state. In 1989 Kentucky leaders were handed a unique state supreme court decision declaring the entire school system unconstitutional, and they responded in 1990 with the Kentucky Education Reform Act, which established many of the mechanisms of "systemic" school reform, based on assessment and accountability, that have since been mimicked by other states. The reform law included a new funding formula and associated tax increases, which pumped millions of new dollars into schools and targeted the more impoverished counties in the state.[5] Other significant reform features included incorporation of site-based decision-making councils at most schools, new state education governance structures (a revamped Department of Education and state board), a statewide technology infrastructure, state support for teacher professional development, funding for remedial education, a preschool program, provision of "highly skilled educators" to help turn around low-performing schools, and family resource and youth services centers to provide social support for needy school communities.

The driving force of the reform, however, has been the assessment and accountability system phased in during the 1990s and tweaked over time. As currently constructed, the Commonwealth Accountability Testing System (CATS) includes several elements. The centerpiece is the Kentucky Core Content Test (KCCT), given each April and featuring open-response and multiple-choice items covering the seven areas of the curriculum mandated by the state—reading, writing, math, science, social studies, arts and humanities, and practical living/vocational arts. As shown in table 9-1, these tests are spread across several grades so as to distribute the accountability burden. The state has four categories of performance on the KCCT: novice, apprentice, proficient, and distinguished (these reflect the National Assessment of Educational Progress [NAEP] categories of below basic, basic, proficient, and advanced). However, score gradations are also provided at each level to better capture student achievement across each category—hence, there are five performance levels below "proficient" for which students can get partial credit. Another CATS component is the CTBS-5 given at grades 3, 6, and 9; this provides the state with national comparisons for its students. Students also complete writing portfolios at grades 4, 7, and 12.[6]

The accountability system associated with these tests determines performance at the school and district levels, but not at the individual student level—that was the philosophical commitment embraced by lawmakers in 1990. The test contractors use a matrix sampling method, such that different forms of the test are given in the same school, so more of the curriculum can be assessed with shorter tests for each student. Results are aggregated into annual "index" scores at the school and district levels. Although tests are administered and index scores calculated each year, accountability results are determined *every two years*, to moderate the effects of score fluctuations, which is particularly important for small schools. Each school and district has performance targets to reach for each biennium, with the goal of reaching "proficiency" (an index score of 100) by 2014. Schools that meet or exceed their performance goals are eligible for recognition. Those that score below their goals but above an "assistance" level

TABLE 9-1

KENTUCKY'S STATE TEST (CATS) CONFIGURATION, SPRING 2006

Core Content Tests	3rd	4th	5th	6th	7th	8th	9th	10th	11th	12th
Reading		x	o		x	o		x		
Mathematics		o	x		o	x			x	
Science		x			x				x	
Social studies			x			x			x	
Arts and humanities			x			x		x	x	
Practical living/ Vocational arts			x			x		x		
Writing (portfolio)		x			x					x
NRT—CTBS/5	x			x			x			

SOURCE: Adapted from Susan Perkins Weston (former executive director of the Kentucky Association of School Councils), "Testing Overview for the 2006–07 School Year," unpublished document prepared for general circulation, 2006.
NOTES: o=Augmented NRT for NCLB calculations.
Beginning in spring of 2007, Kentucky provided Core Content Tests in reading and math for grades 3–8, to replace the augmented NRT for use in NCLB. Beginning in 2008, Kentucky will require the ACT—a college preparedness test—of all eleventh graders.

are deemed to be "progressing." Those below this level are "in assistance," and therefore qualify for remediation and, potentially, sanction under the accountability system.[7]

Between 1994 and 2002, Kentucky paid financial rewards to schools that surpassed performance goals—these were usually distributed as pay bonuses to teachers. But the General Assembly dropped this program when the state budget tightened, and since then Kentucky's primary accountability enforcement mechanism has been embarrassment and the threat of intervention for "assistance" category schools. The lowest-performing schools in the state on CATS are assigned to level 1 (top third), level 2 (middle third), or level 3 (bottom third) for assistance purposes. The various forms of intervention Kentucky uses involve an internally developed "scholastic review and audit" process—a way of examining a school's environment, efficiency, and academic situation in light of eighty-eight standards and indicators for school improvement (SISI)—as well as deployment to assistance schools of highly skilled educators (HSEs), who function like strategic analysts and planners.[8] Though many reviews and audits have been conducted among schools that perform poorly under Kentucky's system, most such schools manage to extricate themselves from this status after one biennium. To this point, no schools have been subjected to the ultimate sanctions under the state system of allowing students to transfer out, or forcing replacement of teachers and administrators.

The accountability index system is widely accepted in the state as a legitimate metric for measuring improvement, and at present many schools and districts seem on trajectory to meet 2014 performance goals. According to 2006 results, about half of Kentucky's schools met or exceeded their goals, several hundred more were progressing, and only forty-one were in assistance.[9] This system seems to be having its intended effects of concentrating school attention on the state curriculum, and enhancing the academic focus of teachers. Kentucky is among the few states with discernible improvements in NAEP results at the fourth and eighth grade levels.[10]

NCLB Comes to the Commonwealth

Into this accountability environment have recently come federal performance mandates, courtesy of NCLB. During the first years of NCLB, the Kentucky Department of Education calculated adequate yearly progress (AYP) across grades 3–8 by augmenting the state's own math and reading tests, and for high schools by using tenth grade reading and eleventh grade math results from the KCCT. Beginning in spring of 2007, Kentucky will add annual reading and math tests to the KCCT across grades 3–8. This will enable annual tracking of AYP that is more consistent with Kentucky's statewide test design. The CATS contractor (for several years it was CTB-McGraw Hill but currently it is Measured Progress) now helps the department produce the various annual NCLB reports.

At the state level, NCLB's effects are beginning to be felt broadly. Statewide, some 766 of 1,187 of schools in 2005–6, or about 65 percent of the total, made AYP under NCLB.[11] Of the remaining schools, 161 had missed AYP for two consecutive years or more and were therefore in the various tiers of sanction under NCLB.[12] In addition, some forty-three districts across the state had entered tier 3 under NCLB as of late summer 2006, and all are taking part in various assistance programs approved or offered by the Department of Education.[13]

In general, the department utilizes the same audit- and review-based process for remediation under NCLB that it does for schools faring poorly under Kentucky's own accountability system. For schools in tiers that require the NCLB school choice option and supplemental educational services (SES), the department provides some guidance. Although Kentucky has a kind of informal school choice system in many districts and has magnet schools in several urban districts, it cannot be described as a choice-friendly state. It has no state policies that explicitly encourage choice among schools, and it does not have a charter school law. Schools in Kentucky have, however, generally complied with the NCLB school choice provisions of the law. For SES, the department has overseen creation of an approved provider list of vendors that is in keeping with state contracting guidelines.

Rural Districts in Focus: Three Case Studies

Whereas urban communities typically deal with large, racially and socioeconomically diverse populations of students in schools that are in close geographic proximity, rural communities tend to have dispersed populations, smaller numbers of schools, less ethnic diversity, and a different array of social and economic problems and concerns. To determine NCLB effects in such communities, the author conducted case studies of three remote school districts in the Commonwealth: Martin County in the Appalachian eastern part of the state, Fulton County in the far western part of the state, and Monroe County in south-central Kentucky (see figure 9-1). These case-study districts were chosen carefully—in consultation with Kentucky Department of Education officials who oversee assistance to needy schools under both CATS and NCLB—to represent different geographic areas of the states, different social and economic settings, and varying experiences with sanctions under NCLB. After identifying the districts, the author secured approval for participation from all three superintendents, conducted site visits during August of 2006, and followed up in October and November of 2006 with additional interviews. The summaries that follow contain a profile of each

FIGURE 9-1
KENTUCKY SCHOOL DISTRICTS

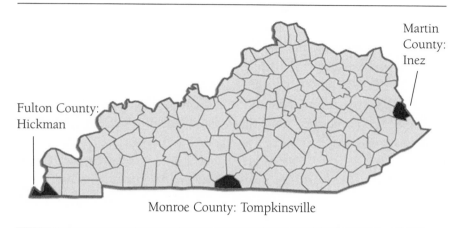

Martin
County:
Inez

Fulton County:
Hickman

Monroe County: Tompkinsville

SOURCE: Author's creation based on basic outline map image by Graphic Maps, a d/b/a of the Woolwine-
Moen Group, available online at www.worldatlas.com/webimage/countrys/namerica/usstates/counties/
ky.htm (June 15, 2007).

district and its schools, how these have fared under Kentucky's accountability system, and how NCLB remedies are being implemented.

Martin County. In many ways Martin County is the stereotypical eastern
Kentucky community. Located deep in the low-slung Appalachian Moun-
tains and bordering West Virginia, Martin County has long depended on
the coal industry for its economic viability. For Inez, the seat of Martin
County, coal mining most recently peaked in the 1980s, and since then economic prospects for many of the 12,000 or so residents have declined.
Median household income in 2003 stood at $22,188, just 60 percent of the
state average.[14] Poverty rates in the county are quite high—slightly more
than one-quarter of the population is at or below the federal poverty line.
Formal education rates are low—only 54 percent of county adults ages
twenty-five and older had completed high school as of the last official
count, and fewer than 9 percent had earned a four-year degree.[15] Nearly all
residents of the county are white. In addition to Inez, the other community
of any size is Warfield, located about eight miles from Inez on the other side
of the mountain that bisects the county.

Martin County schools enroll just over 2,200 students, down from over 3,000 less than a decade ago, spread across six schools—two elementary schools, a middle school, and the high school in Inez, and another elementary school and middle school located in Warfield. The challenges facing Martin County schools have been stark for decades. Martin's 25 percent poverty rate translates into 70 percent eligibility for free or reduced-price lunch, and district schools have long struggled to make headway amidst a populace with low levels of education and few jobs that require high levels of literacy and numeracy.[16] But school reform has provided Martin County with additional resources and accountability tools. As in many other Kentucky districts, Martin's elementary schools perform relatively well under CATS—two of them met their goals in 2006, and the third was in the progressing category.[17] But performance problems have persisted at the middle-school level and at the high school. In 2002, for example, Warfield Middle was in level 3 assistance.[18] By 2004, Warfield had moved out of assistance, but Inez Middle School had dropped into level 3 assistance.[19] In 2006, both middle schools moved slightly above the assistance level, but they were not reducing their numbers of novice performers rapidly enough, and the high school was in level 3 assistance.[20] All of these schools received audits and had assigned HSEs during each level 3 biennium, and all put school improvement plans into place.[21]

As of late 2006, NCLB results in Martin County had roughly mirrored these CATS results. All three Martin County elementary schools had met their AYP targets from 2003 to 2006. But the Martin middle schools had consistently failed to make AYP, although their academic problems differed. Inez Middle School was in level 3 assistance under CATS when NCLB began, so it was designated tier 2 from the beginning. It barely missed its annual measurable objective (AMO) targets in reading and math in 2003 and 2004.[22] By 2005 and 2006, it was missing AMO in more categories, had failed to reach proficiency targets in reading among every subgroup of students, and was listed as tier 5 for the 2006–7 school year.[23] Warfield Middle School, on the other hand, began NCLB with a clean slate, but failed to meet its reading AMO in 2003.[24] In each of the next three cycles, it failed to reach math AMO targets in every subgroup of students and had earned a tier 3 designation for 2006–7.[25] The high school had fluctuated over the years. It did not make AYP in 2003 but did so during 2004. In 2005, it missed math AMO goals with every student subgroup and in 2006 did the same, while also missing AMO reading targets for free or reduced-price lunch and disability students and finally reaching tier 1 under NCLB.[26]

Martin County was, therefore, facing increasing sanctions under both the state and federal accountability systems, and a host of remediation efforts were underway. Superintendent Mark Blackburn, who started his second year at his post in 2006, was himself in place partly as a response to district performance problems. Blackburn worked with school councils to place new principals in both middle schools. Inez Middle had had two audits conducted and a resident HSE for each of the previous four years. Now in tier 5 under NCLB, a district oversight plan was going into effect, with central office administrators rotating through the building so that one was present for at least 60 percent of every school day to help make managerial decisions, meet periodically with teachers and principals, conduct classroom visits, and help supervise the reading instructors. All teachers were participating in professional development on reading instruction, and the school was starting to use small groups for reading practice.[27] After two and a half years without one, Inez Middle had also finally procured a certified math teacher who would be working with Title I–funded math specialists on curricular and instructional improvements in that subject.[28] Warfield Middle, in tier 3 status, had been assigned reading and math specialists, especially targeting free or reduced-price lunch students and disability students. The high school was to be audited during 2006–7, and would be implementing a new math curriculum as well.[29] The district itself was in tier 3 under NCLB and had enlisted in a state assistance program. It would therefore receive strategic planning help from an external team of state-appointed specialists during the 2006–7 school year.[30] The district had recently submitted its revised improvement plan to the department for review.[31]

Although supplemental educational services (SES) had been used by small numbers of Martin Middle School students over the NCLB years, this was clearly not a significant part of district improvement efforts by 2006. During 2004–5, the first year of services availability, the nonproficient performers among Inez Middle's 175 Title I students were eligible, but after the district notified parents of options, held informational meetings, and enrolled students, only seven individuals actually participated in tutoring, all of which was provided online through the Kentucky Virtual High School

(KVHS). The following year nine students enrolled, but only three ended up receiving services, this time from A to Z Tutoring out of Nashville. During 2006–7, Warfield Middle students ran the total number of Title I students at the two schools to about 240, and a total of 11 were participating via three different services providers. The district each year had provided three mailings to Title I families explaining the SES option and announcing dates for meetings of interested students and parents. The district would then determine which providers from the state-approved list would work in Martin County—most years approximately ten companies fit this description—but it would encourage parents to contact the few companies that had been responsive to district queries.[32]

As of 2006, NCLB school choice for Martin County middle school students had been extremely limited, at best. Since both schools had consistently failed to make AYP, or had been in assistance under Kentucky's system, intradistrict transfer between the two had not been an option. Of the school districts that are within an hour of Martin County, only one contains one or more middle schools that had made AYP in recent years or was not in tier 3 status itself. When Martin officials contacted that district about receiving students interested in transferring, the district initially declined to take them. It eventually reversed itself, but informed Martin administrators that it would accept transfer students on a case-by-case basis, implying that it might refuse students who could jeopardize its own status as a high-performing district. In any case, Martin County had been annually notifying families of Inez Middle School since 2003, and Warfield Middle School since 2004, of their option to seek enrollment in the high-performing district, but no parent in any year had contacted the central office about moving his or her child. As the 2006–7 year commenced, Martin's high school students became eligible for transfer to the high school in that other district, and as of late fall a total of seven students were seeking the transfer. But none had yet officially applied for admission, and it was unclear how many would be accepted or how many would actually attend.[33]

Fulton County. At the opposite end of the state—where its tip bumps up against the Mississippi River, right across from Missouri—lies Fulton County, a fertile, rolling area that is an agricultural haven of soybeans and corn, and home to just over 7,000 residents. Though Fulton County is rich in agricultural possibilities, other economic opportunities are clearly limited, as a trip to Hickman, the county seat, attests. Located on a slough—a sort of spur—just off the Mississippi, the portion of Hickman that sits atop a bluff seems typical of small towns in the vicinity, with modest ranch houses, minimarts, and grocery stores. But descend to the old downtown near the water, and one will see crumbling buildings, either boarded up or housing shops selling "antiques" or assorted used goods—the vestiges of a once-vital commerce center that has been dwindling for decades. Unlike that of many Kentucky counties, Fulton's population is racially diverse, with about a quarter comprised of African Americans. Median household income was $26,621 in 2003, or about 73 percent of the statewide average.[34] Some 70 percent of the adult population graduated from high school, and about 12 percent have earned college degrees.[35]

Less than a mile outside of Hickman is the county schools complex, an array of aging structures that includes the high school, the athletic fields, a parking lot, and a middle school that is physically connected to an elementary school. On the edge of the site sits the district office, which includes the county's preschool program as well. The county launched the 2006–7 school year with a total enrollment of only 630 students spread across those three schools, down from about 780 students in 2000. The decline in population prompted the district to combine the elementary and middle schools into one entity recently, and may have further adverse effects on staffing for the high school soon. Some 70 percent of district students are in the free or reduced-price lunch program (FRPL).[36]

Fulton County schools have struggled under Kentucky's accountability system since the late 1990s, with some schools slipping into and out of state assistance and others achieving well enough to receive some state recognition for improvement. At the end of the 1999–2000 school year, for example, Fulton's elementary school was in rewards status, and the high school was progressing as well.[37] After 2002 testing, both the elementary and the high school were in level 3 assistance, and an HSE was placed in each school for the next two years.[38] The high school moved back into progressing status in 2004, but fell back to level 2 assistance in 2006.[39] The elementary school, on the other hand, was still in assistance after 2004, but was then combined with the middle school and assigned a new baseline score under CATS.[40] The K–8 school met its goals under the state system, so as of 2006 only Fulton's high school was considered underperforming and receiving assistance. The district as a whole was performing at the progressing level, although not clearly on track to reach its 2014 goal of an index score of 100 on CATS.[41]

Under NCLB, Fulton County student performance has looked worse overall and achievement gaps more glaring than under CATS, but the picture is complex. In 2002 the elementary school's level 3 status under CATS earned it a tier 1 initial assignment under NCLB, and it slipped to tier 2 in 2003.[42] Though it fell to tier 3 in 2004, the school met its AMO targets for more subgroups than before, failing primarily among African-American students and dramatically increasing proficiency among white students in both reading and math.[43] In 2005, Fulton Elementary met AMO targets with every student group, but failed to make AYP—and moved to tier 4—because it was still categorized as a level 1 assistance school under CATS for the biennium (the "other academic indicator").[44] Fulton Middle failed to make AYP between 2003 and 2005, ending that period at tier 3, but meeting most of its AMO goals.[45] The elementary and middle schools were combined at that point, and in 2006 the new school made its AYP goal.[46] The high school actually made AYP in 2003, but failed to do so in 2004.[47] It scored abysmally in 2005, meeting only six of twelve goals, meeting AMO targets only among white students, and earning tier 1 status.[48] In 2006, the school continued to struggle among non-white students, and reached tier 2 under NCLB.

Hence, Fulton's elementary and middle schools started the NCLB years in trouble but, as of 2006, had seen more recent improvement, finally achieving AYP in the previous year or so and substantially increasing proficiency levels among subgroups. The high school, on the other hand, deteriorated during this period, moving from making AYP to missing AMO targets rather badly, a shift reflected in its being moved to level 2 assistance by the state. These poor performance levels had predictable effects on Fulton's district sanction status under NCLB, moving it from tier 1 in 2004–5 to tier 3 for 2006–7.[49]

Fulton teachers and administrators responded to these accountability pressures through an array of changes and initiatives. First, the district began focusing on individual student achievement. District administrators and teachers in 2005 started meeting one on one with students scoring below proficiency to map and discuss their progress in reading, math, and other subjects based on formative test results. Also, individual schools pursued specific changes based on audits undertaken in the elementary and high schools during the 2002–4 biennium, when both were in level 3 assistance under CATS. The elementary school replaced its principal, began using a program called Project Child to improve instruction in reading, writing, and math, and altered its teacher supervision and evaluation procedures. In addition, the district initiated new computer-based enrichment programs in math, science, and reading, targeting these programs to free or reduced-price lunch and African-American students. The reconfiguration of the middle and elementary schools enabled both to focus on the same academic improvement steps, since both were now under the relatively new principal of the middle school.[50]

The high school responded to its academic problems by selecting a new principal in 2005. He hired seven new teachers since arriving and was experimenting with organizational changes designed by the HSE assigned to that school. For example, to address math and reading problems, teachers in these areas were authorized to pull students from any other class if they needed math and reading remediation. New math teachers were revising the school's math curriculum. Several teachers were being trained to teach advanced placement (AP) courses, which the high school had not been able to offer for several years. And block scheduling for freshmen was eliminated.[51]

At the district level, Fulton County enlisted in the state's voluntary assistance program and, in the winter of 2006, received an audit by its assistance team. Superintendent Chuck Holliday responded, according to state officials, by turning the focus of his work from managing district business to improving instruction in schools and providing better teacher evaluation. The voluntary assistance team would visit his district monthly, meeting with Holliday and his staff before or after every monthly school board meeting.[52]

As of 2006, NCLB school choice had not been a part of remedies in Fulton County. When the elementary school was labeled tier 2 in August of 2003, the district contacted other area schools about taking students who might be interested in transferring. None of the adjacent elementary schools making AYP agreed to take Fulton students, on the grounds that they had neither the staffing nor room to accept such an influx. These area schools were quite distant from Hickman as well, ranging from twenty-one to forty miles away. Similarly, when the high school reached tier 1 in the late summer of 2005, only one area high school had made AYP. It refused to accept

Fulton students, who would also have faced a forty-one-mile trip to school. The district therefore, informed its elementary and high school families that transferring students elsewhere was not an option for them. Given that no private schools exist in the county, the only option available to disgruntled parents seemed to be home-schooling.[53]

Fulton County, along with two other nearby districts, had had difficulty tapping supplemental educational services (SES) as well, as few of the state-approved services providers were eager to work in districts so far from the urban centers. To help meet its needs, Fulton County prevailed upon the nonprofit Western Kentucky Educational Cooperative in Murray, an hour to the east, to create a supplemental educational services program for Fulton and neighbor counties. The cooperative thus created Project Serve, which in 2004–5 served seventeen Fulton elementary and middle school students, and another thirty-one students during 2005–6. About this many students were slated to receive SES again in 2006–7, although Fulton County as of late 2006 had still not found a provider for district high school students, who became eligible in the fall of 2005.[54] Also to that point, district officials had no data to show whether supplemental educational services provision to their students had contributed to test-score improvements.[55]

Monroe County. Yet a different story emerges from Monroe County, located roughly in the middle of the state but in the south, bordering Tennessee. Harboring a relatively stable population of just under 12,000, Monroe County is a small agricultural and manufacturing community about an hour east of Bowling Green, the closest metropolitan area. Dale Hollow Lake, which spans the Kentucky-Tennessee border, is nearby, so that Monroe County partakes of the tourism dollars of the sportsmen and vacationers who come to the area each year. The county seat is Tompkinsville, where about a fifth of the population lives, and where four of the five district schools are located. The only other small towns of note in the county are Gamaliel and Fountain Run. As is characteristic of many such Kentucky communities, there is very little racial diversity—African Americans and Hispanics together comprise less than 5 percent of the population. Household income is only two-thirds of the state average, and two-thirds of the county school students are on free or reduced-price lunch.[56]

Monroe County's approximately 2,200 students are spread across two elementary schools, a middle school, and a high school in Tompkinsville, as well as a satellite elementary in Gamaliel, about ten miles away. In comparative terms, Monroe schools are faring better under both CATS and NCLB than the other two districts. But Monroe illustrates how student scores aggregated to the district level can hurt a district even when individual schools are not under tiers 3 or 4. Under Kentucky's system, the district overall made progress in 2006 but failed to meet its performance goal, although it did not fall into the "assistance" category.[57] All three elementary schools met their goals, but the middle and high schools were only progressing and were flagged for having too many novice-level performers on the state tests.[58] In fact, this had been the pattern in the district for the previous several accountability cycles. In both 2002 and 2004, all three elementary schools met their goal. The high school did so as well in 2002, but by 2004 it had slipped to the progressing level, and the middle school was progressing during both cycles, failing to pull up its low performers quickly enough.[59] But neither the district as a whole nor any individual school had been in assistance under CATS since one of the elementary schools struggled in the mid-1990s.[60]

Against this backdrop of adequate—if lackluster—progress Monroe County encountered difficulties under NCLB. The district itself began having problems making AYP in 2003. That year only one school—an elementary school—failed to make AYP, but because not enough students with disabilities districtwide made their AMO in reading, the entire district failed to make AYP.[61] In 2004, the elementary school that failed to make AYP the previous year made eight of nine AMO targets and slipped to tier 1, while the other four schools made AYP.[62] By 2005, the tier 1 elementary school had not only achieved AYP, but had posted 80 percent proficient in reading among white students and 70 percent among free or reduced-price lunch students.[63] The other two elementary schools also achieved AYP, as did the middle school, although this time the high school failed to meet AYP goals because of poor math performance among all subgroups, which in turn caused the district to reach tier 2.[64] By 2006, a different elementary school failed AYP, due to insufficient math performance among disability students.[65] The middle school missed AYP when free and reduced-price meal students missed their math AMO and disability students missed math and reading

AMO goals.[66] The high school missed its math target for free or reduced-price lunch students, and thus moved to tier 1.[67] Yet again, the district's disability students failed to meet reading and math AMO targets, and students on free or reduced-price lunch missed their math AMO, so the district failed to make AYP and moved to tier 3.[68]

The discrepancy between performance under CATS and NCLB has thus been especially striking in Monroe County, which as of 2006 had attained tier 3 status as a district without individual schools moving into tier 2 or 3, and without the state having intervened at either the school or district level. This happened, as noted, because of low proficiency levels among the district's students with disabilities, and poor math performance among free or reduced-price lunch students. The low math performance came, as well, in the face of tremendous reading scores—in 2006, some 60 percent of the district's eighth graders scored at or above proficient in reading.[69] Superintendent George Wilson, a Monroe County native, attributes the district's strong reading scores to a heavy investment in that subject—thanks in part to state and federal grant programs—and to a university-based consultant who helped design a focused reading effort. But the district's poor showing under NCLB highlights a general complacence toward learning, he avers, a very poor curriculum and effort in math, and too little attention to content knowledge among disability students.[70] These conditions had been masked in his district by Kentucky's more holistic statewide accountability scoring system.

By late 2006, district leaders had developed and were implementing numerous strategies to deal with achievement problems under NCLB. The core of their approach was an effort to align the curriculum across the district using the state's curricular guidelines, and to create the district's own CATS-like formative assessments, called "learning checks." The district was fielding some of these tests that year and by 2007–8 planned to use learning checks once per month, eight times per year, in all subjects, and so track individual student progress in a manner related to the state assessment. The district was also using the web-based Academy of Math and Academy of Reading computer software to shore up skills among underperforming students. With the assistance of Western Kentucky University, it had recently hired several new math teachers and brought in state math specialists to assist it with planning. It had obliged all district teachers to participate in Silver and Strong's Thoughtful Education professional development program. And it was targeting the reading and math achievement problems among its disability students by requiring special education teachers to work with regular teachers on increasing content coverage in the core subject areas.[71]

Monroe County had, therefore, responded to NCLB pressures in several ways. The tier 1 elementary school had recently met AYP and posted strong reading and math gains, and the high school met more AMO goals the previous year. It remained to be seen if the overall district improvement strategy and the focus on disability students would pull the district out of tier 3 status. To this point, the choice and SES remedies of NCLB not yet been a significant part of the district's toolkit; only Title I students from the tier 1 elementary school had technically been eligible for transfer.[72]

An irony here is that Monroe County had for years already allowed district residents to choose among the three elementary schools. Indeed, it had even allowed families from adjacent counties to send their children to these schools, if these families provided transportation. So a modest number of families in the district were already taking advantage of this option. When the district offered families of the tier 1 elementary school—the one ten miles from Tompkinsville—the choice option and to cover transportation costs, no additional families expressed interest in changing schools.[73]

As noted, the high school had by 2006 failed to make AYP twice, but since it is not a Title I school, the choice provisions did not apply. If they had, Monroe County families would have faced the dilemma of leaving their students in an underperforming school, or sending them on a fifty-minute drive (each way) to Burkesville, the location of the nearest high school that made AYP that year, presuming that school would take Monroe students.[74]

Because by 2006 no district Title I schools had yet reached tier 2, Monroe County had not yet had experience with SES.

Discussion: The Feasibility of School Improvement Mandates in Rural Areas

Though these three Kentucky cases offer no basis for generalization, they do illustrate how accountability systems can function on the ground in rural areas of the country. They reveal, first of all, how schools and districts can be caught between rival accountability systems, each of which has a different emphasis and reward structure. In all three districts, and especially in Fulton and Monroe counties, most schools have been making acceptable progress under Kentucky's accountability system—which aggregates scores in seven subject areas to the school level—and none of the districts is "in assistance" under that system, although several individual schools are. But NCLB's focus on individual student proficiency in reading and math, and on subgroups of the population, has revealed several middle and high schools across these districts to be missing the mark to a greater degree than under the state's system. And all three districts have fallen into tier 3 status themselves under NCLB, although for different reasons. While they have ratcheted up their intensity of instruction and increased the coherence of their curriculum in response, the alternative conclusions about performance under the competing accountability systems have led to confusion and frustration in rural communities with such small numbers of schools.

These cases also suggest that many rural districts will have to rely on their own state- or district-developed remediation processes for improvement, and that NCLB's choice and SES provisions will play, at best, only a marginal role in these areas. Each of the three districts contains few schools, and when those schools fail to make AYP, the only out-of-district transfer options available tend to be quite distant, with higher-performing districts sometimes reluctant to accept students from struggling schools. This appears to be partly a matter of logistics; given the relative lack of expressed interest in transferring to other schools when distant options are available, at least in Monroe and Martin counties, rural Kentucky families seem hesitant to send their children forty-five minutes or longer from home. What is unclear is the extent to which limited NCLB choice practices in these rural areas represent a cultural bias in favor of local schools, no matter how they are performing under a given accountability structure, or whether the proportion of transfers will increase as more families gain practice and experience using the option. The limited transfer options in rural areas might benefit from a national initiative to promote out-of-the-box thinking about choice. Under such an initiative, rural schools might explore possibilities for creating a number of smaller school communities out of existing units, or might experiment with virtual-school communities. The latter will become increasingly feasible as broadband Internet availability spreads and computer prices continue to fall. The federal government could usefully fund the development of model virtual-school communities in rural areas, which could, in turn, provide choice options for families.

The potential for supplemental educational services to make an impact might be significant over time. In the cases of Fulton and Martin counties, very small percentages of eligible students have taken advantage of SES, even though the districts have advertised it. Based on the experiences of officials in these counties, few providers have been eager to work in these remote locations. Those that will have had difficulty retaining staff and have preferred offering services online, possibly leading to delivery problems, given limited Internet availability among rural Title I families. SES participation in Kentucky might be depressed because of the mediocre record of the state's own "extended school services" program, a reform-funded effort to provide remedial instruction to underperforming students that has also had very low participation rates. It is possible that as schools gain experience with SES, as an extensive network of providers is built, and as such services are shown to improve school performance, participation will increase. Unfortunately, no data on SES participation in other districts are available for comparison, although the Kentucky Department of Education has calculated that about 9 percent of eligible Title I students statewide enrolled and participated in SES in 2005–6.[75]

In summary, these cases not only reveal the marginal impact of NCLB choice and SES on rural district improvement efforts, but suggest significant barriers to both in rural America as part of NCLB's cascade of remedies. In sparsely populated areas, few schools exist, and some struggle to keep enrollment sufficient to provide a standard array of instruction. These few schools tend to be among the more viable social institutions in rural communities, commanding the loyalty of residents, who may in turn be reluctant to go elsewhere when the schools falter under NCLB. Potential transfer schools are often far away and in communities to which families sometimes feel uncomfortable sending their children. Given the small numbers of eligible students who have sought SES, as well as the distance of these districts from providers and the difficulties of finding and retaining competent tutors, so far the provider market has not begun to flourish in these areas. For the near term, then, it will be up to state- or district-sponsored remediation efforts to meet the escalating proficiency demands of NCLB.

10

Miami-Dade County: Trouble in Choice Paradise

Jane Hannaway and Sarah Cohodes

The Miami-Dade County Public Schools (M-DCPS) system is the largest public school system in Florida and the fourth-largest in the country, with an enrollment of over 350,000 students in 2005–6. As in Florida more generally, the school choice programs operating in M-DCPS are numerous and varied. The school transfer and supplemental educational services (SES) options required by the No Child Left Behind Act (NCLB) add to an already thriving set of choice programs, including magnet schools, charter schools, controlled choice, the corporate tax credit scholarships, the McKay Scholarship, the Opportunity Scholarship Program, and *I Choose!*

This chapter attempts to examine the fit and operation of choice provisions required under NCLB within the overall context of school choice in Miami. The school choice provisions provided by NCLB and the choice programs provided by the state have the same basic objective: to allow parents dissatisfied with the performance of their child's school the option to transfer their child to a better school. The rules governing these programs, however, differ. Most importantly, the school performance ratings provided by the state accountability system, the Florida A+ Accountability Plan, and those provided by the NCLB criteria differ markedly, often presenting parents with conflicting information both about the performance of the school their child attends and the performance of the schools they might choose.

The authors would like to thank Jayanti Owens for her careful assistance in conducting the research reported here. They would also like to thank administrators at the Miami-Dade County Public Schools for their generous access.

We focus on two aspects of the NCLB school choice provisions. First, we explore reasons the utilization of NCLB school choice options by eligible parents is low. After all, this is a community that is well-versed in school choice. Second, we examine the choice behavior of parents to assess the extent to which they are guided by the school performance information that is associated, respectively, with NCLB and with the state A+ Plan.

Miami-Dade County Public Schools

M-DCPS serves over 350,000 students, the majority of whom are from economically disadvantaged backgrounds. Sixty percent of students are eligible for free or reduced-price lunch (FRPL). Hispanic students represent about 60 percent of enrolled students; one-third are African-American; and fewer than 10 percent are white. Approximately 17 percent are English-language learners (ELL), and more than 20 percent are foreign-born.[1]

Student performance levels in Miami are not high, but they have been increasing. The three grades for which we have the longest period of comparable scores are 4, 8, and 10.[2] Between 2000 and 2005, the percentage of fourth grade students who scored "proficient" or above (a numerical score of 3, 4, or 5) on the Florida Comprehensive Assessment Test (FCAT) increased from 40 percent to 69 percent; eighth grade scores rose from 29 percent to 34 percent; and tenth grade moved from 21 percent to 23 percent.[3] For the most part, Miami's student achievement gains have exceeded those of the state of Florida.[4] The number of schools in M-DCPS receiving an A grade, according to the state's A+ accountability program, increased from only 9 in 2003 to 179 in 2006. The district received an overall grade of B in both the 2004–5 and 2005–6 school years, an improvement from its grade of C in 2003–4.

In terms of adequate yearly progress (AYP), according to NCLB, the picture is not so rosy. The district itself has not made AYP in any year since districts began to be rated in 2002–3. In 2002–3, only 8 percent of M-DCPS schools made adequate yearly progress. The proportion went up to 23 percent in 2003–4 and then to 45 percent in 2004–5, but it declined to 35 percent in 2005–6. Indeed, in 2005–6, seventy-nine schools in M-DCPS had not made adequate yearly progress for four consecutive years and were in their third year of school improvement.[5] Their students were therefore eligible for school transfer and supplemental educational services. As the performance bar rises in subsequent years, the situation may well get worse.[6] We discuss the discrepancies between the state's A+ Plan school grades and the NCLB ratings later in this chapter.

School Choice in Florida

Florida has a long and extensive history with school choice, particularly in M-DCPS. Early choice policies in the state were instituted by school districts as a way to remedy residential segregation. Over the years, choice has emerged as a key aspect of state education policy, and its objectives have broadened. In his 2006 state of the state address, Governor Jeb Bush said, "We are committed to school choice because equal opportunity starts with equal options for education and the competition of choice drives positive changes in our public schools." School choice in Florida is seen not only as a way to remedy system inequities for individuals, but also to improve the efficiency and effectiveness of the system as a whole.

The Florida legislature has created three important scholarship-based education programs during Governor Bush's administration. The first is the Opportunity Scholarship Program (OSP), which is part of the state's accountability system (the A+ Plan) and provides choice for students in failing schools. Schools are graded on an A–F scale largely on the basis of student performance on the FCATs, tests used by the state to assess student performance on the Sunshine State Standards. If schools receive an F grade in two out of four years, students in those schools are afforded choice.

Many view the Opportunity Scholarship Program as the state's signature school choice policy. Passed by the legislature in 1999, it is the only statewide voucher program ever created in the nation. OSP allowed students to redeem vouchers at private, including religious, schools as well as higher-performing public schools in the state. The private school option was declared unconstitutional in January 2006 by the Florida Supreme Court, but the public school option remains in place.[7]

The second program, the John M. McKay Scholarships for Students with Disabilities, became a statewide program in the 2000–1 school year.

The McKay Scholarship provides vouchers for parents dissatisfied with the services their special needs children receive in public schools. Parents have an option of choosing other public schools or using the scholarship for their children to attend eligible private schools. While this program is structured similarly to the Opportunity Scholarship Program, it was not included in the supreme court ruling.

The third program is the Corporate Income Tax Credit Scholarship Program. This program allows corporations to take dollar-for-dollar tax credits for donations to scholarship fund organizations.[8] Only students who qualify for the free or reduced-price lunch program are eligible to receive these scholarships, which are valued at up to $3,500 per year. It is noteworthy that each of the state scholarship-based programs is geared to students who, in some way, have special needs or are in circumstances that are likely to disadvantage them.

The state also has more general choice plans. Charter schools began operating in Florida in 1996. By the 2005–6 school year, the state had 334 charter schools in operation, the third-highest number in the country. The schools are authorized and financed by local school districts. Through legislation passed in 1996, the state also requires that school districts have an open-enrollment plan that allows parental choice to be a significant factor in assigning students to schools. A 1985 state law also allows parents to direct home education for their children.[9]

Many of these state programs have had steady and significant growth since their establishment, although the private-school voucher part of the OSP program never took off. A large part of the reason is that the vast majority of schools that received an F grade in 1999 did not receive a second F grade and therefore were never subjected to vouchers. At the time of the state supreme court ruling in January 2006, only 740 students statewide were using OSP vouchers to attend private schools.[10]

The McKay Scholarships have been more popular. Only 970 students used McKay Scholarships in the 2000–1 school year. Five years later (in 2005–6), 16,812 students took advantage of them. By 2005–6, 740 private schools were participating in the program, up from 100 in 2000–1. The Corporate Tax Credit Scholarship Program has held steady, with about 10,000–15,000 students, since it began in the 2002–3 school year.[11]

Charter school enrollment has steadily increased. In the first year (1996–97), there were only 574 students in five charter schools. In the

TABLE 10-1

AYP BY SCHOOL GRADE, ALL FLORIDA SCHOOLS

	2002–3			2003–4		
	A–C	D/F	Total	A–C	D/F	Total
Pass AYP	360	0	360	660	0	660
(%)	(15)	(0)	(14)	(27)	(0)	(25)
Fail AYP	1,973	162	2,135	1,757	231	1,988
(%)	(85)	(100)	(86)	(73)	(100)	(75)
Total	2,333	162	2,495	2,417	231	2,648
(%)	(94)	(6)	(100)	(91)	(9)	(100)

SOURCE: Author's calculations using data from the Florida Department of Education, *School Accountability Report Links*, http://www.firn.edu/doe/schoolgrades/ (accessed May 10, 2007).

2005–6 school year, 92,214 students attended the 334 charter schools in the state. In addition, over 50,000 students in the state were home-schooled, up from a little less than 40,000 in 2000.[12]

On top of the Florida choice programs come the choice options associated with No Child Left Behind. If a school receiving federal Title I funds fails to make adequate yearly progress (AYP) for two years, it is labeled "in school improvement," and parents of students in that school have the option of choosing a school that is not in school improvement, with transportation provided. If a Title I school fails to make AYP for three years, parents of students in that school who are eligible for free or reduced-price lunch have the opportunity to receive supplemental educational services (SES). SES offers tutoring through state-approved providers during flexible times outside the regular school day and on weekends.[13] No Florida schools are yet eligible for restructuring, which occurs after five consecutive AYP failures, but over five hundred are at risk of four consecutive AYP failures with the 2006–7 AYP score calculations.[14]

As noted earlier, academic performance standards determined by the state's A+ Plan differ markedly from those determined by NCLB's AYP criteria. The basic concepts, tests, strategies, and objectives of the two systems are similar.[15] Both test students annually in at least reading and math, and

| | 2004–5 | | | | 2005–6 | | |
A–C	D/F	Total		A–C	D/F	Total
1,059	0	1,059		854	0	854
(43)	(0)	(38)		(32)	(0)	(31)
1,403	308	1,711		1,788	145	1,933
(57)	(100)	(62)		(68)	(100)	(69)
2,462	308	2,770		2,642	145	2,787
(89)	(11)	(100)		(95)	(5)	(100)

NOTE: Schools that did not receive a school grade under Florida's A+ Plan or an AYP designation are excluded from this chart. "Fail AYP" includes schools that received "provisional" AYP in 2006 and 2005.

both establish consequences for low-performing schools, including allowing students in them to transfer to higher-performing schools. But the ways schools are rated often lead to conflicting assessments of performance.

The primary difference between the A+ Plan and NCLB ratings is that A+ gives weight to *learning gains* as well as achievement levels, while NCLB focuses on the percentages of students achieving specified proficiency levels. A school's gains are not taken into account in the NCLB calculation. In addition, while A+ gives special weight to academically low-performing students, NCLB requires that proficiency levels be calculated for a number of student subgroups.[16] While many schools across the country are held responsible for the performance of only a limited number of subgroups because some subgroups have too few students in them, schools in Florida tend to be large and diverse and therefore have a large number of performance hurdles to clear to make AYP.

As a consequence of their different criteria, the school performance appraisals determined, respectively, by the state's A+ Plan and by NCLB often give mixed signals about school quality. In the 2005–6 school year, 74 percent of schools in the state received a grade of either A or B, and 95 percent received a grade of at least C, according to the A+ Plan; but 40 percent of the A/B schools and more than two-thirds of schools with at least a C did not make AYP, according to NCLB. No D or F schools made AYP. Table 10-1 shows the number and percentage of schools in the state that made and failed AYP by school grade (A–C and D/F) by year.[17]

Because the A+ and NCLB ratings were so discrepant, Florida petitioned the U.S. Department of Education in 2005 for amendments to its NCLB accountability plan. Most importantly, and relevant to the discussion here, Florida requested that schools that did not make AYP but received an A or B in the A+ Plan be identified as "Provisional AYP" (P/AYP) schools. Under this proposal, P/AYP schools would be treated differently from other schools that did not make AYP.[18] Specifically, only students in P/AYP schools who did not score proficient or higher in either mathematics or reading would be offered school choice or SES. Such a change would have cut the number of schools fully subject to the NCLB school choice requirements by about half.[19] While the secretary of the U.S. Department of Education was willing to test this change in a limited number of school districts, she was unwilling to grant a statewide approval. Florida declined the offer of a limited test. So while schools in Florida that receive an A or B in the A+ Plan but do not make AYP are designated P/AYP, they are still held to the requirements of schools that do not make AYP. The P/AYP designation may reduce confusion by parents about school performance, and may give some recognition to staff producing student achievement gains, but P/AYP schools still face the full consequences of not making AYP.[20]

School Choice in Miami

All the state choice programs, and more, operate in M-DCPS. The district has a long history of offering choice to students and parents, starting with early desegregation efforts and continuing and expanding since the district was declared unitary in 2002. As early as 1997, the school board established an office to oversee the choice programs of the district. Fully 22 percent of the students in Miami (about 80,000 students) attended a "choice" school in the 2005–6 school year.[21] To put these numbers in perspective, consider that if these choice students constituted a separate school district, it would be among the top thirty-five largest in the country, and larger than Austin, Denver, Cleveland, Boston, San Francisco, or the District of Columbia.[22]

Table 10-2
ENROLLMENT IN SCHOOL CHOICE PROGRAMS

	2002–3	2003–4	2004–5	2005–6	2006–7
Magnet	27,941	28,035	32,651	31,861	—
Charter	7,490	11,607	13,397	18,516	—
NCLB choice	N/A	237	528	633	1,195
Controlled choice	8,328	8,150	7,492	9,417	—
I Choose!	N/A	N/A	6,420	9,940	10,355
McKay Scholarship*	1,896	2,780	3,297	3,607	4,090
OSP Scholarship*	514	558	868	250	—

SOURCES: Miami-Dade County Public Schools, *I Choose 2006–2007 Choice Plan Specialized Programs*, 2006, http://choice.dadeschools.net/images/2006_choice_plan.pdf (accessed May 10, 2007); Miami-Dade County Public Schools district officials, emails to Jayanti Owens, October and November 2006. NOTE: The 2006–7 enrollment figures represent the running total at the time this study was completed, October 26, 2006.
*Program places students in both private and public schools. OSP stopped private school enrollment in 2005–6.

While the total of students exercising choice is large, the extent to which individual programs are utilized varies greatly. Magnet schools and charter schools, part of the district choice program, have the largest enrollments; NCLB and OSP have the smallest, by far (table 10-2). In 2005–6, seventy-six magnet programs in sixty-seven schools served over 30,000 students, and fifty-eight charter schools had a total enrollment of over 18,000 students. An additional thirty-two charter school applications had been approved by the district, and an enrollment of 70,000 students in charter schools in the following few years is likely to be realized.[23]

In contrast, in that same year, OSP served only 250 students, and NCLB school transfer served only 633. Despite being restricted to students with disabilities, the McKay Scholarship Program served over 3,600 students— 330 in public schools and 3,277 in private schools.[24]

No doubt part of the reason for the difference in the take-up rates between magnet and charter schools, on one hand, and OSP and NCLB transfer, on the other, is history. Both magnet and charter schools have had a long history in M-DCPS—the first magnet (Charles R. Drew Elementary Schools) in M-DCPS opened in 1973—and so parents are familiar with them.[25]

The district was also a pioneer with charter schools. Miami opened the first in the state (Liberty City Charter School) the same year state legislation was passed. The Opportunity Scholarship Program has offered choice since 2000, but, as mentioned earlier, relatively few schools in Florida have received two F grades in four years and thereby become eligible for choice under OSP. NCLB transfers only became an option in the 2003–4 school year. Before considering other reasons for the low take-up rate of NCLB school transfer, it is useful to describe more fully the more popular M-DCPC choice programs.

Different types of magnet programs, governed by different rules, operate in M-DCPC. In general, the district attempts to put geographic boundaries around choice options. Dade County covers approximately two thousand square miles of land, so developing efficient transportation systems to support school choice is a challenge. Some magnet programs are open to students from multiple attendance areas but operate in schools that also provide regular programs for students from the school's attendance area. Other magnets are schoolwide programs but open only to students within certain attendance boundaries. Still others are schoolwide without attendance boundaries, but with priority given to students who live in the area, while others serve any eligible students in the district.

Some magnet programs and schools are permitted to take students' achievement levels, talents, and interests into account in determining eligibility for enrollment, but, for the most part, they are randomly selected from applicants in appropriate attendance areas in a process that also takes into account indicators of school performance and socioeconomic status.[26] All magnets are expected to recruit a diverse applicant pool of students. If diversity goals are not met for two years, additional weights may be applied in the random selection process. According to Florida statutes, all students admitted to a magnet program or school are eligible for transportation if they live more than two miles from their school of choice.[27]

The district school choice programs also include controlled choice and *I Choose!* Controlled-choice schools have "an enhanced curriculum focused on an academic theme."[28] They accept applications early each spring for the following fall. Enrollment is based on random selection from applicants within the zone, though priority is given to siblings and to homes closer to the controlled-choice school. In 2005–6, 9,417 students utilized controlled choice, choosing from fourteen designated schools in six controlled-choice zones.[29]

The *I Choose!* program is supported with a grant from the U.S. Department of Education and is designed to foster voluntary within-district school choice by increasing the number of choice schools available. In this five-year plan, the district will identify eight choice zones and support the creation of a number of school options. Currently, there are two choice zones, containing nineteen *I Choose!* schools. Additionally, the *I Choose!* program creates "All Academy" choice schools at underenrolled and under-construction schools that will be open to the whole district. Students are randomly selected for enrollment from the applicant pool.

The district has a number of other, smaller choice programs. For example, K–8 centers are available for parents who prefer that their children complete school through eighth grade in a K–8 setting rather than attend a middle school. With federal grant support, the district has also established a variety of high school initiatives. These include smaller learning communities in sixteen of its high schools, career academies with business partnerships, a lab school in partnership with the University of Miami, three career technical high schools, a dual-enrollment high school/college program for eleventh and twelfth grade students, and satellite learning centers seeking to enable students to attend public school at their parents' workplaces. Under certain circumstances, parents may also request administrative transfers, which allow for routine school changes due to family moves, or other transfers into schools that are not overenrolled.[30]

NCLB School Choice

The above discussion begs the question of why the take-up rate on NCLB choice (school transfer) is so low (table 10-3). Clearly, Miami is a community accustomed to exercising school choice. Indeed, there appears to be a strong acquired appetite for it. Yet fewer than one-half of 1 percent (.47 percent) of students eligible for NCLB school choice in 2005–6 requested and used a transfer. The take-up rate is even lower than the low national estimate

TABLE 10-3

NCLB SCHOOL TRANSFERS, MIAMI-DADE COUNTY

	2003–4	2004–5	2005–6	2006–7
Eligible schools	9	140	148	148
Receiving schools	N/A	108	115	112
Eligible students	7,537	125,738	133,359	125,538
Eligible students requesting	237	528	633	1,195
(%)	(3.1)	(0.4)	(0.5)	(1.0)
Eligible students receiving	237	528	633	1,195
(%)	(3.1)	(0.4)	(0.5)	(1.0)

SOURCES: Miami-Dade County Public Schools, *I Choose 2006–2007 Choice Plan Specialized Programs, 2006,* http://choice.dadeschools.net/images/2006_choice_plan.pdf (accessed May 10, 2007); Miami-Dade County Public Schools district officials, emails to Jayanti Owens, October and November 2006. NOTE: 2006–7 is incomplete.

TABLE 10-4

AYP BY SCHOOL GRADE, ALL MIAMI-DADE COUNTY SCHOOLS

	2002–3			2003–4		
	A–C	D/F	Total	A–C	D/F	Total
Pass AYP	24	0	24	75	0	75
(%)	(9)	(0)	(8)	(29)	(0)	(24)
Fail AYP	231	48	279	187	56	243
(%)	(91)	(100)	(92)	(71)	(100)	(76)
Total	255	48	303	262	56	318
(%)	(84)	(16)	(100)	(82)	(18)	(100)

SOURCE: Authors' calculations using data from the Florida Department of Education, *School Accountability Report Links,* http://www.firn.edu/doe/schoolgrades/ (accessed May 10, 2007).

of 1.6 percent of eligible students using the NCLB school transfer option in 2005–6.[31] We consider five possible explanations for the apparent lack of responsiveness to the NCLB school choice option in Miami below.

Alternatives Are Not Available. Two explanations are commonly cited for the generally low rates of NCLB school choice in large urban districts across the country. The first is that eligible-school alternatives are not available. According to NCLB requirements, students may only transfer into schools that are not in school improvement. In many districts this is a problem: Nationally, 20 percent reported no schools with the AYP rating necessary to accept students, and 25 percent claimed lack of space for transfer students in 2004–5.[32] But in M-DCPS, while only 36 percent of schools made AYP in 2005–6 (table 10-4), 55 percent (180 schools) were not in school improvement. Of these, 115 had the space to accept NCLB transfers. Clearly, these schools could not absorb all the students from all 148 schools in school improvement, but the low demand— only 633 students—could be easily absorbed.[33]

In addition, NCLB school choice is, in many ways, less constrained than other choice programs open to parents in M-DCPS. Because of the

	2004–5				2005–6		
	A–C	D/F	Total		A–C	D/F	Total
150	0	150		119	0	119	
(53)	(0)	(45)		(39)	(0)	(36)	
133	50	183		190	20	210	
(47)	(100)	(55)		(61)	(100)	(64)	
283	50	333		309	20	329	
(85)	(15)	(100)		(94)	(6)	(100)	

NOTE: Schools that did not receive a school grade under Florida's A+ Plan or an AYP designation are excluded from this chart. "Fail AYP" includes schools that received "provisional" AYP in 2006 and 2005.

TABLE 10-5
SCHOOL CHOICE CAPACITY

	Geographic zones	Available schools
Magnet	Some in-zone only; some give proximity advantages	76 programs in 67 schools
Charter	No	58 charter schools
NCLB choice	3	34–48 schools per zone
Controlled choice	6	2–3 schools per zone
I Choose!	2 (up to 8 eventually)	6–13 schools per zone
McKay Scholarship	3	47–85 schools per zone
OSP Scholarship	3	Schools with a grade of C or better

SOURCE: Miami-Dade County Public Schools, I Choose 2006–2007 Choice Plan Specialized Programs, 2006, http://choice.dadeschools.net/images/2006_choice_plan.pdf (accessed May 10, 2007); Miami-Dade County Public Schools district officials, emails to Jayanti Owens, October and November 2006.

expansive physical size of the district, M-DCPS tends to establish geographic boundaries or attendance zones for its choice programs to control transportation costs. For example, in I Choose! and controlled choice, two to thirteen schools are available for choice in a zone. To use these programs, a student must both live in the appropriate zone and choose among the schools in that zone (see table 10-5). In contrast, in NCLB, every student in the district in a school identified for improvement has the school transfer option; and while choice should be within boundaries, the boundaries are large, containing thirty-four to forty-eight schools.

It is notable that 100 percent of the students who requested NCLB school transfers received them, suggesting that shortages in available enrollment spaces or a restricted number of eligible receiving schools are not the issue in M-DCPS, at least not with the current low level of demand.[34]

Ineffective Communication to Parents. A second common explanation for the low use of the NCLB transfer option in large urban school districts is that the districts do not effectively communicate information about the option to parents. This seems to be a hard case to make in M-DCPS. Miami-Dade has extensively promoted NCLB school choice through notification letters sent individually to parents, choice outreach information at schools, advertisements in local media, radio and television commercials, and other targeted dissemination. Outreach efforts are made in English, Haitian Creole, and Spanish. The school transfer application is available in all three languages and is a simple form that requests basic student information and indication of school choice preferences. The district has also promoted NCLB school choice programs directly to parents through local employers, such as those in the hospitality industry, that employ large numbers of parents whose children are likely to be eligible for school transfer. Although the number of students using NCLB school transfer doubled from 633 in 2005–6 to 1,195 in 2006–7, it is still small relative to enrollment in other choice programs and amounts to fewer than 1 percent (.95 percent) of the eligible population.

Distance a Deterrent. A third possibility is that logistical barriers associated with the large geographic region covered by the school district restrict demand for NCLB transfer. But if this were the case, other choice programs would be constrained in the same way. Even if the size of each of the three NCLB school choice zones were a deterrent, the district provides transportation for students when the distance from home to school is more than two miles. It is therefore difficult to attach much weight to this possibility.

Receiving Schools Believed No Better. A fourth possibility is that parents do not think the schools that are available for transfer because they are not in school improvement are any better than those in school improvement that their children already attend. The school improvement designation, which is based on AYP results, may not provide a clear signal of school quality to parents, especially since it is often at odds with the state performance grade. One district official gives an example of this confusion: "Miami High is a sending school under NCLB, so you have a choice out, but by state standards it's a receiving school under the Opportunity Scholarship Program for kids that want to get out of failing high schools." Table 10-4 shows that 61 percent (190) of the schools that did not make AYP received grades between A and C in the state grading system. Indeed, over half (51 percent) of the schools not making AYP received grades of A or B.[35] The rules for making AYP are complicated, since all student subgroups

FIGURE 10-1

SCHOOL CHOICE APPLICATION WINDOWS

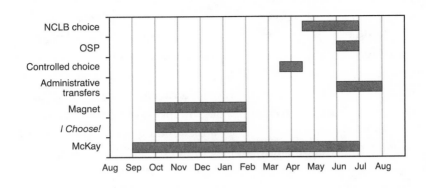

SOURCE: Miami-Dade County Public Schools, *I Choose 2006–2007 Choice Plan Specialized Programs, 2006*, http://choice.dadeschools.net/images/2006_choice_plan.pdf (accessed May 10, 2007).
NOTE: The NCLB choice application period is April 24–May 19. However, for schools unexpectedly in "school improvement" (e.g. schools that districts had informally predicted and reported would not fail AYP), notification is sent to parents and a later deadline extended to them.

must make the proficiency mark. Miami-Dade schools with large subgroup populations may miss AYP by a few criteria, but still be generally high-performing schools. For most parents, the state grading may offer a clearer indication of the value of a school. We explore this issue further when we examine the characteristics of the schools that parents choose.

Choice Offered Too Late. The fifth possible explanation for low participation in school choice is that parents wanting to exercise the option do so well before NCLB school transfer becomes available. Figure 10-1 shows the decision timelines for the major choice programs offered by Miami-Dade.[36] Applications for two of the largest of M-DCPS's programs, *I Choose!* and magnet schools, occur in the fall and winter. This is months before enrollment for NCLB school choice is available. Because NCLB transfer eligibility is based on the cumulative performance of a school, including performance in the year immediately prior, the decision window for parents occurs at the end of the school year—from April 24 to May 19 in 2006–7.

M-DCPS attempts to speed up the process by providing parents with an early notification of schools likely to be eligible for school transfer, allowing parents to register their preferences before final AYP results come out, and in some cases before the school is formally determined as being in school improvement.[37] In 2004–5, M-DCPS was in the 29 percent of districts that managed to notify parents of eligibility to transfer before the beginning of the school year.[38] Even so, the decision window remains considerably later in the school year than those for other programs. One administrator thought that, since most of the other choice programs rely on lotteries for final selection, parents who used NCLB transfer were those for whom it was "the last chance" to leave a school where they were dissatisfied.[39]

M-DCPS recognizes the overall complexity of the array of choice programs it provides to parents, and that this complexity may lead to confusion and low utilization rates of some choice options. The district is currently attempting to work out a system so that parents can apply using a consolidated application at one point in time. The details have yet to be worked out.

The Bases of Choice

In this section we examine the implicit choice behavior in the NCLB transfer program, the magnet program, and the M-DCPS administrative-transfer program that includes *I Choose!* M-DCPS provided us with school transfer files that show at the individual student level the school each was leaving (sending school) and that to which each was transferring (receiving school) for the 2005–6 school year, by program.

Table 10-6 shows the percentage of students leaving and entering schools by AYP status and by state performance grade (A–F).[40] A number of observations are worth noting.

First, many students choosing to transfer left schools with "A" state performance grades. Over one-third using the magnet school option and the administrative-transfer (including *I Choose!*) option left A schools. Similarly, more than one-third of students using the magnet school option and the administrative-transfer option left schools that made AYP. Interestingly, a large fraction of the A school students chose other A schools. In short, much of the choice was being exercised by parents who were fine-tuning their options, probably on the basis of detailed information.

TABLE 10-6

AYP AND SCHOOL GRADES: PERCENTAGE OF TRANSFERS
BY SENDING/RECEIVING SCHOOLS

	NCLB School Ratings			State School Ratings				
Program	Pass AYP	P/AYP	Fail AYP	A	B	C	D	F
NCLB school transfer (N=630)								
Sending school	20	13	68	8	15	45	21	12
Receiving school	31	44	25	50	25	20	5	0
Magnet schools (N=18,839)								
Sending school	34	18	47	35	15	28	16	6
Receiving school	48	12	40	52	7	35	5	1
Administrative transfers, including I Choose! (N=11,630)								
Sending school	35	16	48	34	14	34	15	3
Receiving school	46	23	31	52	15	24	8	1

SOURCE: Authors' calculations based on School Transfer Files, Miami-Dade County Public Schools provided by district officials, and data from the Florida Department of Education, *School Accountability Report Links*, http://www.firn.edu/doe/schoolgrades/ (accessed May 10, 2007).
NOTE: P/AYP stands for Provisional AYP, which means that the school has received an A or B school grade under the Florida A+ Plan but has failed AYP.

Second, A schools were the most likely to be chosen. Over half of the students in each of the three programs for which we have data opted to attend them. In other words, the state A+ ratings either significantly affected parents' choice of schools, or they comported with parents' independent judgments about school quality. A very small fraction chose D or F schools.

Third, a very large percent of parents chose schools in each of the programs that did not make AYP. Indeed, nearly 70 percent of the parents exercising the NCLB school transfer chose a school not making AYP! Forty-four percent of them chose a school with a provisional AYP (P/AYP) rating. Recall that this status is given to schools that received an A or B in the state system, but did not make AYP. And more than half of the students using the magnet option or the administrative-transfer option chose schools that did not make AYP.

The choice behavior of parents does not align with the AYP status of choice schools. Instead, choice patterns indicate that parents give the state ratings more serious consideration when choosing a school for their child.

Supplemental Educational Services

As noted earlier, the request rate for supplemental educational services (28.1 percent) increased dramatically for the 2006–7 school year. On one hand, this is a tribute to the efforts of M-DCPS to generate demand. The district conducted a campaign similar to its choice outreach to inform the public about SES, even including automated telephone calls to homes with a message from a Miami Heat basketball player. Other outreach included media advertisements, flyers, and individual notification letters. The district hosted numerous SES fairs where providers presented their programs, answered parents' questions, and solicited participation. These fairs were held twice a month in at least three different locations during the annual enrollment period. Parents could enroll their child right on the spot at the fair, again using a simple application available in all three major languages spoken in the district.

A new state law spurred these outreach efforts. In 2006, the state legislature augmented the Florida K–12 School Code with regard to "supplemental educational services in Title I schools; school district and provider responsibilities." Under this law, the state Department of Education required and assisted districts to publicize and streamline the SES enrollment process.[41] Miami-Dade responded. One district official commented that the district's outreach endeavors over the 2005–6 school year for SES and NCLB choice had far "outdone previous marketing efforts."[42] The results seemed to bear that out. For the 2006–7 school year, over 25,000 of the over 90,000 students eligible for SES requested services. This represents more than fifty times the number who requested services in 2004–5 (397 students), the first year they were available, and more than a threefold increase in the rate—from 7.8 percent of those eligible to 28.1 percent (table 10-7). While the 2006–7 application numbers were high, it was as yet unclear how many students would actually use the services, but presumably the number was considerably more than it was the previous year. The district office worked overtime to process the more than 25,000 SES applications, as each had to be double-checked to ensure the applicant was both enrolled in an eligible school and met the criteria for free or reduced-price lunch, and then entered into the database by hand. A lack of effort on the part of the district to disseminate information about NCLB school choice options to parents and process applications in a timely way did not appear to be a problem.

TABLE 10-7
SUPPLEMENTAL EDUCATIONAL SERVICES

	2004–5	2005–6	2006–7
Eligible schools	9	95	127
Eligible students	5,122	78,696	92,186
Eligible students requesting	397	8,289	25,918*
(%)	(7.8)	(10.5)	(28.1)
Eligible students receiving	121	4,322	10,854*
(%)	(2.4)	(5.5)	(11.8)

SOURCES: Miami-Dade County Public Schools, *I Choose 2006–2007 Choice Plan Specialized Programs,* 2006, http://choice.dadeschools.net/images/2006_choice_plan.pdf (accessed May 10, 2007); Miami-Dade County Public Schools district officials, emails to Jayanti Owens, October and November 2006. * Data as of January 8, 2007.

At 11.8 percent, however, the use rate for SES remains low.[43] Program administrators have suggested a number of possible explanations. One concern is that parents may not make deliberate choices the way they might if they felt they were paying directly for the services. The fairs put the choices plainly before parents and make it easy to sign up. This, of course, is good. But many parents sign up with multiple providers; after all, the services are "free," and some providers market aggressively. In short, the request rate may be an inflated measure of real interest or reasoned choice. Scheduling also is a problem. Most providers prefer to provide services to students on the school site. However, because of limited space and staff, not all services can be scheduled immediately after school, leaving some students unattended until their SES program begins. This break in schedule may contribute to low actual participation. There have also been reports of providers not showing up for scheduled tutoring sessions, something that is difficult to monitor. M-DCPS has forty-seven providers spread over the city, meeting students in different places at different times.[44] Unreliable scheduling may also contribute to low usage. Many of these issues may simply reflect organizational learning problems that will be overcome with experience and the development of effective and efficient procedures over time.[45] Others may be endemic to the complexity of running SES programs.

Conclusion

M-DCPS operates a system of school choice that involves more students than the total enrollment of many large cities. Yet, even in this "prochoice" environment, the take-up rate on the NCLB options is low.

We have explored various reasons for the low take-up rate and conclude that the most common ones do not hold in M-DCPS, especially for the transfer option. Sufficient spaces seem to be available in higher-rated schools; parents in the community are accustomed to making school choices; and M-DCPS goes to great lengths in informing parents about their options.

Our analysis suggests two problems, one reasonably easy to handle and another that may indicate an inherent and fundamental flaw in the design of the NCLB choice (transfer) policy. The first problem is timing. Because the NCLB choice application period is late in the school year while the other choice plans in the district operate on a much earlier timetable, many students inclined to exercise choice may do so through the other plans before the NCLB possibility is available. If this is the main reason for the low take-up rate of NCLB choice relative to the other options, there may be nothing wrong with the program that timing will not fix. The district is already working on the development of a consolidated application. Time will tell if it will lead to a take-up rate for NCLB closer to that of the other choice plans.

The second problem is more fundamental. The school choice option is triggered and guided by the NCLB-defined performance rating of schools. The option is available to students in Title I schools that have not made AYP for at least two years, and students may choose a school that has not been designated "in need of improvement" (that is, a Title I school that has not made AYP for two or more years). Our results indicate that students (or their parents) may not consider AYP status when making schooling choices, suggesting that they do not consider it a legitimate indicator of school quality. Rather, they seem to use the state ratings for schools (which differ from NCLB's), and probably their own more detailed information. In short, part of the reason NCLB school choice may not be working well is because it is sending parents a misleading signal regarding school quality, and parents as consumers are using what they consider better information to guide their behavior. A market for schooling may be working pretty well in M-DCPS, despite the introduction by NCLB of faulty signals, because other information and choice plans are available. But with its reliance on AYP status as a signal, the submarket for NCLB school choice may never be as vibrant.

PART IV

Restructuring Districts and Schools

11

Remedies in Action:
Four "Restructured" Schools

Julie Kowal and Bryan C. Hassel

One of the most striking provisions of the No Child Left Behind Act is the sequence of increasingly dramatic actions prescribed for schools that chronically fall short of their achievement targets. Under the law, districts must develop a plan for "restructuring" schools that do not make adequate yearly progress (AYP) for five consecutive years. Schools that fail to make AYP for a sixth year in a row must implement the plan to improve student learning. In contrast to previous federal education law, NCLB's restructuring provisions appear on their face to require more than just continued "school improvement" through professional development, new instructional programs, and other standard fare. For schools that have failed year after year, the law envisions change that is more drastic, involving fundamental shifts in the way they are "structured."

So has NCLB led to this kind of drastic change in how districts approach the problem of chronically low-performing schools? To gain preliminary insight into what restructuring looks like "on the ground," we profiled four schools that entered the final stage of restructuring in 2005–6.[1] These case studies offer an account of how these schools (and three districts) have interpreted the restructuring requirements of NCLB and provide the basis for several observations about how these mandates will play out.

Under the law, districts can choose from several tactics for restructuring failing schools:

1. Reopen the school as a public charter school

2. Replace all or most of the school staff

3. Contract with an outside entity to operate the school

4. Turn the operation of the school over to the state educational agency, if permitted under state law and agreed to by the state

5. Engage in another form of major restructuring that makes fundamental reforms, "such as significant changes in the school's staffing and governance."[2] Nonregulatory guidance from the U.S. Department of Education in 2006 further defines this option to include reforms such as diminishing school-based management and decision-making, closing the school and reopening it as a focus or theme school with new staff or staff skilled in the focus area, or dissolving the school and assigning students to other schools in the district.[3]

Each of these restructuring options, hereafter referred to as options 1 through 5, is intended to usher in a significant shift in how the school is governed. Aside from such enumerated lists, however, the Department of Education has provided little guidance on how restructuring should be implemented. As a result, the specific approaches to each alternative vary among states and districts, and the actual implementation looks quite different for each school.[4]

During the 2005–6 school year, approximately 600 schools in the United States entered the final stage of restructuring.[5] This number is modest, in large part because most states have not been tracking AYP long enough for schools to move into the restructuring phase; the few with large numbers of schools in restructuring, such as Michigan and California, established state accountability systems that allowed them to begin calculating AYP earlier than others. According to data compiled by the Center on Education Policy (CEP), only about 15 percent of schools in improvement in 2004–5 exited that status in 2005–6 (1,011 out of 8,646 schools).[6] As most of the other 85 percent continue to fail to make AYP, it is fair to expect the number of schools in restructuring to grow dramatically over the next few years. It is foreseeable, based on current trends, that nearly 2,000 schools will be in restructuring in 2007–8, and more than 3,200 in 2008–9.[7] Meanwhile, approximately 1,000 schools were planning for restructuring in 2006–7, and another 6,150 were in various stages of "corrective action" leading up to restructuring.

To date, restructuring has been largely an urban phenomenon: In 2005–6, about 90 percent of schools in restructuring were located in urban districts. Fifteen districts that accounted for nearly half of all such schools served traditionally disadvantaged populations.[8] In 2004–5, 60 percent of students in restructuring schools qualified for free or reduced-price lunch (compared to 41 percent of students in all public schools), 40 percent were Hispanic, and 37 percent were African-American (compared to 19 and 16 percent, respectively, in all public schools).[9] California, Georgia, New York, Michigan, Pennsylvania, Maryland, and Ohio had the highest proportion—70 percent—in restructuring in 2004–5.[10]

Most schools facing NCLB sanctions are not arbitrary victims of one missed target, but are chronically failing large numbers of students. Of the schools that failed to make AYP in 2004–5, 51 percent missed targets for two or more subgroups or for all students. Less than a quarter of schools that missed AYP did so because only one student subgroup fell short of achievement targets.[11]

Recent surveys suggest that most districts are implementing mild or moderate interventions in restructuring schools—option 5 in the list above—rather than the stronger interventions—options 1 through 4.[12] In Michigan, for example, 93 percent of restructuring schools in 2004–5 used option 5, as did 76 percent in California in 2005–6.[13] In a 2006 review of the effects of NCLB, the Center on Education Policy found that in districts that used these moderate interventions, 42 percent appointed an outside expert to advise the restructuring school, 24 percent extended the school day or year, and 14 percent "restructured the internal organization of the school." Almost no districts invited private firms or state agencies to take over the schools or reopened them as charter schools. Of those schools that implemented more drastic reforms, many used the law to replace staff members who would have been difficult to replace without the power of federal sanctions (14 percent of all restructuring schools replaced some or all staff members in 2004–5).[14]

These national statistics offer a broad picture of how states, districts, and schools are being affected by NCLB. National numbers cannot tell us, however, what restructuring looks like as it is implemented in districts and schools. As more schools become subject to NCLB sanctions each year, our four case studies provide an important picture of how the restructuring requirements of NCLB are being put into practice at the local level.

Methodology and Overview

This chapter profiles the restructuring experiences of four schools in Michigan and California. We chose to profile schools in these states because both have well-established accountability systems that allowed them to begin calculating AYP earlier than most other states. As a result, they also have comparatively large numbers of schools in restructuring. For the same reasons, restructuring experiences in Michigan and California have been the subject of intensive studies by the Center on Education Policy.[15]

For our research, education officials in each state provided lists of "year 5" schools from which we selected four that, at least on paper, represented a diverse set of restructuring approaches. In California, we chose Balboa Elementary and Gompers Middle School (both in San Diego); in Michigan, Buchanan Elementary (Grand Rapids) and Milwood Middle School (Kalamazoo). To gather information about the cases, we conducted structured interviews with officials at the schools in summer or fall 2006 and carried out detailed reviews of relevant state, district, and school-level documents, such as the schools' required restructuring plans.

With only one year of testing data available since Balboa, Buchanan, Gompers, and Milwood implemented their restructuring plans, these case reports offer little evaluation of whether the schools' restructuring has, in fact, put them "back on course to meet state standards," as the law intends. In addition, because of the diversity of schools in restructuring across the country, it is not possible to hold these out as representative of the national population of schools in this phase of NCLB. Instead, the case studies offer a picture of how three districts and four schools have interpreted the restructuring requirements of NCLB and provide the basis for several observations about what restructuring looks like at the school level.

Case Study #1: Buchanan Elementary School

Buchanan Elementary School, located a few miles south of downtown in Grand Rapids, serves approximately 500 students from prekindergarten through fifth grade. While the population of Grand Rapids is roughly 67 percent white and 16 percent Hispanic, at Buchanan in 2005–6, 90 percent of students were Hispanic, 8 percent African-American, and only 1 percent white; 97 percent qualified for free or reduced-price lunch.[16]

Buchanan has struggled for years; until the current principal, Roberto Garcia, joined the school in 1999, it had suffered from constant turnover in administration. Student test scores were consistently low, with as few as 10 percent meeting grade-level standards in English language arts in spring 2003. A large proportion of the student body speaks English as a second language, and an achievement gap between these and English-speaking students has persisted, particularly in reading and writing. In 2004–5, for example, 41.7 percent of students at Buchanan overall met state standards in reading and 24 percent in writing, compared with only 36 percent and 15 percent, respectively, of English-language learners (figure 11-1 shows schoolwide achievement trends from 2002 to 2006).[17] Garcia says that by 2004, when the school entered year 5 of school improvement under NCLB, "We'd had a school improvement team for awhile."[18]

In 2004 the Grand Rapids school district included Buchanan among a group of schools that had failed to make AYP for four or five consecutive years. Principals from these schools were required to meet monthly with their district contact to monitor implementation of a school restructuring plan.[19] As Garcia describes, the schools' restructuring was "basically a district decision. The superintendent developed the plan for all of us in the district. There wasn't a good deal of choice at the building level." There was also no parent or community voice in the development of the restructuring plans. According to Garcia, staff and parents were invited to provide input to a group of staff volunteers from each grade level who comprised the school improvement team, which had been in place for several years. But "in my particular building," he says, "if we decide to implement a program, there really isn't a whole lot of questioning from parents."

District staff met with Garcia in the fall of 2004 and presented their plan to restructure Buchanan. Although NCLB gives schools up to a year to

FIGURE 11-1

BUCHANAN ELEMENTARY SCHOOL:
PERCENTAGE OF STUDENTS MEETING STATE STANDARDS

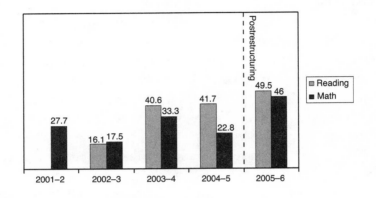

SOURCE: Michigan Department of Education, *Michigan School Report Cards: Buchanan School, 2005–6,* https://oeaa.state.mi.us/ayp/school_one_only_1_2004.asp?ECDid=2345&Grade=6 (accessed May 4, 2007). Data on reading performance from 2001–2 are not publicly available in Michigan.

develop their plans, the CEP has found that many schools in Michigan begin implementing restructuring during their planning year.[20] This was the case at Buchanan as well. In most other ways, however, Buchanan is a classic story of an option 5 restructuring. The district's restructuring plan did not call for changes to governance or staffing, but instead assigned an external review team to the school, required a new instructional model, mandated changes to the school's use of data, and instituted all-day kindergarten.

First, under the plan, an external review team made up of district and intermediate school district staff visited the school regularly to discuss student progress with the school improvement team. "The external review team visited the school periodically to look at achievement data," says Garcia. "They would ask us about how students were doing in every grade level and what kind of intervention plans we had in place for students who were not achieving."

Second, all schools were required to adopt a new instructional model chosen by the district. Garcia was glad for the change, which Buchanan made in 2004. "The previous instructional model didn't work very well for us," he says. With the "four-block framework" as their new instructional model, teachers have begun concentrating on reading and writing and including ESL (English as a second language) strategies in every classroom. Two kindergarten, two first-grade, and two second-grade classrooms at Buchanan now include bilingual education, where students study traditional academic subjects while learning English. To help staff learn the new model, Garcia dedicated extra Title I funds to two new coaches who observe and train teachers in math, language arts, and writing. "We got a lot of Title I money," he says. And while Garcia reports that "some teachers were more comfortable with the coaching than others," this onsite staff development "was probably one of the most effective changes."

According to CEP's national surveys, 95 percent of districts increase the use of student data as part of their restructuring plans. This was true in Grand Rapids, as well. As the third component of its plan, the district required schools to demonstrate regular use of assessment data to guide instruction. This was a major change at Buchanan, according to Garcia. "Teachers always used tests to see how their students are doing, but in the past they would administer a test and keep moving forward. The new focus on data forces them to take a look at how they are doing on a more regular basis. I think it's caused teachers to rethink how they instruct." Teachers now review data four times a year with their colleagues, and at least three times a year with Garcia. Garcia encourages this by establishing collective planning periods for teachers on each grade-level team. "We're all more accountable now to each other, to the district, and to our students," he says.

Finally, Buchanan was required to implement an all-day kindergarten.[21] Garcia says, "I had always wanted an all-day kindergarten, so I was glad it was mandated. Our kids need it."

Garcia remained at the helm throughout Buchanan's restructuring, and there were no staff changes in 2005 aside from the usual turnover. The school received external assistance and extra funds, and implemented a new instructional approach with accompanying professional development. According to Garcia, these changes brought about several improvements, including greater district involvement in the operations of the school and a renewed focus on students' learning needs. Student test scores have risen since 2004: In 2005, the school made AYP for the second year in a row, and in 2006, scores climbed even higher. Still, less than half of the students at Buchanan are meeting state standards in reading and math.

All in all, the changes at Buchanan are hard to distinguish from the "school improvement" efforts underway at thousands of public schools nationwide, including measures taken at Buchanan itself prior to its restructuring. While Garcia says, "These [changes] were good things for us to be involved in," he acknowledges that "we were doing a lot of these things already." Without changes in governance, leadership, or staffing, the same people are still working in largely the same environment. Since Buchanan's challenges are so great, it is not clear that the scope and substance of the changes underway are sufficient to lift the school's achievement over time to meet NCLB's lofty goals for universal proficiency in math and reading by 2014.

Case Study #2: Balboa Elementary School

Located in southwest San Diego about ten miles from the border between the United States and Mexico, Balboa Elementary School operates year-round to serve approximately 800 students in grades K–6. Statistics on Balboa show a school facing a great many challenges. The entire student body qualifies for free or reduced-price lunch. More than 70 percent of students are just learning English. The majority of teachers are in their first or second year of teaching, and turnover is very high—in any given year, principal Sylvia Gonzalez has to use new recruits to fill about one-third of her teaching staff.[22] Recently, Balboa has had to fight to keep its students, too; every year the school loses about 20 percent, most of whom are thought to travel home to Mexico at Christmas and not return.[23] From a peak of nearly 1,000 in 2000–1, the student body declined to just under 800 in 2004–5.

Given this environment, it came as no surprise in 2004 when the school entered its fourth year of program improvement—California's designation for schools that fail to make AYP in the same subject for two consecutive years.[24] English-language learners and socioeconomically disadvantaged students had failed to meet performance expectations for another year. The school's scores as a whole had continued to fall substantially below the districtwide averages for each grade level in both reading and math (see figure 11-2).

The San Diego Unified School District notified Balboa in 2004 that it must propose a plan for restructuring the school in 2005–6, requiring the proposal to be developed by a school restructuring workgroup composed

FIGURE 11-2

BALBOA ELEMENTARY SCHOOL:
PERCENTAGE OF STUDENTS MEETING STATE STANDARDS

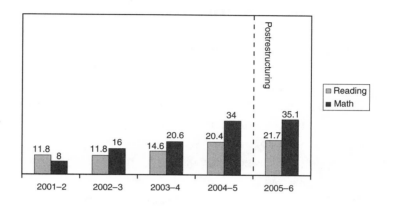

SOURCE: San Diego Unified School District, *School Accountability Report Card: Balboa Elementary School*, 2006. http://studata.sandi.net/research/sarcs/2005-06/SARC013.pdf (accessed May 4, 2007).

of parents, teachers, and community members. So, that fall, Gonzalez hung notices around the school and sent letters home with students to encourage parents, teachers, and community members to attend evening meetings. "Many parents, especially my parents, are not used to having a voice. They believe that what's going on in school is the responsibility of the teachers. They don't get involved in school." But attendance was surprisingly high. Staff hosted parent meetings during evenings and on weekends "so no one would feel left out. This way, everybody felt heard all the time." Gonzalez felt this design was critical to successful implementation of the plan.

Although Gonzalez herself was aware of Balboa's greatest challenges, she involved parents in the process of examining standardized test scores "to see where our deficits were and where our needs were going to be." After a series of about twenty meetings throughout the fall of 2004, the workgroup elected to use option 5 and began fashioning a plan to restructure Balboa. Although it initially considered option 1—the charter option—the workgroup bypassed it because members believed they could implement the necessary changes at Balboa without converting to charter status.

The primary goal of the Balboa plan was to improve student achievement, with a particular focus on overcoming the learning gap between English learners and English-speaking students. A key strategy to meeting this goal was to minimize what had become a constant stream of interruptions during normal class time. Over the years at Balboa, in an effort to meet district requirements, the day had come to include, according to Gonzalez, "a lot of wasted time. We had staff always coming in and out, and we knew that the steps were not developing a quality program for our students."

Balboa's restructuring plan also sought to institute reforms that would help the school retain teachers. "We have a lot of brand new teachers on a regular basis that we have to train. We wanted to look at what it would take to make them want to stay," says Gonzalez. Many teachers "are still in school, finishing certification or working on their master's degree. Others are young parents, and they want to go home to their children." Gonzalez knew that she would have to continue training her teachers every year. But it became clear during the restructuring planning that it would be necessary to include their professional development within the school day.

Parents also wanted their children to have instruction in the arts, which had been dropped several years earlier to allow teachers more time to improve test scores. As Gonzalez explains, "We developed a plan in order to have it all." Under the "Fifth-Day Collaborative Plan" implemented in fall of 2005, grade-level teams of teachers meet for collaborative planning every fifth day. Instead of having substitutes in their classrooms while teachers are planning, Balboa students spend their assigned day cycling through six fifty-minute "extended learning labs" in drama, music, social studies, writing, science, and math. These labs allow time for extra focus on subjects in which they are lagging, while also reintroducing arts into the curriculum. The school day was also extended by thirty-five minutes, which adds the equivalent of twenty days of instruction without adding days to the instructional year.

One of the biggest changes at Balboa in 2005 came as a surprise to everyone involved in developing the plan. Unless they chose to reopen as a charter school, all restructuring schools in San Diego Unified were bound by the district's contract with the local teachers' union, the San Diego Education Association (SDEA), which required all teachers to reapply for their positions. Principals at restructuring schools were allowed to select the first 30 percent of qualified teachers who reapplied; the remaining 70 percent of teaching slots were required to be filled based on seniority.[25] After strug-gling for years with extremely high staff turnover at Balboa, Gonzalez applied immediately for a waiver. In retrospect, had Gonzalez known ini-tially about this districtwide requirement, she might have been more enthu-siastic about pursuing the charter route, which would have allowed the school to make its own hiring and firing decisions. "I had already gone through the process of hiring new people, and I was very happy with the people that we had," says Gonzalez. "Why would I want to go back five years when I've already trained these teachers and gotten them up to par?" The district did not allow the waiver. "Many of my teachers were offended by the district, hurt and angry, and did not reapply. Others who had helped develop the plan ended up having to leave. We made all these changes with these teachers, and then they couldn't stay with us."

The requirement for staff replacement seemed an odd fit at a school that struggled to keep one-third of its staff in any given year. Gonzalez did find ways to keep about 60 percent of her staff in 2005, however, by using her 30 percent primarily to rehire qualified but less senior teachers, and then asking her most experienced teachers to reapply. All of the teachers who started with Gonzalez in the fall of 2005 stayed through to the 2006 school year. Gonzalez attributes this in large part to the targeted professional devel-opment. As for the restructured school day, Gonzalez says, "Students are really enjoying it. They love being able to do things that they wouldn't usu-ally be able to do in the normal classroom. And we've really noticed their self-esteem going up."

Like Buchanan's plan, Balboa's "restructuring" resembles standard school improvement efforts, with its emphasis on professional development and reorganizing instructional time. Leadership, governance, and the school's policy environment have remained largely constant. What staff change there has been was due to turnover and collective bargaining restric-tions, rather than a deliberate effort to refashion the school's teaching force. Will these changes be enough to lift the school out of chronic low per-formance? Test scores are on the rise at Balboa, but passing rates are still very low: In 2005–6, less than a quarter of students met state standards in English; only 35 percent met standards in math. And while the changes have helped the school retain teachers, they have done little to ensure sta-bility in the student population. Only additional time at the restructured

Balboa will show whether the Five-Day Collaborative Plan can usher in the improvements that the district, staff, and parents have hoped for.

Case Study #3: Milwood Magnet School

With a population nearing 80,000, the city of Kalamazoo, Michigan, has two public high schools, three middle schools, sixteen elementary schools, and nine magnet schools. In an environment this small, drops in public school enrollment are perceptible. Administrators felt it at Milwood Middle School, where enrollment dropped in 2004–5 from 540 to 390 students in grades seven and eight. Milwood had experienced a loss of many middle-class families to other options in the district; private and charter schools in the area drew almost half (45 percent) of the students in southeast Kalamazoo in 2005.[26] This, according to principal Kevin Campbell, "starts to signal a downward spiral."[27]

As enrollment at Milwood slipped, so did its test scores. The proportion of eighth graders scoring at proficiency levels on state tests in science dropped by more than eight percentage points between 2002 and 2003; the percentage of seventh graders scoring proficient in reading dropped by thirteen points between 2002–3 and 2003–4 (see figure 11-3).[28] But as state and federal sanctions against the school increased, the philosophy among the teachers remained, according to Campbell: "'Give us different students; we'll give you a different result.'" Many of the teachers at Milwood had been there since the school served a majority-white population, but in 2004, the student body at Milwood was approximately 60 percent African-American, 25 percent white, and 15 percent Hispanic. Most students (80 percent) participated in the free or reduced-price lunch program.[29]

Campbell arrived at Milwood in 2004 after the school failed to make AYP for the fifth year in a row. He was brought in by the district during Milwood's corrective-action phase in an attempt to improve performance at the school. According to Campbell, who had previously served as an elementary school principal in the district, "It didn't take long to realize what was going on. There was a very negative school culture, an entrenched staff. I knew that if we were really interested in fixing this school quickly, we'd need to consider some of the other options available to us." When no significant changes

FIGURE 11-3

MILWOOD MAGNET SCHOOL:
PERCENTAGE OF STUDENTS MEETING STATE STANDARDS

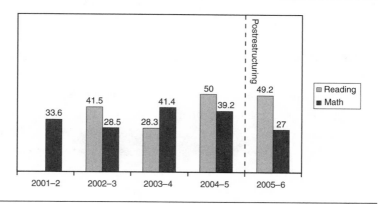

SOURCES: Michigan Department of Education, *Michigan School Report Cards: Milwood Middle School,* 2005–6, https://oeaa.state.mi.us/ayp/school_one_only_1_2004.asp?ECDid=2216&Grade=8 (accessed May 4, 2007). Data on reading performance from 2001–2 are not publicly available in Michigan.

were immediately apparent at the school as a result of Campbell's work in early 2004, he recommended to superintendent Janice Brown that she use the "nuclear option in [her] back pocket: Bomb it and start over."

Campbell and Brown agreed that reconstitution would likely be the best way to restructure the school; the teaching staff had stayed largely the same over the years as the student body had shifted significantly, and many teachers did not have the desire or the skills to work with the new population. "But," Campbell explains, "we knew if that message came from us, it would probably fall on angry ears." So the superintendent appointed a governing board to oversee the development of a restructuring plan and hired external evaluators to assess the school's weaknesses. The governing board was made up of principals, teachers, and parents from Milwood's feeder elementary schools, as well as a union representative and staff and parents from Milwood. Campbell arranged the governing board's first meeting, where, as he describes, "We went to the parents and teachers and said, 'Here is the issue: We are at phase 5 and we want to do some major restructuring at the school. We need your thinking and your input.' Parents' first response was, 'What's wrong?' So the work of the external evaluators was really critical."

Two external evaluators certified by the state's Academic Coaches Registry as school turnaround coaches spent ten days at Milwood in 2004, observing teachers, students, and administration. The evaluators' interview, survey, and walk-through data confirmed Campbell's concerns about the school's climate. At the conclusion of the audit, the evaluators made a presentation to the governing board with ten recommendations. Campbell explains, "After our conversation that night, the board unanimously said, 'We want to act on all of them.'" The evaluators' recommendations allowed the restructuring message to come from an objective source other than the principal or district superintendent. Their recommendations formed the basis of the governing board's proposal to close Milwood Middle at the end of the 2004–5 school year, reconstitute the staff, and reopen the school in 2005–6 to serve grades six through eight.

Campbell points out, however, that "we didn't get into anything about the school being a magnet at that point." That approach mainly arose out of necessity: Reopening as a magnet allowed Milwood to require all staff to reapply for their jobs and bypass contract provisions regarding seniority. "In our district we have favorable language for magnet schools that allows them to staff by matching credentials and interests with the focus of the school. So we decided that would be the best option."

Although the governing board and external evaluators agreed that reconstitution was necessary, the announcement caused an uproar at the school. "I remember the day that everybody got a letter saying, 'The school's closing; you're going to have to reapply for your jobs.' You can't imagine how ugly it got. But I don't blame the teachers. They were a product of the conditions that were created here over time. Still, we had to do it." At the end of the 2004–5 school year, all staff positions were posted with interviews, and placements were completed before students left for the summer.

The school workgroup chose to pursue three further changes in addition to reconstitution at Milwood during restructuring. The school incorporated a new curriculum focused on math, science, and technology. As Campbell explains, before restructuring "the curriculum was entrenched and traditional. But kids today are very tech-savvy. So we threw out a lot of the curriculum and brought in something that is responsive to what kids are going to need to know. They need to know how to use Microsoft Office more than they need to make pillows. So now we teach all the Office tools as part of our curriculum."

With approximately 65 percent new staff at Milwood in the fall of 2005, professional development was also a major focus. "We had a culture that was very much into control, rules, and punishment as a way of trying to maintain order" before restructuring. With this new staff, "we needed to become more relational to kids." The new staff members were hired for their expertise as well as their willingness to learn. Teachers participated in intensive training during the summer of 2005 to set up common expectations and prepare them for working with children from poverty. Still, Campbell says, "It was a pretty ugly year. Every single school structure didn't exist. Even though we got extra time, it didn't even come close to scratching the surface of what we needed to bring everybody together."

As he began a new school year, Campbell was grateful for the changes at Milwood. "Without NCLB," he says, "we probably wouldn't have gone to this extreme. Most schools change principals, and that suffices in terms of meeting a restructuring claim even though they really aren't changing anything; they're just reshuffling. But I told my superintendent: 'I don't want to be in this environment for ten years. You have federal law behind you, and you can use it.'"

Unlike Buchanan and Balboa, Milwood's changes appear to fall more in the category of dramatic change in structure envisioned under NCLB's restructuring provisions. Between 2004 and 2006, Milwood undertook two of the most drastic methods of reform, bringing in a new principal and replacing most of its staff. Its curriculum changes were wholesale, rather than piecemeal. Its new magnet focus did not significantly change Milwood's student population, according to Campbell (in 2005, 53 percent of the students were African-American, 36 were white, and 9 percent were Hispanic). But in 2005 the school made AYP for the first time in over five years. Test scores in reading are improving, with nearly 50 percent of students meeting state standards in 2005–6. But math scores have dropped consistently since 2003–4, and in 2005–6 only 27 percent of students met standards in math. Nonetheless, Campbell is optimistic. "You stripped the school bare. It has to be built back up again. You can't have it be the Taj Mahal in one year. It's going to take three to five years."

Case Study #4: Gompers Middle School

Five rival gangs claim territory in the Chollas View neighborhood surrounding Gompers Middle School in southeastern San Diego. Crime and drugs are common. And in the words of principal Vince Riveroll, Gompers has "some of the student subgroups that need us the most."[30] Most students are poor—in 2004–5, 81 percent qualified for free or reduced-price lunch. Of just over 1,500 students in grades six through nine, 58 percent were Hispanic and 29 percent were African-American; 43 percent were English-language learners.[31] Since the 1980s, when the school served as a magnet for students bused from across town, test scores had dropped dramatically. In 2004, fewer than 20 percent of Gompers students were proficient in language arts and math, ranking the school as one of the lowest-performing in the district (see figure 11-4).[32] There were nearly a thousand suspensions that year, and the school had eighteen teacher vacancies.

Gompers's transformation from this dismal condition in the fall of 2005 hit the national news. Students arrived in August wearing white oxford shirts and ties, plaid skirts and knee socks. Governor Arnold Schwarzenegger, California secretary of education Alan Bersin, the superintendent of schools, the chancellor of the University of California at San Diego (UCSD) and the president of the local Urban League welcomed students from a red carpet to their first day of school. For the first time in the building's history, there were no teacher vacancies on the first day of class.[33] All these changes were the more visible results of Gompers's 2005 restructuring efforts under NCLB.

In 2004, San Diego Unified had classified Gompers Middle School in year 4 of program improvement and called for the creation of a restructuring plan. The process began with a workgroup similar to the group that served at Balboa. "A group of twenty to twenty-five parents, teachers, students and community members signed up to be a part of the group," says Riveroll, who credits much of their restructuring success to this workgroup structure. "People heard about our plans because it wasn't a principal talking; it was parents talking to parents. It was very empowering. Our parents were able to make very informed decisions about what the school was to become."

The Gompers workgroup met weekly and hosted biweekly meetings with students and the general public. "We did a lot of soul-searching in the workgroup. Why is this school low-performing? What are the real issues?"

FIGURE 11-4

GOMPERS CHARTER MIDDLE SCHOOL:
PERCENTAGE OF STUDENTS MEETING STATE STANDARDS

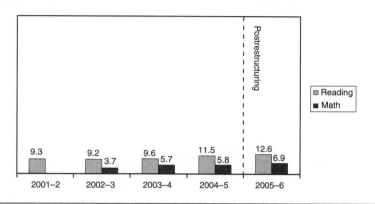

SOURCES: San Diego Unified School District, *School Accountability Report Card: Gompers Secondary School,* 2005, http://studata.sandi.net/research/sarcs/2004-05/SARC335.pdf (accessed May 4, 2007). Data on math performance from 2001–2 are not publicly available.

The meetings revealed that the number one barrier to success at Gompers was the school's inability to hire its own staff.

With this as its primary focus, the Gompers workgroup immediately sought a waiver from the SDEA to allow the school to hire and fire its own teachers. "We asked the SDEA to the workgroup table to negotiate solutions for the school. We believed that this was the best option for us, that this should be our restructuring," Riveroll explains. "We were under the impression that this workgroup was going to recommend what should happen at the school, and that would happen. But [the SDEA's] answer was no."

With their waiver request denied, the workgroup started planning "the next option that met the needs of our school"—becoming a charter school. But "going charter is a very difficult process. It required a lot of work. We faced very hostile responses from the school board at that time. Every time we went to a board meeting, a new obstacle was put in front of us." During this period, the school board was locked in an epic battle with then superintendent Alan Bersin over the direction of change in the district. After the November 2004 election, a new majority of the board opposed Bersin's reforms, including his support for charter schools.

The workgroup knew it would have to offer signatures from 50 percent of parents in support of its charter petition. Parents, teachers, administrators, and community members went door-to-door over the winter holidays to garner more than seven hundred signatures. But then in January, the new school board reversed the district's earlier stance by also requiring 51 percent of Gompers's tenured classroom faculty to approve a change to charter status. The policy change seemed like a fatal setback, another roadblock laid down by a school board hostile to charter schools. But within a day, Riveroll delivered.

"A teacher who had twenty-nine years of service at Gompers was the first to sign the petition," he says. "She told me, 'I can go anywhere. The kids can't.' Many other teachers followed in that sentiment, saying, 'It isn't about the adults, for once. It's about the kids.'"

Despite this show of support for Gompers's charter, the school board removed Mr. Riveroll as principal in early February. Community members viewed Riveroll's removal as another attempt by the school board to derail Gompers's charter effort.[34] "The most wonderful thing, though," says Riveroll, "is that I may have been the starting pitcher in this effort, but I wasn't the closing pitcher. I sat on the bench and watched as parents and community members fought for their school." After a heated board meeting in March of 2005, the board unanimously approved Gompers's charter proposal in the face of strong community pressure. "The community rose to the occasion," says Riveroll. "It was an amazing thing to witness." The new charter board had the authority to make all hiring decisions for the school, and at their first meeting in 2005, the trustees voted unanimously to reappoint Riveroll as principal.

With authority to hire its own staff, Gompers filled its vacancies with many teachers new to the profession, and professional development immediately became a major focus. "We developed a master schedule to make sure that teachers have time built into the day to develop their own learning," says Riveroll. Teachers also engage in three weeks of training with faculty from UCSD during the summer before students arrive.

The swell of community support evident at the 2005 board meeting was one of the most important changes brought about by Gompers's restructuring. According to Michelle Evans, the school's parent-engagement director, many parents had watched for years as the school steadily declined. Before restructuring, parents "were angry at the school. They were angry that nothing was being done."[35] But during the summer of 2005, parents and community members cleaned, painted, and remodeled the Gompers building and grounds in preparation for students' arrival at the new school.

The student population has not changed significantly at Gompers since it became a charter school (in 2005–6, 62 percent of students were Hispanic and 26 percent were African-American, and 45 percent were English-language learners). But the new focus on professional development has helped establish a new culture at the school and greatly increased retention. Between 2005 and 2006, 65 percent of teachers returned to their positions. "That was a complete turnaround," says Riveroll.

Gompers was one of only a handful of schools to "go charter" under NCLB in 2005. According to Riveroll, "It was a very difficult route to take. It's a route that we don't regret, because it's paid out more than we put in— our kids are learning. But it wasn't an easy thing." The state does not compare student test scores at Gompers before and after restructuring because it is classified as a new school, but the school's own internal analysis shows a twenty-four-point gain on California's Academic Performance Index between 2004–5 and 2005–6. Still, passing rates remain dreadfully low. In 2005–6, just under 13 percent of students met standards in English; less than 7 percent did in math. It's clear that "going charter" has not been the solution to all of Gompers's problems. Riveroll is optimistic: "We're definitely on the right track," he says. "It's amazing what can happen when you have quality teaching and learning in the classroom. The same kids that were suspended last year are the ones that are in school now, wearing a tie." Still, the Gompers experience underscores the difficulty of making dramatic improvements in test scores even when implementing the kind of drastic changes enabled by the charter route.

Common Lessons and Conclusions

These four case studies of schools in two states certainly do not provide a representative picture of districts' and schools' implementation of the restructuring provisions of NCLB. They do, however, offer a picture of how these particular communities have been affected by a federal law meant to inspire fundamental school reforms. They also allow us to make several observations about what restructuring can look like at the school level.

NCLB's Restructuring Requirements Provide Schools and Districts an *Opportunity* **to Make Change, but Give Them Wide Flexibility on How to Proceed.** Broad surveys of restructuring have found that most schools nationwide are implementing mild changes, such as option 5, rather than more drastic reforms under NCLB.[36] When compared to national trends, two of our four case-study schools are atypical in their magnitude of change. District and school leaders at Milwood and Gompers initiated major reforms in an attempt to improve student learning through restructuring. The case studies do, however, echo the national finding that NCLB can empower schools choosing drastic restructuring to make changes they would not be willing or perhaps able to make without the power of federal law. Administrators at all four of our case-study schools agreed that without the restructuring requirements of NCLB, they probably wouldn't have gone to this extreme, or it would have taken longer. Specifically, Gompers and Milwood used the more radical restructuring options under NCLB to remove principals or teachers who would otherwise be protected by contracts and bargaining agreements. In Grand Rapids, the district invoked NCLB as the rationale to impose a raft of changes on schools. While school officials perceived the district's plans for restructuring as requirements of the No Child Left Behind Act itself, in fact the imposed changes were just one of a more or less infinite range of responses the district could have pursued.

This flexibility runs in contrast to the inflamed rhetoric on both sides of the NCLB debate. On the one hand, it belies the fear expressed by some that NCLB is forcing localities and schools to engage in disruptive reform that may or may not align with school needs. Instead, NCLB's requirements appear to work more as a symbolic call to action, giving districts and schools extraordinary leeway about how to proceed. It seems clear that any district or school so inclined could simply continue whatever reforms it was undertaking before and call them "restructuring."

On the other hand, flexibility undermines the claim of NCLB proponents that federal law no longer tolerates chronic failure. While the restructuring provisions may nudge districts to take more dramatic action, this nudge falls short of a mandate. The act has, in effect, placed a tool in the hands of local leaders. How (or even whether) they employ that tool remains largely a local decision—and numerous considerations beyond NCLB are likely to influence their choices.

NCLB Is Just One of Many Forces Acting on Failing Schools. Staff and administrators at Buchanan, Balboa, Milwood, and Gompers felt pressure to improve from sources other than NCLB. Changes in neighborhood and district policies in recent years put pressure on Balboa to improve before restructuring, if only to preserve its enrollment (and therefore its funding). Milwood was under similar pressure, lest it be forced to close for lack of enrollment amidst growing competition from private, magnet, and charter schools. At Buchanan, the state accountability system kicked in years before federal restructuring requirements, and brought with it school improvement teams, extra resources, and personnel shifts in an effort to improve performance. In addition, schools operate in the midst of public education's notorious web of constraints, such as collective bargaining agreements and charter school laws requiring faculty votes in favor of charter conversion.

Finally, district and school leaders respond to the restructuring provisions in the context of the wider politics of education reform in their localities. In general, these politics are likely to include numerous pressures *not* to take dramatic actions, especially those that involve replacement of school staff, radical moves like chartering or contracting out, or state takeover. Instead, local leaders face incentives to take more incremental, symbolic actions that may amount more to "spinning wheels" than to true forward motion.[37] While NCLB may place one fairly light weight on the scale in favor of substantial change, it will often not be sufficient to outweigh the heavy load on the other side.

Districts' Involvement in the Planning Process Varies Widely. While the law makes clear that local educational agencies (usually districts) hold primary responsibility for the creation of a restructuring plan, it does not specify the degree to which schools should be involved in the process. Our case studies make clear that, as a result, there is a great deal of variation from one district to the next. For example, in Grand Rapids, all phase 5 schools were required to implement the same or similar restructuring actions under the district's restructuring plan, such as implementing full-day kindergartens.

In San Diego, too, the district required staff at all restructuring schools to reapply for their jobs and laid down several roadblocks before schools that sought to pursue charter status. But also in San Diego, school-level workgroups had a great deal of flexibility in devising their restructuring plans, and the two schools profiled here went in very different directions. In Kalamazoo, an enterprising school principal worked with district leaders to engineer a dramatic change. In just these four schools, then, we see four very different approaches to district engagement—from outright mandates to collaboration to empowerment of school-level teams.

The Restructuring Process Can Offer a Chance for Meaningful Community Involvement. Prior to restructuring, principals in each of our case-study schools were accustomed to very little parental involvement. But in those districts that interpreted restructuring as an opportunity to respond to unique needs at each failing school, principals reported increased community involvement as one of the greatest benefits of the process. In Kalamazoo and San Diego, where workgroups held primary responsibility for developing plan proposals, restructuring gave parents, staff, and community members a concrete reason to meet regularly throughout the planning year, a forum in which to express their concerns, and an opportunity to participate in the creation of strategies to address those concerns. NCLB requires local educational agencies to provide parents and teachers an opportunity to participate in the development of a restructuring plan, but does not specify the means schools and districts must use. School leaders in districts that have fully implemented this provision report that real community involvement is worth the trouble: At Balboa, Milwood, and Gompers, parental commitment and a reinvigorated community reportedly are providing strong and necessary support for the other changes brought about by restructuring.

Ironically, though, parental involvement in restructuring may, in some cases, put a brake on major change. Parents nationwide tend to believe their schools are already serving their children well—in a 2006 survey, 64 percent rated their child's school with a grade of A or B.[38] It is perhaps not surprising, then, that so many schools opt for the less drastic restructuring strategies under NCLB.

Ultimately, the aim of restructuring is to achieve dramatic, measurable improvements in student achievement. In the literature on organizational turnarounds, one of the consistent findings is that in successful turn-arounds, managers achieve relatively quick, measurable wins on important metrics. These wins, while not representing complete organizational turn-arounds, create momentum to take the next steps, leading to a virtual cycle of improvement.[39] One year into the experiences of these four schools, there is little evidence of that kind of improvement in achievement. Yet school leaders are optimistic; they think their schools are going in the right direction. Whether they are right or wrong, what's clear from these case studies is that NCLB's restructuring mandates will be just one part of a much more complex story.

12

District Accountability: More Bark Than Bite?

Joe Williams

Improve your schools, or someone else will. That was supposed to be the bite in the federal No Child Left Behind Act that would leave teeth marks on underperforming school districts, ushering in long-resisted reforms and restructuring in the education systems where they were most needed. As then undersecretary of education Eugene Hickok testified in July 2002 before the House Education and the Workforce Committee, months after the bill was signed into law, "Schools *and school districts* that do not meet these objectives, both for all students and for specific student groups, will be subject to improvement, corrective action, and restructuring aimed at getting them back on track" (emphasis added).

These lofty new goals for district accountability have been viewed in some quarters as harsh, overly punitive, and the governmental equivalent of kicking a school system while it is down and struggling to get up. But nearly five years after No Child Left Behind was signed into law, not a single school district has undergone radical restructuring—nor even seen the state take over its individual schools in response to its failure to get the job done itself—as part of corrective actions for districts under the law.

To date, NCLB has been relatively toothless in terms of holding districts accountable through the use of strong-arm sanctions. From federal guidelines offering tremendous amounts of wiggle-room to states and districts in implementing sanctions to the reality that districts themselves often get the first chance to determine their improvement plans, underperforming districts have encountered little pain under NCLB other than the stigma that comes from being branded failing systems. As Bismarck, North Dakota, superintendent Paul Johnson remarked in 2004 when his district was placed under "program improvement" status for failing to make adequate yearly progress (AYP) under the law, "It actually means very little for the school district. . . . The biggest thing for us is that it's embarrassing and we'd like to remedy it as quickly as possible."[1]

To be fair, restructuring was supposed to be the last resort for districts that had failed to make progress after intensifying levels of state and federal interventions. Because some states didn't begin identifying districts in need of improvement until recently, more radical forms of district restructuring could still loom on the horizon. Nationwide, 1,596 public school districts were identified at some level of "improvement" under the law for the 2005–6 school year, meaning they had failed to show they had made adequate progress on student test scores in 2004–5, according to Consolidated State Performance Reports on file with the U.S. Department of Education.[2] A majority of these districts (1,093) were in their first year of improvement status, and 416 were in their second year; 58 districts were in corrective action; 23 were in their fourth year of improvement status; and 3 were in their fifth year.[3]

Only one state, Maryland, has gone to the extreme measure of rejecting reform plans created by a local district and seeking to seize control of struggling schools as part of corrective actions under NCLB. The political firestorm that erupted in that case, which centered on the Baltimore City Public Schools, ended up exposing the weak position in which many states find themselves when attempting to enforce NCLB at the district level. In fact, the Maryland State Board of Education was at least temporarily thwarted in its bold attempts to require strong corrective actions for a district that had shown both an unwillingness and an inability to correct itself.

But the Baltimore case, as this chapter will show, could still emerge as a reminder that the most important end-result is not whether a state succeeds in taking over failing schools, but whether federal and state educational agencies can effectively use pressure from NCLB to prod districts to make important administrative and pedagogical changes they might not otherwise wish to consider.

NCLB Accountability for Districts: How It Works

Under NCLB, state educational agencies are required to evaluate schools and districts to determine at each level whether adequate progress is being made in academic areas in order to keep schools and districts on schedule to make all students proficient by 2014. Districts that fail to make AYP are generally considered "improvement districts" by their states and must develop plans to correct specific academic deficiencies at the district level. Those that fail to make progress after a set time period—usually two years—must be placed under "corrective-action" status and face more severe reforms imposed by the state educational agency.

State educational agencies are required to identify and designate any district that fails for two consecutive years to make adequate yearly progress under the state's accountability system as being in "LEA improvement." LEA, or local educational agency, is the term federal and state governments generally use for "district." States sometimes use terms other than "improvement districts," which either soften or add urgency to the designation, depending on the state's point of view. Tennessee calls struggling districts "high-priority local educational agencies"; Minnesota declares they are in "continuous improvement"; and Ohio says they are in "academic emergency."

States generally use one of five types of approaches for determining whether or not a district requires improvement. The specific choice of methodology can significantly increase or decrease the number of districts that are potentially captured under the improvement designation and must consider making changes to satisfy federal law. In each option, a "miss" of AYP could be by all students, or students in any subgroup, with reference to either the proficiency target or the proficiency level. A district may be placed in improvement if for two consecutive years it misses AYP in one of the following ways:

- In *any* of its achievement targets (that is, in reading, math, or other academic indicator) in *any* grade span determined by the state.

- In the *same* subject in *any* grade span

- In the *same* subject and *same* grade span

- In the *same* subject in *all* grade spans

- Any combination of the above

The Center on Education Policy notes that an increasing number of states are allowing the fourth option to be used to determine AYP, which has the potential to reduce significantly the number of districts placed in improvement status. Under this approach, states like Delaware have been able to divide up a district's students into three groups, by grade. One group represents elementary students, one represents middle school students, and one represents high school students. The district is only identified for improvement if all three grade spans fail to make AYP for two years in a row.[4] In contrast, some states like New York treat school districts as if they are one giant school, listing them for improvement if any one achievement target is missed.

Interestingly, it is possible under at least one scenario for a district that doesn't have a single school identified as failing under NCLB to be identified for improvement by the state. Because states evaluate districts based on the aggregated results of their academic achievement measures, subgroups too small to be considered for evaluation at the school level can be combined with small subgroups at other schools. Under this scenario, a district can be evaluated based on the cumulative performance of subgroups in multiple schools.

The U.S. Department of Education[5] provides this example: A state may have decided on a minimum group size of thirty for any subgroup to be included in the accountability system. If a district has two elementary schools, each with twenty limited-English-proficient (LEP) students, neither has enough students to be included in its accountability determination. When the performance data are aggregated at the district level, however, there are now assessment results from forty students, exceeding the minimum threshold of thirty students for consideration. In this case, the district is held accountable for the progress of LEP students as a subgroup, even though the schools are not.

Any district identified for improvement within three months must develop (or revise) a written improvement plan in consultation with parents, school staff, and others. According to federal guidelines,

> the purpose of the LEA improvement plan is to address the deficiencies in the LEA that prevent students in its schools from

achieving proficiency in the core academic subjects of reading
and mathematics. Improving the centralized leadership structure of a school district is difficult and complex work. The
improvement plan must analyze and address LEA insufficiencies
as they relate to leadership for schools, governance, and fiscal
infrastructures, and curriculum and instruction. The plan-writing
process should result in a determination of why the LEA's previous efforts to improve were ineffective and a framework of
detailed action steps to improve on those efforts.

The district-developed plans must specifically define measurable
achievement goals and targets for each of the student subgroups; incorporate strategies grounded in "scientific-based" research proven to strengthen
instruction in core academic subjects; include appropriate after-school and
summer learning programs; identify strategies to promote effective parental
involvement in schools; and "include a determination of why the LEA's previous plan did not bring about increased academic achievement."[6]

In addition, districts identified for improvement must reserve at least 10
percent of their federal Title I funding for "high quality professional development" specifically designed to improve classroom teaching.

If the district is able to make AYP for two consecutive years, the state is
no longer required to include it on the improvement list. If, however, a district does not make adequate progress by the end of the second full school
year, it can be placed under "corrective action."

"Corrective Action"

According to the U.S. Department of Education, corrective action refers to
the steps taken by a state educational agency "that substantially and directly
respond to serious instructional, managerial, and organizational problems
in the LEA that jeopardize the likelihood that students will achieve proficiency in the core academic subjects of reading and mathematics."[7] States
must take at least one of the following actions with regard to districts identified as falling under corrective action, depending on what individual state
laws allow:

- Defer programmatic funds or reduce administrative funds

- Institute and fully implement a new curriculum, based on state and local content and academic achievement standards, that includes appropriate, research-based professional development for all relevant staff

- Replace district personnel who are relevant to the ability of the district to make adequate progress

- Remove individual schools from the jurisdiction of the district and arrange for their public governance and supervision

- Appoint a receiver or trustee to administer the affairs of the district in place of the superintendent and school board

- Abolish or restructure the district

The method a state uses to determine AYP can have an impact in triggering corrective-action status, especially if it requires repeated misses in the same subjects and grade spans to warrant more severe sanctions. In Georgia, for example, the 18 (out of 184) districts labeled as "needs improvement" in 2006 would only face corrective action if they failed to make AYP in the same subject and grade span for two consecutive years, a scenario that could have struggling districts languishing on the improvement list for years without more serious sanctions. The state sought and was granted federal approval to use this criterion for evaluating districts in 2004.

The *Atlanta Journal-Constitution* in 2006 explained how generous Georgia's district evaluation system was by examining the fate of the troubled Fulton County School District. Since the state began evaluating districts in 2002, Fulton failed to meet the state's AYP standards in three out of four years. Still, the 80,000-student district had never been placed on the improvement list, despite, for example, repeatedly missing AYP targets for multiple subgroups, though not necessarily for each subgroup and subject matter in consecutive years. Pam Smith, of Governor Sonny Purdue's Office of Student Achievement, told the newspaper that the state's formula for districts might be flawed to the point of being overly generous. "We may need to change our statewide accountability rules if that continues to happen," Smith said.[8]

A school district that has been identified for corrective action may exit from the designation once it makes adequate progress for two consecutive years.

How It Plays Out

The U.S. Department of Education makes clear that states and local districts are the agencies tasked with developing appropriate plans and sanctions for individual school districts, and that the federal government does not intend to exert a heavy hand in driving the specifics of any district improvement plan. "State and local recipients are free to implement the *LEA and School Improvement* requirements based on their own reasonable interpretation of the law," the federal department declares in its guidance documents for states and districts.[9]

As of October 2006, twenty-four of the nation's thirty-six largest school districts were designated by their states for district improvement for various reasons. Eight districts indicated they had been required to implement a new curriculum; four had seen some funding reduced or deferred; five had undergone some minor forms of restructuring; and two had replaced some district personnel.[10]

What state educational agencies can do to improve schools or districts may be limited by their own state laws. For example, thirty-six states do not provide for contracting with third parties to operate low-performing schools, twenty-seven do not authorize state takeovers of schools or districts, and thirty-eight have not provided for closing and reopening low-performing schools as charter schools.[11] The tools available as part of the NCLB toolkit simply may not be powerful enough to provide firm standing for some states that choose to get involved in often volatile political situations over local control of schools. Georgia state law, for example, doesn't allow for state takeovers of school districts, so the most drastic outcome from corrective action down the road would be the removal of district leaders—something the state made clear it wasn't interested in pursuing. "It's something we hope won't happen at all," says Dana Tofig, a spokesman for the Georgia Department of Education. "Our goal is to work with the systems to make sure they don't have to do that."[12]

Most states place the responsibility for developing written district improvement plans with the districts themselves, at least at the start. For a variety of reasons explained below, these districts tend to be more willing to select plans that include introducing new curriculum products and professional development programs over more radical forms of restructuring, such as replacing key employees and initiating school or district takeovers.

This decentralized approach, combined with a cafeteria-style selection of sanctions for district restructuring, often leads to what Jack Jennings of the Center on Education Policy has called "restructuring lite."[13] In 2006, the CEP found that when school systems in Maryland were forced to take corrective action against persistently failing schools, they tended more often than not to choose the least radical option available to them.[14]

Such a structure places the onus on state education officials to overrule local districts, which they avoid because it is often difficult politically. This allows districts to select noncontroversial reforms. "You see districts submitting plans saying they will now teach math differently," says former California secretary of education Alan Bersin.[15]

In California, state superintendent of public instruction Jack O'Connell said in 2005 that education officials in Sacramento had made a "conscious decision" not to force restructuring on districts because of their own ambivalence about some of the particulars of NCLB.[16] Instead, the state took on the role of providing advice to districts about restructuring. O'Connell complained that California was simply unable to help what could amount to hundreds of failing school districts at the same time. "What kind of accountability system do you have when most of the school districts need help?" O'Connell said. "Frankly, we don't have the resources for that."[17]

Although the federal government generally leaves it up to the states to deal with underperforming districts under the law, it will step in if states appear to be excessively dragging their feet. In California's case, the U.S. Department of Education eventually raised concerns that the state was letting too many districts off the hook from having to make improvements by using the weakest forms of measuring overall district AYP. During the 2004–5 school year, for example, the state identified only 14 school districts for program improvement status, which in California involves entering an assistance program that provides additional resources and state support, followed by eventual financial penalties if districts fail to improve.

Ray Simon, an assistant secretary with the U.S. Department of Education, argued that 310 school districts in the state should have been identified as program improvement districts under the state's AYP formula.[18] A compromise between state and federal officials in the spring of 2005 eventually reduced that figure to 184.[19] (In the summer of 2005, an additional 7 districts were identified as needing improvement.)[20]

Advocacy groups like Education Trust West have argued that ambivalence at the state level in California with regard to NCLB sends a message to districts that there is plenty of wiggle-room in how seriously they should take the law, and comments from district leaders often make clear that they have very little respect for the law or its consequences. Some superintendents, for example, upon having their districts placed under improvement status, have issued statements in the press suggesting the problem isn't with their districts, but with the law itself. Comments made by superintendent Eliot Duchon, upon his Jurupa Valley school district in Riverside County being identified for program improvement status in 2005, are illustrative:

> The [Jurupa Valley Unified School District] has shown overall growth in terms of academic performance. Part of the problem is that [No Child Left Behind] is very flawed in how it evaluates districts and how it evaluates schools. I think therein lies a major part of the problem. We were, for the last six years, progressing under the state Public Schools Accountability act, and then [No Child Left Behind] comes along, and it's somewhat different.[21]

Los Angeles Superintendent Roy Romer was also blunt about his displeasure with being identified as the head of a failing district despite what he said was considerable academic progress. "We have been moving the ball down the court faster than most schools in California," Romer said in 2005. "People should be applauding that and assisting us, not saying, 'We're going to cut your legs off.' They ought to give us assistance to improve. This redefinition is just not helpful."[22]

Another frequent response of school districts is to downplay the improvement status by saying their failure to make AYP is limited to small subgroups of students. "Despite the fact that 96.9 percent of Cherokee schools met NCLB accountability goals, the district is labeled as 'Not making adequate yearly progress,'" argued Cherokee County (Georgia) Schools spokesman Mike McGowan in 2006, after limited English proficient students scored low on state exams. "That's borderline preposterous."[23]

Supporting District Stability

A widely accepted belief at the state level holds that major reform of districts is a different ball of wax from reforming individual schools. "It's more difficult for a district to make adequate yearly progress than it is for a building," notes Mary Alice Galloway, a state education official in Michigan.[24]

The tendency to support stability in previously unstable schools and school systems can steer restructuring plans away from any housecleaning of administrators who are deemed responsible. Instead, several state-level administrators note, plans tend to be heavy on supports (new curriculum products and professional development) that can be added to what districts are already trying to do, rather than merely taking away employees who have been involved in previous reform attempts. While NCLB may assume a glass-half-empty approach (replace the people who are responsible), many educators take a glass-half-full approach (these guys are trying hard to make it work, and they just need more support).

Delaware secretary of education Valerie Woodruff says she and her state-level team have viewed dealing with struggling districts as a "collaborative effort." Delaware has two districts facing sanctions for repeated AYP misses, in both cases because of the performance of disabled students within those districts. "We're not in a situation where we are in a takeover mode," says Woodruff, who argues that it makes little sense to take over an entire district if the weak spot is limited to a specific subgroup. Rather, she says, the state and district should work together to make improvements that help students of that particular subgroup. "We need to push and certainly call to their attention areas that need improvement. But we're not in a situation where we say we're going to come in and take over. At the end of the day, the local community should have local authority over their school districts."[25]

These often prevailing attitudes among educators, combined with the obvious potential for political opposition, make it easy to understand why some of the more controversial sanctions (such as reduced funding for low-performing schools, firings, and state takeovers) are seldom realized, even in districts with long track records of failure.

Even in Florida, which has been aggressive about withholding funding from districts that are not in compliance with NCLB regulations, education commissioner John Winn says states don't have the capacity to do more than withhold funding and provide basic technical assistance to districts. "I don't think the state [education] department would be better at running schools—it would probably be less better," Winn said.

One argument often raised against intentionally disruptive restructuring plans for districts is that harsh sanctions and pressure are simply ineffective methods of assisting struggling, undersupported schools. A 2004 report by the National Center for Research on Evaluation, Standards, and Student Testing (CRESST) argued, for example, that the experiences of first-generation accountability systems (those put in place as part of the standards movement but before passage of NCLB in 2002) suggested that low-performing schools and districts were best served not by pressure and sanctions, but by reform programs with a heavy emphasis on support and intervention.[26]

There is even some early anecdotal evidence that the latter approach has worked in some places. In the 2002–3 school year, for example, six of the seven Kansas districts that were placed under improvement status made adequate progress and were removed.[27]

Because the interventions under NCLB are progressively more severe, a district that ends up facing corrective action typically has already undergone some degree of mandated districtwide reform, including school-specific personnel changes, in an attempt to avoid getting blacklisted as failing. To cite one example, thirty of New Jersey's nearly six hundred school districts were placed on the state's first improvement list in 2005. The list included Newark, Jersey City, Camden, Paterson, Trenton, and Atlantic City—districts that were already working under an extensive improvement plan mandated as part of a funding adequacy lawsuit.[28]

Case Study: Baltimore City Schools

The circumstances surrounding the state of Maryland's highly contentious attempt to seize control of eleven failing Baltimore middle and high schools in 2006—the first such attempt by a state education association nationally under NCLB—offer a glimpse at the kinds of district-level factors that can trigger a state agency to seek more radical sanctions than are typically included in LEA improvement plans; but they also expose the weak position of states when they attempt to step in and resolve longstanding cycles of school failure.

Even before NCLB, Maryland had a strong accountability system in place to identify schools that were performing at very low levels. In 2000, for example, two years before NCLB was signed, the Maryland State Department of Education took control of the three lowest-performing public schools in Baltimore. The education management firm Edison Schools was hired to run the schools and given complete control of staffing at the school sites. Maryland state superintendent Nancy Grasmick was instrumental both in constructing the state's "first-generation" accountability system and in overseeing the takeover of the three schools.

Its head start in terms of having a statewide school and district evaluative apparatus in place prior to the passage of NCLB made Maryland more capable than most states of moving quickly to identify districts that were failing to do an adequate job reforming their own struggling schools. In July 2003, in the face of a long period of academic failure in Baltimore schools and the seeming inability of the district to remedy the problem, the Maryland State Board of Education declared the city school system to be a "system in corrective action" under the federal law. The state directed city school leaders to undertake six specific reform measures:

- Conduct a curriculum audit and align the city's curriculum with state standards

- Align professional development for teachers with the curriculum

- Develop a plan to meet the highly-qualified-teacher requirement by the 2005–6 school year (one year before all districts would be required to do so under the law)[29]

- Enact a principal evaluation system

- Establish a special district for low-performing middle schools

• Establish a special district cluster of schools for prekindergarten to grade 12

The original corrective-action plan addressed the concerns of state officials that one reason students in Baltimore schools were not performing well on assessments was a lack of connection between what they were being taught and what they needed to know. There was little curricular coherence, staff development was not helping, and state officials believed that district management bore responsibility for this portion of the district's problems as they related to individual schools.

By the late fall of 2005, however, state officials noted that of the six reform measures mandated by the corrective-action plan, Baltimore school officials had implemented only one—enacting a principal evaluation system. With regard to the requirement that the district meet NCLB's highly-qualified-teacher requirement, for example, only 42 percent of the city's teachers in 2005–6 were considered "highly qualified." In contrast, 78 percent of teachers in Baltimore County and 84 percent of teachers in Anne Arundel County met the criteria.[30]

A master plan for reform submitted by the Baltimore schools was twice rejected by the state—the first time for being woefully inadequate, the second for being so ambitious as to be unrealistic. Baltimore was the only district in the state to see its master plan rejected in such a manner. "System, school, and student performance data reveal alarming results," Maryland superintendent Grasmick wrote in a December 2 letter to the Baltimore City Schools CEO, Bonnie Copeland, informing her of the first rejection. The plan, "as submitted, did not demonstrate how teaching and learning would be improved for each of the 88,401 students who deserve better."

The NCLB process was not entirely clear about what sanctions states could compel districts to accept after failing to reform themselves out of "district improvement" status. "It's one of the weaknesses of the [NCLB] law," Grasmick said in January 2006, as she was contemplating how to handle the Baltimore situation and what the state could do if the city ignored the ordered reforms yet again. "It didn't establish a bottom line."[31]

Under the Maryland statute established to enforce NCLB, state education officials would need either General Assembly or judicial approval to take over the entire system. The political realities of the General Assembly (whose Democratic base resided in the Baltimore area, with close ties to the existing school system's administrative structure) seemed make the possibility of a complete district takeover a nonstarter, and Grasmick herself said she had given up any ideas of seeking help from the courts because they tended to be "too timid."[32]

After quietly considering her options for several months, and with little warning to Baltimore school or political leaders, Grasmick instead announced with the state Board of Education plans to strip the city of its power over eleven of the district's lowest-performing and perennially plagued schools. This was presented as a corrective-action plan not only for the eleven failing schools, but for the district that had failed to take necessary steps in the past to deal with its two-year-old corrective-action status. "Too many schools in the Baltimore City Public School System are not making the grade," said state board president Ed Root on March 29, 2006, in a Maryland State Department of Education press release. "Under federal and state law we are required to intervene when a system falters. We also have the moral responsibility to help strengthen the schools for all of the students and teachers in the system."[33]

The board's decision marked the first time that a state educational agency had moved to take over failing schools under NCLB, and it met with instant hostility from officials in Baltimore. "This is unprecedented," said Mayor Martin O'Malley. "No other state superintendent in the history of the country has ever tried to do what Dr. Grasmick is trying to do in this election year."[34]

Right out of the gate, the plan took on strong political overtones. Mayor O'Malley, a Democrat, was locked in a race for governor against incumbent Robert L. Ehrlich, who had close ties with Grasmick, and even considered her as a running-mate at one point. For his part, Ehrlich said "all extraordinary means" were justified to help improve "a system that is dysfunctional." The battle naturally became a heated issue in the election. The political lines in the sand were drawn even more sharply when Ray Simon, deputy secretary of Republican president George W. Bush's Education Department, issued a statement saying Maryland "should be commended for taking historic and decisive action on the side of the Baltimore students."[35]

Of the eleven schools included in the plan, the state would take responsibility for selecting a third party to run four high schools. The city would have the option for the other seven (middle) schools of selecting a third-party school manager or converting them to charter schools. No one seemed to dispute that the schools in question were a mess, but considerable debate raged over how to fix them and who should be in charge.

While the district had been touting a four-year graduation rate of about 58 percent (which it hailed as a significant improvement), *Education Week* estimated in 2006 that only a sobering 38.5 percent of Baltimore's students emerged with a diploma four years after they began high school, making it the second-worst district in the nation, behind only Detroit.[36] "Data show that the schools are not making enough progress," the state Board of Education's executive summary of its corrective-action plan for Baltimore stated. "According to Maryland and federal law, when a school system is not making adequate progress, the state is not only authorized to act, it is obligated to do so."[37]

The takeover of the eleven low-performing schools got much of the attention; however, the corrective-action plan also included concrete steps that needed to be taken by the district itself to bring it into compliance, including:

- Adopting new middle and high school curricula in reading and math that had been successful in at least one other Maryland school system

- Evaluating and, as necessary, replacing the district's area academic officers

- Hiring two full-time school improvement specialists, reporting to the state, with authority over schools in restructuring

- Developing student support plans for all high school students at risk of failing mandatory high school assessments.

Reaction to the plan stretched far beyond Baltimore, as education-watchers looked for clues as to how such NCLB-driven sanctions could be used. The Council of Great City Schools, a national group representing urban school districts, issued a statement stating that "state takeovers and other dramatic changes in school governance have not proven to be the silver bullet."[38] U.S. education secretary Margaret Spellings weighed in, calling Grasmick a "warrior" and expressing support for the corrective-action plan. "To sit idly by with the kind of data and results and chronic failure that has been demonstrated is educational malpractice," Spellings said. "Account-ability is meaningless if there is no end of the line."[39]

But within hours of the plan's unveiling, forces were at work that would eventually raise significant questions about whether there really was an "end of the line" at all. Within a day, legislators in the General Assembly had introduced in both the state senate and house a bill that would postpone the state intervention in Baltimore for a year. To speed up passage, the details were added to another bill affecting Baltimore schools that was already nearing passage in the final days of the legislative session.[40]

News accounts described heated screaming matches between Grasmick and legislators, who accused her of not working with Baltimore school offi-cials to find a feasible solution.[41] The pressure ratcheted up within a week of the announcement when the Bush administration warned in a letter that $171 million in federal aid to the state could be in jeopardy if the General Assembly blocked the state's corrective-action plan for Baltimore.[42] In response, the office of Maryland attorney general J. Joseph Curran Jr., a Democrat, issued an opinion saying that even under NCLB, the State Educa-tion Department's ability to impose sanctions on a school district was limited by state law, making it an appropriate area for the legislature to pass new laws to intervene. The proposed law postponing the district restructuring "does not restrict the state's authority to 'take appropriate corrective action, includ-ing withholding or redirection of state or federal funding.'" Rather, Curran's office noted in an April 6, 2006, letter from assistant attorney general Bonnie Kirkland to state senator Nathanial McFadden, the bill only prevented the state from imposing new governance structures upon Baltimore city schools.

Grasmick announced the Baltimore plan (and the state Board of Edu-cation simultaneously approved it) on a Tuesday. By Wednesday, the bill to postpone the move for a year had already been drafted, and supporters were lining up votes. By Thursday night, the bill appeared to have enough support for passage, and on Friday it successfully flew through both houses. It was vetoed by the governor within a week, but the House over-rode the veto a day later, and the Senate did the same a day after that. Gov-ernor Ehrlich called the veto overrides "the worst moment for Maryland in my four years as governor" and a "stain on the General Assembly."[43]

What started as the most ambitious example of NCLB enforcement to date was essentially rendered impotent (at least until 2007) within thirteen days of its announcement. The move to take over eleven failing Baltimore schools was stopped despite strong support from some extremely powerful forces in Annapolis and in the nation's capital. Some wondered whether a message had been sent nationally that NCLB hadn't really empowered states to enforce any new measures of accountability on school districts that felt free to ignore the law and its state-imposed sanctions.

It remains to be seen whether the one-year moratorium will mark the end of the state's tough-minded corrective-action plan for Baltimore, or is merely a delay. Time will also tell, however, whether the pressure exerted by the mere threat of more drastic action can be as effective in prompting changes to dysfunctional school districts as the sanctions themselves. "If any good has come out of this, it's focused our attention on the job that's ahead of us," said state senator Nathaniel McFadden, a Democrat from Baltimore who led the charge to halt the state's corrective actions.[44]

The plea from legislators like McFadden and from Mayor O'Malley (who stood at the top of the State House steps lobbying senators on the day the Senate voted to override Ehrlich's veto of the moratorium bill) was to allow the city school district one more chance to try to make things happen with its failing schools. Grasmick as much as declared that Baltimore's schools were now Baltimore's problem because the state's enforcement wings had been clipped by the bill. McFadden, a former school administrator, understood that the burden had shifted. "If we are wrong and voters find we've done something counter-productive, we will have to answer for that," McFadden said.[45]

The Baltimore City Schools subsequently acted with a degree of urgency that some felt had been lacking in previous stages of its corrective-action status. Grasmick's plan didn't seek to have the top administrators who were overseeing the system's failure removed, for example, but in the aftermath of the tense takeover attempt, Baltimore City Schools CEO Bonnie Copeland and the school board reached an agreement regarding Copeland's dismissal. On July 1, 2006, Copeland stepped down and was replaced by Charlene Cooper Boston, the former superintendent of Wicomico County Schools and a previous Baltimore administrator.[46]

Where the previous Baltimore administration shunned the orders of the state, Boston was reportedly working to find ways to make them work. "I think we found an extremely willing partner who understands that these corrective actions are so fundamental to a well-functioning school system, and they were deficiencies that had to be addressed," Grasmick said during the summer of 2006.[47] Boston ran the district until June 2007, when New York City Deputy Chancellor Andres Alonzo was recruited to become the district's sixth CEO in ten years.

Whatever the ultimate lessons learned turn out to be in the Baltimore case, it is important to note that Grasmick repeatedly made clear she wasn't seeking a takeover for the takeover's sake. She consistently argued her clear perception that the Baltimore district itself was creating obstacles that were holding students back from reaching their potential, and that those obstacles needed to be removed. In that sense the takeover, as a tool in the NCLB toolkit, was a means to the end but not the end itself. State takeovers have shown mixed results and have generally been far more successful in cleaning up district-level finances and management practices than in improving student achievement.[48]

If the personnel changes and subsequent internal restructuring result in improvements to Baltimore's schools, it will likely be because of the partnership (even if somewhat forced) between the state and the city over how to handle the corrective measures. Had such a spirit existed under the previous regime in Baltimore, and had the district made good-faith efforts to resolve its clearly identified district deficiencies, it is unlikely that any takeover attempt would have been necessary. The political nature of the equation, however, was such that it exposed a significant weakness in NCLB—namely, that state educational agencies may not be in much of a position to swing some of the law's most drastic and powerful hammers on school systems that fail to comply with it.

Conclusion

The U.S. Department of Education, while establishing the overarching goals and regulations for districts under NCLB, has made the deliberate decision that it is generally up to states to make the law happen. "Our guiding principle in implementing No Child Left Behind is to regulate only when it is absolutely necessary, because non-regulatory guidance tends to provide states and local educational agencies with greater flexibility," then-undersecretary of education Eugene Hickok testified before a congressional committee in July 2002.

As long as the responsibility is on the states, it is at the state level where the will to shake up long-failing districts will succeed or fail. While the law hasn't shown sharp teeth in general, there are cases in which state educational agencies have used it to create pressure that enhances their ability to push districts toward reform. Michigan is widely regarded as having seized upon the potential within the law to creatively prod districts to implement proven strategies for reform even before they find themselves in improvement status. "The intent of restructuring is about governance," says Yvonne Caamal Canul, who oversees school improvement for the Michigan Department of Education. "It's more than just about design and delivery of instruction. We in Michigan believe changing your reading series is not meeting the intent of the law."[49]

Michigan has played hardball with districts in terms of dealing with its struggling schools under NCLB. As a result, forty-one of the state's sixty-nine schools that had been forced to undergo restructuring by 2004 chose to replace their principals or other school staff as part of their plans. About twenty schools chose to hire outside turnaround specialists or coaches to work directly with districts on launching improvement plans.[50] All of this restructuring within the schools has taken place without having yet to rely on interventions associated with "improvement district" status—that is, Michigan has been working to put the teeth in early interventions with "improvement schools" that are designed to help districts overall in the end.

Caamal Canul explains how NCLB has changed the dynamic, in terms of the state's ability to effect reform at the local level in persistently struggling districts: "Our role before was to move money [to districts]. Our role now is to keep the money moving but have very developed guidelines as to how the money should be spent and what programs are viable."[51]

Controlling the money may also be the one way the federal government can exercise its clout in applying pressure to districts resistant to more painful forms of restructuring. Where state laws prevent district takeovers or other forms of heavy-handed action by the state, the continued threat of reduced federal funding may be the easiest means of rendering the political climate conducive to pushing for the changes in state law necessary to bolster the position of state educational agencies. The political tendency to support local control of schools might have to rub up against the political tendency to favor maintaining federal funding.

Conclusion: Can This Law Be Fixed?
A Hard Look at the NCLB Remedies

Frederick M. Hess and Chester E. Finn Jr.

Here's how we size things up, based on the research presented in this volume and evidence and analyses encountered elsewhere. Ten points are fundamental.

First, it appears clear in retrospect that educational accountability under the No Child Left Behind Act is less about any conventional notion of educational improvement or "reinventing government" and more about proclaiming fealty to a noble, even millennial, aspiration. Rather than simply seeking to ensure that schools and school districts effectively serve their students, NCLB's authors set the extraordinarily ambitious goal that every single American child will be proficient in reading and math by 2014. In so doing, they took the language and mechanisms of standards-based education reform and married them to a policy agenda that owes more to Great Society dreams and the civil rights initiatives of the sixties than to any contemporary vision of disciplined education governance. In short, educational accountability à la NCLB is more a form of moral advocacy than a sensibly designed set of institutional improvement mechanisms and incentives. Indeed, NCLB's aspirations call to mind the grandly ambitious "National Education Goals" that the nation's governors (led by Arkansas's Bill Clinton) and the first Bush administration crafted in 1990. Those millennial goals, including the declaration that the United States would lead the world in math and science by the year 2000, quietly sank from view and are now mostly remembered for their naiveté and earnest unseriousness.

Yet the political calculus and compromises that produced NCLB meant that its soaring aspirations were coupled with outdated machinery, weak "sanctions," and uncertain "interventions." Rather than sharp slaps to the faces of districts and schools that lose students, for example, NCLB choice and SES are more like wet noodles dragged across the cheek. NCLB choice implies no consequences for any educator at the school or district level, and the only "pressure" it brings on districts is the mandate that they may have to spend some of their Title I dollars on transportation. SES may mean that a small portion of Title I money flows to private providers, but there's no evidence that this spending has cost a single educator a job or pay raise—and most of the SES outlays, even by for-profit providers, flow back to local teachers who teach after hours for these firms. In short, as designed, the rhetorical nods that NCLB's proponents pay to "competition" are empty flourishes.

Effective behavior-changing regimes are rooted in realistic expectations. That pragmatism leads self-interested workers to take goals seriously, to focus relentlessly on outcomes, and to employ the levers at their disposal. When goals are patently unreachable, the logic of accountability changes in important ways. If managers and workers know they are unlikely to reach their objectives, then their primary motivation becomes avoiding trouble when they fail. Since unrealistic goals make failure inevitable, they have the perverse effect of focusing employees on compliance and on keeping out of trouble—rather than on the ostensible goals. We sense—and fear—that NCLB's aspirational framework has created a system in which the prospect of likely failure by many schools gives educators more reason to focus on obeying rules and following procedures than on delivering results.

Second, almost everywhere, compliance-style activity is underway as state and local officials attempt, sometimes cynically and sometimes in good faith, to fulfill NCLB's formal requirements, fill out the forms, and keep the money flowing. NCLB's remedies don't actually require states, districts, or schools to do better; they require only that they comply with the remedies spelled out in the law. The law is frequently misunderstood as *requiring* student academic proficiency. In fact, it only requires that states and districts comply with its guidelines regarding reporting of data, spending, planning, and adoption of interventions. So long as officials do those things, whatever their progress or lack of progress in reading and math achievement, they are home free. It appears that the compliance mentality that long infused the Elementary and Secondary Education Act (ESEA) has made the leap to NCLB, and that most districts and schools are again focused more on obeisance to the law's procedural requirements (including its remedy provisions) than on its spirit or results. While Casserly's unprecedented data show growing compliance with NCLB in urban districts,[1] other analyses in this volume show how unenthusiastic and formulaic most such activity appears to be. This is particularly perilous for the remedy provisions, as the impact of public choice, SES, or school restructuring depends almost entirely on determined execution.

Federal officials bear much responsibility here. Lawmakers assembled their bipartisan majority by agreeing to vague statutory language, and the executive branch has generally been unwilling to stand firm on implementation of the remedies. After strong initial promises—that "lack of capacity," for example, would not be an acceptable excuse for failing to provide school choice, and that districts "in need of improvement" could not provide SES—the Department of Education instead offered waivers, accepted half-measures, and backed away from fights with states or districts. Some of this may be due to the particular challenges of NCLB and political decisions by the administration, but much can be attributed to decades of bureaucratic inertia in an agency built around regulatory compliance and monitoring.

It doesn't help that the NCLB remedies themselves are blurry. For example, is public school choice intended primarily to allow children to switch to schools where most peers are currently scoring at grade level, to move to a demonstrably more effective school environment, or to create pressure on the schools that lose students? At times these impulses conflict, leaving state and local officials legitimately to ask themselves, "Why exactly are we doing this, and how do we know if we're succeeding?"

The school "restructuring" mandate is even more perplexing. What exactly does it mean to "restructure" a school? NCLB creates so many options and loopholes as to provide no clear answer to that key question. Can a school retain the same staff and still have been restructured? Does restructuring presuppose new leadership? A new curriculum? Does it require emptying out the students and repopulating the building so as to establish a new culture? Is there any reason to believe that "restructuring" can succeed on a large scale? We've seen scant evidence that even acclaimed restructuring systems are equal to the task. New Jersey, for example, touts its Collaborative Assessment and Planning for Achievement (CAPA) program as a stellar example of "technical assistance" to schools needing improvement, yet there's no evidence that it makes a difference. Kentucky has boasted a pioneering system of school improvement and restructuring for more than fifteen years, but there's little to suggest that the Bluegrass State has found a way consistently to improve troubled schools—much less provide an exportable model for other states.

In the end, NCLB's "action-oriented" remedies appear to have reinforced the habits of ESEA, becoming yet one more set of rules and procedures with which districts half-heartedly comply. That situation is particularly perilous for NCLB because the efficacy of its remedies requires states and districts to embrace them in spirit. Old-style ESEA measures dealt with distribution of inputs, so formal compliance generally meant that federal resources went approximately where they were supposed to (although that regime led in time to such absurdities as schools reserving certain staplers for use with Title I students). The NCLB remedies, precisely because they are supposed to be about outcomes, cannot be made to work merely through guidance and reporting requirements.

Third, this compliance mindset has, unsurprisingly, been accompanied by a notable creativity vacuum. NCLB's architects hoped that school choice, supplemental educational services, corrective action, and restructuring would foster ingenuity and creative problem-solving. Such activity is almost uniformly absent, however. Instead, implementation has tended toward the grudging and predictable. Few districts are making heroic efforts to create more openings in high-performing schools into which students can transfer; are using technology to provide new options; or are aggressively using supplemental educational services or restructuring as tools of reform. Whether this failure is due to lack of knowledge, lack of real consequences, lack of will, lack of resources, or some other factor—or a combination of these—is not yet clear.

It doesn't suffice to say that schools and school districts are uniquely impervious to change. In a multitude of sectors, established organizations have found it difficult to adapt to new challenges and to take advantage of new tools and opportunities. That's why so many of today's leading airlines, retailers, technology firms, automobile companies, and media outlets are not the same as the leaders of forty years ago. Embedded routines, organizational cultures, union contracts, and expensive infrastructure can make it difficult even for relatively nimble organizations to meet new challenges and adapt to changing circumstances. In such instances, it may be necessary to erect new organizations rather than continuously seek to reform familiar ones. It seems unlikely that even sending new principals, "turnaround" specialists, tutoring, and some additional resources to the same old schools in troubled communities is going to fulfill the hopes of NCLB's proponents. In fact, it's likely that many of today's schools and districts will not be up to the challenge, and that new providers and institutions—free from the baggage that weighs upon them—must emerge to replace them. Yet federal, state, and district officials show no such appetite, outside a few much-noted locales like New York City, Philadelphia, and Indianapolis.

Fourth, NCLB's remedies are not, in fact, being much used (notably school choice and SES), or they are being deployed in their mildest forms (as with school and district restructuring). Little NCLB-inspired choice is occurring; SES participation rates, though higher than before, remain laughably low in most places; and we see scant evidence of systematic school restructuring. Nor do states and districts appear to have the *capacity* to restructure more than a handful of schools—certainly not the hundreds, soon to be thousands, that NCLB has flagged as warranting such interventions.

Given Washington's failure to recognize, give incentive to, or reward states or districts that aggressively wield the remedy provisions, and the potential political backlash and headaches for those that do, this is no great surprise. Yet there is a companion surprise: Across the nation, much standards-based and choice-based reforming is occurring separate and apart from NCLB. Most of this action is state-initiated, some locally inspired. This belies the view that NCLB is the only game in town, or that tempering its aspirations would weaken the nation's education reforms. In practice, NCLB may have caught a reform wave more than it caused such a wave.

Fifth, on the plus side, there are places where NCLB has created political cover for state, district, or school officials to take bolder actions than they otherwise might. Plank and Dunbar, for example, suggest that the imagined threat of NCLB restructuring in Michigan (as toothless as it may actually be) has fostered a sense of urgency at low-performing schools.[2] Clements, in the case of Kentucky, and Kowal and Hassel, in examining a quartet of schools under restructuring, also report that the federal law has brought an urgency and focus that had previously been lacking.[3] It is possible that the actual design and operation of the remedies aren't as important as their mere existence—and the mythology that envelops them. We may be witnessing a "Wizard of Oz" phenomenon, in which NCLB matters not for what it actually does, but because it creates a scary presence "behind the curtain" that can be used to prompt otherwise painful changes and blamed for difficult decisions.

But can such an illusion last? As the curtain is pulled back and the NCLB wizard is revealed to wield little real power, the "political cover" it supplies seems likely to fade. As more schools are slated for NCLB remedies at the same time, it becomes apparent to all that neither federal nor state nor local officials have much idea how to "fix" schools nor any desire to sanction perpetual low-performers. Educators and local officials will see the little man behind the curtain struggling futilely to scare them, and the law's remedies will lose credibility. This may also undermine non-NCLB accountability in the process.

Sixth, NCLB works very differently from state to state. In some places, its prescriptiveness impedes the state's own approach to standards-based reform, as in Florida, where NCLB mandates the restructuring of some schools that are simultaneously earning honors grades from the Sunshine State's own widely admired accountability system. Certainly, NCLB sows confusion where, as in California, there are discrepancies in school ratings between state and federal models. In particular, the crude AYP/not-AYP trigger of NCLB, the law's mandated restructuring cascade, and its emphasis on the procedures of choice, serve to complicate homegrown improvement strategies in such leading reform states as Florida, Texas, Massachusetts, and California.

Less is known about NCLB's potential stimulus effect in those states— such as Oklahoma, Mississippi, South Dakota, Nebraska, and Idaho—that had done little by way of standards-based, accountability-style education reform as of 2002. The task for NCLB proponents is to demonstrate that the benefits in such states are substantial enough to outweigh the difficulties wrought in those that had already forged coherent accountability systems of their own.

Nobody should be too surprised by unevenness in implementing the NCLB remedies, given the extensive decentralization assumed by the law. The law is, in fact, almost a Rorschach test of state and local attitudes toward education reform. It does the most good where gung-ho educators seize upon its remedies, where tough-minded state leaders leverage its political muscle, or where technical support and intense focus have been targeted on a limited set of schools. NCLB has vocal fans among some leading superintendents and school reformers precisely because it provides moral authority and some political cover for their own struggles against the inertia, bureaucracy, and resistance that characterize troubled school systems. The corollary, however, is that NCLB seems not to make much difference in places where state and/or local leaders lack gumption, imagination, and political courage. That's probably inherent in any federal law that relies on state and local implementation, but it holds out scant hope of driving improvement in the majority of districts or improving thousands upon thousands of schools.

Seventh, supplemental educational services (SES) pose a particular challenge. Districts want tutoring that boosts their math and reading scores but doesn't inconvenience them. They don't like losing money (which happens when parents opt for outside providers to deliver SES), but they don't mind their teachers earning extra dollars on the side. Providers are loath to be monitored or regulated by hostile state authorities and may not teach in ways aligned to district curricula or state tests—but definitely want to maximize their enrollments. Parents get information through the school and likely trust its staff, yet the school has little reason to steer families to outsiders that will take district funds and not necessarily help it make AYP.

Here, too, compliance reigns. Those charged with making SES work follow the letter of the law, even though realizing the uncertain potential of this provision requires an aggressive commitment to its spirit. That is evident in places like Dade County, where a concerted effort to reach out to parents and boost participation has had evident impact. Yet even after Dade's leadership mounted an outreach effort that tripled the number of students enrolled in SES, only about one-third of all students requesting the program were actually receiving services.

Across the land, evaluation and quality control have received scant attention, parental outreach has been half-hearted, and the SES machinery has proved balky. These developments are not simply a consequence of lackluster implementation and perverse incentives; they're also a result of the hodgepodge of theories and compromises baked into the SES program itself. Jeff Henig's analysis illumines the tensions among competing notions of what it was intended to accomplish.[4] One faction views SES as a stalking horse for vouchers and, believing in competition as a tool of school improvement, holds that the ability of private tutoring providers to compete for Title I dollars will press low-performing districts to improve. A second group regards SES chiefly as a way to provide extra instruction to students in low-performing schools, crafted to avoid harming either those students or their schools. A third cadre sees it as a mechanism for nurturing an industry of for-profit and nonprofit providers and encouraging innovative approaches to serving at-risk students.

Unfortunately, these disparate theories and strategies work at cross-purposes and have meant, in practice, an awkward reliance on national chains and local nonprofits, a staffing model that relies on teachers from the same districts supposedly being subjected to competition, lack of synergy between tutoring curricula and district standards, little quality control (to avoid squelching innovation), and reliance on outdated district machinery to manage an unprecedented set of awkward responsibilities. In the end, there has not been competition, demonstrably effective remediation, or much evidence of innovation. We conclude that the SES provision is unworkable as presently designed, and that efforts to improve its "implementation" are unlikely to change that.

Eighth, parts of NCLB are providing a wealth of data, sunlight, and transparency with regard to school, district, and state-level performance. This has empowered public officials and parents to lean on schools and districts, has equipped educators with new tools, and has brought greater resonance to discussions of school reform. This is a good but imperfect thing, both because a lot of other needed data don't yet exist or aren't available in comparable and readily accessible fashion, and because some of the ways that NCLB insists on judging schools (especially the "pass-fail" nature of AYP) are out of whack with how parents and states judge them.

Such transparency is precisely what the Clinton-era ESEA reauthorization (the "Improving America's Schools Act" of 1994) and Goals 2000 legislation sought but mostly failed to provide. Despite AYP-related flaws, we welcome the flood of additional information, and we suspect that, in the long run, NCLB's greatest accomplishment may be the school-performance data it furnishes to parents, educators, and state and local officials, data on the basis of which they can make desirable changes in their own schools and their choices among schools. We also note the irony of suggesting that

NCLB-style overkill was needed to get states and districts to produce the data sought by previous, less invasive legislation and implying that NCLB might have been unnecessary had educators and state officials been less intransigent and more eager to promote transparency in the preceding decade.

Yet while it has generated reams of information regarding pupil achievement and school performance, NCLB does a woeful job of gathering other kinds of data pertaining to its own implementation, the nature and use of its "remedies," and their effectiveness. In other words, NCLB is good at telling America how students and schools (and districts and states) are faring today when it comes to math and reading, but bad at telling anyone *what* they are doing, how they are changing, how much students are benefiting, what remedies are being used in which ways where, and what difference (if any) those remedies are making. Descriptive information and hard data are scarce. This means that very little can be learned about what to do more of—and less of—by way of *altering* the present achievement picture.

Ninth, evaluation of the NCLB remedies (and the theories and models on which they're based) is weaker still. Today, there's little evidence that remedies even have much bearing on the law's larger student-achievement goals. They're more theories of change than proven methods of altering school/educator/child/district/state behavior. That doesn't mean they're not worth trying, but it does mean that their implementation and effectiveness ought to be rigorously monitored, meticulously appraised, and honestly reported. Yet there's startlingly little such evaluation underway to determine whether, how, and under what circumstances these remedies "work." In public presentations and private discussions, federal officials have seemed more than a little blasé about evaluating these features of NCLB. Especially given that statute's emphasis on what it calls "scientifically based" research and evaluation, and the Education Department's aggressive calls for such research in areas like reading and math, this inattention shows a worrisome blind spot if not a troubling hypocrisy. In fact, experience with these sorts of remedies outside the NCLB context provides little cause to believe that they reliably yield heightened student achievement or school improvement. Moreover, because the versions crafted by Congress were compromised and constrained from the outset (by, for example, limited choices and reconstitution loopholes), and because they entail what could fairly be termed unnatural and unfamiliar acts by districts and states, it would seem doubly important that careful monitoring and rigorous evaluation be conducted.

Tenth, and finally, the problems of implementing NCLB's remedies raise fundamental issues of federalism and whether the circa 1965 architecture of ESEA, relying as it does on state educational agencies (SEAs) and local educational agencies (LEAs) for implementation, is even suitable for a "reform" regimen (as opposed to a funding program), when it is the behavior of those very agencies that is meant to be altered. Such change-forcing steps require *somebody* to drop the hammer. As ESEA has been structured for four decades, that somebody is the district in the case of schools and the state in the case of districts; yet neither hammer-wielder has shown much inclination to take politically tough steps. Save where state or local leadership is exceptional, they lack the political muscle, the stomach, or the know-how to fix things. Meanwhile, schools of education have done an abysmal job of providing school or district leaders with the skills to turn around troubled schools or districts, while licensure arrangements ensure that the vast majority of principals and superintendents have been trained in those institutions. There's a crying need to inject somewhere into this closed circuit a healthy dollop of fresh thinking on organizational leadership and improvement. On this count, the best of today's nontraditional providers of leadership, such as New Leaders for New Schools, the Knowledge Is Power Program (KIPP), and the Broad Superintendents program, are welcome departures, indeed.

In the private sector, outmoded competitors can ultimately be bypassed, bankrupted, restructured, bought out, or otherwise rendered irrelevant. In the public sector, this almost never happens. Yet NCLB's remedies seem to take for granted that it will. That is a strategic error that threatens to undo the promise of the restructuring provision.

Thus, we find a truly mixed picture. Parts of NCLB may be working, but its "remedies" are, at best, an iffy proposition when it comes to catalyzing changes that boost school effectiveness and student achievement. Meanwhile, there is cause for concern that the remedies, as the law stands, may impede school effectiveness, damage morale, confound promising practices and functioning reform programs, and ask for such unrealistic acts that they breed compliance and cynicism.

Recommendations

There are two ways to draw guidance from what has been learned to date about the NCLB remedies. One is to consider them narrowly—to ask how Congress might retool them to make them work better within the law's current structure and basic design. This is the path that Washington is most apt to follow at reauthorization time, the path of least resistance. It is the path charted by President George W. Bush in his 2007 NCLB proposals, by the Commission on No Child Left Behind in its February 2007 report, and by most of the congressional leaders who have signaled their intentions. It is also consistent with a long tradition of refining major laws on the basis of experience rather than fundamentally reconstructing them. And it places boundaries around the political tussles ahead.

A very different approach is to rethink the law's basic structure and design. Though politically less likely, that approach would probably do children more good; for the lessons to be learned from NCLB's remedies over these past five years beg for fundamental changes based on a clear-eyed assessment of what roles Washington can (and cannot) usefully play when it comes to improving troubled schools and creating options for children.

The ten recommendations that follow draw from both the incremental and more radical perspectives.

First, federal policymakers ought to be more realistic regarding what they can cause to happen in K–12 education, acknowledging that Uncle Sam isn't good at managing the kind of calibrated, escalating sanctions that NCLB currently expects states and districts to execute. His capabilities are better aligned with a simpler, clearer model that leaves more room for state and local policy entrepreneurs to devise creative solutions. This may be an unwelcome message to advocates frustrated by the glacial pace of education change and eager to make a big difference in one giant leap, but it is a message they should heed.

Rather than imposing an incremental cascade of interventions and remedies, Washington should insist that states label schools that need help; that they act to strengthen such schools; and that they shut, replace, or turn inside out those schools that resist improvement. That kind of mission is much more attuned to Washington's strengths—and more closely resembles the recipe that Uncle Sam has used to excellent effect in reforming welfare.

In education, the key is to make clear that states—working through districts as they see fit—are to assist schools that they identify as low-performing, and help to clear away the barriers that stymie change-agents from improving such schools and districts. Simultaneously, choice programs should provide decent options to students, without any notion that they will improve malfunctioning schools. After a certain trigger point is reached, however—when schools have gone several years without making sufficient improvement—the interventions that follow should be draconian. Such schools should be closed, with their buildings recycled to house new schools. In other words, there ought to be a presumption of good intention in the initial years, with the law geared to providing essential political cover and local muscle to clear-eyed reformers; thereafter, the law should be designed to *replace* persistently ineffective schools. We believe this sequence—presumption of competence, followed by swift and sure action—can provide the clarity of purpose and design that is currently lost amid NCLB's scattered components and disparate theories of action.

Second, although Washington should trust states to turn around their own schools, all should be measured against a single set of national standards and uniform national tests, at least in the core subjects of math and reading. (This presupposes that such standards and tests can be competently and coherently designed—and not by politicians.) This would permit parents, educators, and officials to see clearly how their school, district, or state is doing. That strategy has the great merit of sorting out roles and responsibilities in the school reform domain. Were they compulsory, national standards and tests would prove unpalatable to many on Capitol Hill; but the bipartisan Commission on No Child Left Behind has outlined a voluntary approach, keyed to the National Assessment of Educational Progress, that has merit and may attract support on both sides of the aisle. While the corollary of "trusting states," though much favored by the Council of Chief State School Officers and the Heritage Foundation, is not likely to win many Democratic votes, and neither the NCLB Commission nor Bush administration has proposed moving in that direction, it is urgent to distinguish the actions that Washington is truly capable of doing well from those that must be entrusted to others. It is equally urgent to recognize that the "others" do not necessarily have to be state and district educational agencies—the old ESEA architecture. The 2001 assumption that the "state educational agencies" and "local educational agencies" that had long been entrusted with implementing ESEA could now be charged with implementing NCLB needs to be rethought.

It may be that governors, mayors, nonprofit organizations, for-profit firms, regional authorities, and other such entities are better suited to handling the task of school reform. If Washington is serious about making NCLB effective, it might envision a contracting and multiple-provider regime in which a variety of nontraditional players is empowered to provide and monitor schooling.

Because states differ so dramatically in their approaches (and commitment) to education reform, Washington should adopt an "alpha-state" model, in which the feds provide greater freedom for states that earn it. States that can document success in providing options to eligible populations or delivering effective school improvement deserve greater flexibility and the opportunity to serve as models and laboratories for other jurisdictions.

Third, at least in the "alpha" states, and preferably everywhere, instead of mandating "one step per year" over a seven-year sequence of remedies, NCLB should afford states and districts the option of "corrective action" spanning several years. So, for example, if a school fails to "make AYP" (properly calculated), even for a single year, it would go into "corrective action" *and* its students would have access to SES *and* they would have the right to leave for other schools. But that phase would last four or five years, during which time the state or district would be able to do pretty much whatever it liked to improve the school's effectiveness—and any and all federal rules, mandates, and spending restrictions that got in the way should be waived. The goal is to empower hard-charging superintendents and principals—and encourage others to charge harder, mindful that Washington will abet rather than impede them. States must do the same. For example, they should set aside provisions of collective bargaining contracts that impede the reform of faltering schools.

AYP would still be calculated each year (modified as described below) but a school's status would not change as a result of additional "misses." When and if the school did "make AYP," it would emerge from corrective action and have the option of continuing or not continuing SES, and its students would no longer have the right to exit if they have not already done so (though those who left during the "corrective-action" phase might remain where they have gone if they wish to). If, however, the school did not begin to "make AYP" during the four- to five-year "corrective-action" period, a hammer would come down, allowing no loopholes and scant flexibility. Essentially, the failing school would have to be turned over to someone else to run, or else closed and its students reaccommodated in new or different schools. The key point is that, if district efforts fail to strengthen a school, the district should lose "ownership" of that school. (Similar logic should apply to state efforts to strengthen low-performing districts.)

Fourth, for any of this to work as intended, both parents and educators need to have confidence in the reliability of AYP as an identifying mechanism; any version of this scheme goes to pieces if states or districts are ordered to shutter schools that fair-minded observers regard as reasonably effective. While NCLB's AYP-designation process has not been our focus in this volume, the collected analyses make clear that any thoughtful effort to address the remedies requires major surgery to the AYP model. Right now, the law identifies hundreds of generally competent schools as "failing" and pushes states either to set unrealistic targets that ensure that this designation will apply to many more schools, or else dumb down their standards; and it does so based not on how much students are learning, but on a model that holds schools responsible for overcoming all challenges in children's lives.

AYP determinations and reporting must be better attuned to schools' effectiveness (that is, "growth" or "value-added" as well as absolute performance)[5] and better at distinguishing between schools (and districts) in serious trouble and those that are succeeding with most of their students. So long as this law threatens to ensnare reasonably effective schools in a confusing web of remedies, it will prove difficult for even the best-intentioned and most skillful of implementers to make work. (The Bush administration's 2007 NCLB reform recommendations point toward the possibility of AYP "growth models" for all states, as does the report of the national NCLB Commission; two states are actually piloting them today.)

What's more, the annual identification of school status needs to happen far faster than it does now, so that educators, policymakers, and parents know the results well before the next school year commences. The incapacities of the testing industry must not be allowed to perpetuate the dysfunctional practice of delaying the provision of such information until

August, September, or October. *All* of the NCLB remedies currently require that a school's status be determined annually. (Note, though, that our "multiyear" recommendation would ease the problem of timely data-reporting.) Ensuring the accuracy of such determinations has combined with the problems posed by overburdened, underaccountable testing firms and balky data systems to produce an unworkable timetable. Manna reports that sixteen states failed to finish identifying their "need-improvement" schools from the 2005–6 school year before September, when the 2006–7 school year had already begun.[6] For the remedies to work as conceived, it is imperative that states radically alter their testing and data management processes so that school identification is executed—and made known to all interested parties—in weeks instead of months. These problems are aggravated by the strain placed upon testing companies (and states) by a regime of fifty separate state exams. It goes without saying a well-designed set of high-quality national tests could potentially capture massive economies of scale, streamline the testing and reporting process, and permit the construction of a high-quality set of online assessments that could provide rapid, instructionally relevant feedback to teachers and parents.

Fifth, parents, in particular, need better, faster, clearer information regarding their SES and school choice options. These remedies also demand monitoring of SES providers, focused on actual delivery of services, better templates for communication and evaluation, and support for districts that do their best to make them work. States should conduct regular audits to encourage districts and schools to pay attention to customer service. They might, for example, usefully examine the availability of materials on district websites and the responsiveness of district personnel, and survey parents to ensure they are receiving timely and useful communications about the status of their current schools and the options available to them. It also makes sense to provide both SES and school choice simultaneously to students whose schools "need improvement"—particularly since few districts have been able to provide viable choice options even when required to do so. (The administration's recent NCLB reform proposals would make this change.)

A longstanding concern is the conflicted dual role that districts play as both SES providers and "gatekeepers" charged with negotiating agreements with alternative providers. This needs fixing. It asks districts to do unnatural things, work against their own interests, manage responsibilities for which they're not equipped, and engage in activities they regard as peripheral. The cleanest solution is for districts to cease controlling access to SES. Instead, states should explore how they can provide for other public or private entities to assume those responsibilities. Meanwhile, states must be required to monitor and report on the effectiveness of their SES providers. (One option might be an open-source national provider registry wherein families and officials can provide feedback that will be systematically available and warehoused, and which will be available for third-party analysis in order to increase provider accountability.)

Sixth, SES should come to be regarded not as a source of competition, but as a provider of extended learning time for students who need it. If the district itself is "making AYP" (according to a sensibly redefined AYP metric), it should be able to provide SES directly to students who need such help. If the district is not doing so, it should lose control of SES and SES dollars, and other providers should be invited (by the state or by entities chosen by the state to manage the program and inform parents of their options) to shoulder this responsibility. That responsibility should include careful evaluation of the performance of such providers and "de-listing" of those that don't boost student achievement.

Seventh, if choice is to be a serious element of NCLB, as we believe it should be, more options are essential, including interdistrict choice, the creation of greater capacity via a flood of high-performing charter schools, and the inclusion of academically effective private schools. (The Bush administration's 2007 NCLB reform proposals move in this direction, though the bipartisan NCLB Commission was all but silent on the subject of school choice.) Part of this entails the Department of Education's living by its stated position that lack of capacity is not a valid excuse for failing to provide choices. For instance, Washington might require that districts find ways to offer feasible options—for example, virtual schooling, expanding the capacity of effective schools, or raising state charter school "caps." If the feds want to show that NCLB is more than a collection of happy sentiments, they should inform states that they risk losing federal dollars if their own statute books restrict (for instance, through charter school caps) the provision of new options for children who are entitled to NCLB choice but currently can't find acceptable options. Washington should make clear that—at the very least—such states need to get out of the way and allow entrepreneurs to try to meet the existing need. Steve Clements' research in rural Kentucky revealed that local officials whose districts lack viable options for children eligible for NCLB choice don't even consider virtual schooling. Overall, there's been little effort to get creative about new options. This must change if NCLB is to keep its promise that children can exit low-performing schools for better ones. Ratcheting up the pressure on state and local officials to provide such opportunities—and, in the process, making it politically easier for them to propose disruptive measures like new charter schools or an expansion of virtual schooling—is vital to that effort.

We see no conflict between exhorting Washington to get tough on promoting NCLB choice and our earlier advice to "be more realistic." It is folly to imagine that every student can go to the school of his or her choice, or that we can wish enough good-quality schools into existence to serve all families. But it is wholly realistic to push states and districts to remove barriers that limit NCLB choice. Congress might, for example, require states to lift charter school caps if those limit access to viable options in communities where too many students are chasing too few seats in desirable schools. They can push districts to be more creative about scheduling, finding extra spaces in good schools, and providing students with transportation, and they can be more creative about rewarding good schools that make an effort to accept transfers. One promising proposal touted by the Bush administration in early 2007 was the requirement that districts actually spend the Title I dollars set aside for NCLB choice and SES for those purposes or risk losing the money. Much else is possible. Frankly, if there's a desire to increase NCLB choice, there's *a lot* more that can be done.

Eighth, many states and districts need expert help in fixing their troubled schools. Most lack the capacity. But that's not just an education problem. We know of no sector, public or private, in which thousands of entities are capable of assembling the know-how, talent, and organizational machinery to "turn around" troubled operations. Instead, such capabilities tend to be concentrated in a handful of specialized organizations such as "turnaround specialists" and niche consultants. If revitalizing a large number of low-performing schools (and districts) is actually to occur with any consistency at scale, education must also develop that capability. The nation would benefit greatly from a collection of highly effective operators with broad reach that are capable of contracting with multiple districts or states to provide the oversight, leadership, knowledge, and personnel to drive restructuring. That kind of scale would permit specialization and cooperation, allow providers to build knowledge and deep expertise, and yield a competitive market composed of public and private actors; but getting to that point calls for many more participants and a critical mass of research and knowledge. Washington cannot create this capacity or provide the knowledge, but it can provide resources, underwrite research, and encourage states to embrace nonprofit and for-profit entities that show a record of success.

As we observed previously, answering the challenge of persistently failing schools requires a degree of institutional flexibility and imagination that few state educational agencies, school districts, or schools presently possess. Hence, it would help to increase sharply the public and philanthropic funding flowing to those independent and "nontraditional" organizations that are taking steps to meet the challenge or provide the tools to do so—including such efforts as KIPP, the Big Picture Company, Green Dot Public Schools, K–12, Teach for America, New Leaders for New Schools, The New Teacher Project, and kindred entrepreneurial efforts.

Ninth, in reauthorizing NCLB, Congress should introduce real consequences for failure—and incentives for success. NCLB's current rewards and sanctions create little urgency for individual educators or school or district leaders. Collective bargaining agreements still protect the jobs of educators even in schools that pass beyond the restructuring horizon. (This problem is the result of political timidity on Capitol Hill and at the Education Department, though in early 2007 President Bush proposed changing course.) The requirement that schools spend money on SES or NCLB choice includes no hint that such expenditures should affect staff compensation. Failure to comply with the law or to drive improvement holds no clear consequences for the pay or job security of teachers or principals. The threat of federal dollars being withheld is all but toothless, mainly because Congress restricted this penalty to "administrative dollars"—and didn't apply it to weak academic performance, only to failure to submit acceptable "plans" to Washington.

We recommend that federal policymakers encourage states and districts to adopt personal consequences for inadequate performance and failure to improve. Superintendents and principals should be held responsible for their schools' outcomes and should be professionally and monetarily rewarded when those outcomes are good—and penalized when they're not. While many of today's calls for performance pay focus on rewarding teachers for test-score results, the easier task is to begin by ensuring that managers have skin in the game.

Tenth, and finally, districts and states must gather and report far more hard data and descriptive information regarding every phase of NCLB implementation, including the uses of the various remedies—and the marriage of NCLB's student achievement data to "remedy" information in ways that will advance our understanding of what's actually working. This is not only a challenge of data collection and reporting, but also of encouraging and supporting research and analysis that track the implementation and impact of the various remedies. At least four audiences need to be better served: parents, education practitioners, state and local (and federal) policymakers, and analysts and researchers. Such activity requires support, and providing it is a role that Washington is uniquely equipped to play.

Closing Observations

NCLB began with the noble yet naive promise that every U.S. schoolchild would attain "proficiency" in reading and math by 2014. While there is no doubt that the percentage of "proficient" students can and should increase dramatically from the current 30-ish percent (according to the definition of proficiency used by the National Assessment of Educational Progress [NAEP]), and while the achievement of children below the proficient level also can and should rise closer to proficiency, no educator in America believes that universal proficiency will, in fact, be attained by 2014. Only politicians promise such things. The inevitable result is cynicism and frustration among educators, and a "compliance" mentality ("We have to pretend that we're really doing these things or we'll get in trouble, maybe even lose money") among state and local officials.

In critical ways, today's NCLB amounts to a civil rights manifesto dressed up as an accountability system. This provides an untenable basis for serious reform, rather as if Congress declared that every last molecule of water or air pollution would vanish by 2014, or that all American cities would be crime-free by that date. There is evidence from states such as

Florida and California that the act will force them to restructure reasonably good schools, set back their own school improvements, and undermine coherent state leadership. The law is also pushing states to move aggressively in too many schools at once, ensuring that capacity won't be up to the challenges at hand. In this light, revamping the remedies begins with the need to refashion NCLB as a clear-minded accountability system, rather than an aspirational one. The failure to do so will ensure that NCLB does not work as hoped. It will also make likely an eventual public backlash that will topple NCLB and may discredit, as well, the years of hard, clear thinking and coalition-building that have characterized educational accountability since the release of *A Nation at Risk* nearly a quarter-century ago.

Whatever the political value of promising to "leave no child behind," the results thus far threaten to undermine two decades of hard-won gains on educational accountability. NCLB's dogmatic aspirations and fractured design are producing a compliance-driven regimen that recreates the very pathologies it was intended to solve. It's time to relearn the lessons of the Great Society, when ambitious programs designed to promote justice and opportunity were undone by utopian formulations, unworkable implementation structures, and a stubborn unwillingness to acknowledge the limits of federal action in the American system. In the end, Washington is not well-positioned to effect change to a program that depends on state and local action, or successfully to require states and districts to adopt measures whose efficacy hinges on gusto and creativity rather than compliance.

Finally, no matter how finely NCLB is tuned or how artfully refashioned, powerful cultural and political forces will continue to impede school improvement. A sense of urgency and outsized aspirations is commendable, but there's a world of difference between determination and delusion. In reforming NCLB, it is important neither to overpromise nor to overreach. We have spent forty years learning how hard school reform actually is. Yet too many otherwise serious people, such as the members of the national NCLB Commission, sustain that very pretense, indeed worsen it by suggesting that sixty-plus technocratic changes and considerably more federal control will cure what ails this law.

We disagree that such tinkering will be enough. What Washington can do best, given the structure of the American federal system, is deploy its "bully pulpit" to change the political climate, set common standards, collect and disseminate data, cultivate research and technical expertise, nurture pioneering state efforts and cast a spotlight upon them, and promote a clear understanding of what constitutes unacceptable school performance. Given different machinery, Washington might be able to do more. Until that day comes, however, responsible governance demands that the feds do what they can do well—and not sacrifice hard-won gains in the service of sloganeering.

Notes

Preface

1. Frederick M. Hess and Chester E. Finn, Jr. (eds.), *Leaving No Child Behind? Options for Kids in Failing Schools* (New York: Palgrave Macmillan, 2004).

Introduction

1. *No Child Left Behind Act of 2001*, Public Law 107-110, 107th Cong., 1st sess. (January 8, 2002).

2. *Elementary and Secondary Education Act of 1965*, Public Law 89-10, 89th Cong., 1st sess. (April 11, 1965).

3. *New York Times*, "Excerpts from Gore's Speech Outlining His Plans for Improving Education," April 29, 2000, late edition, sec. A.

4. National Commission on Excellence in Education, *A Nation at Risk: The Imperative for Educational Reform* (Washington, D.C.: Government Printing Office, 1983).

5. For a full description of the scope and details of Title I, visit the *Education Week* online research center, www.edweek.org/rc/issues/title-i/ (accessed June 12, 2007).

Chapter 1: NCLB in the States:
Fragmented Governance, Uneven Implementation

1. P.L. 103-382.

2. On NCLB's theory of action see Frederick M. Hess and Michael J. Petrilli, *No Child Left Behind Primer* (New York: Peter Lang, 2006), 23. The distinction between high-stakes and suggestive accountability is in Frederick M. Hess, "Refining or Retreating? High-Stakes Accountability in the States," in *No Child Left Behind? The Politics and Practice of School Accountability*, eds. Paul E. Peterson and Martin R. West (Washington, D.C.: Brookings Institution Press, 2003), 57–58.

3. For historical and more recent analysis arguing that federal control remains limited see Paul Manna, "Control, Persuasion and Educational Accountability: Implementing the No Child Left Behind Act," *Educational Policy* 20, no. 3 (2006): 471–94; Paul Manna, *School's In: Federalism and the National Education Agenda* (Washington, D.C.: Georgetown University Press, 2006). Other perspectives, which stress a more dominant federal role, appear in Christopher T. Cross, *Political Education: National Policy Comes of Age* (New York: Teachers College Press, 2004); Richard F. Elmore, "Unwarranted Intrusion," *Education Next* 2, no. 1 (2002): 31–35; Patrick McGuinn, "The National Schoolmarm: No Child Left Behind and the New Educational Federalism," *Publius* 35, no. 1 (2005): 41–68; Patrick J. McGuinn, *No Child Left Behind and the Transformation of Federal Education Policy, 1965–2005* (Lawrence, Kans.: University of Kansas Press, 2006).

4. An overview of the grants tool is in David R. Beam and Timothy J. Conlan, "Grants," in *The Tools of Government: A Guide to the New Governance*, ed. Lester M. Salamon (New York: Oxford University Press, 2002). Political scientists and economists often refer to the challenge of controlling grant recipients as a "principal-agent problem." For numerous specific examples of this dynamic that involve the ESEA, see John E. Chubb, "The Political Economy of Federalism," *American Political Science Review* 79, no. 4 (1985): 994–1015; Michael Cohen, "Unruly Crew," *Education Next* 2, no. 2 (2002): 43–47; William J. Erpenbach, Ellen Forte Fast, and Abigail Potts, *Statewide Accountability under NCLB* (Washington, D.C.: Council of Chief State School Officers, 2003); Ellen Forte Fast and William J. Erpenbach, *Revisiting Statewide Educational Accountability under NCLB* (Washington, D.C.: Council of Chief State School Officers, 2004); Manna, *School's In*; Diane Ravitch, "The History Lesson in Bush's School Plan," *New York Times*, January 27, 2001.

5. For a general treatment of delegation and its challenges see Jonathan Bendor, Amihai Glazer, and Thomas Hammond, "Theories of Delegation," *Annual Review of Political Science* 4 (2001): 235–69.

6. Stephen Goldsmith and William D. Eggers, *Governing by Network: The New Shape of the Public Sector* (Washington, D.C.: Brookings Institution Press, 2004); NASBE Study Group on Education Governance, *A Motion to Reconsider: Education Governance at a Crossroads* (Alexandria, Va.: National Association of State Boards of Education, 1996).

7. Also see chapters 5, 6, 7, and 8 for more detailed analyses.

8. Albert O. Hirschman, *Exit, Voice, and Loyalty: Responses to Decline in Firms, Organizations, and States* (Cambridge, Mass.: Harvard University Press, 1970).

9. General discussion of the importance of timing and the states' role appears in U.S. Government Accountability Office, *No Child Left Behind Act: Improvements Needed in Education's Process for Tracking States' Implementation of Key Provisions* (GAO-04-734) (Washington, D.C.: Author, 2004), 19–23; U.S. Department of Education, *LEA and School Improvement: Non-Regulatory Guidance*, July 21, 2006, 2, http://www.ed.gov/policy/elsec/guid/schoolimprovementguid.pdf (accessed March

29, 2007). Regarding appeals, see NCLB Section 1116(b)(2) "Opportunity to Review and Present Evidence"; Time Limit.

10. Diane Stark Rentner, Caitlin Scott, Nancy Kober, Naomi Chudowsky, Victor Chudowsky, Scott Joftus, and Dalia Zabala, *From the Capital to the Classroom: Year 4 of the No Child Left Behind Act*, Center on Education Policy, March 2006, 126–27.

11. Lynn Olson, "Citing New Tests, Many States Late with AYP Results," *Education Week*, August 31, 2006.

12. A description of the required elements of these letters appears in U.S. Department of Education, *No Child Left Behind Public School Choice: Non-Regulatory Guidance*, February 6, 2004 draft, question D-2, http://www.ed.gov/policy/elsec/guid/schoolchoiceguid.doc (accessed May 2, 2007). Criticism regarding the content of local letters is reported in Center on Education Policy, *From the Capital to the Classroom: Year 3 of the No Child Left Behind Act*, March 2005, 121–22.

13. Julia Crouse, "Transfers Threaten Class Size Balance," *Ledger*, August 9, 2006.

14. U.S. Department of Education, *No Child Left Behind Public School Choice*, question E-9.

15. Quoted in Julia Crouse, "Transfers Threaten Class Size Balance".

16. Ibid.

17. U.S. Department of Education, *No Child Left Behind Supplemental Educational Services: Non-Regulatory Guidance*, June 13, 2005, question B-1, http://www.ed.gov/policy/elsec/guid/suppsvcsguid.doc (accessed May 2, 2007).

18. U.S. Government Accountability Office, *No Child Left Behind Act: Education Actions Needed to Improve Local Implementation and State Evaluation of Supplemental Educational Services*, GAO-06-758, August 2006, 20, 22, 44, http://www.gao.gov/new.items/d06758.pdf (accessed March 26, 2007).

19. U.S. Department of Education, *No Child Left Behind Supplemental Educational Services*, C-2.

20. U.S. Government Accountability Office, *Education Actions Needed to Improve Local Implementation*, 34. Additionally, in its fourth year study of NCLB implementation, the Center on Education Policy found that "41 states reported that monitoring the quality and effectiveness of supplemental educational services was a moderate or serious challenge. In fact, more states viewed this as a moderate or serious challenge than any other challenge related to SES. . . . More than two-thirds of states also said it was moderately or seriously challenging to determine whether providers' services are effective in raising student achievement (40 states), whether providers' instruction is research-based (34 states), and whether providers' instructional strategies are of high quality (34 states)"; Rentner et al., *From the Capital to the Classroom: Year 4 of the No Child Left Behind Act*, 131, 142.

21. U.S. Department of Education, *No Child Left Behind LEA and School Improvement*, D-15.

22. Quoted in Jessica Foster, "More Schools Falling Short," *Sun News*, October 6, 2006.

23. U.S. Department of Education, *No Child Left Behind LEA and School Improvement*, H-8.

24. Ibid. Regarding limited state involvement, for example, in California, no single state agency checks for school compliance with corrective action plans, and on-site state monitoring of districts is relatively infrequent, involving district visits once every four years; Cadonna Peyton, "Failing Schools Aren't Watched," *Press Enterprise*, August 31, 2006.

25. U.S. Department of Education, *No Child Left Behind LEA and School Improvement*, K-6.

26. Quoted in Diane Rado, "217 Illinois Schools Face U.S. Sanctions," *Chicago Tribune*, November 17, 2005.

27. Quoted in Greg Gelpi, "5 Local Schools Facing Reform," *Augusta Chronicle*, May 11, 2006.

28. Quoted in Steven Carter, "State Schools Test Law's Limits," *Oregonian*, September 3, 2006.

29. Ron Matus, "Progress on FCAT Has Federal Caveat," *St. Petersburg Times*, June 15, 2006.

30. Nivri Shah, "Education Overhaul May Delay Local Reforms," *Palm Beach Post*, July 31, 2006.

31. Examples of the work of turnaround specialists appear in Karen A. Davis, "State Joins Effort to Improve 8 Schools," *Providence Journal*, December 16, 2005; Kelly Hinchcliffe, "Most Durham Schools Miss Federal Targets," *Herald-Sun*, July 20, 2006; Linda Conner Lambeck, "Laggers Include Beardsley, Columbus," *Connecticut Post*, December 7, 2005; James Vaznis, "More Schools Falling Short," *Boston Globe*, September 13, 2006. The quote from Chamberlain is from Judy Kroeger, "Cahs to Submit Action Plan to State," *Pittsburgh Tribune Review*, December 21, 2005.

32. For general discussion of the restructuring loophole, see Sara Mead, "Easy Way Out: 'Restructured' Usually Means Little Has Changed," *Education Next* 7, no. 1 (2007): 52–56.

33. See Eleanor Chute, "Schools on Track to Meet Standards," *Pittsburgh Post-Gazette*, September 1, 2006.

34. Helen Gao, "Charter Schools Group Gets Grant," *San Diego Union-Tribune*, October 4, 2006.

35. Brenda Neuman-Sheldon, *Building on State Reform: Maryland School Restructuring*, Center on Education Policy, September 2006, 5–6. See also Sara Neufeld, "City Judge Orders School-Cost Detail," *Baltimore Sun*, May 16, 2006.

36. See Kate N. Grossman, "185 Failing Schools to Undergo $5 Million in Changes," *Chicago Sun-Times*, May 22, 2006; Linda Shaw, "Schools That Need to

Improve," *Seattle Times*, September 1, 2006; Kenneth K. Wong and Francis X. Shen, "Does School District Takeover Work? Assessing the Effectiveness of City and State Takeover as a School Reform Strategy," *State Education Standard*, Spring 2002.

37. Arnold F. Shober, Paul Manna, and John F. Witte, "Flexibility Meets Accountability: State Charter School Laws and Their Influence on the Formation of Charter Schools in the United States," *Policy Studies Journal* 34, no. 4 (2006): 563–87.

38. Associated Press State and Local Wire, "Six Kentucky Schools Facing Possible Sanctions," May 3, 2006.

39. A general treatment of collective bargaining and its impact on reform is Jane Hannaway and Andrew J. Rotherham, eds., *Collective Bargaining in Education: Negotiating Change in Today's Schools* (Cambridge, Mass.: Harvard Education Press, 2006). Analyses of teacher certification are in Kati Haycock, "The Elephant in the Living Room," in *Brookings Papers on Education Policy*, ed. Diane Ravitch (Washington, D.C.: Brookings Institution, 2004); Frederick M. Hess, *Tear Down This Wall: The Case for a Radical Overhaul of Teacher Certification* (Washington, D.C.: Progressive Policy Institute, 2001).

40. Discussion of the increasing demands on state agencies appears in Steve Kaagan and Michael D. Usdan, "Leadership Capacity for State Reform: The Mismatch between Rhetoric and Reality," *Education Week*, May 5, 1993; Manna, *School's In*.

41. Jacqueline Reis, "More Schools Are Falling Behind," *Telegram and Gazette*, September 13, 2006.

42. See chapter 2.

Chapter 2: America's Great City Schools:
Moving in the Right Direction

1. U.S. Department of Education, National Center for Education Statistics, *National Assessment of Educational Progress, The Nation's Report Card: Trial Urban District Assessment Reading 2005*, NCES 2006-455, http://nces.ed.gov/nationsreportcard/pdf/dst2005/2006455r.pdf (accessed June 8, 2007); and U.S. Department of Education, National Center for Education Statistics, *National Assessment of Educational Progress, The Nation's Report Card: Trial Urban District Assessment Mathematics 2005*, NCES 2006-457, http://nces.ed.gov/nationsreportcard/pdf/dst2005/2006457r.pdf (accessed June 8, 2007).

2. Council of the Great City Schools, "No Child Left Behind Reauthorization in the Great City Schools," unpublished internal survey, 2006.

3. Districts responding included Albuquerque, Anchorage, Atlanta, Baltimore, Birmingham, Boston, Broward County, Charlotte-Mecklenburg, Chicago, Clark County (Las Vegas), Cleveland, Columbus, Denver, Detroit, East Baton Rouge, Fresno, Fort Worth, Guilford County (Greensboro, North Carolina), Hillsborough

County (Tampa), Houston, Indianapolis, Jackson (Mississippi), Jefferson County (Louisville), Los Angeles, Memphis, Miami-Dade County, Milwaukee, Minneapolis, Nashville, Newark, New York City, Norfolk, Omaha, Palm Beach County, Philadelphia, Portland (Oregon), Providence, Salt Lake City, San Diego, and St. Paul.

4. Data on the forty cities from internal data banks of the Council of the Great City Schools.

5. Council of the Great City Schools, "No Child Left Behind Reauthorization in the Great City Schools,"1.

6. See, for example, chapter 1.

7. Council of the Great City Schools, "No Child Left Behind Reauthorization in the Great City Schools," letters to parents.

8. Ibid.

9. Ibid.

10. Ibid., SES contracts.

Chapter 3: The Political Economy of Supplemental Educational Services

1. Edmund W. Gordon and Beatrice L. Bridglall, "The Idea of Supplementary Education," *Pedagogical Inquiry and Praxis*, no. 3 (March 2002), http://iume.tc.columbia.edu/reports/praxis3.html (accessed March 26, 2007).

2. Ibid.

3. The timing of the SES trigger, particularly the question of whether SES should be instituted before the parental choice option, which currently kicks in after the second year of inadequate progress, is the subject of considerable debate, and some exceptions to the standard sequencing have been approved on an experimental basis.

4. Unlike the most common entitlement programs, SES eligibility is defined less by the individuals' personal characteristics than by the characteristics of the schools they are assigned to attend. While some entitlement programs create an open-ended obligation on public revenues, districts are not required to spend more than 20 percent of their Title I allotments on SES plus student choice, so SES does not present the same threat of budget uncontrollables.

5. U.S. Government Accountability Office, *No Child Left Behind Act: Education Actions Needed to Improve Local Implementation and State Evaluation of Supplemental Educational Services*, GAO-06-758, August 2006, http://www.gao.gov/new.items/d06758.pdf (accessed March 26, 2007).

6. U.S. Government Accountability Office, *No Child Left Behind Act: Education Needs to Provide Additional Technical Assistance and Conduct Implementation Studies for School Choice Provision*, GAO-05-7, December 2004, http://www.gao.gov/new.items/d057.pdf (accessed March 26, 2007).

7. U.S. Government Accountability Office, *No Child Left Behind Act: Education Actions Needed to Improve Local Implementation*.

8. While some of that will be spent on transportation for children whose parents choose to move them to better public schools under the NCLB provision, the actual uptake on the choice option, as noted, has been quite limited, leaving most of the money available for SES.

9. U.S. Department of Health and Human Services, Administration for Children and Families, Office of Head Start, "Head Start Program Fact Sheet, Fiscal Year 2006," http://www2.acf.dhhs.gov/programs/hsb/research/2006.htm (accessed March 26, 2007).

10. Siobhan Gorman, "Selling Supplemental Services," *Education Next*, Fall 2004, 32.

11. Searches were run using ProQuest Direct for each year, with the key terms being George (or President) Bush, PLUS Education PLUS either <"No Child Left Behind" or "Leave No Child Behind"> or <"Supplemental Education" or Tutors or Tutoring>. Searches were restricted to "major newspapers." One set run was restricted to "citation and abstract"; these searches presumably picked up articles in which either NCLB or SES were a major focus. A second included searches for references within the article text, which could uncover less prominent references.

12. Patrick McGuinn, *No Child Left Behind and the Transformation of Federal Education Policy 1965–2005* (Lawrence, Kans.: University Press of Kansas, 2006).

13. Daniel Patrick Moynihan, *Maximum Feasible Misunderstanding: Community Action in the War on Poverty* (New York: The Free Press, 1969).

14. Martin L. Needleman and Carolyn Emerson Needleman, *Guerrillas in the Bureaucracy: The Community Planning Experiment in the United States* (New York: John Wiley & Sons, 1974).

15. Senator Judd Gregg, speaking for himself and Senator Hagel, "Statements on Introduced Bills and Joint Resolutions" *Congressional Record* S11731, September 30, 1999.

16. Andrew Rudalevige, "The Politics of No Child Left Behind," *Education Next*, Fall 2003, 62–69.

17. Ibid.

18. In *Mueller v. Allen*, 463 U.S. 388, the U.S. Supreme Court in 1983 upheld Minnesota's tax credit program, which provided tuition tax credits to parents of private school students in part because it also provided aid to public school parents for their educational expenses.

19. Andrew Rotherham, phone interview conducted by the author, May 25, 2006.

20. Gorman, "Selling Supplemental Services."

21. Anonymous SES provider, phone interview conducted by the author, June 5, 2006.

22. Ibid.

23. Ronald Brownstein, "The No Child Left Behind Act Granted Children the Right to Transfer out of Failing Schools. The Question Is, Will School Districts Let Them?" *Education Next*, no. 3 (2003): 40–46.

24. U.S. Government Accountability Office, *No Child Left Behind Act: Education Actions Needed to Improve Local Implementation*.

25. See chapter 10.

26. U.S. Department of Education, *Creating Strong Supplemental Education Services Programs* (Washington, D.C.: Government Printing Office, 2004).

27. See chapter 2.

28. New York City, Memphis, and Anchorage subsequently were granted similar discretion.

29. Richard J. Condon to Joel Klein, "RE: Platform Learning Inc. SCI Case #2004-2153," March 2006.

30. In 615 cases the provider names were too generic to allow for meaningful coding. Examples of this type include "Advantage Tutoring Service"; "ACE Tutoring Services Inc."; "Da Vinci Learning Center"; and "Howe Tutoring Associates." It is important to recognize that not coding these providers is not quite the same as counting them as "missing" data. The fact that some providers choose names that do not identify a particular market niche is interesting and important in and of itself.

31. Anonymous SES provider, interview.

32. Paul Manna, *School's In: Federalism and the National Education Agenda* (Washington D.C.: Georgetown University Press, 2006).

33. Katrina E. Bulkley, "Bringing the Private into the Public: Changing the Rules of the Game and New Regime Politics in Philadelphia Public Education," *Educational Policy* 21 (1): 155–84.

34. Gorman, "Selling Supplemental Services."

35. In at least some, and probably most, districts, specific endorsements by principals and teachers would be against policy. But informal recommendations could easily go unnoticed, and for many providers even a generic recommendation ("You should consider sending your child to one of the several SES providers working in this neighborhood") would be extremely valuable.

36. U.S. Department of Education, Office of Planning Evaluation and Policy Development, *Case Studies of Supplemental Services under the No Child Left Behind Act: Findings from 2003–04*, by Leslie M. Anderson and Katrina G. Laguarda, 2005, http://eric.ed.gov/ERICDocs/data/ericdocs2/content_storage_01/0000000b/80/31/be/36.pdf (accessed May 23, 2007).

Chapter 4: The Problem with "Implementation Is the Problem"

1. Sam Dillon, "As 2 Bushes Try to Fix Schools, Tools Differ," *New York Times*, September 28, 2006.

2. Office of Senator Edward M. Kennedy, "Senate Democrats Call for Effective Implementation of School Reforms," press release, September 13, 2004, http://kennedy.senate.gov/newsroom/press_release.cfm?id=71490759-029C-4BD9-A2C4-F821BF274157 (accessed March 29, 2007).

3. George Miller, testimony from "The Fourth Annual No Child Left Behind Forum: Assessing Progress, Addressing Problems, Advancing Performance," Business Roundtable, September 20, 2006, http://www.businessroundtable.org//task-Forces/taskforce/document.aspx?qs=7075BF159F849514481138A77EC1851159169FEB56A36B7AE (accessed March 29, 2007).

4. Kati Haycock, testimony from "Is No Child Left Behind Working? A Progress Report," Business Roundtable, December 3, 2003, http://www.businessroundtable.org/pdf/NCLBFinalTranscript.pdf (accessed March 29, 2007).

5. This is not unique to No Child Left Behind or even to the Education Department; see, for example, Jeffrey L. Pressman and Aaron Wildavsky, *Implementation* (Berkeley, Calif.: University of California Press, 1973).

6. See, for example, Matthew Carr, "Viewpoint: New EdChoice Voucher Program a Success," Buckeye Institute, June 12, 2006, http://www.buckeyeinstitute.org/article/715 (accessed March 29, 2007).

7. NCLB, 1116(6).

8. NCLB, 1116(E)(i).

9. NCLB, 1116(E)(2).

10. U.S. Department of Education, *Public School Choice Draft Non-Regulatory Guidance*, December 4, 2002, question D-4, http://dese.mo.gov/divimprove/fedprog/schoolchoiceguid.pdf (accessed June 8, 2007).

11. U.S. Department of Education, *Supplemental Educational Services Draft Non-Regulatory Guidance*, December 12, 2002, question E-2, http://www.nsba.org/site/docs/9000/8950.pdf (accessed March 29, 2007).

12. U.S. Department of Education, *Supplemental Educational Services Non-Regulatory Guidance*, draft, final guidance, August 22, 2003, https://www.nsba.org/site/docs/31900/31834.pdf (accessed June 11, 2007).

13. U.S. Department of Education, Office of Innovation and Improvement, *Innovations in Education: Creating Strong District School Choice Programs*, May 2004, http://www.ed.gov/admins/comm/choice/choiceprograms/report.pdf (accessed March 29, 2007).

14. Black Alliance for Educational Options, "About Us," http://www.baeo.org/programs?program_id=7 (accessed October 13, 2006).

15. Anonymous Department of Education official, email message to the author,

October 2006; the official would only provide info on condition of anonymity.

16. Nina Shokraii Rees, email message to the author, October 26, 2006.

17. JM Consulting Inc., *BAEO Project Clarion Three Year Final Evaluation Report*, May 2006.

18. Margaret Spellings letter to Thomas M. Jackson Jr., "Request for a flexibility agreement to provide supplemental educational services in lieu of public school choice, to students attending Title I schools in the first year of school improvement," August 25, 2005, http://www.ed.gov/admins/lead/account/letters/acva5.html (accessed June 8, 2007).

19. Margaret Spellings, letter to Joel I. Klein, "Flexibility Agreement on Behalf of the New York City Department of Education (NYCDOE) to Permit NYCDOE to Provide Supplemental Educational Services," November 7, 2005.

20. *Wall Street Journal*, "Spellings Exemptions," October 31, 2006.

21. See, for example, Lynn Olson, "Department Raps States on Testing," *Education Week*, July 12, 2006; Julie Blair, "Critics Question Federal Funding of Teacher Test," *Education Week*, October 8, 2003; Joetta L. Sack, "Utah Passes Bill to Trump 'No Child' Law," *Education Week*, April 27, 2005; and Christina A. Samuels, "Alternate Assessments Proving to Be a Challenge for States," *Education Week*, October 11, 2006.

22. Rees, email.

23. Frederick M. Hess and Chester E. Finn Jr. (eds.), *Leaving No Child Behind?: Options for Kids in Failing Schools* (New York, N.Y.: Palgrave Macmillan, 2004).

24. NCLB, 1116(E)(i).

25. Lisa Snell, "No Way Out: The No Child Left Behind Act Provides Only the Illusion of School Choice," *Reason* 36, no. 5 (October 1, 2004): 34.

26. Rod Paige, letter to education officials, June 14, 2002, http://www.ed.gov/policy/elsec/guid/secletter/020614.html (accessed March 29, 2007).

27. Mary Leonard and Anand Vaishnav, "Few So Far Use Law Allowing School Transfers," *Boston Globe*, August 29, 2002.

28. Duke Helfand, "School Choice Falling Short," *Los Angeles Times*, August 17, 2002.

29. National Archives and Records Administration, *Federal Register* 67, no. 231, December 2, 2002, Part IV: Department of Education, 34 CFR Part 200.44.

30. Ibid.

31. U.S. Department of Education, *Public School Choice Draft Non-Regulatory Guidance*, question E-7.

32. Rees, email.

33. U.S. Department of Education, *Public School Choice Draft Non-Regulatory Guidance*, question E-8.

34. Travis Hicks, "Lawyer: NCLB Guidance May Pave Way for Vouchers," *Education Daily*, May 6, 2004.

35. NCLB, 1116(8) (B).

36. Ibid.

37. NCLB, 1116(9).

38. National Archives and Records Administration, *Federal Register* 67, no. 151, August 6, 2002, Part IV: Department of Education, 34 CFR Part 200.54, proposed rules.

39. As reported by the Education Intelligence Agency, September 23, 2002, http://www.eiaonline.com/archives/20020923.htm (accessed March 29, 2007).

40. National Archives and Records Administration, *Federal Register* 67, no. 231, December 2, 2002, Part IV: Department of Education, 34 CFR Part 200, discussion of comments, section 200.54.

41. U.S. Department of Education, *LEA and School Improvement: Non-Regulatory Guidance*, July 21, 2006, question G-14, http://www.ed.gov/policy/elsec/guid/schoolimprovementguid.pdf (accessed March 29, 2007).

42. *Title I Monitor*, "School Improvement Guidance Takes Tough Stance on Restructuring," August 1, 2006.

43. U.S. Department of Education, *LEA and School Improvement: Non-Regulatory Guidance*, question G-8.

Chapter 5: California: Does the Golden State Deserve a Gold Star?

1. Ed-Data Education Data Partnership, *State of California Education Profile Fiscal Year 2005–2006*, http://www.ed-data.k12.ca.us/Navigation/fsTwoPanel.asp?bottom=%2Fprofile%2Easp%3Flevel%3D04%26reportNumber%3D16 (accessed August 2006).

2. One notable exception is the California High School Exit Examination (CAHSEE), which California has designated as an additional educational goal under NCLB. Having originally presented it as a binding requirement on the graduating class of 2004, the state announced in mid-2003 that in order to graduate in 2004, students need not have passed the CAHSEE. Since that time, the exam standards have been slightly watered down, and in spring 2006, for the first time, grade 12 students were prevented from graduating if they had yet to pass the revised CAHSEE.

3. For more information on California's own educational accountability system, see, for example, Julian R. Betts and Anne Danenberg, "The Effects of Accountability in California," in *No Child Left Behind? The Politics and Practice of Accountability*, ed. Paul E. Peterson and Martin R. West (Washington, D.C.: Brookings Institution, 2003),197–212.

4. Melissa McCabe, "State of the States: Overview," *Education Week*, January 5, 2006, "Standards & Accountability" (table).

5. D. McLaughlin and V. Bandeira de Mello, "How to Compare NAEP and State Assessment Results: NAEP State Analysis Project" (paper, National Conference on Large-Scale Assessment, San Antonio, Texas, June 18, 2005).

6. See Julian R. Betts and Anne Danenberg, "San Diego: Do Too Many Cooks Spoil the Broth?" in *Leaving No Child Behind? Options for Kids in Failing Schools*, ed. Frederick M. Hess and Chester E. Finn (New York: Palgrave Macmillan, 2004). Given the short timeframe of one or two weeks that California districts have between the announcement of new PI schools and the start of the school year, Betts and Danenberg suggested that the U.S. Department of Education consider requiring that schools offer supplemental educational services in the first year they are deemed in need of improvement, and the choice program, which is more difficult to organize, in year 2. The Department of Education has recently authorized several states to experiment with this approach.

7. California Department of Education, "Parent Notification Letter Template," http://www.cde.ca.gov/ta/ac/ti/documents/1parenttempdist.doc (accessed March 30, 2007).

8. See David J. Hoff, "Complaint Targets NCLB Transfers in Calif. Move is Step in Campaign to Include Private Schools in Law's Choice Provisions," *Education Week*, March 29, 2006.

9. Julian R. Betts, Lorien A. Rice, Andrew C. Zau, Y. Emily Tang, and Cory R. Koedel, *Does School Choice Work? Effects on Student Integration and Achievement* (San Francisco: Public Policy Institute of California, 2006).

10. Charles Weis (superintendent, Ventura County schools), personal communication to the author, November 2006.

11. Christine Quinn (associate superintendent, Hayward Unified School District), personal communication to the author, November 2006.

12. Some of the first evidence is likely to come from the RAND Corporation, which is under federal contract to evaluate the effects of both NCLB school choice and supplemental educational services in a sampling of districts nationwide.

13. Betts et al., *Does School Choice Work?*

14. This description is based on the California Department of Education, "2006 Supplemental Educational Services Provider Request for Applications (RFA)," http://www.cde.ca.gov/ta/ac/ti/documents/suppapp06.doc (accessed March 30, 2007).

15. Betts and Danenberg, "San Diego: Do Too Many Cooks Spoil the Broth?"

16. Insights from Camille Maben and Ann Just reported here and later in this chapter derive from an interview the author conducted jointly with them in October 2006.

17. See California Department of Education, *California Title 5 Supplemental Educational Services (SES) Regulations (Section 13075.2 (c) (1) – (21))*, September 2005, http://www.cde.ca.gov/ta/ac/ti/documents/sesduties.doc (accessed June 11 2007).

18. When asked if the state's application process seemed too time-consuming, the representative replied that he thought the screening was necessary, and that it had not been a burden thus far.

19. Julian R. Betts, Andrew C. Zau, and Kevin King, *From Blueprint to Reality: San Diego's Education Reforms* (San Francisco: Public Policy Institute of California, 2005).

20. There are no districts or county offices in their third year of PI status because the state and federal departments of education disagreed about the optimal way to identify PI districts in 2004–5. The disagreement hinged upon the California Department of Education's decision to focus on the economically disadvantaged subgroup, while the federal law states that if a LEA fails to make AYP in a given subject for two years in a row *in any student subgroup*, it must be labeled as being in need of improvement. As a result, the state's initial list of 14 LEAs from 2004 increased by 141 in April 2005, based on the guidance of the federal Department of Education. Because of this late notice, LEAs that were designated as PI in 2004–5 were deemed to be entering their first, rather than second, year of PI status in fall 2005.

21. For details see California Education Code Section 52055.57, http://www leginfo.ca.gov/cgi-bin/displaycode?section=edc&group=52001-53000& file=52055.57.

22. See, for instance, California Department of Education, *Academic Program Survey—Elementary School Level,* http://www.cde.ca.gov/ta/lp/vl/documents/egaps. doc (accessed April 2, 2007).

23. California Department of Education, *District Assistance Survey for Use by Local Education Agencies in Program Improvement,* http://www.cde.ca.gov/ta/lp/vl/ documents/distassistsrvy1.doc (accessed April 2, 2007). The nine components include the degree of alignment of curriculum with state content standards; adherence to suggested minimum times per day for math and English language arts; indicators for whether the school's principal has completed the state-mandated training program; measures of teachers' professional development; indicators for whether the school uses testing every six to eight weeks to feed back into instructional lesson plans; measures of content support for teachers; the degree of principal-led collaboration; the use of pacing schedules; and the extent to which the school can pay for the elements of its plan. The Academic Program Survey is similar for middle and high schools.

24. California also started a pilot program in four districts in 2006 in which teams from county offices of education work with senior district administrators to find ways to focus available categorical funds on the schools most in need.

25. California Education Code Section 52055.57.

26. Charles Weis (superintendent, Ventura County schools), interview conducted by the author, October 2006.

27. California Department of Education, *District Assistance Survey*.

28. Association of California School Administrators, *Recommendations for the 2007 Reauthorization of the No Child Left Behind Act* (Sacramento, Calif.: Association of California School Administrators, 2006).

29. See Julian R. Betts, "The Promise and Challenge of Accountability in Public Schooling," in *Urban School Reform: Lessons from San Diego*, ed. Frederick M. Hess (Cambridge, Mass.: Harvard Education Press, 2005), 157–76.

30. See California Department of Education, "O'Connell Announces Significant Gains in State API Results, Mixed Progress in Federal AYP Results," press release, August 31, 2005, http://www.cde.ca.gov/nr/ne/yr05/yr05rel103.asp (accessed April 2, 2007).

31. Carl A. Cohn, "Kids Don't Count: What Happens When Washington Decides How to Count Kids?" *San Diego Union Tribune*, September 29, 2006, http://www.signonsandiego.com/uniontrib/20060929/news_lz1e29cohn.html (accessed April 2, 2007).

32. Association of California School Administrators, *Recommendations for the 2007 Reauthorization*, 3.

33. Ibid.

Chapter 6: New Jersey: Equity Meets Accountability

1. In *Robinson*, the court found that school funding disparities violated the education clause of the New Jersey constitution, which declares that "the Legislature shall provide for the maintenance and support of a thorough and efficient system of free public schools." In 1976, however, the court declared it would assess not just financing, but substantive educational content. William Firestone, Margaret Goertz, and Gary Natriello, *From Cashbox to Classroom: The Struggle for Fiscal Reform and Educational Change in New Jersey* (New York: Teachers College Press, 1997), 22; *Robinson v. Cahill*, 69 N.J. 133, 351 A.2d 713 (N.J. 1975).

2. The system established forty-three different indicators of school performance—including minimum proficiency standards in reading, writing, and math—which were monitored by the state Department of Education. Districts that did not perform satisfactorily were placed under closer supervision (Level II or Level III monitoring); ibid., 40.

3. *Abbott v. Burke*, 119 N.J. 287, 575 A.2d 359 (N.J. 1990); *Abbott v. Burke*, 153 N.J. 480, 710 A.2d 450 (N.J. 1998).

4. Gordon MacInnes (Abbott commissioner), statement to the New Jersey Senate Education Committee, February 3, 2005, http://www.state.nj.us/njed/abbotts/info/statement.shtml (accessed July 25, 2006).

5. New Jersey Department of Education, "DOE Approves Six New Charter

Schools, Renews 12," press release, January 23, 2006, http://www.state.nj.us/education/news/2006/0123chart.htm (accessed June 6, 2007).

6. *Education Week*, "Quality Counts: New Jersey State Report Card," January 2007. http://www.edweek.org/ew/toc/2006/01/05 (accessed June 6, 2007).

7. John Mooney, "N.J. Lawmakers Want the State to Join Education Law Protest," *Star-Ledger*, March 26, 2005, 25.

8. U.S. Department of Education, Office of Inspector General, "Audit of NJDOE's Compliance with Public School Choice and SES Provisions," Final Report ED-OIG/A02-F0006, September 14, 2005, http://www.ed.gov/about/offices/list/oig/auditreports/a02f0006.doc (accessed April 2, 2007).

9. Emma Smith, "Raising Standards in American Schools: The Case of No Child Left Behind," *Journal of Education Policy* 20, no. 4 (July 2005): 515.

10. *Education Week*, "Quality Counts."

11. Wayne Dibofsky (associate director of government relations, New Jersey Education Association), telephone interview conducted by the author, August 23, 2006.

12. Gayle Griffin (assistant superintendent, Newark School District), telephone interview conducted by the author, October 18, 2006.

13. A recurring concern in New Jersey is that the state has essentially been penalized for its initial decision to set high academic standards and to meet the spirit of NCLB, in particular with regard to subgroups. Sean Hadley, a lobbyist at the New Jersey Principals and Supervisors Association (NJPSA), notes that "New Jersey chose to go with the low n, while other states chose a high n. New Jersey chose to make many other adjustments in their calculations that were overinclusive of school districts and students. . . . The state took a very difficult path by not taking full advantage of the flexibility already offered in the law at the time that the regulations came forward." A number of subsequent requests by the state for additional flexibility in its accountability plan were rejected by the U.S. Department of Education.

14. When the 2003–4 AYP results were finalized (which did not occur until October 2004), the AYP status of 151 schools changed, with 66 moving from early warning to school choice status, 9 moving from choice to SES status, and 16 moving from SES to corrective action.

15. U.S. Department of Education, Office of Inspector General, "Audit of NJDOE's Compliance."

16. Ibid.

17. New Jersey Department of Education, "New Jersey 2004–05 No Child Left Behind Act AYP Report," press release, August 10, 2005, http://www.state.nj.us/njded/news/2005/0810aypreport.htm (accessed April 6, 2007), and New Jersey Department of Education, "New Jersey 2005–06 No Child Left Behind Act AYP Report," press release, August 22, 2006, http://www.state.nj.us/njded/news/2006/0822ayp.htm (accessed April 6, 2007).

18. Data accessed from *Education Week*, "Preliminary NCLB Results Show Slippage in 2006." http://www.edweek.org/media/04ayp.pdf (accessed June 6, 2007). The large number of New Jersey schools labeled as in need of improvement led to vocal opposition to the law among many educators and politicians in the state. In June 2005, a bill entitled the "No School Left Behind Act," which required state education officials to press the federal government for more flexibility in NCLB, passed the state assembly. A legislative proposal (modeled on one from Utah) was also put forward that would have permitted the state DOE to ignore NCLB when it conflicted with state education laws, but this proposal failed to pass, and the state legislature has basically stayed out of NCLB implementation, leaving it almost entirely in the hands of the state DOE.

19. The state requires that a proposal to convert to charter status receive majority support from the school's teachers and parents. The NJDOE's website on choice notes that "many districts do lack capacity to offer choice. New Jersey is the most densely populated state in the country. This is reflected in the high enrollments and over-crowding in some schools. Unfortunately, many schools and districts will not be able to offer intra-district choices"; http://www.state.nj.us/education/parents/title1.htm (accessed June 6, 2007). The website encourages parents in such districts to investigate charter schools in their area, but, as noted, there are only fifty-one charter schools operating in the entire state. State support for the creation of new charter schools is poor—the Fordham Foundation gave New Jersey a grade of "C" in this area because of the funding discrepancy between charter and district schools. Thomas B. Fordham Foundation, *How Well Are States Educating Our Neediest Children? The Fordham Report 2006,* November 2006, http://www.edexcellence.net/doc/TFR06FULLREPORT.PDF (accessed April 6, 2007).

20. New Jersey Department of Education, *School Choice and Supplemental Services Survey*, http://www.state.nj.us/education/grants/nclb/choice/surv_results.htm (accessed August 1, 2006).

21. John Mooney, "Feds: Speed Reforms for N.J. Schools," *Star-Ledger*, September 16, 2002.

22. New Jersey Department of Education, *School Choice and Supplemental Services Survey*.

23. New Jersey Department of Education, *Consolidated State Performance Report Part 1: For Reporting on School Year 2003–2004*, 63, http://www.nj.gov/njded/grants/nclb/app/per05/performance.pdf (accessed April 6, 2007).

24. Data provided by Judy Alu, NJDOE Office of Title I Program Planning and Accountability, in correspondence of November 13, 2006. Even when choice has been exercised to this point, it has been of dubious efficacy. In the Vineland School District, for example, forty-seven of the fifty-two students who exercised school choice transferred from schools identified as in need of improvement to other schools needing improvement. Six students actually transferred from schools making AYP to schools not making AYP.

25. The picture painted of choice utilization by the 2005 federal audit is similar: In the sample of twenty-five schools reviewed, only 62 of 10,944 eligible students (0.6 percent) exercised their right to school choice; U.S. Department of Education, Office of Inspector General, "Audit of NJDOE's Compliance."

26. All five of the districts had serious deficiencies with their choice notification letters, with two (Upper Deerfield and Vineland) not sending letters at all, two (Newark and Camden) sending timely but insufficient letters, and one (Plainfield) sending a late and deficient letter. The report found that the letters did not clearly inform parents of their eligibility for choice and SES, how to utilize the services, or what options were available to them. Camden did not send the letters through the mail as required, but relied on students to deliver them to parents. Plainfield did not send its letter to parents until January 2005—more than three months after it was notified by NJDOE of its being in need of improvement status. U.S. Department of Education, Office of Inspector General, "Audit of NJDOE's Compliance."

27. All data in this section were provided by Gayle Griffin (assistant superintendent, Newark School District), in correspondence with the author during October 2006.

28. Mayra Rosner (director of federal programs, Perth Amboy School District, and NJ NCLB Advisory Council member), telephone interview conducted by the author, August 24, 2006.

29. Sean Hadley (assistant director of government relations, New Jersey Principals and Supervisors Association, and NJ NCLB Advisory Council member), telephone interview conducted by the author, August 24, 2006.

30. Rosner, interview.

31. Gene Wade (director, Platform Learning), telephone interview conducted by the author, August 29, 2006.

32. Ibid.

33. Ibid.

34. Ibid.

35. As Wade observes, "Now, where it gets dicey is when you can't touch the form, and you don't know how many kids are going to sign up. Then it's a black hole, and I think a lot of companies shy away from making that kind of investment when they don't know what the outcome is and when there's no correlation between the effort and the investment. I've had instances in Camden in particular where I've trained more teachers than students because I geared up for a larger program, and then what came back didn't bear any relation to the number of kids we serve"; ibid.

36. New Jersey Department of Education, "Memo: District Evaluation of SES Providers," October 27, 2004, accessed online at http://www.state.nj.us/education/grants/nclb/guidance/ses/letter.pdf (accessed June 6, 2007).

37. U.S. Department of Education, Office of Inspector General, "Audit of NJDOE's Compliance."

38. Wade, telephone interview.

39. School administrator requested anonymity in telephone interview conducted by the author.

40. As Wade puts it, "I wouldn't describe it as competition—there certainly are other providers in New Jersey, national companies like Catapult Learning, which is a part of Educating/Sylvan, and Newton Learning, which is a part of Edison Schools. And then there are a host of what I would call regional and local players that are in the various markets, but in terms of tutoring large numbers of people, large numbers of students, there aren't a lot of providers doing it, mainly because it's a large investment before they ever see any revenue"; Wade, interview. Platform is the largest SES provider in Newark and one of the largest in the state, with major operations in Camden, Trenton, Jersey City, and Bridgetown City, but it has only enrolled approximately 2,200 students.

41. Data provided by Judy Alu, NJDOE Office of Title I Program Planning and Accountability, in correspondence of November 13, 2006.

42. New Jersey Department of Education, Office of Title I Program Planning and Accountability, "SES in NJ: Technical Assistance for Prospective Providers," January 11, 2006, http://www.nj.gov/education/title1/tech/pp/ses.ppt (accessed May 31, 2007).

43. John Mooney, "Rash of Tutor Programs Spurring New Concerns," *Star-Ledger*, December 22, 2003, 17.

44. Data provided by Judy Alu, NJDOE Office of Title I Program Planning and Accountability in correspondence of November 13, 2006.

45. U.S. Department of Education, Office of Inspector General, "Audit of NJDOE's Compliance."

46. In the first two years of SES, however, a large number of students who enrolled were not ultimately served, though it is unclear why this was the case. While 2,313 enrolled in SES in Newark in 2003–4, for example, only 1,639 were served; and in 2004–5, 3,963 students enrolled, but only 2,715 were served. While the gap closed in 2005–6 (4,426 enrolled and 4,325 served), over 2,000 students who enrolled for SES during the three-year period in the district did not ultimately receive services.

47. Data provided by Gayle Griffin (assistant superintendent, Newark School District), in correspondence with the author during October 2006.

48. Sarah Kohl (lobbyist, New Jersey School Boards Association, and NJ NCLB Advisory Council member), telephone interview conducted by the author, August 28, 2006.

49. NCLB Advisory Council Meeting Minutes, Friday, February 21, 2003. Minutes provided by Diane Schonyers (director, Office of Strategic Initiatives & Accountability, N.J. Department of Education), in correspondence with the author, October 2006.

50. The teams are organized, trained, and supervised by the state Department of Education and typically are comprised of seven to ten members, including a team leader, principal, parent, representative from higher education, and specialists in language arts literacy, mathematics, special education, and bilingual education. Team members are drawn from NJDOE staff, district administrators, staff from high-performing schools in the district, and staff from high-performing schools outside of the district. For additional information on the CAPA process, see State of New Jersey Department of Education, "Collaborative Assessment for Planning and Achievement," http://www.state.nj.us/njded/capa (accessed May 23, 2007).

51. The state DOE has established guidelines for this process in the form of CAPA Core Standards and Indicators for assessing school and district performance. The nine standards cover curriculum, classroom assessment, instruction, school culture, student, family, and community support, professional development, school leadership, organizational structure and resources, and planning. The state has created a 174-page CAPA team member handbook to guide the onsite school assessment process, http://www.state.nj.us/education/capa/docs/handbook.pdf (accessed June 6, 2007).

52. State of New Jersey Department of Education, "DOE Identifies 60 NCLB 'Districts in Need of Improvement,'" press release, December 5, 2006, http://www.state.nj.us/education/news/2006/1205dini.htm (accessed May 23, 2007).

53. These numbers include a handful of low-performing Abbott schools which were not necessarily in corrective action or in year 3 supplemental educational services. Patricia Mitchell (New Jersey Office of Title I Program Planning and Accountability, N.J. Department of Education), telephone interview conducted by the author, September 19, 2006.

54. Gordon MacInnes (assistant commissioner of education, Division of Abbott Implementation, N.J. Department of Education), telephone interview conducted by the author, August 28, 2006.

55. Mitchell, interview.

56. Dibofsky, interview.

57. Andrew Babiak (assistant counsel, New Jersey Association of School Administrators, and NJ NCLB Advisory Council member), telephone interview conducted by the author, August 24, 2006.

58. Kohl, interview.

59. Hadley, interview.

60. Babiak, interview.

61. Mitchell, interview.

62. Since many schools or districts fail to make AYP because of one or two subgroups, many of the improvement and restructuring plans focus specifically on improving the performance of these particular students. NJSBA's Kohl stated that

the early intervention on the part of the state DOE has been particularly helpful for struggling schools. "From what the department has told us this process has been very, very effective in terms of troubleshooting. Last year they had three hundred–odd districts in year 3, and they tried to identify those that they thought needed the most help and were most likely to become year 4, because there was going to be no way that they were going to be able to do three hundred assessments. So they did a lot of early intervention. They were able to go into schools and really do an inventory of their programs and their curriculum and their administration and offer recommendations and follow up and support or find ways for support to really help those schools"; Kohl, interview.

63. Ibid.

64. Mitchell, interview.

65. MacInnes, interview.

Chapter 7: Colorado: The Misapplication of Federal Power

1. Data on NCLB-identified schools and supplemental educational services and school choice participation rates were provided to the author electronically by staff of the Consolidated Federal Programs Office from the Colorado Department of Education in July 2006; analysis is by the author.

2. Ibid.

3. Ibid.

4. Brad Jupp (senior academic policy advisor to the superintendent for Denver Public Schools), interview conducted by the author, July 2006.

5. Colorado Department of Education (CDE), "2005 Pupil Membership By School and Grade" (table), http://www.cde.state.co.us/cdereval/download/spreadsheet/2005PM/SCHOOL/05-06PMBYGRADE.xls (accessed May 11, 2007).

6. CDE, "Fall 2005 Pupil Membership by County, District, Race/Ethnicity and Percent Minority" (table), http://www.cde.state.co.us/cdereval/download/spreadsheet/2005PM/DISTRICT/05PercentMinority.xls (accessed May 11, 2007).

7. CDE, "Fall 2005 K-12 Free and Reduced Lunch by District" (table), http://www.cde.state.co.us/cdereval/download/spreadsheet/2005PM/DISTRICT/05BaseK-12FRED.xls (accessed May 11, 2007).

8. CDE, "2005 Pupil Membership By School and Grade."

9. Ibid.

10. Ibid.

11. Colorado State Constitution, Article IX, Section 15.

12. Colorado League of Charter Schools, "General Overview," http://www.coloradoleague.org/general_overview_of_charter.htm (accessed October 2006).

13. CDE, "Fall 2005 Pupil Membership: Students Attending Public Schools Not in Their Parent's District of Residence,"(table),http://www.cde.state.co.us/cdereval/

download/spreadsheet/2005PM/DISTRICT/NonResstudentsATTENDANCE.
xls (accessed May 11, 2007).

14. CDE, "Non-Public School Membership By District/School/Grade Fall 2005,"
http://www.cde.state.co.us/cdereval/download/spreadsheet/2005PM/SCHOOL/
Fall2005Non-Publicschoolmembership.xls (accessed May 11, 2007).

15. The actual number of students home-schooled in Colorado is likely to be
significantly larger, due to underreporting by parents. Figures reported here
from CDE, "Home Based Education Fall 2001–2005" (table), http://www.
cde.state.co.us/cdereval/download/spreadsheet/2005PM/DISTRICT/
FINALHOMEBASED05-06.xls (accessed May 11, 2007).

16. Alex Medler, "Colorado: Layered Reforms and Challenges of Scale," in *Leaving No Child Behind? Options for Kids in Failing Schools*, ed. Frederick Hess and
Chester Finn (New York: Palgrave Macmillan, 2004).

17. Data on NCLB-identified schools provided to the author electronically by
staff of the Consolidated Federal Programs Office in the Colorado Department of
Education in July 2006. Data reflecting school enrollment, location, demographics,
revenue, SAR designations, and state assessment results compiled by the Colorado
Children's Campaign (CCC) from various data released by CDE from 2001 to 2007
and combined with NCLB-related data for this analysis by the author. This dataset
is subsequently referred to as "CCC dataset."

18. Ibid.

19. Medler, "Colorado: Layered Reforms and Challenges of Scale."

20. According to interview with staff from the Consolidated Federal Programs
Office from the Colorado Department of Education in July 2006.

21. See chapter 1.

22. Colorado Senate, Committee on Education, "Final Bill Summary for SB05-050,
Senate Committee on Education," http://www.leg.state.co.us/Clics2005a/commsumm.
nsf/IndSumm/AE001F7DDDD5D83187256F95005A6435?OpenDocument
(accessed June 2, 2007).

23. CCC dataset.

24. This reduced set was necessary to accommodate problems in the comparability of data across data systems and ambiguity in the identification of targeted
programs serving special populations and small schools operating within
schools. For example, the schools listed in NCLB datasets represented extremely
small subgroups of students within the state's school for the deaf. Data from
statewide programs for specific populations, or schools within schools, could not
be compared to other state datasets used for the analysis.

25. CCC dataset.

26. Ibid.

27. Ibid.

28. Ibid.

29. Ibid.

30. Ibid.

31. Ibid.

32. Of the one hundred schools in this study identified under NCLB, nine were in small districts with very few or no other schools to choose from. The other ninety-one were in districts where at least one other school served the same grades. Among the ninety-one schools where choice was technically possible, there was generally little choice attributed to NCLB.

33. CCC dataset.

34. Ibid.

35. Ibid.

36. Alex Medler, *Breaking Up Is Hard To Do: Lessons Learned from the Experience of Manual High School* (Denver, Colo.: Colorado Children's Campaign and the Colorado Small Schools Initative, April 2005).

37. CCC dataset.

38. Ibid.

39. Ibid.

40. Colorado Department of Education Competitive Grants and Awards Unit, *Overview (Characteristics and Outcomes) of the Colorado 21st Century Community Learning Centers Program 2003–2004* (Denver, Colo.: Colorado Department of Education Competitive Grants and Awards Unit, August 2006).

41. Colorado Department of Public Health and Environment, *Tony Grampsas Youth Services Program 2005–2006 Annual Report* (Denver, Colo.: Colorado Department of Public Health and Environment, January 2007).

42. Data on SES providers were provided to the author by staff from the Consolidated Federal Programs Office from the Colorado Department of Education in July 2006. The most recent data on approved providers and their characteristics are available from Colorado Department of Education, "Supplemental Service Providers 2006–2007" (table), http://www.cde.state.co.us/FedPrograms/improvement/download/ss_providers.pdf (accessed May 21, 2007).

43. Medler, "Colorado: Layered Reforms and Challenges of Scale."

44. CCC dataset.

45. The KIPP program is a national model based on highly successful charter schools created in Texas and New York. The KIPP program relies heavily on strong school leaders. The schools involved mix high expectations for student behavior and achievement with an emphasis on discipline among students, hard work by staff, and strong school leaders.

46. Anderson, Amy Berk and Dale DeCesare. *Opening Closed Doors: Lessons from Colorado's First Independent Charter School*. Denver, Colo.: Donnel-Kay Foundation and the Piton Foundation, September 5, 2006.

47. Precisely measuring the incremental costs of providing transportation is difficult. Financial reporting and recordkeeping are not designed to accommodate such analysis. According to interviews with CDE staff, the state tracks initial allocations within Title I budgets but does not gather precise figures on reallocations for each school if the spending on one or both of the components fails to exhaust the full amount initially allocated for that purpose. This means there are no official state figures for how much money districts actually spend on transportation or supplemental services. When trying to estimate expenditures based on participation rates, the variation in fees, billing schemes, and the amount of time provided to each student by different SES providers complicates the process. Nevertheless, given these caveats, we can still estimate the expenses associated with the number of students who take advantage of either choice or SES under NCLB for each school. The method of calculating costs in this study excludes some costs borne by the district for administering choice and SES. This model assumes the district's administrative portion of Title I funding can cover costs associated with negotiating and finalizing contracts with providers, overseeing their services, or answering parents' questions about the programs, and it includes $5 for producing and mailing each packet of materials required for a student eligible for choice or SES. The cost of providing transportation and associated mailings is set at $405 per year per student. This assumes there are no further costs in adjusting staffing at the sending and receiving schools. We can also assume, conservatively, that a student using SES has the maximum amount spent on services allowed in that district for tutoring services. The maximum rate per served child is set by formula and averages around $1,360. In this estimate, the incremental cost of providing transportation is set at $400 per year per student. This is increased by $5 per student in each school eligible for choice for mailing. Using each district's maximum rate to calculate the SES costs for each school is conservative, given the large number of students who are listed as participating but who only participate for part of the prescribed time and thus do not generate the "billable hours" for the maximum amount an SES provider can charge in that district.

48. The schools' operating budgets are derived by multiplying each district's average per-pupil operating revenue by each school's enrollment. Per-pupil operating revenue is available from Colorado Department of Education (CDE), untitled table, http://www.cde.state.co.us/cdefinance/download/spreadsheet/RevExp2005/ComparisonofRevenueandOtherSources.xls (accessed May 11, 2007).

49. CCC dataset.

50. Jupp, interview.

51. Information on the CDE School Improvement Grant is available from CDE, "Title I School Improvement Grant,"http://www.cde.state.co.us/FedPrograms/improvement/schimp_tia.asp (accessed May 11, 2007). Data on grant recipients provided to the author electronically by staff from the Consolidated Federal Programs Office at CDE in July 2006.

52. All money is not the same. Schools identified under NCLB must reallocate funds from other activities to support public school choice and SES, whereas school improvement grants are generally restricted to restructuring activities. Nevertheless, this approach provides insight into the overall financial impact of these programs on schools.

53. Figures do not sum due to variation in the number of applicable schools.

54. CCC dataset. Basic data on DPS are available from Denver Public Schools, various pages accessed from homepage, http://www.dpsk12.org (accessed May 22, 2007). Demographic data on DPS are available in CDE datasets, including Colorado Department of Education (CDE), "Fall 2005 Pupil Membership by County, District, Race/Ethnicity and Percent Minority."

55. CCC dataset. Data on most revenue sources for Colorado schools are available from Colorado Department of Education (CDE), untitled table.

56. CCC dataset.

57. Lee, Chungmei. *Denver Public Schools: Resegregating Latino Style.* Cambridge, Mass.: Harvard Civil Rights Project, January 2006, and Author. "Study Documents the Resegregation of Denver Public Schools," *The Term Paper.* Denver, Colo: Piton Foundation, January 2006.

58. Nancy Connor (director of federal programs, Denver Public Schools) and Ethan Hemming (School Choice Office, Denver Public Schools), interviews conducted by the author, July 2006.

59. Ibid.

60. CCC dataset.

61. DPS intradistrict choice figures based on Connor and Hemming, interviews.

62. Students from the recently closed Manual High School are transported on school buses.

63. CCC dataset.

64. The total is greater than the total number of DPS schools because individual schools can offer multiple programs.

65. Connor, Hemming, and Jupp, interviews.

66. CDE, "2005 Pupil Membership By School and Grade."

67. CDE, "Fall 2005 Pupil Membership by County, District, Race/Ethnicity and Percent Minority."

68. CDE, "Fall 2005 K–12 Free and Reduced Lunch by District."

69. CCC dataset.

70. Colorado Department of Education, "Fall 2005 Pupil Membership: Students Attending Public Schools Not in Their Parent's District of Residence."

71. CCC dataset.

72. David Cruz (assistant superintendent, Cortez District), interview conducted by the author, July 2006.

73. CCC dataset.

74. Cruz, interview.

75. Ibid.

Chapter 8: Michigan: Over the First Hurdle

1. See, for example Richard Elmore, *School Reform from the Inside Out: Policy, Practice, and Performance* (Cambridge, Mass.: Harvard Educational Review, 2004).

2. See, for example John E. Chubb and Terry M. Moe, *Politics, Markets, and America's Schools* (Washington, D.C.: Brookings Institution, 1990).

3. Unless otherwise indicated, all unattributed quotes are from these interviews, which were conducted with the understanding that we would not identify our informants by name.

4. For the MEA's endorsement interviews see Michigan Education Association, *MEA Voice*, Fall 2006, http://www.mea.org/voice/fall2006/lettertomembers.html (accessed October 12, 2006).

5. David N. Plank and Christopher Dunbar Jr., "Michigan: False Start," in *Leaving No Child Behind? Options for Kids in Failing Schools*, ed. Frederick M. Hess and Chester E. Finn (New York: Palgrave MacMillan, 2004).

6. Michigan Education Association, *MEA Voice*, Fall 2006.

7. Plank and Dunbar, "Michigan: False Start."

8. David N. Plank, "School Grades Spark Questions about Michigan Evaluations," *Detroit News*, September 16, 2004.

9. Susan Vela, "Parents Dismiss Schools' Ratings: *Education YES!* Grading by State Draws Criticism," *Lansing State Journal*, October 2, 2006.

10. Plank and Dunbar, "Michigan: False Start."

11. ISDs provide a variety of services, including vocational education, special education, and some administrative services to school districts within their service areas. Their boundaries generally correspond to county boundaries. Outside Michigan's metropolitan areas, ISDs often comprise more than one county.

12. The list of approved SES providers can be accessed from Michigan Department of Education, "Supplemental Educational Services," http://www.michigan.gov/mde/0,1607,7-140-5235-49582—,00.html (accessed June 11, 2007).

13. Plank and Dunbar, "Michigan: False Start."

14. See chapters 3 and 5.

15. Data on enrollments in SES opportunities were provided to the authors by the MDE.

16. See Plank and Dunbar, "Michigan: False Start."

17. This faith is not always well-placed. To take a single notorious example, the Detroit Public Schools reported to MDE that they had replaced principals in all district schools required to "restructure" under NCLB. MDE subsequently discovered

that many Detroit principals had not in fact been replaced, despite the district's reports.

18. Michigan Department of Education, Office of School Improvement, *Michigan School Improvement Framework*, http://www.michigan.gov/documents/SIF_4-01-05_130701_7.pdf (accessed June 11, 2007).

19. This set of documents can be found at Michigan Department of Education, http://www.michigan.gov/mde/0,1607,7-140-28753_33424—,00.html (accessed June 11, 2007).

20. According to one official in the MDE, the department is under pressure from the U.S. Department of Education to "recreate" persistently failing schools as charters—"without closing the building or moving the kids."

21. The number of schools receiving a grade of "not accredited" is relatively small, and many of these are alternative programs. None of the phase 7 schools received a grade of "not accredited" in 2005–6.

22. Some principals were, in fact, replaced as well, through retirement and "attrition."

23. With a recent change in superintendents, the responsibility for coaching has been assumed by a "lead principal" in each group of six schools, instead of central office staff.

24. See chapter 11 for additional information on Grand Rapids and the process of restructuring in one GRPS elementary school.

25. Per agreement, we have changed the name of this school.

26. MDE's approach clearly relies on the implicit threat of sanctions. The department's attention to specific schools increases as the number of years of failure to make AYP increases, and it has begun publicly to explore the possibility of abrogating union contracts and establishing "hybrid charters" in schools that cannot turn themselves around.

Chapter 9: Rural Kentucky Districts: "Do-It-Yourself" School Improvement

1. U.S. Department of Education, National Center for Education Statistics, "Local Education Agency Universe Survey," the NCES Common Core of Data (CCD) survey, 2003–4, http://nces.ed.gov/ccd/pubagency.asp (accessed May 22, 2007); and U.S. Department of Agriculture, "Table 1. Number of Public School Districts by 2003 Rural–Urban Continuum (Beale) Count Code and State: 2003–04," http://nces.ed.gov/surveys/RuralEd/TablesHTML/1bealedistricts.asp (accessed May 12, 2007). According to this table, some 3,222 districts are categorized as "completely rural" or as having an "urban population of 2,500 to 19,999 and not adjacent to a metro area."

2. U.S. Department of Education, "Table 1." The first number here is the count of Kentucky districts in the three most rural categories, and the second is the number reported in the "urban population of 2,500 to 19,999, adjacent to a metro area."

3. U.S. Department of Education, "Table 7. Number and Percentage of Rural and Non-Rural Public Elementary and Secondary Students, by District Locale (Locale Code) and State: Fall 2003," http://nces.ed.gov/surveys/RuralEd/TablesHTML/7localerural_nonrural.asp (accessed May 12, 2007).

4. Author calculations based on information in U.S. Census Bureau, *State and County QuickFacts: Data Derived from Population Estimates, Census of Population and Housing, Small Area Income and Poverty Estimates, State and County Housing Unit Estimates, County Business Patterns, Nonemployer Statistics, Economic Census, Survey of Business Owners, Building Permits, Consolidated Federal Funds Report.* Kentucky data at http://quickfacts.census.gov/qfd/states/21000.html. Illinois data at http://quickfacts.census.gov/qfd/states/17000.html Ohio data at http://quickfacts.census.gov/qfd/states/39000.html (accessed May 12, 2007).

5. In the first few years of reform implementation, these spending increases boosted Kentucky to around thirty-third place among the states in terms of per-pupil spending, according to a reputable estimate; National Education Association, "Table H-11: Current Expenditures for Public Elementary and Secondary Schools Per Pupil in Fall Enrollment, 1993–94," in *Rankings of the States, 1994* (West Haven, Conn.: NEA, Research Division, 1994), 61. But spending in other states has outpaced that of Kentucky since the early 1990s, and Kentucky has now slipped to thirty-eighth place, according to a recent national estimate; Editorial Projects in Education Research Center, "Quality Counts at 10: A Decade of Standard-Based Education," data table: Resources: Spending, 2006, accessible from Melissa McCabe, "State of the States: Overview," *Education Week*, January 5, 2006, http://www.edweek.org/ew/articles/2006/01/05/17sos.h25.html (accessed May 12, 2007).

6. Summarized from the complete description of Kentucky's assessment system as of the 2005–6 academic year, found in Kentucky Department of Education, Office of Assessment and Accountability, *2005 CATS Interpretive Guide*, v. 3.1., 2007. http://www.kde.state.ky.us/KDE/Administrative+Resources/Testing+and+Reporting+/CATS/Accountability+System/2005+CATS+Interpretive+Guide+version+31.htm (accessed May 12, 2007).

7. Ibid.

8. So-called "level 1" schools—the highest-performing third of schools below the assistance line—must receive a scholastic review using SISI from a team headed by a district official, with assistance by Kentucky Department of Education staff, and their school councils must adopt improvement plans based on recommendations from the review team. Schools in the next third of low performers, level 2 schools, receive a review headed by an appointee of the commissioner of education's choosing, and must also alter their improvement plans

in light of the review findings. Level 3 schools are usually assigned an HSE, and must receive an audit by an external team, which can recommend improvement steps that include additional evaluations of teachers and principals. Students in schools that remain at level 3 for two successive biennia are eligible for transfer to nearby (public) schools that are above the assistance line. A more detailed description of Kentucky's assistance system can be found in Commonwealth of Kentucky, Legislative Research Commission, "703 KAR 5:120. Assistance for Schools; Guidelines for Scholastic Audit," Kentucky administrative regulations, Frankfort, Kentucky, http://www.lrc.ky.gov/kar/703/005/120.htm (accessed May 12, 2007).

9. Kentucky Department of Education, "All Schools Performance Judgment by CATS Biennium" (table), *Briefing Packet, State and Regional Release: Commonwealth Accountability Testing System, 2006*, 9, http://www.education.ky.gov/KDE/Administrative+Resources/Testing+and+Reporting+/Reports/CATS+Briefing+Packets/2006+CATS+Briefing+Packet.htm (accessed May 12, 2007).

10. Between 1992 and 2005, for example, Kentucky fourth graders moved from 14 percent proficient or above in math to 27 percent, and eighth graders from 16 percent proficient or above to 26 percent. In reading during the same period, fourth graders in Kentucky moved from 26 percent proficient or above to 38 percent. Between 1998 and 2005, Kentucky eighth graders moved from 32 percent proficient or above in reading to 34 percent; U.S. Department of Education, National Center for Education Statistics, "History of NAEP Participation and Performance," Kentucky State Profile, http://nces.ed.gov/nationsreportcard/states/profile.asp (accessed April 30, 2007).

11. Kentucky Department of Education, *Briefing Packet-State Release, No Child Left Behind (NCLB) Adequate Yearly Progress Report, 2006*, 6, http://www.kde.state.ky.us/KDE/Administrative+Resources/Testing+and+Reporting+/Reports/No+Child+Left+Behind+Reports/2006+No+Child+Left+Behind+NCLBBriefing+Packet+and+Reports.htm (accessed May 13, 2007).

12. Kentucky Department of Education, Office of Leadership and School Improvement, unpublished spreadsheet shared with author.

13. Stephen Schenck (associate commissioner, Kentucky Department of Education), interview conducted by the author, September 14, 2006.

14. U.S. Census Bureau, *State and County QuickFacts: Data Derived from Population Estimates*, Martin County data at http://quickfacts.census.gov/qfd/states/21/21159.html (accessed May 12, 2007).

15. Kentucky Council on Postsecondary Education, "Martin County, Kentucky, Postsecondary Education Profile 2006–07," website data portal, http://cpe.ky.gov/info/county/default.htm (accessed May 12, 2007).

16. Mark Blackburn (superintendent, Martin County), interview conducted by the author, August 23, 2006.

17. Kentucky Department of Education, Martin County, Kentucky performance report, 2006, 3, http://apps.kde.state.ky.us/secure_cats_reports_06/index.cfm (accessed November 28, 2006).

18. Kentucky Department of Education, Martin County, Kentucky performance report, 2002, 3, http://apps.kde.state.ky.us/secure_cats_reports/index.cfm? action=display_cards (accessed May 13, 2007).

19. Kentucky Department of Education, Martin County, Kentucky performance report, 2004, 3, http://apps.kde.state.ky.us/secure_cats_reports_04/index.cfm (accessed May 13, 2007).

20. Kentucky Department of Education, Martin County, Kentucky performance report, 2006, 3.

21. These remedies are required under Kentucky's accountability regulations, discussed above.

22. Kentucky Department of Education, No Child Left Behind reports for Eden Elementary, Inez Elementary, and Warfield Elementary, 2003, 1; 2004, 1; 2005, 1; 2006, 1, http://apps.kde.state.ky.us/secure_cats_reports_06/index.cfm (accessed May 13, 2007).

23. Kentucky Department of Education, No Child Left Behind reports for Inez Middle School, 2003, 1, http://apps.kde.state.ky.us/secure_cats_reports_03 (accessed November 28, 2006); 2004, 1, http://apps.kde.state.ky.us/secure_cats_reports_04 (accessed November 28, 2006); 2005, 1, http://apps.kde.state.ky.us/secure_cats_reports_05 (accessed November 28, 2006); 2006, 1, http://apps.kde.state.ky.us/secure%5Fcats%5Freports%5F06 (accessed November 28, 2006).

24. Kentucky Department of Education, No Child Left Behind report for Warfield Middle School, 2003, 1, http://apps.kde.state.ky.us/secure_cats_reports_03 (accessed November 28, 2006).

25. Kentucky Department of Education, No Child Left Behind reports for Warfield Middle School, 2004, 1, http://apps.kde.state.ky.us/secure_cats_reports_04 (accessed November 28, 2006); 2005, 1, http://apps.kde.state.ky.us/secure_cats_reports_05 (accessed November 28, 2006); 2006, 1, http://apps.kde.state.ky.us/secure%5Fcats%5Freports%5F06 (accessed November 28, 2006).

26. Kentucky Department of Education, No Child Left Behind reports for Sheldon Clark High School, 2003, 1, http://apps.kde.state.ky.us/secure_cats_reports_043 (accessed November 28, 2006); 2004, 1, http://apps.kde.state.ky.us/secure_cats_reports_04 (accessed November 28, 2006); 2005, 1, http://apps.kde.state.ky.us/secure_cats_reports_05 (accessed November 28, 2006); 2006, 1, http://apps.kde.state.ky.us/secure%5Fcats%5Freports%5F06 (accessed November 28, 2006).

27. Blackburn, interview.

28. Greg Cornette (principal, Inez Middle School), interview conducted by the author, August 23, 2006.

29. Carl Kirk (assistant superintendent, Martin County), interview conducted by the author, August 23, 2006.

30. Sue Davis (Achievement Gap coordinator for Eastern Kentucky region), interview conducted by the author, November 10, 2006; Barbara Kennedy (Office of Leadership and School Improvement, Kentucky Department of Education), interview conducted by the author, November 10, 2006.

31. Blackburn, interview.

32. All information about supplemental educational services in Martin County provided by Michael Kessinger (district financial officer), interviews conducted by the author, August 23, 2006, and November 15, 2006.

33. NCLB choice information on Martin County provided by Kessinger, interviews, and Blackburn, interview.

34. U.S. Census Bureau, *State and County QuickFacts: Data Derived from Population Estimates*, Fulton County data at http://quickfacts.census.gov/qfd/states/21/21075.html (accessed May 13, 2007).

35. Kentucky Council on Postsecondary Education, "Fulton County, Kentucky Postsecondary Education Profile 2006–07," *Kentucky Postsecondary Education County Profiles*, http://cpe.ky.gov/NR/rdonlyres/8B55AFFB-E7EB-4D0B-BA09-A25CA4F9C8D8/0/Fulton.pdf (accessed May 13, 2007).

36. Charles Holliday (superintendent, Fulton County), interview conducted by the author, September 1, 2006.

37. Ibid.

38. Kentucky Department of Education, Fulton County, Kentucky performance report, 2002, 3, http://apps.kde.state.ky.us/secure_cats_reports/index.cfm?action=display_cards (accessed May 13, 2007).

39. Kentucky Department of Education, Fulton County, Kentucky performance report, 2004, 3, http://apps.kde.state.ky.us/secure_cats_reports_04 (accessed May 13, 2007); 2006, 3, http://apps.kde.state.ky.us/secure_cats_reports_06/index.cfm (accessed May 13, 2007).

40. Kentucky Department of Education, Fulton County, Kentucky performance report, 2004, 3.

41. Kentucky Department of Education, Fulton County, Kentucky performance report, 2006, 3.

42. Kentucky Department of Education, No Child Left Behind report for Fulton County Elementary School, 2003, 1, http://apps.kde.state.ky.us/secure_cats_reports_03 (accessed May 13, 2007); 2004, 1, http://apps.kde.state.ky.us/secure_cats_reports_04 (accessed May 13, 2007).

43. Kentucky Department of Education, No Child Left Behind report for Fulton County Elementary School, 2005, 1, http://apps.kde.state.ky.us/secure_cats_reports_05 (accessed May 13, 2007).

44. Ibid.

45. Kentucky Department of Education, No Child Left Behind report for Fulton County Elementary School, 2003, 1; 2004, 1; 2005, 1.

46. Kentucky Department of Education, No Child Left Behind report for Fulton County Elementary School, 2006, 1; Kentucky Department of Education, No Child Left Behind report for Fulton County Middle School, 2006, 1, http://apps.kde.state.ky.us/secure_cats_reports_06 (accessed May 13, 2007).

47. Kentucky Department of Education, No Child Left Behind report for Fulton County High School, 2003, 1, http://apps.kde.state.ky.us/secure_cats_reports_03 (accessed May 13, 2007); 2004, 1, http://apps.kde.state.ky.us/secure_cats_reports_04 (accessed May 13, 2007).

48. Kentucky Department of Education, No Child Left Behind report for Fulton County Elementary School, 2005, 1.

49. Kentucky Department of Education, No Child Left Behind report for Fulton County District, 2004, 1, http://apps.kde.state.ky.us/secure_cats_reports_04 (accessed May 13, 2007); 2006, 1, http://apps.kde.state.ky.us/secure_cats_reports_06 (accessed May 13, 2007).

50. District improvement strategies provided by Holliday, interview, and Sheila Haynes (Student Learning Support Services, Fulton County), interview conducted by the author, September 1, 2006.

51. Gary Meredith (principal, Fulton County High School), interview conducted by the author, September 1, 2007.

52. Kay Brown (Achievement Gap coordinator for western Kentucky), interview conducted by the author, November 10, 2007.

53. District choice information supplied by Holliday, interviews, September 1, 2006, and November 1, 2006.

54. Holliday, email to the author, December 20, 2006.

55. Holliday, interview, November 1, 2006.

56. U.S. Census Bureau, *State and County QuickFacts: Data Derived from Population Estimates*, Monroe County data at http://quickfacts.census.gov/qfd/states/21/21171.html (accessed May 13, 2007). FRP data provided by George Wilson (superintendent, Monroe County), interview conducted by the author, August 25, 2006.

57. Kentucky Department of Education, Monroe County, Kentucky performance report, 2006, 3, http://apps.kde.state.ky.us/secure_cats_reports_06/index.cfm (accessed May 13, 2007).

58. Ibid.

59. Kentucky Department of Education, Monroe County, Kentucky performance report, 2002, 3, http://apps.kde.state.ky.us/secure_cats_reports_02/index.cfm (accessed May 13, 2007); 2004, 3, http://apps.kde.state.ky.us/secure_cats_reports_04/index.cfm (accessed May 13, 2007).

60. Wilson, interview, August 25, 2006.

61. Kentucky Department of Education, No Child Left Behind report for Monroe County, 2003, 1, http://apps.kde.state.ky.us/secure_cats_reports_03 (accessed May 13, 2007).

62. Kentucky Department of Education, No Child Left Behind report for Monroe County, 2004, 1, http://apps.kde.state.ky.us/secure_cats_reports_04 (accessed May 13, 2007).

63. Kentucky Department of Education, No Child Left Behind report for Gamaliel Elemenary School, 2005, 1, http://apps.kde.state.ky.us/secure_cats_reports_05 (accessed May 13, 2007).

64. Kentucky Department of Education, No Child Left Behind report for Monroe County High School, 2005, 1, http://apps.kde.state.ky.us/secure_cats_reports_05 (accessed May 13, 2007).

65. Kentucky Department of Education, No Child Left Behind report for Tompkinsville Elementary School, 2006, 1, http://apps.kde.state.ky.us/secure_cats_reports_06 (accessed May 13, 2007).

66. Kentucky Department of Education, No Child Left Behind report for Monroe County Middle School, 2006, 1, http://apps.kde.state.ky.us/secure_cats_reports_06 (accessed May 13, 2007).

67. Kentucky Department of Education, No Child Left Behind report for Monroe County High School, 2006, 1, http://apps.kde.state.ky.us/secure_cats_reports_06 (accessed May 13, 2007).

68. Kentucky Department of Education, No Child Left Behind report for Monroe County, 2006, 1, http://apps.kde.state.ky.us/secure_cats_reports_06 (accessed May 13, 2007).

69. Kentucky Department of Education, Tested and Accountable report for Monroe County, 2006, 2, http://apps.kde.state.ky.us/secure_cats_reports_06 (accessed May 13, 2007).

70. Wilson, interview, August 25, 2006.

71. School improvement strategies described by Wilson, interviews, August 25, 2006, and October 31, 2006, and by Elizabeth Willett (district assessment coordinator, Monroe County), interview conducted by the author, August 25, 2006.

72. Kentucky Department of Education, No Child Left Behind report for Gamaliel Elementary School, 2006, 2, http://apps.kde.state.ky.us/secure_cats_reports_06 (accessed May 13, 2007).

73. Ibid.

74. Ibid.

75. Claude Christian (Kentucky Department of Education), interview conducted by the author, October 31, 2006.

Chapter 10: Miami-Dade County: Trouble in Choice Paradise

1. Miami-Dade County Public Schools, *Statistical Abstract 2005–2006*, 13–37, http://drs.dadeschools.net/Abstract/Abstract_2005-06.pdf (accessed May 10, 2007).

2. These grades were the only grade levels tested prior to the state instituting annual testing in 2001.

3. The FCAT is administered to students in grades 3–11 and contains two basic components: criterion-referenced tests (CRT), measuring selected benchmarks in mathematics, reading, science, and writing from the Sunshine State Standards (SSS), the Florida state standards for student achievement; and norm-referenced tests (NRT) in reading and mathematics, measuring individual student performance against national norms. Students' performance is reported using a 1–5 scale, with 5 being the highest. Students who receive a 3 are considered "proficient." They answer many of the questions successfully, but not the most challenging ones. In 2003, Florida was the only state in the country that had significantly higher National Assessment of Educational Progress (NAEP) reading scores in fourth grade, providing some independent evidence to corroborate the large increase cited here; Florida Department of Education, "K12 NAEP Highlights," http://www.firn.edu/doe/sas/naep/k12/k12states.htm (accessed May 10, 2007).

4. Michael Casserly, *Beating the Odds VII: City-by-City Profiles: Miami*, Council of Great City Schools, 2006, http://www.cgcs.org/BTO7/Miami.pdf (accessed May 10, 2007).

5. Authors' calculations. AYP results are available at Florida Department of Education, "Florida School Grades: School Accountability Report Links," http://schoolgrades.fldoe.org/reports/ (accessed May 22, 2007).

6. States specify each year the percentage of students who need to be academically proficient in order for schools to make AYP, with the goal that by the 2013–14 school year, all students (100 percent) will be proficient. Florida has established ten intermediate goals that increase annually in equal increments (seven percentage points) for determining adequate yearly progress, beginning in the 2004–5 school year with 37 percent proficient.

7. *Bush et al. v. Holmes et al.*, 919 So.2d 392 (Fla. 2006). In a 5–2 opinion, the Florida Supreme Court held that the Opportunity Scholarship Program (OSP) law violates the state constitutional requirement of a uniform system of free public schools. The opinion held that OSP violates Article IX of the state's constitution because

> it diverts public dollars into separate private systems parallel to and in competition with the free public schools that are the sole means set out in the constitution for the state to provide for the education of Florida's children. This diversion not only reduces money available to the free schools, but also funds private schools that are not "uniform" when compared with each other or the public system. Many standards

> imposed by law on the public schools are inapplicable to the private schools receiving public monies. In sum, through the OSP the state is fostering plural, nonuniform systems of education in direct violation of the constitutional mandate for a uniform system of free public schools.

However, in response to the court decision, Governor Jeb Bush signed into law a bill that would allow many low-income students using the OSP program to transfer into the Corporate Tax Credit Scholarship program and continue to exercise school choice; *Alliance for School Choice*, "Florida Governor Signs Bill Giving Displaced Students a Lifeline to a New School Choice Program and More Accountability to Private Schools," June 7, 2006, http://www.allianceforschoolchoice.org/media_center.aspx?IITypeID=3&IIID=2691 (accessed April 19, 2007).

8. The tax credit may be up to 75 percent of their state income tax liability. The legislation limits the aggregate amount the state may award to $88 million.

9. Florida Department of Education, *School Choice Options: Florida Continues to Lead the Nation*, 2006, 7, https://floridaschoolchoice.org/district/files/School_Choice_Options.pdf (accessed May 10, 2007), 7.

10. Ibid., 4.

11. Ibid., 2, 6.

12. Ibid., 7.

13. School districts must set aside an amount equal to 20 percent of the Title I funds to provide choice options.

14. Authors' calculations. AYP results are available at Florida Department of Education, "Florida School Grades."

15. Jane Hannaway and Kendra Bischoff, "Florida: Confusions, Constraints, and Cascading Scenarios" in *Leaving No Child Behind? Options for Kids in Failing Schools*, eds. Frederick M. Hess and Chester E. Finn, Jr. (New York: Palgrave Macmillan, 2004).

16. These subgroups include racial and ethnic categories of students (white, black, Hispanic, Asian-American, American Indian), and students who are economically disadvantaged, have limited English proficiency, or have disabilities.

17. Authors' calculations. AYP results are available at Florida Department of Education, "Florida School Grades."

18. The state also requested that the number of students required for determination of subgroup performance remain at least thirty, but that the students represent at least 15 percent of the student body. The secretary of education approved this change.

19. Of schools in the state, 35 percent made P/AYP, and 34 percent failed to make AYP.

20. Interestingly, a recent study examined the learning gains of students in schools that made AYP and schools that did not, and also schools that received different letter grades in the A+ Plan; Paul Peterson and Martin West, "Is Your Child's

School Really Effective?" *Education Next*, no. 4 (2006), www.hoover.org/publications/ednext/3853947.html (accessed May 25, 2007). The researchers found that the A+ Plan more accurately measured school quality than the AYP determination of the NCLB program. Governor Bush was reported as saying, "With all due respect to the federal system, our accountability system is really the better way to go"; Sam Dillon, "As Two Bushes Try to Fix Schools, Tools Differ," *New York Times*, September 28, 2006.

21. Anonymous official, Miami-Dade County Public Schools, interview conducted by Jane Hannaway, Miami, Florida, November 8, 2006. All district officials asked to remain anonymous.

22. National Center for Education Statistics, *Characteristics of the 100 Largest Public Elementary and Secondary School Districts in the U.S. 2001–02*, table 1, http://nces.ed.gov/pubs2003/2003353.pdf (accessed May 22, 2007).

23. Miami-Dade County Public Schools, *I Choose! 2006–2007 Choice Plan Specialized Programs, 2006*, 12, 28, http://choice.dadeschools.net/images/2006_choice_plan.pdf (accessed May 10, 2007).

24. Of course, the motivation of parents with children with special needs may be particularly compelling; ibid., 33, 37.

25. Indeed, the M-DC School Board established in 1991 the Magnet Educational Choice Association Inc. (MECA), a community-based organization, to provide support and advice on the district's choice initiatives; ibid. 7.

26. Race, ethnicity, and gender are not used as selection factors.

27. Miami-Dade County Public Schools, *I Choose!*, 22–24.

28. Ibid., 18.

29. Controlled open enrollment is required in all Florida school districts by state law passed in 1996; ibid., 18.

30. These transfers are individually approved and can only occur when at least one of these conditions is met: "The parent or guardian can substantiate that a health or other type of hardship exists; the student requests admission into a vocational program or a course of study that does not exist in their assigned school; it can be determined that a change of school assignment may alleviate emotional problems or that an exceptional student can be better served by reassignment to a special program or class" Ibid., 40.

31. Diane Stark Rentner, Caitlin Scott, Nancy Kober, Naomi Chudowsky, Victor Chudowsky, Scott Joftus, Dalia Zabala, *From Capital to the Classroom: Year 4 of the No Child Left Behind Act*, March 2006, 117, http://www.cep-dc.org/nclb/Year4/CEP-NCLB-Report-4.pdf (accessed May 1, 2007). In 2003–4, the Institute of Education Sciences estimates, 1 percent of eligible students used NCLB school transfer; U.S. Department of Education, National Center For Education Evaluation and Regional Assistance, Institute of Education Sciences, *National Assessment of Title I: Interim Report to Congress. Volume I Implementation*, NCEE 2006-4000, February 2006, 64,

http://www.ed.gov/rschstat/eval/disadv/title1interimreport/index.html (accessed May 1, 2007).

32. U.S. Department of Education, National Center For Education Evaluation and Regional Assistance, Institute of Education Sciences, *National Assessment of Title I: Volume I*, 67.

33. Authors' calculations. AYP results are available at Florida Department of Education, "Florida School Grades."

34. Anonymous official, interview.

35. Authors' calculations. AYP results are available at Florida Department of Education, "Florida School Grades."

36. Charter schools set their own application time period.

37. If a school is unexpectedly found to be in school improvement, or if a school can no longer be transferred into because it gets on the school improvement list, the district notifies parents, and they have a second chance to enroll their child.

38. U.S. Department of Education, National Center For Education Evaluation and Regional Assistance, Institute of Education Sciences, *National Assessment of Title I: Volume I*, 67.

39. Anonymous official, interview.

40. More detailed tables are available from the authors.

41. Section 1008.331, Florida Statutes, http://www.leg.state.fl.us/statutes/index.cfm?mode=View%20Statutes&SubMenu=1&App_mode=Display_Statute&Search_String=1008.331&URL=CH1008/Sec331.htm (accessed May 10, 2007). A technical assistance paper from the Florida Department of Education regarding the new law is available at Florida Department of Education, *Technical Assistance Paper Regarding Supplemental Educational Services (SES) in Title I Schools, October 2006*, http://info.fldoe.org/docushare/dsweb/Get/Document-4044/k12_06_150att1.pdf (accessed May 10, 2007).

42. Anonymous official, interview.

43. According to the Center on Education Policy, in 2005–6, 20 percent of eligible students received SES. The U.S. Government Accountability Office estimate is comparable, with 19 percent of eligible students said to have received SES in 2004–5, while the Institute of Education Sciences estimates participation at 17 percent for that same year; see Rentner et al., *From Capital to the Classroom: Year 4 of the No Child Left Behind Act*; U.S. Government Accountability Office, *No Child Left Behind Act: Education Actions Needed to Improve Local Implementation and State Evaluation of Supplemental Services*, GAO-06-758, August 2006, 3, http://www.gao.gov/new.items/d06758.pdf (accessed May 1, 2007); U.S. Department of Education, National Center For Education Evaluation and Regional Assistance, Institute of Education Sciences, *National Assessment of Title I: Volume I*, 64.

44. A provider must first meet state standards to become state-approved. Then it must negotiate a contract with the district itself. Providers must also create an individual Parent District Provider Agreement (PDPA) for each child enrolled to customize the more general goals and expectations outlined by the SES program.

45. The payment process, for example, is complicated, with payment and processing handled individually for each session of tutoring, as the district cannot pay when the student does not attend.

Chapter 11: Remedies in Action: Four "Restructured" Schools

1. See chapter 2 for an overview of several large districts' approach to restructuring.

2. *No Child Left Behind Act*, 2001.

3. U.S. Department of Education, *LEA and School Improvement: Non-Regulatory Guidance*, July 21, 2006, http://www.ed.gov/policy/elsec/guid/schoolimprovement-guid.pdf (accessed March 29, 2007).

4. The federally funded Center for Comprehensive School Reform and Improvement has commissioned a series of resources on restructuring, including four white papers reviewing the literature on approaches to restructuring and a guide for district leaders making restructuring decisions. See Emily A. Hassel, Bryan C. Hassel, Matthew Arkin, Julie Kowal, and Lucy Steiner, *School Restructuring Under NCLB: What Works When* (Naperville, Ill.: Learning Point Associates, 2005). Available online at http://www.centerforcsri.org/index.php?option=com_content&task=view&id=282&Itemid=88.

5. Diane Stark Rentner, Caitlin Scott, Nancy Kober, Naomi Chudowsky, Victor Chudowsky, Scott Joftus, Dalia Zabala, *From Capital to the Classroom: Year 4 of the No Child Left Behind Act*, Center on Education Policy, March 2006, 58, http://www.cep-dc.org/nclb/Year4/CEP-NCLB-Report-4.pdf (accessed May 1, 2007).

6. Ibid., 60

7. Analysis based on current trends reported in ibid., 57–60.

8. Kerstin Carlson Le Floch, James Taylor, and Yu Zhang, *Schools in NCLB Restructuring: National Trends* (Washington, D.C.: American Institutes for Research, 2006).

9. Ibid.; U.S. Department of Education, National Center for Education Statistics, *Participation in Education* (Washington, D.C.: NCES, 2005).

10. Le Floch, Taylor, and Zhang, *Schools in NCLB Restructuring*.

11. U.S. Department of Education, National Center for Education Evaluation and Regional Assistance, Institute of Education Sciences, *National Assessment of Title I Interim Report: Volume I: Implementation of Title I*, by Stephanie Stullich, Elizabeth Eisner, Joseph McCrary, and Collette Roney (Washington, D.C.: Government Printing Office, 2006), xi, citing data from the Study of State Implementation of

Accountability and Teacher Quality under NCLB and the National Longitudinal Study of NCLB; Le Floch, Taylor, and Zhang, *Schools in NCLB Restructuring.*

12. Rentner et al., *From the Capital to the Classroom: Year 4 of the No Child Left Behind Act*; Center on Education Policy, *From Capital to the Classroom: Year 3 of the No Child Left Behind Act*, March 2005, http://www.cep-dc.org/pubs/nclby3/press/cep-nclby3_21Mar2005.pdf (accessed May 1, 2007); Rebecca Wolf DiBiase, *State Involvement in School Restructuring Under No Child Left Behind in the 2004–05 School Year.* (Denver, Colo.: Education Commission of the States, 2005).

13. Caitlin Scott, Nancy Kober, Diane Stark Rentner, Jack Jennings, *Hope but No Miracle Cures: Michigan's Early Restructuring Lessons*, Center on Education Policy, November 2005, 2, http://www.cep-dc.org/fededprograms/michiganNov2005/HopebutNoMiracleCure.pdf (accessed May 2, 2007); Center on Education Policy, *Wrestling with the Devil in the Details: An Early Look at Restructuring in California*, February 2006, 2, http://www.cep-dc.org/nclb/Year4/CEP-NCLB-Report-4.pdf (accessed May 2, 2007).

14. Rentner et al., *From the Capital to the Classroom: Year 4 of the No Child Left Behind Act*, 59; DiBiase, *State Involvement in School Restructuring.*

15. Scott et al., *Hope but No Miracle Cures*; Center on Education Policy, *Wrestling the Devil in the Details.* CEP also studied the effects of NCLB in Brenda Neuman-Sheldon, *Building on State Reform: Maryland School Restructuring*, Center on Education Policy, September 2006, http://www.cep-dc.org/pubs/mdschoolSep2006/CEP-MdSchlRestruct.pdf (accessed May 2, 2007). Chapters 5 and 8 offer an overview of restructuring schools in California and Michigan, respectively, and the CEP analyses provide valuable contextual information about how restructuring works in these two states.

16. Grand Rapids Public Schools, *Buchanan Elementary School Statistics, 2006*, http://web.grps.k12.mi.us/Elementary/Buchanan/aboutbuchanan.html (accessed November 16, 2006).

17. Buchanan Elementary School, *School Action Plan for Learning, 2005–6* (Grand Rapids, Mich.: Grand Rapids Public Schools, 2006).

18. Roberto Garcia (principal, Buchanan Elementary School), phone interview, August 28, 2006.

19. Bert R. Blake, "Focus, Consistency, and Commitment Drive Change in Grand Rapids Schools," *Leading Change*, Fall 2004, http://cenmi.org/LeadingChange/F04/article1A.asp.

20. Scott et al., *Hope But No Miracle Cures.*

21. Blake, "Focus, Consistency, and Commitment Drive Change."

22. Sylvia Gonzalez (principal, Balboa Elementary School), phone interview, September 12, 2006.

23. San Diego Unified School District, *School Accountability Report Card: Balboa Elementary School*, 2006, http://studata.sandi.net/research/sarcs/2005-06/SARC013.pdf (accessed May 4, 2007).

24. California Department of Education, *Title I Program Improvement Status Determinations*, http://www.cde.ca.gov/ta/ac/ay/tidetermine.asp (accessed May 22, 2007).

25. Balboa Elementary School, Proposal to Restructure Balboa Elementary School, March 7, 2005, http://www.sandi.net/board/reports/2005/0307/e5d_3.pdf (accessed May 4, 2007).

26. Kalamazoo Public Schools website, http://www.kalamazoopublicschools.com/education/district/district.php?sectionid=1 (accessed November 16, 2006).

27. Helen L. Burz and Richard E. Wood, *School and Instructional Audit: Milwood Middle School*, December 2005, http://www.milwoodmiddle.org/info/audit/index.html (accessed May 4, 2007).

28. Michigan Department of Education, *Michigan School Report Cards: Milwood Middle School, 2005–6*, https://oeaa.state.mi.us/ayp/school_one_only_1_2004.asp?ECDid=2216&Grade=8 (accessed May 4, 2007).

29. Burz and Wood, *School and Instructional Audit*, 1.

30. Vince Riveroll (principal, Gompers Charter Middle School), phone interview, September 26, 2006.

31. San Diego Unified School District, *School Accountability Report Card: Gompers Charter Middle School*, 2006, http://studata.sandi.net/research/sarcs/2005-06/SARC747.pdf (accessed May 4, 2007).

32. San Diego Unified School District, *School Accountability Report Card: Gompers Secondary School*, 2005, http://studata.sandi.net/research/sarcs/200405/SARC335.pdf (accessed May 4, 2007).

33. Helen Gao, "Red Carpet Opening at Gompers Charter," *San Diego Union-Tribune*, September 7, 2005.

34. Helen Gao, "Popular Principal to Return to Gompers," *San Diego Union-Tribune*, June 2, 2005.

35. Erik W. Robelen, "School Reopened as Charter under NCLB Winds Up Year 1," *Education Week*, June 14, 2006.

36. Rentner et al., *From the Capital to the Classroom: Year 4 of the No Child Left Behind Act*; Center on Education Policy, *From the Capital to the Classroom: Year 3 of the No Child Left Behind Act*; DiBiase, *State Involvement in School Restructuring*.

37. Frederick M. Hess, *Spinning Wheels: The Politics of Urban School Reform* (Washington, D.C.: Brookings Institution Press, 1998).

38. Lowell C. Rose and Alec M. Gallup, *The 38th Annual Phi Delta Kappa/Gallup Poll of the Public's Attitudes Toward the Public Schools*, August 2006, http://www.pdkintl.org/kappan/k0609pol.

39. Sudi Sudarsanam and Jim Lai, "Corporate Financial Distress and Turnaround Strategies: An Empirical Analysis," *British Journal of Management* 12, no. 3 (2001): 183–99; Rob Paton and Jill Mordaunt, "What's Different about Public and Non-Profit 'Turnaround'?" *Public Money & Management*, August 2004. For a summary of this research as it relates to the NCLB school restructuring context, see also Julie Kowal and

Emily Ayscue Hassel, *Turnarounds with New Leaders and Staff*, Center for Comprehensive School Reform and Improvement, 2005, http://www.centerforcsri.org/pubs/restructuring/KnowledgeIssues4Turnaround.pdf (accessed May 23, 2007).

Chapter 12: District Accountability: More Bark Than Bite?

1. Sheena Dooley, "Schools Put on Program Improvement," *Bismarck Tribune*, September 17, 2004.

2. A tally of all state reporting was provided to the author on November 15, 2006, by Chad Colby, of the U.S. Department of Education's media relations office.

3. Three other school districts were reported by states as being "in improvement"; however, the states did not indicate which year of improvement they were in.

4. Naomi Chudowsky and Victor Chudowsky, *Identifying School Districts for Improvement and Corrective Action*, Center on Education Policy, March 2005, http://www.cep-dc.org/nclb/identifying_school_districts.pdf (accessed May 2, 2007).

5. For specifics listed in the next few paragraphs, see U.S. Department of Education, *LEA and School Improvement: Non-Regulatory Guidance*, July 21, 2006, http://www.ed.gov/policy/elsec/guid/schoolimprovementguid.pdf (accessed March 29, 2007), 46–48.

6. Ibid., 46–47.

7. Ibid., 48.

8. Heather Vogell and Bridget Gutierrez, "Long Road to School Sanctions," *Atlanta Journal-Constitution*, July 15, 2006.

9. U.S. Department of Education, *LEA and School Improvement: Non-Regulatory Guidance*, ii.

10. See chapter 2.

11. Information on school restructuring contained in Bonnie A. Kirkland (Maryland assistant attorney general) letter to Nathaniel J. McFadden (Maryland state senator), April 6, 2006.

12. Vogell and Gutierrez, "Long Road to School Sanctions."

13. Daniel de Vise, "Lite Choice in School Reform," *Washington Post*, September 20, 2006.

14. Brenda Neuman-Sheldon, *Building on State Reform: Maryland School Restructuring*, Center on Education Policy, September 2006, http://www.cep-dc.org/pubs/mdschoolSep2006/CEP-MdSchlRestruct.pdf (accessed May 2, 2007).

15. Alan Bersin, comments, American Enterprise Institute conference on NCLB, Washington, D.C., November 30, 2006.

16. Michael Kolber, "Districts Find Wiggle Room In Education Law," *Sacramento Bee*, April 10, 2005.

17. Duke Helfand, "U.S. May Force California to Call More School Districts Failures," *Los Angeles Times*, February 17, 2005.

18. Nanette Asimov, "No Child Left Behind: California," *San Francisco Chronicle*, March 9, 2005.

19. Alexis Young, "Five Inland Valley School Districts Could Face State Takeover," *Inland Valley Daily Bulletin*, March 13, 2005.

20. California Department of Education, "O'Connell Releases List of 2005–06 PI Schools and Districts," press release, September 20, 2005, http://www.cde.ca.gov/nr/ne/yr05/yr05rel112.asp (accessed June 7, 2007).

21. Ibid.

22. Helfand, "U.S. May Force California to Call More Districts Failures."

23. Vogell and Gutierrez, "Long Road to School Sanctions."

24. Mark Hornbeck, "109 School Districts Fail to Make Federal Progress," *Detroit News*, January 13, 2005.

25. Valerie Woodruff, interview conducted by the author, November 28, 2006.

26. Heinrich Mintrop and Tina Trujillo, "Corrective Action in Low-Performing Schools: Lessons for NCLB Implementation from State and District Strategies in First-Generation Accountability Systems," *Education Policy Analysis Archives* 13, no. 48 (2005), http://epaa.asu.edu/epaa/v13n48 (accessed May 24, 2007).

27. John Milburn, "Seven Districts/33 Schools Listed 'On Improvement,'" Associated Press, August 12, 2003.

28. Josh Davidson and Chris Lundy, "30 of New Jersey School Districts Fail Federal Standards," *Ocean County Observer*, March 10, 2005.

29. NCLB requires teachers to be "highly qualified," meaning they are adequately trained in the subject areas they are teaching.

30. Sara Neufeld, "City Fails Reform Test; Fewer than Half of Teachers Meet Federal Standards," *Baltimore Sun*, January 26, 2006.

31. Ibid.

32. Liz Bowie and Sara Neufeld, "Md. Acts To Seize 11 City Schools; Grasmick Seeks Control Under No Child Left Behind," *Baltimore Sun*, March 29, 2006.

33. Maryland State Board of Education, "State Board Takes New Action to Strengthen Baltimore City Schools," press release, March 29, 2006.

34. Diana Jean Schemo, "Maryland Acts to Take Over Failing Baltimore Schools," *New York Times*, March 30, 2006, 16.

35. Quotes in this paragraph taken from Nick Anderson, "Control of 11 Schools Seized; Md. Board Moves Against Baltimore," *Washington Post*, March 30, 2006, B1.

36. Sara Neufeld, "Schools Challenge Report; Journal Says City Graduates 38.5 Percent of Students; Only Detroit Fared Poorer," *Baltimore Sun*, June 27, 2006, 1B.

37. Maryland State Board of Education, *Proposed State Actions in Baltimore Public Schools*, executive summary, March 2006, http://www.marylandpublicschools.org/NR/

rdonlyres/407FF8E5-C710-4A64-881C-CA1641821E78/9354/BaltCityProposed_
March2006_exexsummary1.pdf (accessed May 29, 2007).

38. Liz Bowie, "U.S. Education Secretary Applauds State Move," *Baltimore Sun*,
March 31, 2006, 6A.

39. Ibid.

40. John Wagner and Nick Anderson, "Bill Would Block State Takeover of Baltimore Schools," *Washington Post*, March 31, 2006, B9.

41. Liz Bowie, "Fight Over City Schools Promised; Baltimore Leaders Criticize
State Takeover Plan Proposal," *Baltimore Sun*, March 31, 2006, 1A.

42. Liz Bowie and Jill Rosen, "School Aid Faces Threat," *Baltimore Sun*, April 6,
2006.

43. Jill Rosen, "House Blocks Veto on Schools; Senate Next To Vote On Overrid-
ing Governor Over Takeover Measure," *Baltimore Sun*, April 10, 2006, 1A.

44. Jill Rosen, "School Takeover Delay Gets A Veto; Ehrlich Rejects Nine Measures On Deadline Day," *Baltimore Sun*, April 9, 2006, 1A.

45. Jill Rosen, "Veto Killed, Takeover Of Schools Halted," *Baltimore Sun*, April 11,
2006, 1A.

46. Sara Neufeld and Liz Bowie, "School CEO Leaving; Copeland to Step Down
July 1 after Turbulent 3 Years," *Baltimore Sun*, June 20, 2006, 1A.

47. Sara Neufeld, "School Reform Claim Reduced," *Baltimore Sun*, July 22, 2006, 1A.

48. Kenneth K. Wong and Francis X. Shen, "Do School District Takeovers
Work?" *State Education Standard* 3, no. 2 (Spring 2002), 19–23.

49. Kolber, "Districts Find Wiggle Room."

50. Tim Martin, "Restructuring Schools Opt to Replace Staff, Make Other
Changes, State Says," Associated Press, August 10, 2004.

51. Ledyard King, "Failing Schools Pushed to Restructure," Gannett News Service, August 3, 2006.

Conclusion: Can This Law Be Fixed?
A Hard Look at the NCLB Remedies

1. See chapter 2.

2. See chapter 8.

3. See chapters 9 and 11, respectively.

4. See chapter 3.

5. "Growth" measures gauge the extent to which children or schools gain knowledge and skills during the course of a year (or other time period), whereas
"absolute performance" compares their present achievement to a fixed standard
and does not indicate change over time. Thus, growth models are generally viewed
as better indicators of schools' true effectiveness.

6. See chapter 1.

About the Authors

Julian Betts is a professor of economics at the University of California, San Diego, a research associate at the National Bureau of Research, and an adjunct fellow at the Public Policy Institute of California. He has written extensively on the link between student outcomes and measures of school spending, including class size, teachers' salaries, and teachers' education levels, and is the coeditor of *Getting Choice Right: Ensuring Equity and Efficiency in Education Policy* (Brookings Institution Press, 2005). His work on accountability has appeared in the *American Economic Review, Journal of Urban Economics, Journal of Public Economics, The Economics of Education Review*, and *Educational Evaluation and Policy Analysis*.

Michael Casserly is the executive director of the Council of the Great City Schools, the primary national organization exclusively representing the interests of large urban public school districts. Before assuming this position, Casserly served as the organization's director of legislation and research for fifteen years. He is currently spearheading efforts to boost academic performance in the nation's big-city schools, strengthen management and operations, challenge inequitable state financing systems, and improve the public's image of urban education.

Stephen Clements is associate director of the University of Kentucky's Institute for Educational Research. His recent projects have included grant program coordinator duties for the Title II Teacher Quality Enhancement Grant at Kentucky's Education Professional Standards Board, and an education data system improvement project for the Kentucky Department of Education. His research interests have included the politics of the creation and passage of Kentucky's 1990 education reforms, state-level school reforms enacted since the mid-1980s, the role of political culture in state education changes, the status of the teacher workforce, and data needs for effective education policymaking.

Sarah Cohodes is a research assistant at the Education Policy Center of the Urban Institute. Her work there focuses on an extensive study of Florida's accountability system, and she has contributed to several U.S. Department of Education reports on the flexibility provisions of the No Child Left Behind Act. An article she coauthored while at Swarthmore College on out-of-field teachers and student achievement is forthcoming in the *Public Finance Review*.

Christopher Dunbar Jr. is an associate professor of educational administration at Michigan State University. His research focuses on issues of equity, with a particular focus on children most vulnerable to academic and social failure. He is the author of *African American Males and Alternative Education: Does Anyone Know We're Here?* (Peter Lang, 2001), which explores the school experiences of African-American males placed in an alternative school. His scholarly efforts during the past few years have focused on issues of race in education, zero-tolerance policy, and, most recently, No Child Left Behind.

Chester E. Finn Jr. is president of the Thomas B. Fordham Foundation and Thomas B. Fordham Institute, senior fellow at Stanford's Hoover Institution, and senior editor of *Education Next*. Previously, Finn served as assistant secretary for research and improvement at the U.S. Department of Education, senior fellow at the Hudson Institute, and founding partner and senior scholar with the Edison Project (which later grew into Edison Schools Inc.). The author of fourteen books and over 350 articles, his work has appeared in *The Wall Street Journal, The Washington Post, The Public Interest, Harvard Business Review, The New York Times*, and many other major publications, journals, and newspapers.

Jane Hannaway directs the Education Policy Center of the Urban Institute. She is also director of a newly formed research center, the Center for the Analysis of Longitudinal Data in Education Research (CALDER). Hannaway is a sociologist whose work focuses on structural reforms in education, particularly those promoting competition and choice. She is the past editor of *Educational Evaluation and Policy Analysis* and has coauthored five books and numerous articles in education and management journals. Previously, she served on the faculty of Columbia, Princeton, and Stanford universities and was twice vice president of the American Educational Research Association.

Bryan C. Hassel is co-director of Public Impact, a North Carolina–based education policy and management consulting firm. He conducts research and consults with leading organizations on topics such as school restructuring, charter schooling, and the human capital pipeline for public education. Hassel is the coauthor of *Picky Parent Guide: Choose Your Child's School with Confidence* (Armchair Press, 2004) and author of *The Charter School Challenge: Avoiding the Pitfalls, Fulfilling the Promise* (Brookings Institution Press, 1999).

Jeffrey R. Henig is a professor of political science and education at Teachers College, Columbia University. His research has focused on the boundary between private and public action in addressing social problems. He is the author of several books, including *The Color of School Reform: Race, Politics, and the Challenge of Urban Education* (Princeton University Press, 1999) and *Building Civic Capacity: The Politics of Reforming Urban Schools* (University Press of Kansas, 2001), and most recently, coeditor of *Mayors in the Middle: Politics, Race, and Mayoral Control of Urban Schools* (Princeton University Press, 2004).

Frederick M. Hess is director of education policy studies at the American Enterprise Institute and executive editor of *Education Next*. His many books include *No Child Left Behind: A Primer* (Peter Lang, 2006), *With the Best of Intentions* (Harvard Education Press, 2005), *Common Sense School Reform* (Palgrave Macmillan, 2004), and *Spinning Wheels* (Brookings Institution Press, 1999). His scholarly work has appeared in publications including *Urban Affairs Review, Social Science Quarterly, American Politics Quarterly,* and *Teachers College Record*. Hess is a research associate at the Harvard University Program on Education Policy and Governance, as well as a former high school social studies teacher and education professor.

Julie Kowal is a consultant with Public Impact. She has conducted extensive policy research on school restructuring, including coauthoring *Reopening as a Charter School, Contracting with External Education Management Providers,* and *Turnarounds with New Leaders and Staff* in the *School Restructuring Under NCLB: What Works When?* series for the Center for Comprehensive School Reform and Improvement. Kowal earned her law degree with honors from the University of North Carolina at Chapel Hill.

Paul Manna is an assistant professor in the Department of Government and a faculty affiliate with the Thomas Jefferson Program in Public Policy at the College of William and Mary. His research and teaching focus on American public policy, elementary and secondary education, federalism, and applied research methods. He has written and published on No Child Left Behind, school vouchers, charter schools, teachers' unions, and education governance. His book, *School's In: Federalism and the National Education Agenda* (Georgetown University Press, 2006), analyzes the development of the federal role and federal-state relationships in K–12 education since the 1960s.

Patrick McGuinn is assistant professor of political science at Drew University and author of *No Child Left Behind and the Transformation of Federal Education Policy, 1965–2005* (University Press of Kansas, 2006). He was previously a visiting assistant professor at Colby College, a postdoctoral fellow at the Taubman Center for Public Policy and American Institutions at Brown University, a predoctoral fellow at the Miller Center for Public Affairs, University of Virginia, and a high school teacher. His work on education policy has been published in journals, including *The Public Interest, Teachers College Record,* and *Educational Policy.*

Alex Medler is vice president for research and analysis at the Colorado Children's Campaign, a nonprofit, nonpartisan children's advocacy group based in Denver. Medler has written extensively on education reform and worked with policymakers at the local, state, and national levels. He directed national activities to support charter schools for the U.S. Department of Education from 1997 to 2001. From 1992 to 1997 he was an analyst for the Education Commission of the States, where he directed an initiative to track major state education reforms. Medler is completing his PhD in political science at the University of Colorado at Boulder.

Michael J. Petrilli is vice president for national programs and policy at the Thomas B. Fordham Foundation, a school reform organization based in Washington, D.C., and a research fellow at Stanford University's Hoover Institution. He served as a Bush administration appointee in the U.S. Department of Education, where he helped coordinate the public school choice and supplemental educational services provisions of the No Child Left Behind Act and oversaw discretionary grant programs for charter schools, alternative teacher certification, and high school reform. His work has appeared in *The New York Times*, *The Wall Street Journal*, *Education Next*, *Education Week*, *The Public Interest*, and other publications.

David N. Plank is executive director of policy analysis for California Education (PACE), based at Berkeley. He was previously on the faculty of the College of Education at Michigan State University, where he directed the Education Policy Center. He has published widely in a variety of fields, including economics of education, history of education, and politics of education. He has also served as a consultant in the areas of educational finance and educational policy to organizations including the World Bank, the United Nations Development Programme (UNDP), the Organisation for Economic Co-operation and Development (OECD), the United States Agency for International Development (USAID), and the Ford Foundation; and to governments in Africa and Latin America.

Joe Williams, a New York City–based journalist, is executive director of Democrats for Education Reform, a political action and advocacy group. Previously, he wrote about education issues for the *New York Daily News* and the *Milwaukee Journal Sentinel*. Williams has won numerous state, local, and national awards for reporting on Milwaukee's private school choice program in the 1990s, and recently published the book *Cheating Our Kids: How Politics and Greed Ruin Education* (Palgrave Macmillan, 2005).

Index

Abbott districts, 153–54, 155, 160, 174
Abbott v. Burke (N.J.), 153
Academic Coaches Registry (Mich.), 280
Academic Performance Index (Calif.),
    122
    differs from federal AYP system,
      123–25
Academic Program Survey (Calif.), 140
Academy of Math and of Reading com-
puter software, 240
Accountability, 5–7, 18–19, 176
    in California, 122–25, 128
    in Colorado, 183
    Florida A+ Accountability Plan,
      244–46
    in Kentucky, 227–30
    of SES providers, 32
    See also District accountability
Adequate yearly progress, 5–6, 7–8,
    250, 260
    designation process needs major
      revisions, 322–23
    in great city schools, 44–46
    in New Jersey, 156–57
    results, timely notification to
      parents, 21–27
    See also Parental notification
Advocacy groups supported by
    Department of Education, 101–2
After School Youth Development
    Program (N.J.), 167

Alaska, 38, 40
Albion, Mich., 211
Alliance for School Choice, 175
Alonzo, Andres, 307
"Alternative governance" and restructur-
    ing, 114
American Federation of Teachers, 112–13
America 2000, 3
Anchorage, 48, 103
Annual measurable objectives targets
    (Ky.), 232–33, 236, 239–41
Asbury Park, N.J., 154
Association of California School
    Administrators, 142–43, 146–47
Atlanta, 101
Atlantic City, 300
A to Z Tutoring, 234
AYP, *see* Adequate yearly progress

Babbage Net School, 53
Babiak, Andrew, 170, 171–72
Balboa Elementary School, San Diego
    arts instruction, 276
    focus on English learners, 276
    involvement of parents, 275
    lessons learned, 285–89
    restructuring process, 274–78
    strategies to retain teachers, 276
Baltimore, 38, 107, 291
Baltimore City Schools, case study of
    district accountability, 300–307

Bandeiro de Mello, V., 124
Bayard Rustin Academy, 219–20
Beacon Schools (Denver), 196
Benton Harbor, Mich., 211
Bersin, Alan, 282, 283, 297
Betts, Julian, 11–12, 128, 131,
    133, 139
Big city schools, *see* Great city schools
Big Picture Company, 326
Bill and Melinda Gates Foundation, 196
Bi-partisanship in NCLB bill, 3–5, 6, 66
    creates policy paradoxes difficult to
        implement, 98, 105, 110
    results in vague language and
        contradictions, 97–98, 311
Black Alliance for Educational Options,
    100–101
Blackburn, Mark, 233
Bolick, Clint, 130
Boston, 45, 47, 51, 103, 106, 196
Boston, Charlene Cooper, 306–7
Boys and Girls Clubs of Indianapolis, 53
Buchanan Elementary School,
        Grand Rapids
    increased use of assessment data, 273
    lessons learned, 285–89
    new instructional model (from
        district), 272
    restructuring process, 271–74
    started all-day kindergarten, 273
    use of external review team, 272
Bush, George H. W., 3, 309
Bush, George W., 2, 3, 4, 71, 74, 79,
        305, 319, 320, 322, 324, 325,
        326
Bush, Jeb, 246
Brainfuse, 53
Broad Superintendents program, 318
Brown, Janice, 279

California, 37, 38, 121–52, 268, 269,
    270, 297–98, 314, 328

unintended consequences of NCLB,
    145–48
California Charter School Association,
    38
California Standards Test, 137
California State Department of
        Education
    dealing with NCLB requirements,
        143–45, 149–50
    districts in need of improvement,
        139–43
    and SES providers, 132–37
    tools for local education agencies in
        program improvement status,
        140–41
Camden, N.J., 154, 300
Campbell, Kevin, 278–81
Canul, Yvonne Caamal, 308
CAPA, *see* Collaborative Assessment and
        Planning for Achievement
Capacity in high-performing schools
        lacking, 50, 105–9, 255–56
"Capacity is no excuse" position, 105–9
Casserly, Michael, 11, 83, 112–13, 311
Castillo, Susan, 36
Center on Education Policy, 268,
    269, 293
Central Michigan University, 219–20
Chamberlain, Sally, 37
Charles R. Drew Elementary Schools,
    252
Charter School Program grants, 116
Charter schools, 109, 154, 215, 324
    in Colorado, 191
    in Florida, 247–48
    in Miami, 251–52
    in Michigan, 203
    See also Bayard Rustin Academy,
        Gompers Middle School
Charter Schools Office (Mich.), 219–20
Cherokee County, Ga., Schools, 298–99
Chicago, 51, 56, 85, 103, 106

Clements, Stephen, 13, 313, 325
Clinton, Bill, 3, 101, 309, 316
Club Z, 53
Cohn, Carl, 146
Cohodes, Sarah, 13, 83
Cole Middle School (Colo.), 191
Collaborative Assessment and Planning
    for Achievement teams (N.J.),
    168–73, 173–74, 177, 311
Collective bargaining, 39, 326
    loophole in NCLB, 110–13
Colorado, 28, 179–201
    accountability, 183
    case studies of districts, 194–99
    conflicts with state and federal
        designations, 183–85
    costs of NCLB interventions, 192–93
    demographics, 187–89
    geography presents problems, 181–82
    local control strong, 182
    recommendations for future
        interventions, 199–201
    rural districts a challenge for NCLB
        implementation, 185–86
    schools in need of improvement,
        186–92
Colorado Student Assessment Program,
    183
    and problems with AYP timelines,
        184–85
Columbus, Ohio, 48
Commission on No Child Left Behind,
    320, 322, 324, 328
Commonwealth Accountability Testing
    System (Ky.), 227–29
    discrepancies with NCLB in
        performance designations, 239–40
Community Action Program, 72
Community involvement in restructur-
    ing process, 288–89
Compliance-style activity and mindset,
    310, 312

Compton Unified School District
    (Calif.), 130
Connecticut, 25, 26, 40
Consolidated State Performance
    Reports, 291
Controlled-choice schools in Miami--
    Dade, 252–53, 256
Copeland, Bonnie, 302, 306
Corporate Income Tax Credit Scholar-
    ship Program, 247
Corrective action, 7, 294–96
    in great city schools, strategies used,
        58–60, 63–64
    need to change present sequence of
        remedies, 321–22
    in New Jersey, 167–73
    state oversight of and action on,
        33–41
    state plans for, 301–2, 304, 307
Cortez, Colo., implementing NCLB,
    case study, 197–99
Council of Chief State School Officers,
    320
Council of Great City Schools, 44, 51,
    58, 103, 112, 304
Cowan, Kristen Tosh, 109
Cruz, David, 198
Curran, J. Joseph, 305

Danenberg, Anne, 128, 133, 139
Delaware, 23, 24, 28, 40, 293, 299
Democrats, 175, 303, 320
    and localism, 77–78
    and market metaphor, 78–79
    and passage of NCLB, 3–5, 6, 66,
        73–75
Denver, 56, 180, 186, 191, 193
Denver Public Schools, 181, 186, 188–89
    implementing NCLB, case study,
        194–97
Department of Education, see U.S.
    Department of Education

Detroit, 48, 101, 207, 214
Detroit Public Schools, 209–12
Dibofsky, Wayne, 155, 170
District accountability, 290–91, 307–8
    in Baltimore Public Schools, 300–7
    harsh sanctions ineffective method
        of assistance, 300
    how it works under NCLB, 292–94
    improvement plans, 293–94, 297
    political overtones of state and
        district accountability struggle in
        Baltimore, 303, 305
    role of state education agencies,
        296–300, 301
Districts (local education agencies), 35
    implementation problems, 40–41
    improvement status among great
        city schools, 60–61
    lack of capacity for school choice,
        106–9
    in need of improvement in
        California, 139–43
    responses to SES requirement, 80–85
    See also District accountability,
        Obsolescent localism
District Assistance Survey (Calif.), 140–42
Duchon, Eliot, 298
Dunbar, Christopher Jr., 12, 313
Duncan, Arne, 106
Dyslexia Institute of Indiana, 53

Edison, 53
Education Station, 53, 70, 167
Education Trust West, 298
Education YES! 205–6, 215, 219
Edvisions, 220
Ehrlich, Robert L., 303, 305, 306
Elementary and Secondary Education
        Act, 2, 18–19, 202–3, 310, 312,
        316, 318, 320
English language learners, 53, 147–48
    in California, 121, 123–25, 130, 14

in Miami, 245
in New Jersey, 176
in San Diego, 274, 277
Evaluation of NCLB and concerns
    aspirational framework not realistic
        or effective, 309–10
    civil rights manifesto dressed up as
        an accountability system, 327–28
    conflicts with Individuals with
        Disabilities Act, 146–46
    creates political cover for state/
        district officials to take action,
        313–14
    deficiencies in serving English—
        learner students, 147–48
    does not foster creativity, 312–13
    focuses on compliance, not better
        performance, 310–11, 312–13
    operations vary from state to state,
        314–15
    provides transparency but little
        data on its own effectiveness,
        316–17
    remedies not used or evaluated,
        313, 317–18
    SES concept unworkable, 315–16
    state and federal systems incompat-
        ible, 145–46, 318
    tinkering with act is not enough,
        319, 328
Evans, Michelle, 284
Extended Day Reading Program, 139

Federalism, is it suitable for a reform
        regime? 4, 145–46, 318
Federal power limits to change, demon-
        strated in Colorado, 179–81
Fifth-Day Collaborative Plan
        (San Diego), 276, 278
Flanagan, Mike, 205
Flint City School District, 216–17
Flint, Mich., 203, 211, 215

Florida, 22, 26–27, 36, 37, 177,
    244–64, 300, 314, 328
  school choice history, 246–50
Florida A+ Accountability Plan,
    244–46, 248–50
Florida Comprehensive Assessment
    Test, 245
Florida State Department of Education
    and SES, 261
Food and Drug Administration, 1
Fresno, 48
Fulton County, Ga., School District, 295
Fulton County, Ky., schools, under
    NCLB, 230, 234–38, 243
Fund for the Improvement of Education
    grants (Department of Educa-
    tion), 101

Galloway, Mary Alice, 299
Gamaliel, Ky., 238, 239
Garcia, Roberto, 271–74
Georgia, 22, 36, 295, 296
Goals 2000, 3, 101, 316
Gompers Middle School (San Diego)
    became chartered, 283–84
    lessons learned, 285–89
    restructuring process, 282–85
    workgroup met weekly, 282
Gonzalez, Sylvia, 274–77
Gore, Al, 3
Gorman, Siobhan, 71
Grand Rapids, Mich., 203
Grand Rapids Public Schools, 217–19,
    270, 274–78
Granholm, Jennifer, 205
Grasmick, Nancy, 38, 301–5, 307
Great City Schools, 43–65
  AYP status in, 44–46
  corrective action and restructuring,
    58–60
  discussion of progress, 61–65
  district improvement status, 60–61

school choice, 46–50
SES, 50–58, 103
student achievement, 64–65
transfer rates in, 46–47, 62
Greater Educational Opportunities
Foundation, 101
Green Dot Public Schools, 326
Gregg, Judd, 66, 73
Griffin, Gayle, 156

Hadley, Sean, 162, 170, 171
Hammel, Patti, 35
Hannaway, Jane, 13, 83
Harris, Wendy, 139
Hassel, Bryan C., 13, 313
Hawaii, 22
Haycock, Kate, 96
Hayward, Calif., Unified School District,
    131, 135, 137, 138, 144
Hazel, Charles, 73
Head Start, 70
Henig, Jeffrey R., 11, 315
Heritage Foundation, 320
Hickman, Ky., 235
Hickok, Eugene, 290, 307
Highly skilled educators (Ky.), 229,
    235, 236
Hillsborough County, Fla., 103
Hispanic Council for Reform and
    Educational Options, 101
Hispanic students, 181, 186–88, 245
Hoff, David J., 130
Holliday, Chuck, 237

I choose! schools (Miami), 252–53,
    256, 258, 259–60
Idaho, 314
Illinois, 36
Implementation of NCLB
  in Colorado, reasons for problems
    with, 183–86
  lessons learned to date, 115–16

in Michigan, weak but achieved goals, 203–4, 221–22
in New Jersey, problems and promising projects, 173–76
problems with, 96–97
Improving America's Schools Act, 18, 316
Indianapolis, 313
Indiana State Council of Opportunities
Industrialization Centers of America, 53
Individuals with Disabilities Education Act, 146–47
Inez, Ky., 232, 233, 234
Innovations in Education: Creating Strong District School Choice Options, 100, 102
Iowa, 24, 28, 39
Irvington, N.J., 154

Jefferson County, Ky., 108
Jennings, Jack, 297
Jersey City, 154, 300
John M. McKay Scholarships for Students with Disabilities, 246–47, 251
Johnson, Lyndon B., 2
Johnson, Paul, 291
Jurupa Valley (Calif.) Unified School District, 298
Just, Ann, 134, 136, 143–44

Kalamazoo, Mich., 270, 278–81
Kaplan, 78
Kennedy, Edward M., 4, 5, 66, 75, 96
Kentucky, 108, 168, 225–43, 311–12, 313, 325
reform efforts in, 226–29
in rural district problems, 230–43
Kentucky Core Content Test, 227–28
Kentucky Education Reform Act, 226–27
Kentucky Virtual High School, 233–34
King, Kevin, 139

Kirkland, Bonnie, 305
Kit Carson District (Colo.), 185–86
Klein, Joe, 86
Knowledge Is Power Program, 191, 318, 326
Knowledge Learning Corporation, 70
Kohl, Sarah, 167, 170–71, 172
Kowal, Julie, 13, 313

Lansing, Mich., 211
LEA and School Improvement Non-Regulatory Guidance, 113–14
Leadership training lacking, 318, 325
Liberty City Charter School (Miami), 252
Librera, William, 156
Lieberman, Joe, 73
Local
control, 182, 308
educational agencies, *see* Districts
leadership, 40
See also Obsolescent localism
Los Angeles, 47, 83, 106–7, 130, 298
Louisville, Ky., 108

Maben, Camille, 134, 136, 152
MacInnes, Gordon, 153, 169, 175–76
Magnet schools
in Miami-Dade, 251–52, 258, 259–60
See also Milwood Magnet School
Manna, Paul, 10–11, 90, 185, 323
Manual High School (Colo.), 189
Market metaphor, 66–67, 75–76, 78–82, 92
market responses, 86–89
Martin County (Ky.) schools under NCLB, 230–34, 242, 243
Maryland, 38, 291, 297, 300–309
Maryland State Board of Education, 301–4, 305

Maryland State Department of Education attempt to take over failing Baltimore schools, 38, 300–7
Massachusetts, 27, 28, 40, 314
McFadden, Nathaniel, 305, 306
McGowan, Mike, 299
McGuinn, Patrick, 12
McLaughlin, D., 124
McLaughlin, Michelle, 113
Measured Progress, 229
Medler, Alex, 12
Miami-Dade County, 244–64
  choice behavior, 259–60
  description of student performance levels, 245–46
  enrollment in choice options, 251t
  problems and recommendations, 263–64
  school choice, 250–53
  school choice under NCLB, 253–59
  and SES, 83, 261–62, 315
Michigan, 202–22, 268, 269, 270, 30
  ambiguous account of NCLB implementation, 221–22
Michigan Department of Education, 205, 210, 211–12
  strategies to aid low-performing schools, 212–15
  use of sanctions, 204, 206–9, 215
Michigan Educational Assessment Program, 220
Michigan Education Association, 205, 214
Michigan School Improvement Framework, 213–14
Michigan State University, 214
Miller, George, 4, 5, 96
Milwood Magnet School (Kalamazoo)
  external evaluators, 279
  focus on professional development, 281

lessons learned, 285–89
reconstitution (school closed, new staff), 280
restructuring process, 278–81
MI-Map Game (Mich.), 213–14
Minneapolis, 56
Minnesota, 292
Mississippi, 314
Mitchell, Patricia, 169, 170, 172
Monroe County (Ky.) schools under NCLB, 238–41, 242
Moynihan, Daniel Patrick, 5, 72

National Assessment of Educational Progress, 43, 124, 320, 327
National Center for Research on Evaluation, Standards and Student Testing, 300
National Education Association, 96
National Education Goals, 309
Nation at Risk, A, 3
NCLB, see No Child Left Behind Act
Nebraska, 314
Newark, 154, 160–61, 166–67, 300
New Jersey, 27, 28, 153–78, 300, 311
New Jersey Assessment of Skills and Knowledge, 156
New Jersey Department of Education
  active role in assisting low-performing schools, 168–73
  current promising projects, 174–75
  established CAPA teams, 168–73
  failed to provide initial guidance, 177
  implementation of NCLB complications, 155–57
  inadequacies in SES management, 164–65
  reasons for poor performance under NCLB, 173–74, 176–77
  support for revising restructuring process, 177

New Jersey NCLB advisory council,
    168, 172
New Leaders for New Schools, 318, 326
Newspaper coverage of NCLB and SES,
    71–72
New Teacher Project, 326
Newton Learning, 53
New York, 293
New York City, 47, 86, 313
No Child Left Behind Act
    future of, 327–28
    passage of in 2001, 2–5
    See also Evaluation of, Implementa-
        tion of, Reauthorization of
Norfolk, 51
North Carolina, 37, 39–40, 40–41, 115
North Dakota, 22
Notification letters of options, 23–32,
    130
    excerpts from school choice letters,
        24–25
    excerpts from SES letters, 28–29

Obsolescent localism, 66–67, 75–78,
    79–82, 90
    overblown concept, 82–85
O'Connell, Jack, 145, 297
Office of Innovation and Improvement,
    108
Ohio, 292
Oklahoma, 314
Omaha, 51
O'Malley, Martin, 303, 307
Opportunity Scholarship (D.C.), 98
Opportunity Scholarship Program
    (Miami-Dade County), 246, 251,
    252
Oregon, 36

Paige, Rod, 103, 107, 112
Parental choice behavior in Miami-Dade
    County, 259–60

Parental notification of choice
    options, 21–27, 323
    failure of school districts to provide
        adequately, 98–105
    in great city schools, 47–50, 52, 62
    methods used in California, 129–30
    in Miami-Dade, outreach efforts
        made, 256–59, 261
    in New Jersey, 160–61, 163
    under scrutiny in California,
        143–44, 150
    U.S. Department of Education
        strategies to force implementa-
        tion, 99–105
    See also Notification letters
Parent Information and Resource
    Centers program, 101–2, 116
Paterson, N.J., 154, 167, 300
Pennsylvania, 37, 38
Petrilli, Michael J., 11
Philadelphia, 38, 47, 101, 313
Plank, David N., 12, 313
Platform Learning, 163, 167
PLATO Learning, 53
Polk County (Fla.) School District,
    26–27
Portland, Ore., 48
Pressman, Jeffrey L., 80
Princeton Review, 53, 69, 78, 92
Private school clause option in Florida,
    246, 247
Private-sector and SES, 69–70, 318
Professional training for education
    leadership lacking, 318, 325
Project Child, 237
Project Clarion, 101
Providers (SES), 29
    in California (complaints from and
        about), 132–37, 144–45
    in Colorado, 190–91
    in Miami-Dade County, 262
    in Michigan, 210–11

in New Jersey (complaints from and against), 161–67
number and variety of, 86–89
private sector, 69–70, 81–82, 167
program elements reviewed, 84–85
state-approved, lists of, 30–32
types of, 88t
urban school districts tutoring, 103
use of school facilities, 55, 91
Provisional AYP designation in Florida, 250, 260
Public School Accountability Act (Calif.), 122
Public School Act (N.J.), 153
Public school choice, *see* School choice
Public School Choice Non-Regulatory Guidance, 99, 108–9

Quality Single Accountability Continuum (N.J.), 174
Quinn, Christine, 131, 137, 138

RAND Corporation national study, 139, 152
Reading First, 64
Reagan, Ronald, 74
Reauthorization
cascade of sanctions needs revision, 65, 116–17
lessons for, learned in California, 151–52
lessons for, learned in New Jersey, 175–76
ten recommendations for changes, 319–26
Rees, Nina Shokraii, 101, 104, 108
Remedies
applied in California, 139–43
concept of in NCLB, 6–10, 18, 311–12
expectations for cascade of, 18–21
role of states, 21, 22–32, 41–42

See also Sanctions, specific remedies
Republicans
and localism, 77–78
and market metaphor, 78–79
and passage of NCLB, 3–5, 6, 66, 73–75
Restructured schools
Balboa Elementary School, San Diego, 274–78
Buchanon Elementary School, Grand Rapids, 271–74
case studies, 271–85
common lessons learned, 285–89
Gompers Middle School, San Diego, 282–85
methodology and overview of case studies, 270
Milwood Magnet School, Kalamazoo, 278–81
Restructuring process, 7–8, 114, 267–70, 290–91
in Colorado, 180–81, 191–9
concept blurry and perplexing, 311–12
in Denver Public Schools, 196
district involvement in planning process varies widely, 287–88
loopholes in bill requirements, 37, 110–11
in Michigan, 211–12
in New Jersey, 167–74
offers wide flexibility for change, 286–87
problems with forcing districts to take action, 110–14
state oversight of and action on, 33–41
Riveroll, Vince, 282–85
Robinson v. Cahill (N.J.), 153
Rochester, 83
Romer, Roy, 107, 298
Root, Ed, 303

Rosner, Mayra, 161, 162
Rotherham, Andy, 75
Rural districts and NCLB, 185–86,
        230–43
Russo, Carmen, 107

Salt Lake City, 51
San Diego, 45, 83, 128, 130–32, 133–35,
        137–39, 145, 146, 148, 270,
        274–78, 282–85
San Diego Education Association,
        276–77, 283
Sanctions, 290
    inefficient way of improving district
        performance, 65, 299–300
    in Michigan, 204, 206–9, 215
    use of "soft" sanctions, 63–64, 269,
        310
    See also Remedies
School Accountability Reports (Colo.)
        conflicts with AYP designations,
        183–85
School choice, 7, 105–9, 313, 324
    in California, 126–32, 149
    in Colorado, 179–80, 182, 188–89
    in Cortez, Colo., 197–98
    in Denver Public Schools, 195
    in Florida, 246–50
    in great city schools, 46–50
    in Kentucky, 230, 241, 242
    in Miami-Dade, 250–64
    in Michigan, 209
    in New Jersey, 157–61
    problems with, 105–9
    role of states in implementing, 21–27
    See also Parental notification of
        choice options
School Improvement Grants (Colo.),
        192–93
School-performance data, NCLB
        provides a wealth of, but little
        analysis of effectiveness, 316–17

Schwarzenegger, Arnold, 282
SES, see Supplemental educational services
Silver and Strong's Thoughtful Educa-
        tion professional development
        program, 241
Simon, Ray, 298, 303
Smith, Pam, 295
Socratic Learning, 53
South Dakota, 314
Spellings, Margaret, 96, 102, 103,
        304–5
Stabenow, Debbie, 205
State education agencies, 17
    "alpha state" model, 321
    and district accountability, 296–300,
        301–7, 308
    oversight of corrective action and
        restructuring, 35–38
    policies and NCLB remedies, 38–40
    provider lists, 29–32
    role in implementation of NCLB
        remedies, 21, 22–32, 41–42
    role in improving schools and
        districts, 40–41, 296–99
    variability among, as to policy
        infrastructure, 19–21
Sunshine State Standards (Fla.), 246
Supplemental educational services, 7
    concept is unworkable, 315–16
    districts should not be both pro-
        viders and "gatekeepers," 323–24
    future of, 92–95
    in great city schools, provision and
        evaluation, 50–58, 62–63
    as local contracting regime, 56–57,
        90–95
    and local district action, 82–85
    as major policy intervention, 68–71
    and market metaphor, 78–82
    and obsolescent localism, 79–81
    offered before choice in trial
        districts, 102–4

origins of, 71–75
participation rates, 86, 313
program defined, 67–71
response to by local districts, 80–85
role of states in implementing, 21,
  27–32
See also Parental notification of
  choice options, Providers
Supplemental educational services
  in states
  in California, 132–39, 144–45, 149
  in Colorado, 180, 189–91
  in Cortez, Colo., 198
  in Denver Public Schools, 195
  in Kentucky, 230, 238, 241, 242,
    243
  in Miami-Dade County, 261–62
  in Michigan, 209–11
  in New Jersey, 158–67
*Supplemental Educational Services Non-
  Regulatory Guidance*, 99–100
Supplemental Educational Services
  Quality Center, 87
Sylvan, 69, 78

Teachers unions, 112–13, 205, 217,
  276–77
Teach for America, 326
Tennessee, 292
Texas, 4, 115, 314
Title I, 19, 57–58, 63, 73, 107, 113
  schools in California, 126–29, 132,
    143
  schools in improvement stages,
    19–21, 33–35, 127
Tofig, Dana, 36, 296
Toledo, 83
Tompkinsville, Ky., 238, 239
Tony Grampsas Youth Services
  Program, 190
Transfer rates, *see* School choice
True, Mariam, 135, 137–38, 152

Turnaround specialists, 37
Tutoring, *see* Supplemental educational
  services
21st Century Community Learning
  Centers, 190, 198–99, 200

U.S. Department of Education, 29, 51,
  63, 74, 85, 97–98, 151–52, 307,
  311, 317, 324, 326
  actions to boost local education
    agencies to implement school
    choice, 99–105
  and district accountability, 296–98
  and lack of capacity in good schools,
    106–9
  and petition from Florida for provi-
    sional AYP, 250
  and pilot SES projects, 102–4
  requirements for information from
    California, 143–45, 297–98
  and teachers unions battle over col
    lective bargaining, 111–13
University of Miami, 253

Ventura County, Calif., 130–31,
  144
Vigil, Dale, 144
Virginia, 102
Voluntary Public School Choice
  program, 116

Wade, Gene, 163–65, 167
Warfield, Ky., 232, 233, 234
Washington, 24
Watkins, Tom, 205
Watts, Becky, 36
Weis, Charles, 130–31, 141–42, 144,
  148
Western Kentucky Educational
  Cooperative, 238
Western Kentucky University, 240
West Virginia, 24, 25–26, 40

2712 Gift

Wildavsky, Aaron, 80
Williams, Joe, 13
Wilson, George, 240
Winn, John, 36, 37, 30

Wisconsin, 22
Woodruff, Valerie, 299

Zau, Andrew C., 139